# Fundamental Applied Mathematics

## 2nd Edition

**Oliver Murphy**

## Dedication

This book is dedicated to all the students I have taught, especially in Castleknock College. You have taught me a lot and have kept me young. Most importantly, you have helped me to be happy in my work. Thank you.
- Oliver Murphy

## Acknowledgements

I wish to thank many people for making this book possible. To Jonathan Foley and Jim McElroy and their students for testing the book in class and giving me excellent advice. To Dirk Folens and Margaret Burns for their keen interest and dedication to bringing the project to fruition. To Warren Yeates for his excellent work in designing the layout of the book.

## Editor, Layout & Mathematical typesetting

Dirk Folens

## Design

Bookworks

## Illustrations

Bookworks et al.

© 2011 Oliver Murphy

ISBN: 1-84741-187-8
EAN: 978-1-84741-187-7
Folens Publishers,
Hibernian Industrial Estate,
Greenhills Road,
Tallaght,
Dublin 24

# Contents

# Preface

The original Fundamental Applied Mathematics, with its chocolate brown cover, served its purpose well for over 25 years. It was popular with both teachers and students.

Even though the course has not changed, there was need for a new edition to reflect changes of emphasis in the exams and the course. This new edition of Fundamental Applied Mathematics is better than the original in many ways:

- It reflects more closely the kind of question which has been asked in the Leaving Cert exams in recent years.
- It emphasises the techniques required for success in exams.
- It omits questions which the State Examinations Commission has said will not be examined, such as Thrust on a vertical surface.
- It uses the notation of Project Maths, with capital letters for points and lower case letters for lines.
- At the beginning of each chapter there is a list of contents, an inventory of the mathematics required, and (most importantly) a list of the learning outcomes of that chapter.
- Each chapter ends with a summary of important points as well as tips for the exam associated with that topic, showing students the key points to watch and the common pitfalls to avoid.
- There are plenty of well-graded questions on every sub-topic. These have all been class-tested.
- There is advice for revision and for the exam itself, as well as a detailed index and answers to all questions.
- The book is not crowded. There are plenty of diagrams to help students understand clearly what is going on.
- This book explains clearly not just the techniques of solving problems, but what are the underlying concepts which determine such techniques. It shows where formulae come from. This enables students to understand what they are doing and helps them to solve a variety of problems, with new twists and turns.
- 'Projectiles' is split into two chapters so that students meet the difficulties of 'Projectiles on the inclined plane' and 'Projectiles which bounce' when they have the required knowledge of trigonometry and Newton's Law of Restitution.

Applied Mathematics is a beautiful and challenging subject. It can be the most satisfying subject on the Leaving Cert. It serves students well because it gives them a skill – to solve real-life problems using mathematics as the tool – which they can later apply to any other field such as medicine, architecture, economics, pharmacy, engineering, design, technology, business and actuarial studies.

I hope that this book helps teachers in their task of inspiring young people to love their subject. I hope especially that it helps young people to develop the skill of problem-solving which will serve them through the Leaving Cert and beyond into whatever field they choose as a career. Applied Mathematics can change your life.

Oliver Murphy
March 2011

# Advice for the exam

## In the exam...

**Marking scheme:**

You start with 300 marks (6 × 50 =300)

1. Any 'slip' is –1 marks:  e.g. $4 \times 0 = 4$  or $\sin \pi = -1$

2. Any 'blunder' is –3: e.g. $\dfrac{v_2 - v_1}{u_2 - u_1} = e$ or $\dfrac{d}{dx}(\cos x) = \sin x$

3. You get the 'attempt mark' for any correct step: it is one third of the marks to the nearest whole number.  You cannot get less than the attempt mark no matter how many mistakes you make, so long as you do one correct step.

4. In Applied Maths exams, nearly all questions are broken into 10 parts which get 5 marks each, with attempt mark 2 in each case.

5. Do the easiest question first – it will help build your confidence.

6. **Attempt** every part of every question.  Avoid leaving out whole parts.

7. Don't do rough-work.  Show all your work.

8. Don't use Tippex, just cross it out and work on.

9. 'Trial & error' methods or 'proof by example' get the attempt mark only.

10. Don't hop from question to question doing only bits from each.

11. If questions don't work out right – don't panic. Just go straight on to the next question.  It's the method that counts, not the answer.

12. If you have time you can do another question and you'll get the marks for your best six questions. But is it worth it?  Could you use the time better to perfect other questions?

## Topics: Do 6 of these 10 questions

1. Uniform acceleration

2. Relative velocity

3. Projectiles

4. Pulleys & wedges

5. Collisions & impacts

6. Circular motion & Simple Harmonic Motion

7. Statics

8. Moments of Inertia

9. Hydrostatics

10. Differential equations

Occasionally, topics have been mixed around, but this is rare.  For example, look at question 4(a) in the 2002 paper: it's about Simple Harmonic Motion!

## Revision:

1. Be systematic.  Work out a revision schedule.

2. Prepare at least 7 questions.  Give them all enough time in your revision schedule.

3. Do as many questions as you have time for from the past papers.  It is more useful to solve problems yourself than to read someone else's solutions.

4. When you can't do a question, ask someone.  This is when you learn the most.

5. At exam time, ease off.  The evening before, play a game of tennis or golf or go for a walk or a swim. You want a clear brain – as well as knowing all the formulae etc.

# Vectors

αγεωμετρητος μηδεις εισιτω

(Do not enter if you do not understand geometry.)

*Notice at the entrance to Plato's Academy*

## Contents

## Learning outcomes

**In this chapter you will learn...**

- What a vector is, and what it represents

- The difference between a vector and a scalar

- How to draw vectors

- How to add vectors

- How to multiply a vector by a scalar

- How to represent a vector on the Cartesian plane

- How to calculate the magnitude and direction of a given vector

## You will need to know...

- Pythagoras' theorem
- The Cartesian plane (i.e. the $x - y$ plane)
- Sine, Cosine and Tangent

## Scalars

In our study of Applied Mathematics we will come across physical quantities which have magnitude only. We call such quantities **scalar** quantities, since they can be measured on a scale. Scalars are, in fact, real numbers.

Here are some examples:

### 1. Height

Height = 2 metres

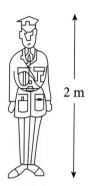

2 m

Fig. 1.1

### 2. Length and Area

Length of Circumference = $6\pi$ cm

Area of Circle = $9\pi$ cm$^2$

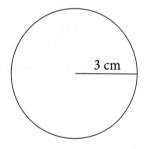

3 cm

Fig. 1.2

### 3. Speed

Speed = 40 km per hour or 40 km/h.

Fig. 1.3

## Vectors

But we will also come across physical quantities which have both magnitude and direction.

We call such quantities **vector** quantities. They are represented by tipped arrows and denoted by letters with arrows on top.

For example:

### 1. Velocity

Velocity = $\vec{v}$

= 20 km/h in an easterly direction

or

20 km/h, E.

Fig. 1.4

### 2. Acceleration

Acceleration = $\vec{a}$ = 9.8 m/s$^2$ towards the centre of the earth.

Fig. 1.5

### 3. Displacement

(or position relative to a given point)

Displacement = $\vec{d}$

= 200 kilometres, South West

(or 200 km, SW).

Fig. 1.6

## 4. Force

Force = $\vec{F}$

      = 40 newtons, 20° North of East
      or 40 N, E 20° N

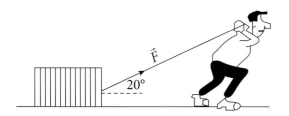

Fig. 1.7

**Notes:**

(i)   The magnitude (or 'bigness') of a physical quantity is represented by the length of the vector: a longer vector represents a stronger force. For example, Fig 1.8 shows two equal apples, one growing on the earth, one on the moon, with the force due to gravity shown.

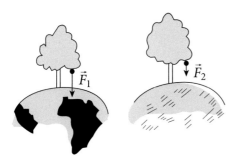

Fig. 1.8 Why is the earth's vector longer than the moon's?

(ii)  Velocity is a vector with magnitude and direction (e.g. 20 km/h due East) but speed is a scalar with magnitude only (e.g. 20 km/h)

## The sum of two vectors

Imagine a ship that is being towed into a harbour by two tug boats, with tug boat A pulling with greater force than tug boat B.

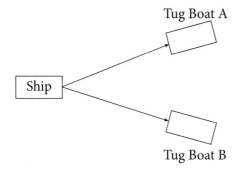

Fig. 1.9

In vector notation we represent the forces on the ship in this way:

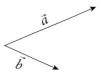

Fig. 1.10

The longer vector represents the stronger pull (not, of course, the length of the rope). But the ship will travel in the direction of neither $\vec{a}$ nor $\vec{b}$. In what direction will it go? How can we "add" the two vectors? Here's how:

### Adding two vectors

**The parallelogram method:**

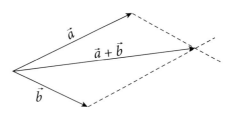

Fig. 1.11

**Method:**

(i)   Draw a line parallel to $\vec{b}$ through the tip of $\vec{a}$.

(ii)  Draw a line parallel to $\vec{a}$ through the tip of $\vec{b}$.

(iii) Join the intersection of $\vec{a}$ and $\vec{b}$ to the point where these two lines intersect.

(iv) This new vector is called "$\vec{a} + \vec{b}$".

The ship will travel in the direction of $\vec{a} + \vec{b}$.
We call $\vec{a} + \vec{b}$ the **resultant** or **sum** of $\vec{a}$ and $\vec{b}$.

**Notes:**

(i)   A vector represents any physical quantity with magnitude and direction.

(ii)  Any two vectors which have the same magnitude and direction are equal — indeed we can say they are the same vector.

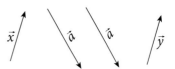

Fig. 1.12

We can say $\vec{x} = \vec{y}$ or simply call the two equal vectors by the same name; in this case two of them are called $\vec{a}$.

(iii)  If $\vec{a}$ is a vector, then $-\vec{a}$ is a vector with the same magnitude but in the opposite direction.

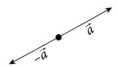

Fig. 1.13

(iv)  $\vec{a} + \vec{a}$ can be written as $2\vec{a}$, as you would expect. Similarly $\vec{a} + \vec{a} + \vec{a}$ can be written as $3\vec{a}$.

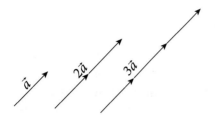

Fig. 1.14

## Worked Example 1.1

Copy this diagram and construct the vector $3\vec{a} - 2\vec{b}$.

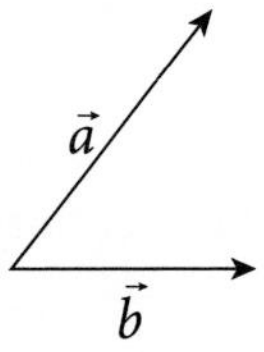

Fig. 1.15

Solution:

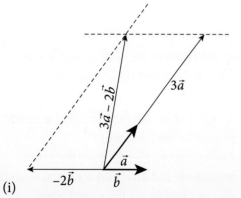

(i)

Fig. 1.16

(i)  Draw $3\vec{a}$ by trebling the length of $\vec{a}$.

(ii)  Show $-2\vec{b}$ by reversing $\vec{b}$'s direction and doubling its length.

(iii)  Add $3\vec{a}$ and $-2\vec{b}$ by the parallelogram method.

(iv)  Label the resultant vector clearly.

## Exercise 1 A

1.  Add $\vec{a}$ and $\vec{b}$ in each case, denoting your answer $\vec{a} + \vec{b}$ :

(i)

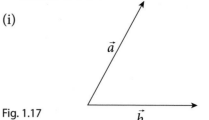

Fig. 1.17

(ii)

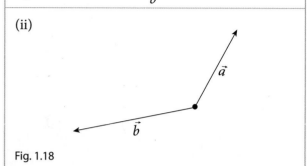

Fig. 1.18

(iii)

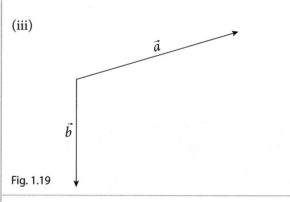

Fig. 1.19

(iv)

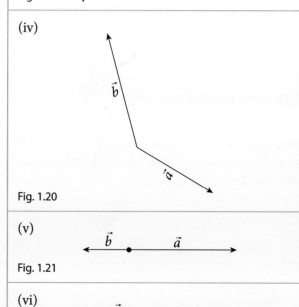

Fig. 1.20

(v)

Fig. 1.21

(vi)

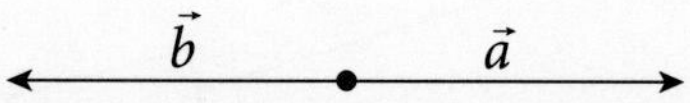

Fig. 1.22

2. Show the vector $2\,\vec{a} + \vec{b}$.

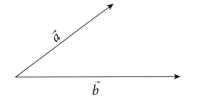

Fig. 1.23

3. Construct $4\,\vec{x} - \vec{y}$.

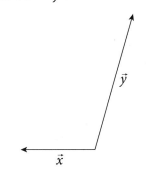

Fig. 1.24

4. Construct the vector $\frac{1}{2}\,\vec{x} - \frac{1}{2}\,\vec{y}$

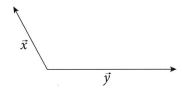

Fig. 1.25

5. Copy this diagram accurately and show $\left(\vec{a} + \vec{b}\right) + \vec{c}$

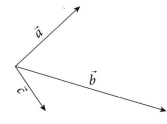

Fig. 1.26

6. Using the same vectors as in Question 5, show $\vec{a} + \left(\vec{b} + \vec{c}\right)$.
   Is $\left(\vec{a} + \vec{b}\right) + \vec{c} = \vec{a} + \left(\vec{b} + \vec{c}\right)$?

7. Show $3\,\vec{x} + 1\frac{1}{2}\,\vec{y}$

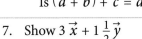

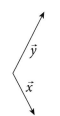

Fig. 1.27

8. Show $\left(\vec{x} - \frac{1}{2}\,\vec{y}\right)$ and also $\left(\vec{y} - \frac{1}{2}\,\vec{x}\right)$

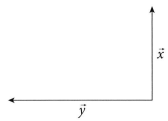

Fig. 1.28

9. $\vec{u}$ is a vector 3 cm long in an easterly direction. $\vec{v}$ is a vector 4 cm long in a northerly direction. Draw them accurately and, using a ruler and protractor, find the length (or magnitude) and direction of $\vec{u} + \vec{v}$ as accurately as possible.

10. $\vec{x}$ is a vector 5 cm long in a direction 30° North of East. $\vec{y}$ is a vector 4 cm long in a SE direction. Draw $\vec{x}$, $\vec{y}$, and $\vec{x} + \vec{y}$ using a ruler and protractor. Find the length and direction of $\vec{x} + \vec{y}$ as accurately as you can.

11. $\vec{x}$ is a vector 12 cm long and due East. $\vec{y}$ is a vector 5 cm long and due South. Find the magnitude (or length) of $\vec{x} + \vec{y}$.

## The $\vec{i} - \vec{j}$ plane

In order to avoid drawing a diagram for each question or using the rather cumbersome notation for directions (e.g. 20° North of West), we can impose vectors onto the Cartesian or $x - y$ plane.

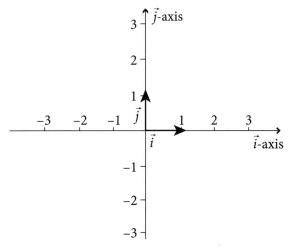

Fig. 1.29

$\vec{i}$ is a vector one unit long, which is drawn along the $x$-axis, which we will now call the $\vec{i}$-axis.
$\vec{j}$ is a vector one unit long, which is drawn along the $y$-axis (now called the $\vec{j}$-axis).
$\vec{i}$ and $\vec{j}$ are orthogonal unit vectors:

**Note:**
(i) **orthogonal** means they are at right angles to one another, represented by the symbol $\perp$.
(ii) **unit** vectors are one unit long.

---

**Worked Example 1.2**

Show the vector $3\vec{i} + 4\vec{j}$ on a diagram and find its magnitude and direction.

**Solution:**

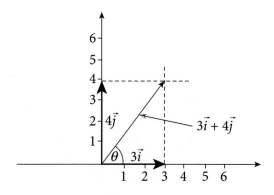

Fig. 1.30

(i) $3\vec{i} + 4\vec{j}$ is simply the sum of $3\vec{i}$ and $4\vec{j}$, as shown.

(ii) To find the magnitude, or length, of $3\vec{i} + 4\vec{j}$, use Pythagoras' Theorem.
Let $l$ be the length of the resultant vector.
$$l^2 = 3^2 + 4^2$$
$$\Rightarrow l^2 = 25$$
$$\Rightarrow l = 5.$$
The magnitude of $3\vec{i} + 4\vec{j}$ is 5 units.

We write this as $|3\vec{i} + 4\vec{j}| = 5$ units.

(iii) The angle $\theta$ can be found in this way.
$$\text{Tan } \theta = \frac{\text{opposite}}{\text{adjacent}}$$
$$= \frac{4}{3}$$
$$= 1.3333$$
$$\therefore \theta = 53.13° \text{ (or } 53° 8')$$
The direction of $3\vec{i} + 4\vec{j}$ is 53.13° North of East, or E53.13°N.

**Note:**
In general, the magnitude of $x\vec{i} + y\vec{j}$ is $\sqrt{x^2 + y^2}$ (by Pythagoras' Theorem).

---

**Worked Example 1.3**

$$\vec{a} = -3\vec{i} + \vec{j}$$

(i) Illustrate $\vec{a}$.
(ii) Find $|\vec{a}|$, the magnitude of $\vec{a}$.
(iii) Find the direction of $\vec{a}$.

**Solution:**

(i) $\vec{a}$ is the sum of $-3\vec{i}$ and $\vec{j}$.

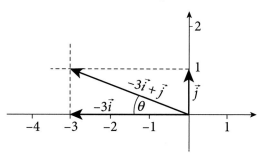

Fig. 1.31

(ii) By Pythagoras' Theorem
$$|\vec{a}| = \sqrt{(-3)^2 + (1)^2} = \sqrt{9 + 1} = \sqrt{10}$$

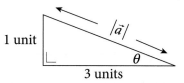

Fig. 1.32

(iii) We can find $\theta$ by $\tan \theta = \frac{\text{opposite}}{\text{adjacent}} = \frac{1}{3}$
$$\therefore \theta = 18.43° \text{ (or } 18°26')$$
$\therefore$ The direction of $\vec{a}$ is 18.43° North of West, or W18.43° N.

---

**Worked Example 1.4**

If $\vec{x} = 3\vec{i} - 2\vec{j}$ and $\vec{y} = 4\vec{i} + \vec{j}$.

(a) Write in terms of $\vec{i}$ and $\vec{j}$, the orthogonal unit vectors, the following:
(i) $\vec{x} + \vec{y}$
(ii) $3\vec{x} - \vec{y}$
(iii) $\vec{y} - \vec{x}$

(b) Find the magnitude of $2\vec{x} + \vec{y}$.

(c) Find the values of the scalars $t$ and $k$ such that $t\vec{x} + k\vec{y} = 2\vec{i} - 5\vec{j}$.

(d) Find a unit vector in the same direction as $\vec{x}$

(e) Investigate if $\vec{x} \perp \vec{y}$

**Solution:**

(a)

(i) $\quad \vec{x} + \vec{y} = (3\vec{i} - 2\vec{j}) + (4\vec{i} + \vec{j})$
$= 7\vec{i} - \vec{j}$

(ii) $\quad 3\vec{x} - \vec{y} = 3(3\vec{i} - 2\vec{j}) - (4\vec{i} + \vec{j})$
$= 9\vec{i} - 6\vec{j} - 4\vec{i} - \vec{j}$
$= 5\vec{i} - 7\vec{j}$

(iii) $\quad \vec{y} - \vec{x} = (4\vec{i} + \vec{j}) - (3\vec{i} - 2\vec{j})$
$= 4\vec{i} + \vec{j} - 3\vec{i} + 2\vec{j}$
$= \vec{i} + 3\vec{j}$

(b) Firstly, write $2\vec{x} + \vec{y}$ in terms of $\vec{i}$ and $\vec{j}$.
$2\vec{x} + \vec{y} = 2(3\vec{i} - 2\vec{j}) + (4\vec{i} + \vec{j})$
$= 6\vec{i} - 4\vec{j} + 4\vec{i} + \vec{j}$
$= 10\vec{i} - 3\vec{j}$

$\therefore \quad |2\vec{x} + \vec{y}| = \sqrt{10^2 + (-3)^2}$
$= \sqrt{109}$ units

(c) $\quad\quad\quad\quad\quad t\vec{x} + k\vec{y} = 2\vec{i} - 5\vec{j}$
$\therefore t(3\vec{i} - 2\vec{j}) + k(4\vec{i} + \vec{j}) = 2\vec{i} - 5\vec{j}$
$\therefore 3t\vec{i} - 2t\vec{j} + 4k\vec{i} + k\vec{j} = 2\vec{i} - 5\vec{j}$
$\therefore (3t + 4k)\vec{i} + (-2t + k)\vec{j} = 2\vec{i} - 5\vec{j}$

$\therefore$ Equation I:
($\vec{i}$ component on left = $\vec{i}$ component on right)
$\Rightarrow 3t + 4k = 2$

Equation II:
($\vec{j}$ component on left = $\vec{j}$ component on right)
$\Rightarrow -2t + k = -5.$

Solve these simultaneous equations:

I: $\quad\quad\quad 3t + 4k = 2$

$-4 \times$ II: $\quad 8t - 4k = 20$

Adding $\quad \therefore 11t = 22$

$\quad\quad\quad\quad \therefore t = 2, k = -1$: Answer.

(d)

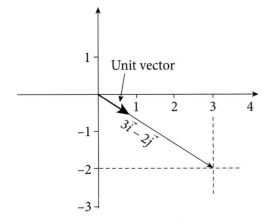

Fig. 1.33

We want a vector, one unit long, along $3\vec{i} - 2\vec{j}$.
The magnitude of $3\vec{i} - 2\vec{j}$ is
$|3\vec{i} - 2\vec{j}| = \sqrt{3^2 + (-2)^2}$
$= \sqrt{9 + 4}$
$= \sqrt{13}$ units.

Therefore, we have to divide $3\vec{i} - 2\vec{j}$ by $\sqrt{13}$ to get a vector in the same direction, but one unit long.
The unit vector we want is

$$\frac{3\vec{i} - 2\vec{j}}{\sqrt{13}} = \frac{3}{\sqrt{13}}\vec{i} - \frac{2}{\sqrt{13}}\vec{j}$$

(e) The slope of a vector is given by $\dfrac{\vec{j}\text{ - component}}{\vec{i}\text{ - component}}$

$\therefore$ the slope of $\vec{x} = \dfrac{-2}{3} = -\dfrac{2}{3} = m_1$

The slope of $\vec{y} = \dfrac{1}{4} = m_2$

$m_1 \times m_2 = -\dfrac{2}{3} \times \dfrac{1}{4} = -\dfrac{1}{6} \neq -1$

$\therefore \vec{x}$ is not perpendicular to $\vec{y}$

---

**Exercise 1 B**

1. In each of the following examples, draw the vector and find its magnitude and direction.

   (i) $5\vec{i} + 2\vec{j}$
   (ii) $2\vec{i} + 2\vec{j}$
   (iii) $4\vec{i} - 3\vec{j}$
   (iv) $-5\vec{i} - 12\vec{j}$
   (v) $-4\vec{i} + 2\vec{j}$
   (vi) $\vec{i} + \vec{j}$
   (vii) $\frac{1}{2}\vec{i} - \frac{1}{2}\vec{j}$
   (viii) $-\frac{3}{5}\vec{i} - \frac{4}{5}\vec{j}$
   (ix) $-\sqrt{3}\vec{i} + \vec{j}$
   (x) $3\vec{i} - \sqrt{3}\vec{j}$
   (xi) $-4\vec{i}$ .

2. If $\vec{a} = 3\vec{i} - \vec{j}$ and $\vec{b} = 2\vec{i} - 3\vec{j}$, write in terms of $\vec{i}$ and $\vec{j}$:

   (i) $\vec{a} + \vec{b}$
   (ii) $\vec{a} - \vec{b}$
   (iii) $\vec{b} - \vec{a}$
   (iv) $2\vec{a} - 3\vec{b}$ .

3. If $\vec{x} = 2\vec{i} + 3\vec{j}$ and $\vec{y} = 10\vec{i} + 2\vec{j}$, write in terms of $\vec{i}$ and $\vec{j}$ the vector $\vec{x} + \vec{y}$.

   (i) Find $|\vec{x}|$

(ii)   Find $|\vec{y}|$

(iii)  Find $|\vec{x} + \vec{y}|$

(iv)   Show that $|\vec{x} + \vec{y}| < |\vec{x}| + |\vec{y}|$

4.   $\vec{a} = 3\vec{i} + \vec{j}$, $\vec{b} = \vec{i} + 7\vec{j}$.

(i)   Write $\vec{a} + \vec{b}$ in terms of $\vec{i}$ and $\vec{j}$.

(ii)  Evaluate $|\vec{a} + \vec{b}|$

(iii) Show that $|\vec{a} + \vec{b}| < |\vec{a}| + |\vec{b}|$

5.   Given that $\vec{p} = 4\vec{i} - 2\vec{j}$ and $\vec{q} = 2\vec{i} - \vec{j}$, show that $|\vec{p} - \vec{q}| > |\vec{p}| - |\vec{q}|$.

6.   Find unit vectors in the same direction as these:

(i)   $3\vec{i} + 4\vec{j}$

(ii)  $\vec{i} + 2\vec{j}$

(iii) $\vec{i} - \vec{j}$

(iv)  $-3\vec{i} - \vec{j}$

(v)   $\sqrt{3}\,\vec{i} + \vec{j}$

7.   If $\vec{m} = 2\vec{i} - \vec{j}$ and $\vec{p} = 4\vec{i} + 3\vec{j}$, find scalars $k$ and $l$ such that $k\vec{m} + l\vec{p} = 2\vec{i} - 11\vec{j}$.

8.   $\vec{a} = 4\vec{i} - 2\vec{j}$, $\vec{b} = 7\vec{i} + 5\vec{j}$, find a scalar $t$ such that $\vec{a} + t\vec{b}$ is along the $\vec{i}$ – axis.
     (Hint: The $\vec{j}$-component must be zero.)

9.   If $|8\vec{i} - \vec{j}| = |7\vec{i} + k\vec{j}|$, find two possible values for $k \in$ R.

10.  If $|7\vec{i} + \vec{j}| = |p(\vec{i} + \vec{j})|$, find two possible values for $p \in$ R.

11.  If $|11\vec{i} - k\vec{j}| = |5(2\vec{i} + \vec{j})|$, find two possible values for $k \in$ R.

12.  If $|k(\vec{i} - \vec{j})| = |\sqrt{5}(3\vec{i} + \vec{j})|$, find two possible values for $k \in$ R.

13.  $\vec{x} = 4\vec{i} + 3\vec{j}$ and $\vec{y} = 6\vec{i} - 8\vec{j}$.
     Prove that $\vec{x} \perp \vec{y}$

14.  Prove that $5\vec{i} - 2\vec{j}$ is perpendicular to $8\vec{i} + 20\vec{j}$.

15.  Prove that $\vec{i} + 3\vec{j}$ is perpendicular to $6\vec{i} - 2\vec{j}$

16.  If $9\vec{i} - t\vec{j} \perp 2\vec{i} + 6\vec{j}$, find the value of $t$.

17.  If $4\vec{i} + p\vec{j}$ is perpendicular to $(p + 1)\vec{i} - 2\vec{j}$, find the value of $p$.

## Adjacents & Opposites

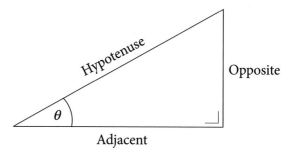

Fig. 1.34

Take any right angled triangle, like the one shown here.

$$\sin\theta = \frac{\text{Opposite}}{\text{hypotenuse}}$$

$$\Rightarrow \text{Opposite} = \text{hypotenuse} \times \sin\theta$$

$$\cos\theta = \frac{\text{Adjacent}}{\text{hypotenuse}}$$

$$\Rightarrow \text{Adjacent} = \text{hypotenuse} \times \cos\theta$$

These two results should become rules-of-thumb. They can speed up calculations considerably.

### Worked Example 1.5

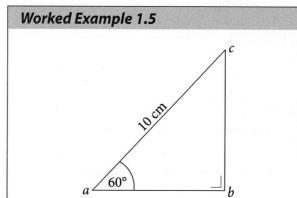

Fig. 1.35

In the triangle shown, find the lengths $|ab|$ and $|bc|$.

**Solution:**

$$|ab| = \text{Adjacent}$$
$$= \text{Hypotenuse} \times \cos\theta$$
$$= 10\cos 60°$$
$$= 10 \times \frac{1}{2}$$
$$= 5 \text{ cm.}$$

$$|bc| = \text{Opposite}$$
$$= \text{Hypotenuse} \times \sin\theta$$
$$= 10\sin 60°$$
$$= 10 \times \frac{\sqrt{3}}{2}$$
$$= 5\sqrt{3} \text{ cm.}$$

## Worked Example 1.6

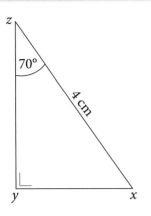

Fig. 1.36

In the given triangle, find $|xy|$ and $|yz|$ correct to two decimal places.

**Solution:**

$|xy|$ = Opposite = Hypotenuse × sin θ
= 4 × sin 70°
= 4 × 0.9397
= 3.7588
= 3.76 cm.

$|yz|$ = Adjacent = Hypotenuse × cos θ
= 4 × cos 70°
= 4 × 0.3420
= 1.3680
= 1.37 cm.

## Worked Example 1.7

If $\tan A = \dfrac{8}{15}$, find sin A and cos A without using mathematical tables, where 0°< A < 90°.

**Solution:**

$$\tan A = \frac{8}{15} = \frac{\text{Opposite}}{\text{Adjacent}}$$

∴ If the Opposite is 8 units long, the Adjacent must be 15 units long (or at least in the ratio 8:15).

Put these results onto a model triangle. To find the missing length, $x$, use Pythagoras' Theorem.

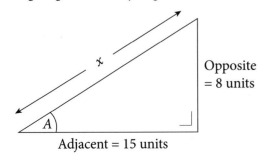

Opposite = 8 units

Adjacent = 15 units

Fig. 1.37

$$x^2 = 8^2 + 15^2$$
$$\Rightarrow x^2 = 64 + 225$$
$$\Rightarrow x^2 = 289$$
$$\therefore x = 17.$$

(i.e. the Hypotenuse is 17 units long)

$$\therefore \sin A = \frac{\text{Opposite}}{\text{Hypotenuse}} = \frac{8}{17}$$

and $\qquad \cos A = \dfrac{\text{Adjacent}}{\text{Hypotenuse}} = \dfrac{15}{17}$

## Worked Example 1.8

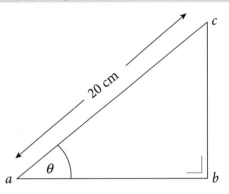

Fig. 1.38

If $\theta = \tan^{-1}\dfrac{4}{3}$ (i.e. $\tan \theta = \dfrac{4}{3}$) find the lengths $|ab|$ and $|bc|$.

**Solution:**

Before we start, we will need to know the values of Sin θ and Cos θ.

$$\tan \theta = \frac{4}{3} = \frac{\text{Opposite}}{\text{Adjacent}}$$

∴ $\qquad$ Opposite = 4

and $\qquad$ Adjacent = 3 (or at least in the ratio 4:3)

Put these onto a model triangle:

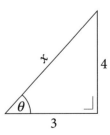

Fig. 1.39

By Pythagoras' Theorem
$$x^2 = 4^2 + 3^2$$
$$\therefore x^2 = 25$$
$$\therefore x = 5$$

(i.e. the Hypotenuse is 5 units long.)

$\therefore$

$$\sin \theta = \frac{\text{Opposite}}{\text{Hypotenuse}} = \frac{4}{5}$$

$$\cos \theta = \frac{\text{Adjacent}}{\text{Hypotenuse}} = \frac{3}{5}$$

Now:

$$|ab| = \text{Adjacent}$$
$$= \text{Hypotenuse} \times \cos \theta$$
$$= 20 \times \frac{3}{5}$$
$$= 12 \text{ cm}$$

$$|bc| = \text{Opposite}$$
$$= \text{Hypotenuse} \times \sin \theta$$
$$= 20 \times \frac{4}{5}$$
$$= 16 \text{ cm}$$

## Exercise 1 C

1.  Write down the length of the missing sides in terms of $H$, $\sin \theta$ and/or $\cos \theta$. (e.g. $H \sin \theta$, $H \cos \theta$, etc.)

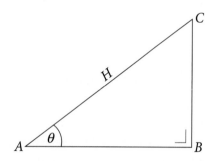

Fig. 1.40

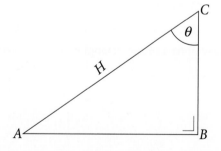

Fig. 1.41

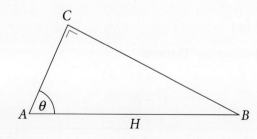

Fig. 1.42

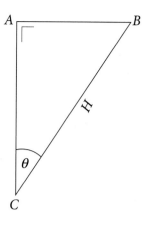

Fig. 1.43

2.  All of the following parts should be done without finding the value of $A$, and assuming $0° < A < 90°$.

    **Note:** answers should be left where necessary in surd form.

    (i)   If $\tan A = \frac{5}{12}$, find $\cos A$ and $\sin A$.

    (ii)  If $\tan A = \frac{12}{35}$, find $\cos A$ and $\sin A$.

    (iii) If $\cos A = \frac{3}{4}$, find $\sin A$ and $\tan A$.

    (iv)  If $\sin A = \frac{9}{41}$, find $\cos A$.

3.  Find the lengths of the missing sides in each case. Use surd (i.e. square root) form where the angle appears on Page 13 of the "Formulae and Tables"; otherwise give your answer correct to 2 decimal places.

    (i)

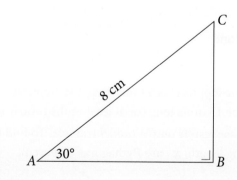

Fig. 1.44

(ii)

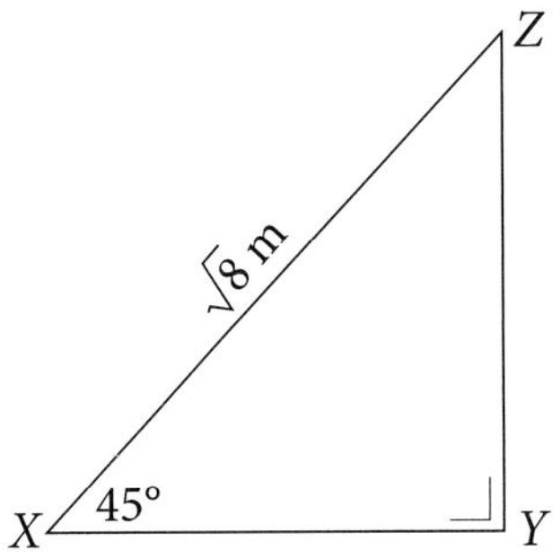

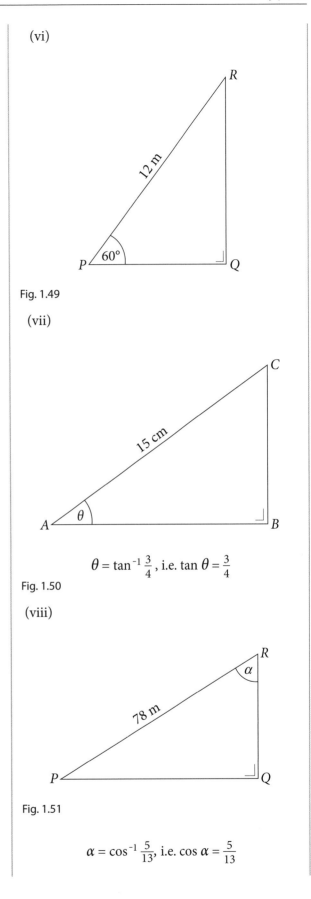

Fig. 1.45

(iii)

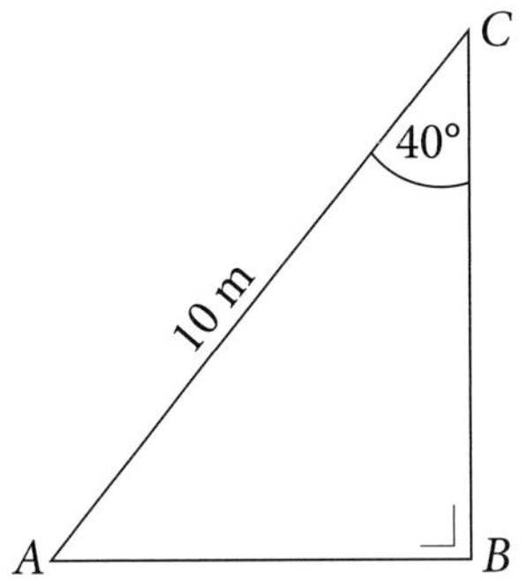

Fig. 1.46

(iv)

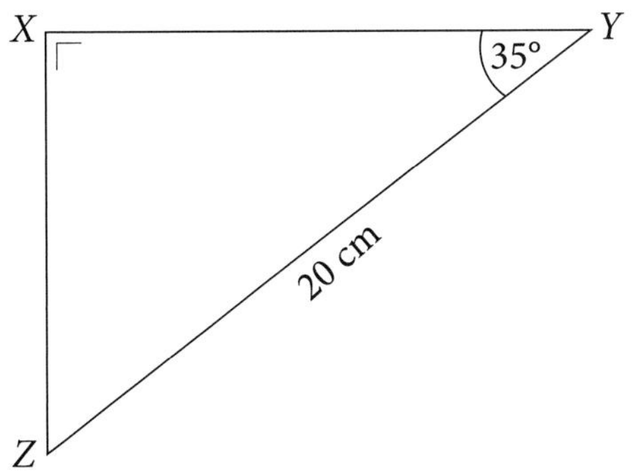

Fig. 1.47

(v)

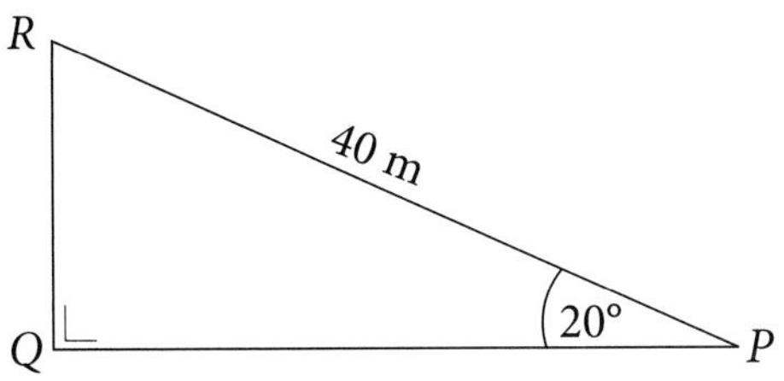

Fig. 1.48

(vi)

Fig. 1.49

(vii)

$\theta = \tan^{-1} \frac{3}{4}$, i.e. $\tan \theta = \frac{3}{4}$

Fig. 1.50

(viii)

$\alpha = \cos^{-1} \frac{5}{13}$, i.e. $\cos \alpha = \frac{5}{13}$

Fig. 1.51

(ix)

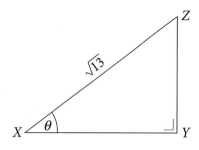

Fig. 1.52

$$\theta = \tan^{-1}\frac{2}{3}. \text{ i.e. } \tan\theta = \frac{2}{3}$$

(x)

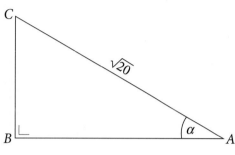

$$\alpha = \tan^{-1}\frac{1}{2}. \text{ i.e. } \tan\alpha = \frac{1}{2}$$

Fig. 1.53

4. (a) Write $X$ in terms of $H$, $\theta$ and $\phi$.

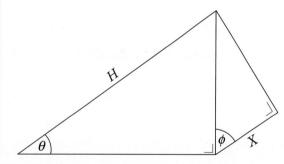

Fig. 1.54

(b) If $\tan\theta = \frac{3}{4}$ and $\tan\phi = \frac{12}{5}$ and $H = 13$, find $X$.

5. (a) Write $X$ in terms of $H$, $\alpha$ and $\beta$.

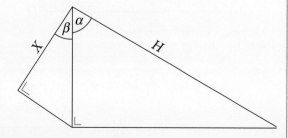

Fig. 1.55

(b) If $\tan\alpha = \frac{1}{7}$ and if $\beta = 45°$, find the ratio $H : X$.

## Writing Vectors in terms of $\vec{i}$ and $\vec{j}$

### Worked Example 1.9

$\vec{v}$ is a vector of magnitude 4 units in a direction 30° South of East . Write $\vec{v}$ in terms of $\vec{i}$ and $\vec{j}$, the orthogonal unit vectors.

**Solution:**

**Step** 1: Sketch $\vec{v}$ and calculate the missing sides in the right–angle triangle formed by $\vec{v}$ and the perpendicular dropped onto the $\vec{i}$ -axis.

**Step** 1

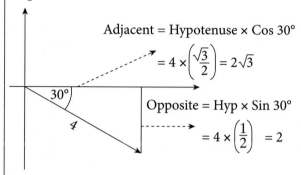

Adjacent = Hypotenuse × Cos 30°
$$= 4 \times \left(\frac{\sqrt{3}}{2}\right) = 2\sqrt{3}$$

Opposite = Hyp × Sin 30°
$$= 4 \times \left(\frac{1}{2}\right) = 2$$

Fig. 1.56

**Step 2**

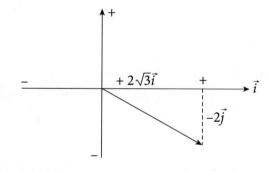

Fig. 1.57

Decide on the correct signs:

$\vec{i}$ component is positive, $\therefore + 2\sqrt{3}\ \vec{i}$

$\vec{j}$ component is negative, $\therefore - 2\ \vec{j}$

Answer: $\vec{v} = 2\sqrt{3}\ \vec{i} - 2\vec{j}$

## Worked Example 1.10

$\vec{u}$ is a vector of magnitude 20 units in a direction 42° South of West. Write $\vec{u}$ in terms of the orthogonal unit vectors $\vec{i}$ and $\vec{j}$.

**Solution:**

**Step** 1: Rough sketch and find missing sides.

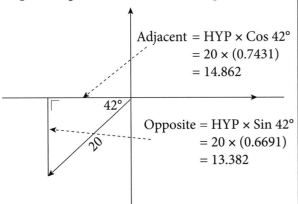

Adjacent = HYP × Cos 42°
= 20 × (0.7431)
= 14.862

Opposite = HYP × Sin 42°
= 20 × (0.6691)
= 13.382

Fig. 1.58

**Step** 2: Decide on the signs. In this case both are negative.

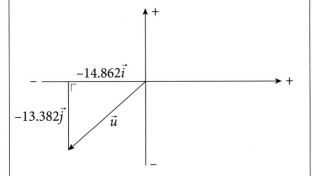

Fig. 1.59

Answer: $\vec{u} = -14.862\,\vec{i} - 13.382\,\vec{j}$

## Exercise 1 D

1. Write these vectors in terms of $\vec{i}$ and $\vec{j}$, given their magnitude and direction.
   Use surd form where possible.

   |      | Magnitude | Direction          |
   |------|-----------|--------------------|
   | (i)  | 2         | 60° North of East  |
   | (ii) | 10        | 18° North of East  |
   | (iii)| 8         | SE                 |
   | (iv) | 20        | 20° North of West  |
   | (v)  | $\sqrt{50}$ | SW               |
   | (vi) | 12        | 39° South of East  |

2.

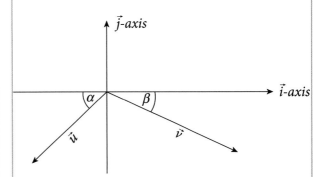

Fig. 1.60

   If $|\vec{u}| = 10$ units and $|\vec{v}| = 13$ units while $\alpha = \tan^{-1}\frac{3}{4}$ and $\beta = \tan^{-1}\frac{5}{12}$, find $\vec{u}$ and $\vec{v}$ and $(\vec{u} + \vec{v})$ in terms of $\vec{i}$ and $\vec{j}$.

   (i) Find $\vec{w}$ in terms of $\vec{i}$ and $\vec{j}$ if $\vec{u} + \vec{v} + \vec{w} = \vec{0}$

   (ii) Find, also, the magnitude and direction of $\vec{w}$ correct to one decimal place and the nearest degree respectively.

3.

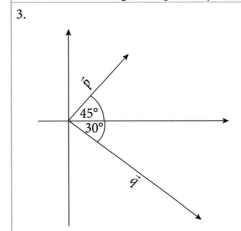

Fig. 1.61

   If $|\vec{p}| = \sqrt{8}$ and $|\vec{q}| = 4$, write $(\vec{p} + \vec{q})$ in terms of the unit vectors $\vec{i}$ and $\vec{j}$.

**4.**

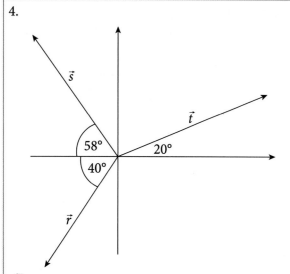

Fig. 1.62

$|\vec{s}| = |\vec{r}| = 10$ units. $|\vec{t}| = 11$ units.

Find $\vec{r} + \vec{s} + \vec{t}$ in terms of $\vec{i}$ and $\vec{j}$ correct to one decimal place.

**5.**

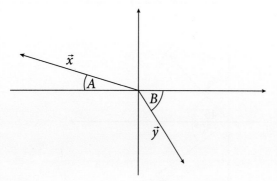

Fig. 1.63

If $|\vec{a}| = 12$ and $|\vec{b}| = 13$ and $\tan \theta = \frac{5}{12}$, find
(i) $\vec{a}$ and $\vec{b}$ in terms of $\vec{i}$ and $\vec{j}$
(ii) show that $(\vec{a} + \vec{b})$ is along the $\vec{j}$-axis.
(iii) find the magnitude of $(\vec{a} + \vec{b})$.

**6.**

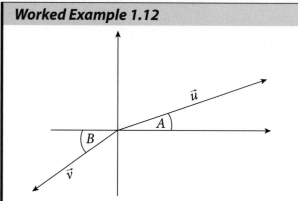

Fig. 1.64

$\vec{x}$ has magnitude 25 units and $\vec{y}$ has magnitude 17 units. If $A = \tan^{-1}\frac{3}{4}$ and $B = \tan^{-1}\frac{15}{8}$
(i) write $\vec{x}$ and $\vec{y}$ in terms of $\vec{i}$ and $\vec{j}$
(ii) show that $(\vec{x} + \vec{y})$ has no $\vec{j}$-component.
(iii) find the magnitude of $(\vec{x} + \vec{y})$.

## Solving for missing angles

### Worked Example 1.12

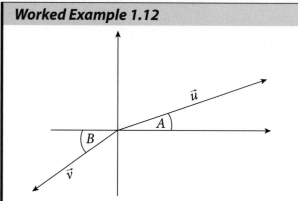

Fig. 1.65

$\vec{u}$ has magnitude 34 units; $\vec{v}$ has magnitude 20 units and $\tan B = \frac{4}{3}$.
   (i) If $(\vec{u} + \vec{v})$ has no $\vec{j}$-component (i.e. $(\vec{u} + \vec{v})$ is along the $\vec{i}$-axis) find $\tan A$.
   (ii) Hence find $(\vec{u} + \vec{v})$ in terms of $\vec{i}$ and $\vec{j}$.

**Solution:**

**Step** (1): We know that $\tan B = \frac{4}{3} = \dfrac{\text{Opposite}}{\text{Adjacent}}$

Put these results onto a model triangle.

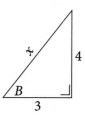

Fig. 1.66

By Pythagoras' Theorem
$$x^2 = 4^2 + 3^2$$
$$= 16 + 9$$
$$= 25$$
$$\therefore x = 5$$
$$\therefore \sin B = \frac{4}{5} \text{ and } \cos B = \frac{3}{5}$$

**Step** (2): To find $\vec{v}$ in terms of $\vec{i}$ and $\vec{j}$.

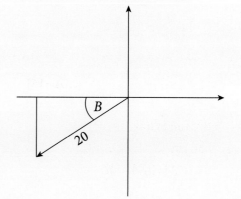

Fig. 1.67

Opposite = Hypotenuse × Sin B

$$= 20 \times \frac{4}{5}$$

$$= 16 \text{ units}$$

Adjacent = Hypotenuse x Cos B

$$= 20 \times \frac{3}{5}$$

$$= 12 \text{ units}$$

$$\therefore \vec{v} = -12 \vec{i} - 16 \vec{j}$$

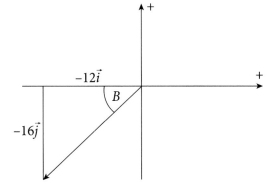

Fig. 1.68

**Step** (3): To find $\vec{u}$ in terms of $\vec{i}$ and $\vec{j}$.

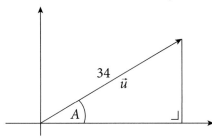

Fig. 1.69

Opposite = Hypotenuse × Sin A

$$= 34 \sin A$$

Adjacent = Hypotenuse × Cos A

$$= 34 \cos A$$

Since the $\vec{i}$ -direction is positive and the $\vec{j}$ -direction is also positive we can write:

$$\vec{u} = 34 \cos A \vec{i} + 34 \sin A \vec{j}$$

**Step** (4):

$$\therefore \vec{u} + \vec{v} = \left(34 \cos A \vec{i} + 34 \sin A \vec{j}\right) + \left(-12 \vec{i} - 16 \vec{j}\right)$$

$$\therefore \vec{u} + \vec{v} = 34 \cos A \vec{i} + 34 \sin A \vec{j} - 12 \vec{i} - 16 \vec{j}$$

$$\therefore \vec{u} + \vec{v} = (34 \cos A - 12) \vec{i} + (34 \sin A - 16) \vec{j}$$

Eqt 1

**Step** (5): But the $\vec{j}$ component must equal zero.

$$\therefore 34 \sin A - 16 = 0$$

$$\therefore 34 \sin A = 16$$

$$\therefore \sin A = \frac{16}{34}$$

$$= \frac{8}{17}$$

$$= \frac{\text{Opposite}}{\text{Hypotenuse}}$$

Put these measurements onto a model triangle.

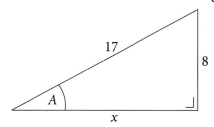

Fig. 1.70

$$x^2 + 8^2 = 17^2$$

$$\therefore x^2 = 289 - 64$$

$$\therefore x^2 = 225$$

$$\therefore x = 15$$

$$\therefore \tan A = \frac{8}{15}, \text{ and } \cos A = \frac{15}{17}$$

Putting this into Equation 1 we get

$$\vec{u} + \vec{v} = \left(34 \left(\frac{15}{17}\right) - 12\right) \vec{i} + \left(34 \left(\frac{8}{17}\right) - 16\right) \vec{j}$$

$$= 18 \vec{i} + 0 \vec{j}$$

Answer: (i) $\tan A = \frac{8}{15}$

(ii) $(\vec{u} + \vec{v}) = 18 \vec{i}$

## Exercise 1 E

1.

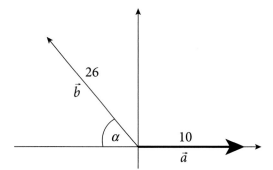

Fig. 1.71

Find tan α if $(\vec{a} + \vec{b})$ has no $\vec{i}$ -component.
Find, also, the magnitude of $(\vec{a} + \vec{b})$.

2.

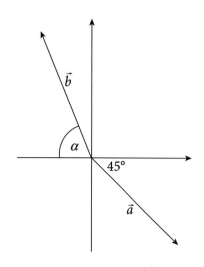

Fig. 1.72

$|\vec{a}| = \sqrt{32}$, $|\vec{b}| = 5$

Find $(\vec{a} + \vec{b})$ if it is parallel with the $\vec{j}$-axis.

3.

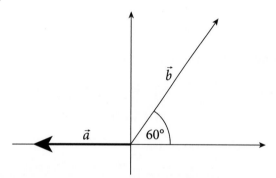

Fig. 1.73

$|\vec{a}| = 4$ cm.

Find the magnitude of $\vec{b}$ if $(\vec{a} + \vec{b})$ is parallel with the $\vec{j}$-axis. Find, also, the magnitude of $(\vec{a} + \vec{b})$.

4. $\vec{r}$ is a vector of magnitude 10 units in a direction 70° North of West.
$\vec{s}$ is a vector along the positive $\vec{i}$-axis.
Find the magnitude of $\vec{s}$ if $(\vec{r} + \vec{s})$ has no $\vec{i}$-component.

5.

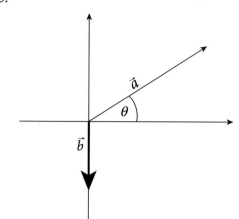

Fig. 1.74

$\vec{a}$ is a vector of magnitude 10 units; $\vec{b}$ is a vector along the negative $\vec{j}$-axis, as shown. Find the value of $k$ if $\vec{a} + \vec{b} = k\,\vec{i}$, given that $\tan \theta = \frac{3}{4}$.

6.

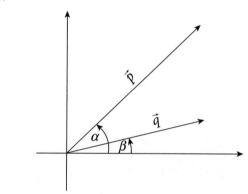

Fig. 1.75

$\vec{p}$ is a vector of magnitude 35 cm; $\vec{q}$ is a vector of magnitude 13 cm. If $\tan \alpha = \frac{4}{3}$ and $\tan \beta = \frac{5}{12}$,
(i) Write $\vec{p}$ and $\vec{q}$ in terms of $\vec{i}$ and $\vec{j}$, the orthogonal unit vectors.
(ii) Show that $(\vec{p} + \vec{q})$ makes an angle 45° with the $\vec{i}$-axis.

7. $\vec{r}$ is a vector of magnitude 10 units in a direction 70° North of West. $\vec{s}$ is a vector in a direction 10° North of East. Find the magnitude of $\vec{s}$, correct to one decimal place, if $(\vec{r} + \vec{s})$ must be in a NE direction.

8. $\vec{p} = 8\,\vec{i} + \vec{j}$
   $\vec{q} = -7\,\vec{i} + 4\,\vec{j}$

   (i) Show that $\vec{p}$ and $\vec{q}$ are of equal magnitude.
   (ii) Show that $\vec{p}$ and $\vec{q}$ are not perpendicular to each other.

9. If $(-7\,\vec{i} + \vec{j})$ and $p\,(\vec{i} + \vec{j})$ have equal magnitude where $p \in R$, $p > 0$, find the value of $p$.

10. $\vec{a}$ is a vector of magnitude 10 units with direction 80° North of East. $\vec{b}$ is a vector such that $\vec{b} = k\,\vec{i}$.

    Find the value of $k$ if $(\vec{a} + \vec{b})$ has direction 21.8° North of East, giving your answer correct to two decimal places.

## Do's and Don't for the exam

**Do**
- Do draw large diagrams on graph paper
- Do use a ruler to draw vectors
- Do put arrowheads on all vectors
- Do label every vector
- Do show all calculations

**Don't**
- Don't draw small unclear diagrams
- Don't forget to answer precisely what you were asked
- Don't mix up minutes and decimals, when dealing in parts of degrees
- Don't omit to put in units in all answers.

## Summary of important points

1. The magnitude of $a\,\vec{i} + b\,\vec{j} = \sqrt{a^2 + b^2}$

2. The angle $\theta$ which $a\,\vec{i} + b\,\vec{j}$ makes with the positive $\vec{i}$ - axis is given by: $\tan \theta = \dfrac{b}{a}$

3. In a right angled triangle

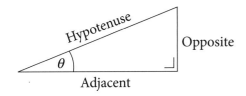

Fig. 1.76

Adjacent = Hypotenuse × cos $\theta$
Opposite = Hypotenuse × sin $\theta$

4. The slope of $p\,\vec{i} + q\,\vec{j}$ is given by $\dfrac{q}{p}$.

# Uniform acceleration

παντα ρει ουδεν μενει

(Everything is moving, nothing stays as it is.)

*Heraclitus*

## Contents

## Learning outcomes

**In this chapter you will learn...**

- What uniform acceleration is

- The formulae for uniform acceleration

- How to draw time-velocity graphs

- How to use time-velocity graphs

- How to solve problems where particles travel under gravity

## You will need to know...

- How to manipulate a formula
- How to solve simultaneous equations
- How to solve quadratics by factorising and by using the formula

$$\frac{-b \pm \sqrt{b^2 - 4ac}}{2a}$$

## Uniform acceleration

Imagine a car passing a set of traffic–lights at a speed of 8 metres per second. One second later it has increased its speed to 10 metres per second; yet another second later it has increased its speed to 12 metres / sec. After a third second it has increased its speed to 14 m/s.

**Note**: we substitute the symbol "/" for "per".

We see that it is accelerating, or increasing its speed, by 2 m/s every second, that is 2 metres per second per second or 2 m/s$^2$ (Spoken: "2 metres per second squared".)

We call such motion "**uniform acceleration**".

If we were to draw a graph of the car's velocity as time passes by, it would look like this:

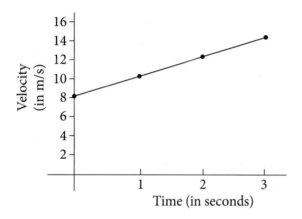

Fig. 2.1

This is a **time–velocity graph**

In general, letters are assigned to the quantities involved, in this way:

$u$ = the initial velocity (in this case 8 m/s)
$v$ = the final velocity (in this case 14 m/s)
$a$ = the acceleration (in this case 2 m/s$^2$)
$t$ = the time taken (in this case 3 s)
$s$ = the distance covered (in this case – we don't know yet).

**Acceleration**, $a$ is defined as the rate at which the velocity is changing.

$$a = \frac{(v - u)}{t}$$

In our case
$$a = \frac{(14 - 8)}{3}$$
$$a = \frac{6}{3}$$
$$a = 2 \text{ m/s}^2$$

Multiplying equation 2.1 out, and isolating $v$ we get
$$v = u + a t \qquad \textbf{Equation 2.1}$$

But how far did our car go in those 3 seconds? It started, at 8 m/s and ended at 14 m/s. The distance

covered would be the same if it had travelled at a constant velocity which is the average of 8 and 14 m/s, *i.e.*

$$= \frac{(8 + 14)}{2}$$
$$= 11 \text{ m/s}.$$

If it had travelled for 3 seconds at 11 m/s it would have covered a distance of $3 \times 11 = 33$ m.

In general the **distance** covered, $s$, is given by the average speed multiplied by the time.

i.e. $\qquad s = \frac{(u + v)}{2} t \qquad \textbf{Equation 2.2}$

We can eliminate $v$ by substituting $v = u + at$ into equation 2.3.

In this way we get
$$s = \frac{(u + u + at)}{2} t$$
$$s = \frac{1}{2}(2 u t + a t^2)$$
$$s = u t + \frac{1}{2} a t^2 \qquad \textbf{Equation 2.3}$$

Similarly we can eliminate $t$ from our system of equations by modifying equation 2.2

$$v = u + a t$$
$$t = \frac{(v - u)}{a}$$

Eq: 2.3 $\quad s = \frac{(u + v)}{2} t$

Replacing (substituting) $t$ into this equation
$$s = \frac{(u + v)(v - u)}{2 a}$$
$$s = \frac{v^2 - u^2}{2 a}$$
$$2as = v^2 - u^2$$
$$v^2 = u^2 + 2as \qquad \textbf{Equation 2.4}$$

| Formula | Equation |
|---|---|
| $v = u + a t$ | 2.1 |
| $s = \frac{(u + v)}{2} t$ | 2.2 |
| $s = u t + \frac{1}{2} a t^2$ | 2.3 |
| $v^2 = u^2 + 2 a s$ | 2.4 |

**Note:** these appear on page 50 of "Formulae and Tables"

Given any three of the variables $u$, $v$, $a$, $t$, $s$, we can find the other two.

For example, if a car is travelling at 20 m/s and slows down to 5 m/s in 3 seconds, we know that $u = 20$, $v = 5$ and $t = 3$.

Therefore the acceleration

$$a = \frac{(v - u)}{t}$$

$$a = \frac{(5 - 20)}{3}$$

$$a = -5 \text{ m/s}^2$$

The acceleration is negative because the car is slowing down. We can say either

"The acceleration is –5 m/s$^2$" or

"The deceleration or retardation is 5 m/s$^2$".

We have now found $a$. To find the remaining unknown $s$, use Eq: 2.3. Try it yourself.

### Worked Example 2.1

A girl on a bicycle accelerates from 2 m/s to 12 m/s over 4 seconds. Draw a velocity–time graph and calculate:

1. her acceleration

2. the distance covered.

**Solution**

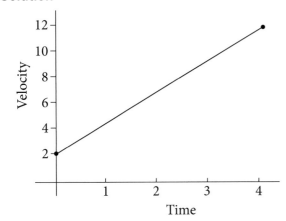

Fig. 2.2

1. her acceleration

We know $u = 2$

$v = 12$

$t = 4$

Use $a = \frac{(v - u)}{t} \Rightarrow a = \frac{12 - 2}{4}$

$\therefore a = -\frac{10}{4}$

Answer $= -2.5 \text{ m/s}^2$

2. the distance covered

$$s = ut + \frac{1}{2}at^2$$

$$s = 2(4) + 0.5(2.5)4^2$$

$$s = 8 + 20$$

Answer: 28 m.

### Worked Example 2.2

While slowing down from 40 m/s to rest, a car covers a distance of 100 m.

Find:

(i) the time taken

(ii) the deceleration

(iii) the distance the car would take to stop from 40m/s if its deceleration were doubled.

**Solution**

(i) The time taken

We know $u = 40$

$v = 0$

$s = 100$

Use $s = \frac{(u + v)}{2}t$

$100 = \frac{(40 + 0)}{2}t$

$100 = 20t$

$t = \frac{100}{20} = 5$

Answer: 5 sec

(ii) The deceleration

We know $u = 40$

$v = 0$

$t = 5$

Use $a = \frac{(v - u)}{t}$

$a = \frac{(0 - 40)}{5}$

$a = -\frac{40}{5} \text{ m/s}^2$

Answer: deceleration = 8 m/s$^2$

(iii) the distance the car would take to stop from 40 m/s if its deceleration were doubled.

We know $u = 40$

$v = 0$

$a = -16 \text{ m/s}^2$

(= twice value in (ii) above)

Use $v^2 = u^2 + 2as$

$s = \frac{(v^2 - u^2)}{2a}$

$s = \frac{(0^2 - 40^2)}{2 \times (-16)}$

$$s = \frac{-1600}{-32} \text{ m}$$

Answer:                    50 m

### Exercise 2 A

1.  A car accelerated uniformly from rest to 10 m/s in 5 seconds.
    Draw a time-velocity graph and find
    (i)   the acceleration
    (ii)  the distance covered.

2.  A car, driving on a straight road, accelerates with an acceleration of 3 m/s² from rest to a speed of 24 m/s.
    Find:
    (i)   the time taken
    (ii)  the distance covered.

3.  A car starts from rest and accelerates at 3 m/s². Find its speed when it has travelled a distance of 6 m.

4.  A train accelerates from 50 m/s to 70 m/s over a distance of 300 m.
    Find the acceleration and the time taken.

5.  A car, accelerating uniformly at 0.5 m/s², travels a distance of 600 m in 40 seconds.
    What was its initial speed?

6.  A cyclist accelerates uniformly from 3 m/s to 11 m/s during a 6 second period.
    Find the distance covered.

7.  A lift decelerates from 3 m/s to rest during the last 6 metres of its motion.
    Find the deceleration and the time taken.

8.  A train slows down from 70 m/s to 50 m/s over an eight-second time interval.
    (i)   Find the deceleration and the distance covered.
    (ii)  If the train continues to decelerate at the same uniform rate, how much further will it travel before it comes to rest?

9.  A car has maximum deceleration of 8 m/s².
    Find the shortest possible distance it will take to stop if it is travelling at:
    (i)   24 m/s
    (ii)  48 m/s.

10.
    (i)   Convert 72 km/hour to metres per second.
    (ii)  A train decelerates from 72 km/hour to 48 km/hour over a distance of $\frac{1}{2}$ km.
          Find the deceleration as a fraction.
          Find also the time taken.
    (iii) If the train continues to decelerate at this rate find how much further it will travel before it comes to rest.

11. Show that a speed of 1 km/hour is equivalent to $\frac{5}{18}$ m/s. The speed of a car is reduced from 72 km/hour to 54 km/hour over a distance of 35 m.
    (i)   Find the retardation, assuming it is uniform throughout.
    (ii)  If the retardation continues, how much further will the car travel before coming to rest?

12. $P$ and $Q$ are points 162 m apart. A body leaves $P$ with initial speed 5 m/s and travels towards $Q$ with uniform acceleration 3 m/s². At the same instant another body leaves $Q$ and travels towards $P$ with initial speed 7 m/s and uniform acceleration 2 m/s².
    After how many seconds do they meet and what, then, is the speed of each body?

13. $X$ and $Y$ are 400 metres apart.
    $X$ is travelling towards $Y$ with initial speed 3 m/s and acceleration 4 m/s². At the same time $Y$ is travelling towards $X$ with initial speed 7 m/s and acceleration 2 m/s².
    Find
    (i)   the time which elapses before they meet
    (ii)  the distance which each travels in this time.

14. A particle starts from rest with uniform acceleration 2 m/s².
    Calculate the following, giving your answers as rational numbers (fractions):
    (i)   After how many seconds will its speed be 30 km/hour?
    (ii)  How far from its starting point will the particle be when its speed is 60 km/hour?
    (iii) If the particle is then brought to rest in 2 metres, what is the deceleration?

# Distance travelled from the velocity - time graph

You should observe, at this stage, that the area under a velocity - time, curve is equal to the distance travelled. We will prove this in the case of uniform acceleration:

**To prove**: The area under a velocity - time graph is equal to the distance travelled.

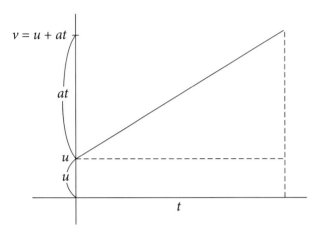

Fig. 2.3

## Proof

Since $v = u + at$ the gap between "$u$" and "$v$" is of length "$at$". The area under the curve is the sum of a rectangle and a triangle.

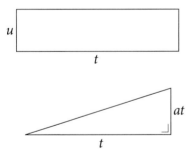

Fig. 2.4

Area of rectangle
= length × breadth
= $u \times t$

Area of triangle is

$= \frac{1}{2} t \times at$

$= \frac{1}{2} at^2$

∴ Total Area $= ut + \frac{1}{2} a t^2$, which is $s$ the distance covered; see Eq. 2.3 **Q.E.D.**

This is true whether the object is accelerating uniformly or not,

## The Area under Velocity - Time Curve = Distance Travelled

We use this to help solve questions, especially where there is NOT a uniform acceleration throughout; here are some examples:

### Worked Example 2.3

A particle starting from rest moves in a straight line with an acceleration of $\frac{1}{2}$ m/s$^2$ for 8 seconds. It then decelerates uniformly to a speed of 3 m/s in the next 4 seconds. It maintains this speed for 5 seconds and then comes to rest with a deceleration of 2 m/s$^2$ Draw a time–velocity graph for this motion. Hence, or otherwise find:

 (i)   The greatest velocity reached during the journey.

 (ii)  The total time for the journey.

 (iii) The total distance travelled.

 (iv)  The average speed, correct to three decimal places.

### Solution

We draw a time–velocity graph showing acceleration for 8 seconds, deceleration for 4 seconds, steady speed for the next 5 seconds, and a deceleration to rest for an unknown time.

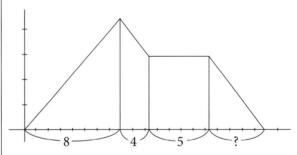

Fig. 2.5

 (i)   The greatest velocity reached during the journey.

To find the greatest velocity reached we examine our information for the first 8 seconds of motion.

We know
$$u = 0$$
$$t = 8$$
$$a = \frac{1}{2} \text{ m/s}^2$$

Use
$$v = u + at$$
$$v = 0 + \left(\frac{1}{2}\right) 8$$
$$v = 4 \text{ m/s}$$
Answer: $v = 4$ m/s

(ii)  The total time for the journey.

The only missing time interval is the time taken to decelerate to rest from 3 m/s. The deceleration is given as 2 m/s$^2$

We know
$$u = 3$$
$$v = 0$$
$$a = 2$$

Use
$$v = u + at$$
$$\therefore 0 = 3 + (-2)\, t$$
$$\therefore t = 1.5 \text{ s}$$
Answer: $t = 1.5$ s

Therefore, the total time for the journey = 8 + 4 + 5 + 1.5 = 18.5 s. We can now complete an accurate time–velocity graph:

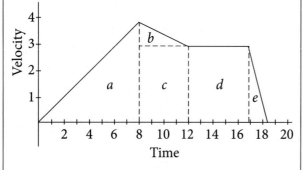

Fig. 2.6

(iii)  The total distance covered

The total distance covered = the area under the curve. We will break it up into 5 parts, as shown.

| Part | Area | Calc | Result |
|---|---|---|---|
| a. | $\frac{1}{2}$ base × height | $= \frac{1}{2} \times 8 \times 4$ | = 16 |
| b. | $\frac{1}{2}$ base × height | $= \frac{1}{2} \times 4 \times 1$ | = 2 |
| c. | length × breadth | $= 4 \times 3$ | = 12 |
| d. | length × breadth | $= 5 \times 3$ | = 15 |
| e. | $\frac{1}{2}$ base × height | $= \frac{1}{2} \times \frac{3}{2} \times 3$ | = 2.25 |
| | Total area = | Distance covered | 47.25 m |

(iv)  Average speed = total distance/total time
$$= \frac{47.25}{18.5}$$
$$= 2.446 \text{ m/s}$$

Answer(s)    4 m/s, 18.5 sec, 47.25 m, 2.446 m/s

### Worked Example 2.4

A cyclist starts a 100 m race at a speed of 4 m/s and accelerates to his maximum speed of 16 m/s. He continues at this speed for the rest of the race. The total time for the race is 7 seconds. Find

(i)  the time spent accelerating

(ii)  the rate of acceleration.

**Solution**

Draw a rough time–velocity graph, Fig 2.10

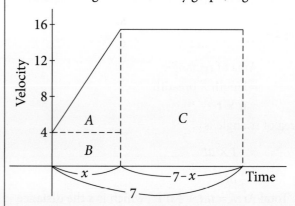

Fig. 2.7

(i)  Let $x$ = the time spent accelerating.

$\therefore$    $7 - x$ = the time spent at a uniform speed. The area under the curve must be 100.

$100 = $ Sum of $A + B + C$

$100 = \frac{1}{2} x (16 - 4) + x (4) + (7 - x) 16$

$100 = 6 x + 4 x + 112 - 16 x$

$100 = 112 - 6 x$

$6 x = 12$

$x = 2$ s

Answer: time spent accelerating is 2 seconds

(ii)  the acceleration

To find the acceleration "$a$" we examine our information for the first part of motion:

We know       $u = 4$

$v = 16$

$t = 2$

$a = ?$

Use       $v = u + at$

$\therefore a = \frac{(v - u)}{t}$

$\therefore a = \frac{(16 - 4)}{2}$

$\therefore a = 6$ m/s$^2$

Answer: $a = 6$ m/s$^2$

## Exercise 2 B

1.  A car, travelling in a straight line, accelerates uniformly from rest with an acceleration of 2 m/s$^2$ to a maximum speed of 30 m/s. It drives at a constant speed for 12 seconds and then decelerates to rest in a further 10 seconds. Find:

    (i)   the time spent accelerating

    (ii)  the total distance covered

    (iii) the magnitude of the deceleration.

2.  A car accelerates from rest to a speed of 20 m/s over a 5–second time interval. It then continues at this constant speed. Calculate:

    (i)   the acceleration

    (ii)  the distance covered during acceleration

    (iii) the total time taken, given that the total distance covered was $\frac{1}{4}$ km.

3.  A car accelerates at 5 m/s$^2$ from rest to a speed of 50 m/s. It then travels at a steady speed of 50 m/s for 25 $s$ and finally decelerates to rest with a deceleration of 10 m/s$^2$. Find:

(i)   the total distance travelled

(ii)  the average speed.

4.  A car accelerates at 3 m/s$^2$ from rest to a speed of 60 m/s. It then travels at a steady speed of 60 m/s for 75 s. It finally decelerates to rest, covering a distance of 150 m while decelerating.
Find

    (i)   the time spent decelerating

    (ii)  the total distance covered

    (iii) the average speed for the entire journey.

5.  A car accelerates at 2 m/s$^2$ from rest to a speed of 40 m/s. It then travels at a steady speed and finally decelerates to rest with a deceleration of 5 m/s$^2$.
Find:

    (i)   the distance covered during acceleration

    (ii)  the distance covered during deceleration.

    (iii) If the entire journey, from rest to rest, was 1 km long, find the total time taken.

6.  A car starts from rest with a uniform acceleration and reaches a velocity of 27 m/s in 9 seconds. The brakes are then applied and it comes to rest with uniform deceleration after travelling a further 54 m.
Calculate:

    (i)   the uniform acceleration

    (ii)  the uniform deceleration

    (iii) the average speed of the car for the journey

    (iv)  the two times that the velocity of the car will be 15 m/s.

7.  A car travelling towards $P$ at a steady speed of 15 m/s, accelerated at a constant rate between $P$ and $Q$. At $Q$ its speed was 25 m/s. This speed was maintained as far as $R$ (see Fig. 2.8)
If $|PR| = 980$ m and the time from $P$ to $R$ was 40 seconds, draw a time–velocity graph of the motion and hence, or otherwise, calculate the acceleration.

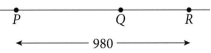

Fig. 2.8

8. An athlete runs a 100 m race in 12 seconds. Starting from rest, she accelerates uniformly to a speed of 10 m/s. She then continues at this speed for the rest of the race.
Calculate the acceleration.

9. A cyclist covers a distance of 350 m in 18 seconds. Starting from rest, he accelerates uniformly to a speed of 25 m/s. He then continues at this speed for the rest of the distance.
Calculate the time spent accelerating.

10. The maximum speed of a car is 40 m/s. Its maximum acceleration is 2 m/s$^2$ and its maximum deceleration is 8 m/s$^2$. This car has to travel a distance of 700 m from rest to rest. What is the minimum possible time?

11. A racing car covers a distance of 8.8 km from rest to rest. It accelerates uniformly in the first minute to reach its maximum speed of 40 m/s. It holds this speed for a certain time and then slows uniformly to rest with a retardation of magnitude three times that of the acceleration.
   (i) Draw a rough time–velocity graph and find the distances travelled in the three stages of the journey. Find also the total time taken.
   (ii) If the maximum speed over the final kilometre of the journey had been restricted to 20 m/s, show that the time taken from rest to rest would have been at least 22.5 seconds longer than before, assuming that the rates of acceleration and deceleration are the same as before.

## Worked Example 2.5

A train covers 24 m in the first two seconds after it passes a signal post. It then covers 51 m in the following 3 seconds. Assuming that the train is accelerating uniformly, find out how far it will go in the next 3 seconds.

### Solution

Let the initial speed be $u$.

Let the acceleration be $a$

We know $\qquad t = 2$

$\qquad\qquad s = 24$

Use $\qquad\qquad s = u\,t + \frac{1}{2}\,a\,t^2$

$\therefore 24 = u\,(2) + \frac{1}{2}\,a\,(4)$

$\therefore 24 = 2\,u + 2\,a$

$u + a = 12 \qquad$ Equation X

Now looking at the information over the first 5 seconds (not the next three seconds because the initial velocity for that period would not be $u$).

$\qquad\qquad t = 5$

$\qquad\qquad s = (51+24)$

$\qquad\qquad s = 75$

$\qquad\qquad s = u\,t + \frac{1}{2}\,a\,t^2$

$\therefore 75 = u\,(5) + \frac{1}{2}\,a\,5^2$

$\therefore 75 = 5\,u + 12.5\,a$

$\therefore 150 = 10\,u + 25\,a$

$\therefore 2\,u + 5\,a = 30 \qquad$ Equation Y

Equations X and Y are simultaneous equations in $u$ and $a$ and hence can be solved.

$\qquad 2\,u + 2\,a = 24 \qquad$ Eq. X × 2

$\qquad 2\,u + 5\,a = 30 \qquad$ Eq.Y

$\qquad\qquad \therefore 3\,a = 6$

$\qquad\qquad \therefore a = 2 \text{ m/s}^2$

But $\qquad\qquad u + 2 = 12 \qquad$ Eq. X

$\qquad\qquad u = 10 \text{ m/s}$

How far will it go in the first 8 seconds?

$\qquad\qquad s = u\,t + \frac{1}{2}\,a\,t^2$

$\qquad\qquad s = (10)(8) + \frac{1}{2}(2)\,8^2$

$\qquad\qquad s = 80 + 64$

$\qquad\qquad s = 144 \text{ m for the whole 8 secs.}$

The question asked was how far will it travel in the last 3 seconds. Since it travelled 75 m over the first 5 seconds and 144 m over the first 8 seconds, the answer is:

$\qquad\qquad s = 144 - 75$

$\qquad\qquad = 69 \text{ m.}$

$\qquad\qquad$ Answer: $s = 69$ m

### Worked Example 2.6

A car starts from rest at a traffic light and accelerates at 3 m/s$^2$. As it starts it is passed by a cyclist who is moving at a constant speed of 12 m/s. After how long will the car overtake the cyclist and how far from the traffic light will overtaking occur?

**Solution**

The key is that at the moment of overtaking (say when the time $= T$), the distances travelled by both are the same.

| Cyclist | Car |
|---|---|
| $u = 12$ | $u = 0$ |
| $a = 0$ | $a = 3$ |
| $t = T$ | $t = T$ |
| $s = ?$ | $s = ?$ |
| $s = ut + \frac{1}{2}at^2$ | $s = ut + \frac{1}{2}at^2$ |
| $s = (12)T + \frac{1}{2}(0)T^2$ | $s = (0)T + \frac{1}{2}(3)T^2$ |
| $s = 12T$ | $s = \frac{3}{2}T^2$ |

But at overtaking $s_{cyclist} = s_{car}$

$\therefore$
$$12T = \frac{3}{2}T^2$$
$$12 = \frac{3}{2}T$$
$$24 = 3T$$
$$T = 8 \text{ s.}$$

The distance travelled by the cyclist and the car is the same but as the cyclist is not accelerating the calculation is easier:

$$s = 12t$$
$$s = (12)(8)$$
$$s = 96 \text{ m.}$$

### Worked Example 2.7

A Mini starts from rest at a point $P$ and moves with acceleration 2 m/s$^2$, in a straight line. Twenty seconds later a Fiat passes through $P$ at a speed of 10 m/s, moving with acceleration 4 m/s$^2$

(i) What is the greatest distance the Mini will ever be ahead of the Fiat?

(ii) After how long and how far from $P$ will overtaking occur?

**Solution:**

(i) The greatest gap occurs when their speeds are equal. This is because before this critical moment, the Mini is going faster and after this moment, the Fiat is going faster. Hence the greatest gap occurs when their speeds are equal.

Let $t =$ the time the Mini has spent on the road when the greatest gap occurs. Hence $(t - 20)$ is the time the Fiat is on the road when this happens.

At this time, the speeds of both cars are the same, $v_1 = v_2$
$$v = u + at$$
Speed Mini = Speed Fiat
$$(u + at)_{Mini} = (u + at)_{Fiat}$$
$$0 + 2(t) = 10 + 4(t - 20)$$
$$2t = 10 + 4t - 80$$
$$2t - 4t = -70$$
$$2t = 70$$
$$t = 35 \text{ s.}$$
$$s_{mini} = 0(35) + \frac{1}{2}(2)(35)^2 = 1225 \text{ m}$$
$$s_{Fiat} = 10(15) + \frac{1}{2}(4)(15)^2 = 600 \text{ m}$$
$$\therefore \text{ Gap} = 1225 - 600 = 625 \text{ m.}$$

Once again at the moment of overtaking (let's again say when time $= T$), the distances travelled by both cars are equal:

| Mini | Fiat |
|---|---|
| $s_1 = 0(T) + \frac{1}{2}(2)T^2$ | $s_2 = 10(T-20) + \frac{1}{2}(4)(T-20)^2$ |
| $s_1 = T^2$ | $s_2 = 10T - 200 +$ $2(T^2 - 40T + 400)$ |
| | $s_2 = 2T^2 - 70T + 600$ |

But at the moment of overtaking $s_1 = s_2$

| Substitute for $s_1$ & $s_2$ | $\therefore T^2 = 2T^2 - 70T + 600$ |
|---|---|
| Simplify | $T^2 - 70T + 600 = 0$ |
| Factorise | $(T - 60)(T - 10) = 0$ |
| | $T = 60$ or $T = 10$ |

Chapter 2 – Uniform acceleration

$T = 10$ is unacceptable, since the Fiat has not, in fact, started to move at $T = 10$.

The answer is then $T = 60$ s. The Mini will have travelled a distance of $T^2 = (60)^2$ = 3,600 m. (The Fiat, will, of course, also have travelled this distance.)

A time–velocity graph is given here:

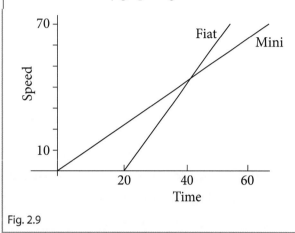

Fig. 2.9

## Worked Example 2.8

A passenger train leaves a station. It starts from rest and moving with uniform acceleration $\frac{1}{2}$ m/s$^2$ until it reaches 40 m/s. It then continues at this speed uniformly. As it was leaving, a goods train passed it, moving at a constant speed 24 m/s on a parallel track in the same direction.

After how long and how far from the station will overtaking occur? (Neglect the lengths of the trains.)

### Solution:

In this case we CANNOT use the formula $s = ut + \frac{1}{2} a t^2$ because the passenger train does not have uniform acceleration throughout its motion. In such cases we revert to a time–velocity graph, using one set of axes for both trains:

**Step** 1: Let $T$ = the time at which overtaking occurs

We know
$$u = 0$$
$$a = \frac{1}{2}$$
$$v = 40$$
$$t = ?$$

Use
$$v = u + at$$
$$40 = 0 + \frac{1}{2} t$$
$$t = 80 \text{ s.}$$

The rest of the time during which it travelled at a uniform speed, is therefore, $T - 80$

Put these details into the time–velocity graph.

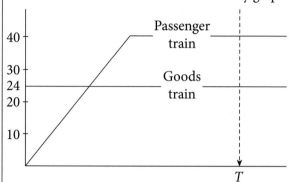

Fig. 2.10

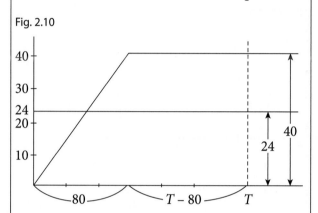

Fig. 2.11

The areas under both curves must be equal, since the distances travelled are equal.

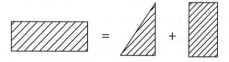

Fig. 2.12

$$24\,T = \frac{1}{2}(80)(40) + (T - 80)\,40$$
$$24\,T = 1600 + 40\,T - 3200$$
$$1600 = 16\,T$$
$$T = 100 \text{ s}$$

The distance travelled by the goods train will be
$$= 24T$$
$$= (24)(100)$$
$$= 2400 \text{ m.}$$

Answer(s):     100 s, 2400 m

## Note

In questions where there is uniform acceleration followed immediately by uniform deceleration, let $v$ = the top speed reached.

Then find the following in terms of $v$:

The time spent accelerating

The time spent decelerating

Now, form an equation in $v$ and solve it!

## Worked Example 2.9

A car accelerates at 2 m/s$^2$ from rest to a maximum speed. It immediately decelerates with deceleration 5 m/s$^2$ to rest. If the total time taken is 21 seconds, find the distance covered.

**Solution:**

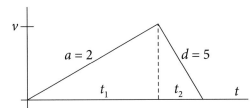

Fig. 2.13

Let the top speed reached $= v$

The time spent accelerating $t_1$ is $= \dfrac{v}{2}$ s

The time spent decelerating $t_2$ is $= \dfrac{v}{5}$ s

The time taken is $t_1 + t_2 = 21$ s

$$\frac{v}{2} + \frac{v}{5} = 21$$

$$\frac{(5v + 2v)}{10} = 21$$

$$\frac{7}{10}v = 21$$

$$7v = 210$$

$$v = 30 \text{ m/s}$$

The time spent accelerating is, therefore,

$$= \frac{v}{2}$$

$$= \frac{30}{2}$$

$$= 15 \text{ s}$$

The time spent decelerating is

$$= \frac{v}{5}$$

$$= \frac{30}{5}$$

$$= 6 \text{ s}$$

Distance travelled = Area of triangle

$$= \frac{1}{2}(15 + 6)(30)$$

Answer: $= 315$ m

## Worked Example 2.10

A car can accelerate with acceleration 2 m/s$^2$, and decelerate with deceleration 3 m/s$^2$. Find the least possible time it takes to cover a distance of 375 m, from rest to rest,

(i) subject to a 24 m/s speed limit

(ii) subject to no speed limit.

**Solution: (i)**

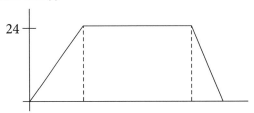

Fig. 2.14

The car can accelerate to 24 m/s, then drive at a constant speed, and then decelerate to rest. Simple calculations show that the time for acceleration at 2 m/s$^2$ is 12 seconds, but for deceleration at 3 m/s$^2$ is 8 seconds.

We'll say that the time spent moving at a constant speed is $= x$

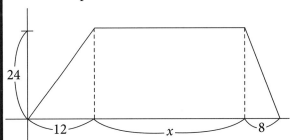

Fig. 2.15

The area under the time/velocity graph must be 375, the distance travelled.

$$375 = \frac{1}{2}(12)(24) + 24x + \frac{1}{2}(8)(24)$$

$$375 = 144 + 24x + 96$$

$$24x = 135$$

$$8x = 45$$

$$x = 5.625$$

Total time $= 12 + 5.625 + 8$

Answer $= 25.625$ s

**Solution: (ii)**

In this case there is no speed limit, so the car accelerates to a maximum speed and immediately decelerates again to rest. We follow these 3 steps:

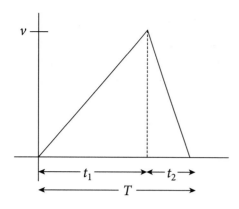

Fig. 2.16

Let the top speed $= v$

The time spent accelerating is $t_1$ $= \dfrac{v}{2}$ m/s

The time spent decelerating is $t_2$ $= \dfrac{v}{3}$ m/s

The distance travelled $= 375$ m

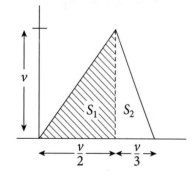

Fig. 2.17

$$s_1 + s_2 = 375$$

$$\frac{1}{2}\left(\frac{v}{2} + \frac{v}{3}\right) v = 375$$

$$\frac{1}{2}\frac{(3v + 2v)}{6} v = 375$$

$$\frac{1}{2}\left(\frac{5v}{6}\right) v = 375$$

$$\frac{5}{12} v^2 = 375$$

$$5v^2 = 4500$$

$$v^2 = 900$$

$$v = 30$$

Time taken $= \dfrac{v}{2} + \dfrac{v}{3}$

$= \dfrac{30}{2} + \dfrac{30}{3}$

Answer: $= 25$ s

## Exercise 2 C

1. A cyclist accelerates from rest with acceleration 2 m/s² to a maximum speed of 10 m/s, and then continues at this speed. Show this motion on a time–speed graph and hence, or otherwise, find out how long it will take the cyclist to cover 100 m.

2. A car accelerates from rest for 15 seconds with a uniform acceleration of 1.5 m/s² and immediately decelerates with a uniform deceleration of 5 m/s² to rest.
   (i) How long does the deceleration take?
   (ii) How far will the car go during the entire journey?

3. A car accelerates from rest at 2 m/s² to a maximum speed of 24 m/s. It immediately decelerates to rest covering a distance of 48 m during deceleration. Find:
   (i) the time used up during each part of the journey
   (ii) the average speed throughout.

4. A car starts from rest at a point $P$ and moves with acceleration 4 m/s². As it starts, another car passes $P$ moving in the same direction at a uniform speed of 20 m/s.
   Find at what time overtaking will occur and how far from $P$.

5. Two cars travelling in the same direction side by side pass a traffic light simultaneously. Car $A$ is travelling at 10 m/s with acceleration 3 m/s²; Car $B$ is travelling with speed 20 m/s and acceleration 2 m/s².
   Write in terms of the time, $t$:
   (i) the velocity of each car at time $t$
   (ii) the distance travelled by each car.
   Hence find the time at which:
   (iii) they are travelling at the same speed
   (iv) they are side by side again.

6. A car moving with constant acceleration passes three posts, $A$, $B$ and $C$ on a straight road. The distance from $A$ to $B$ is 48 m and from $B$ to $C$ 102 m. The car takes 4 $s$ to go from $A$ to $B$ and 6 $s$ to go from $B$ to $C$. Find the acceleration of the car.

7. A train, which is accelerating uniformly, passes a point $P$ at speed. In the next two seconds it covers a distance 18 metres and in the two seconds after that it covers a further 30 metres. Find:
   (i) its acceleration
   (ii) its speed as it passes $P$
   (iii) the distance it will travel in yet another two seconds.

8. A particle starts from rest and moves in a straight line with uniform acceleration. It passes three points $A$, $B$ and $C$ where $|AB| = 105$ m and $|BC| = 63$ m. If it takes 6 seconds to travel from $A$ to $B$ and 2 seconds to travel from $B$ to $C$. Find
   (i) its acceleration
   (ii) the distance of $A$ from the starting position

9. A train travels 39 metres, 37 metres, 35 metres in each of 3 consecutive seconds along a straight railway track. Show that this is consistent with motion under constant deceleration.
   Find how much further the train will travel before coming to rest.

10. A sprinter runs a race with constant acceleration throughout. During the race he passes four posts $A$, $B$, $C$, $D$ in a straight line such that $|AB| = |BC| = |CD| = 20$ m. If the sprinter takes 5 seconds to go from $A$ to $B$, and 3 seconds to go from $B$ to $C$, find how long, to the nearest tenth of a second, it takes him to run from $C$ to $D$.

11. A train starting from rest at $P$ accelerates uniformly for 10 seconds, travels at a uniform speed for 32 seconds and decelerates for 6 seconds to rest at $Q$. Draw a rough time velocity graph of this motion. If the distance $|PQ|$ is 1 km find the maximum speed reached and the distance travelled during each part of the journey.

12. A car moves from rest with uniform acceleration of 1 m/s$^2$ followed by an immediate deceleration of 3 m/s$^2$ to rest. The total time taken is 20 $s$. Find:
   (i) the time spent on each part of the journey
   (ii) the maximum speed reached
   (iii) the total distance covered.

13. A Japanese monorail train leaves Showajima Station where it had stopped and accelerates at 2 m/s$^2$ to a maximum speed and immediately decelerates at 7 m/s$^2$ to reach Oi–keibajo–mae Station. If the journey takes $1\frac{1}{2}$ minutes find the distance between the two stations in kilometres.

14. A train travels from rest at $A$ to rest at $B$ in one minute. It starts by accelerating uniformly for 12 seconds and finishes by decelerating uniformly for 8 seconds. In between it travels with uniform velocity.
   (i) If the distance covered is 1 km, find the maximum speed reached.
   (ii) As it was leaving $A$, another train passed it moving in the same direction on a parallel track with a uniform speed of 14 m/s. After how long, and how far from $A$, will overtaking occur? (Neglect the length of the trains.)

15. An underground train accelerating uniformly passes 4 signals in a straight line, each 24 m apart. If it takes the train 2 seconds to go from the first to the second, 1 second to go from the second to the third, how long (correct to 3 decimal places) will it take to go from the third to the fourth?

16. A car can accelerate at 1 m/s$^2$ and decelerate at 2 m/s$^2$. How long will it take to travel a distance 300 m from rest to rest
   (i) subject to a 16 m/s speed limit
   (ii) subject to no speed limit?

17. Cyclists $A$ and $B$ leave the same spot from rest and travel in opposite directions. Cyclist $A$ accelerates at 0.5 m/s$^2$, whilst cyclist $B$ accelerates at 1 m/s$^2$.
   (i) How far apart will they be after 10 seconds?
   (ii) After how long more will they be 108 m apart?

18. The maximum acceleration of a body is 4 m/s$^2$ and its maximum retardation is 8 m/s$^2$. What is the shortest time in which the body can travel a distance of 1200 m from rest to rest?

19. A cyclist, travelling at a constant speed of 12 m/s, passes a point $p$. Five seconds later a car starts from $p$ from rest and travels in the same direction as the cyclist with a uniform acceleration of 1 m/s$^2$.
    What is the greatest distance by which the cyclist is ever ahead of the car?

20. A car $P$ starts from a point $O$ with an initial speed of 8 m/s and then travels with a uniform acceleration of 4 m/s$^2$. Two seconds later a second car $Q$ starts from $O$ with an initial velocity of 30 m/s and then moves with a uniform acceleration of 3 m/s$^2$.
    Show that, after passing $P$, $Q$ will never be ahead by more than 74 m.

21. At a certain moment in the Tour de France, Alberto is 22 m behind Gustav. Alberto is cycling at 12 m/s and accelerating at 1 m/s$^2$ Gustav, who has just fixed a puncture, starts from rest and accelerates with acceleration 2 m/s$^2$.

    (i) After how long will Alberto catch up with Gustav?

    (ii) After how long more will Gustav overtake Alberto again?

22. A body starts from rest at $P$, travels in a straight line and then comes to rest at $Q$ which is 696 m from $P$. The time taken is 66 seconds. For the first 10 seconds it has uniform acceleration $a_1$. It then travels at a constant speed and is finally brought to rest by a uniform deceleration $a_2$ acting for 6 seconds. Calculate $a_1$ and $a_2$.
    If the journey from rest at $P$ to rest at $Q$ had been travelled with no interval of constant speed, but subject to $a_1$ for a time $t_1$ and followed by $a_2$ for time $t_2$, show that the time for the journey is $8\sqrt{29}$ seconds.

23. A passenger train, which is travelling at 80 m/s is 1,500 m behind a goods train which is travelling at 30 m/s in the same direction on the same track. At what rate must the passenger train decelerate to avoid a crash? (Ignore the lengths of the trains.)

24. The driver of a car travelling at 20 m/s sees a second car 120 m in front, travelling in the same direction at a uniform speed of 8 m/s.

    (i) What is the least uniform retardation that must be applied to the faster car so as to avoid a collision?

    (ii) If the actual retardation is 1 m/s$^2$, calculate:
        (a) the time interval in seconds for the faster car to reach a point 66 m behind the slower
        (b) the shortest distance between the cars.

## Motion under gravity

One of the most common examples of uniformly accelerated motion is when an object falls under gravity. It accelerates towards the ground at 9.8 m/s$^2$, which is known as $g$ m/s$^2$.
Here is an example:

### Worked Example 2.11

A particle is projected vertically downwards from the top of a tower with speed $u$ m/s. It takes the particle 4 seconds to reach the bottom of the tower. During the third second of its motion the particle travels 29.9 metres.
Find

(i) the value of $u$

(ii) the height of the tower.

**Solution**

(i) We know that the particle travels 29.9 m in the second from $t = 2$ to $t = 3$.
So, its average speed over that second is 29·9 m/s. Since the acceleration is a constant, we can state that it is travelling at exactly 29.9 m/s at $t = 2.5$ s.

We know at $t = 2.5$

$$u = u$$
$$t = 2.5$$
$$v = 29.9$$
$$a = 9.8$$

Use $v = u + a\,t$
$$\therefore 29.9 = u + (9.8)\,2.5$$
$$\therefore 29.9 = u + 24.5$$
$$\therefore u = 5.4 \text{ m/s}$$

(ii) Let $h$ = the height of the tower.

$$u = 5.4$$
$$t = 4$$
$$a = 9.8$$
$$s = h$$

Using $\quad s = ut + \frac{1}{2}at^2$

$$\therefore h = 5.4\,(4) + \frac{1}{2}\,(9.8)\,4^2$$
$$= 21.6 + 78.4$$

Answer $\qquad h = 100$ m.

## Exercise 2 D

1. A stone is thrown vertically upwards from ground level with an initial speed of 35 m/s.
   (i) After how long will the stone hit the ground?
   (ii) Find the greatest height reached.

2. A stone is projected vertically upward from ground level with initial speed $u$ m/s. After 1 second it reaches a height of 16.1 m. Find
   (i) the value of $u$
   (ii) the greatest height reached
   (iii) the time spent in the air before it hits the ground

3. A particle falls freely under gravity from rest at a point $P$. After it has fallen for 1 second another particle is projected vertically downwards from $P$ with speed 14.7 m/s.
   (i) Find the time at which they collide.
   (ii) How far below $P$ do they collide?
   (iii) Show the motion of both particles on a speed–time graph.

4. A particle $P$ is projected upwards from the ground with an initial speed of 47 m/s. Two seconds later a second particle $Q$ is projected upwards from the same point with initial velocity 64.6 m/s. Calculate
   (i) how long $Q$ is in motion before it collides with $P$
   (ii) the height at which the collision occurs.

5. A stone projected vertically upwards with an initial speed of $u$ m/s rises 70 m in the first $t$ seconds and another 50 m in the next $t$ seconds.
   Find the value of $u$ and the value of $t$.

6. A stone is thrown vertically upwards under gravity with a speed of $u$ m/s from a point 30 metres above the horizontal ground. The stone hits the ground 5 seconds later.
   (i) Find the value of $u$
   (ii) Find the speed with which the stone hits the ground

7. A particle is projected vertically upwards from ground level with velocity 49 m/s. It is at a height 78.4 m above the ground at times $t_1$ and $t_2$.
   Prove that $t_1 + t_2 = 10$.

8. A particle is projected vertically upwards from ground level with velocity 70 m/s. It is at a height of 210 m above the ground at times $t_1$ and $t_2$
   Prove that $7\,t_1\,t_2 = 300$.

## Harder examples: Dealing with letters instead of numbers

When faced with problems in which the quantities are given as letters rather than numbers, the problem is harder to solve. Just imagine, "How would I solve this problem if these letters were numbers" – and proceed in the same way.

### Worked Example 2.12

A train accelerates uniformly from rest to a speed of $v$ m/s. It continues at this speed for a period of time and then decelerates to rest.

In travelling a total distance of $d$ metres the train accelerates through a distance $pd$ metres and decelerates through a distance $qd$ metres, where $p < 1$ and $q < 1$.

Draw a speed–time graph for the motion of the train.

If the average speed for the whole journey is $\dfrac{v}{p + q + b}$, find the value of $b$.

**Solution**

Let $t_1$ = the time spent accelerating

Let $t_2$ = the time spent at a constant speed

Let $t_3$ = the time spent decelerating

We will try to get $t_1$, $t_2$, $t_3$ in terms of the variables given, namely $d$, $v$, $p$ and $q$.

Firstly: $\frac{1}{2} t_1 v = pd$ (since $pd$ is the distance travelled while accelerating)

$$\therefore t_1 v = 2 pd$$

$$\therefore t_1 = \frac{2 p d}{v}$$

The distance travelled at a constant speed

$$= d - pd - qd$$

$$= d (1 - p - q)$$

Hence, $\qquad t_2 v = d (1 - p - q)$

$$t_2 = \frac{d (1 - p - q)}{v}$$

Finally, $\qquad \frac{1}{2} t_3 v = q d$

(since $qd$ is the distance travelled while decelerating)

$$t_3 v = 2 q d$$

$$t_3 = \frac{2 q d}{v}$$

But the average speed is $\dfrac{v}{p + q + b}$ is given

$$\therefore \frac{\text{Total distance}}{\text{Total time}} = \frac{v}{p + q + b}$$

$$\therefore \frac{d}{t_1 + t_2 + t_3} = \frac{v}{p + q + b}$$

$$\therefore d (p + q + b) = v (t_1 + t_2 + t_3)$$

$$\therefore d (p + q + b) = v \left( \frac{2pd}{v} + \frac{d (1 - p - q)}{v} + \frac{2qd}{v} \right)$$

$$\therefore d (p + q + b) = 2pd + d (1 - p - q) + 2qd$$

$$\therefore p + q + b = 2p + (1 - p - q) + 2q$$

(dividing by $d$)

$$\therefore p + q + b = 2p + 1 - p - q + 2q$$

$$\therefore p + q + b = p + q + 1$$

$$\therefore b = 1$$

## Exercise 2. E

1. A car, starting from rest and accelerating uniformly, travels a distance $d$ in the first $n$ seconds of motion and a distance $k$ in the next $n$ seconds. Prove that $k = 3d$.

2. A car can move with acceleration $3a$ and deceleration $5a$. Find, in terms of $k$, the time taken to cover a distance of $90 \, ak^2$ from rest to rest.

   (i)   subject to speed limit of $15 \, ak$

   (ii)  subject to no speed limit.

3. A particle is projected vertically upwards with velocity $u$ m/s. Its height is $h$ after $t_1$ and $t_2$ seconds. Prove that

   $$t_1 t_2 = \frac{2h}{g}$$

4. A particle moving in a straight line with constant acceleration passes three points $P$, $Q$, and $R$, where $Q$ is the midpoint of $|PR|$. The speeds at $P$ and $R$ are $u$ and $7u$, respectively.

   (i)   Find its speed at $Q$ in terms of $u$.

   (ii)  Show that the time taken to go from $P$ to $Q$ is twice the time taken to go from $Q$ to $R$.

5. A car has to travel a distance $s$ on a straight road. The car has maximum acceleration $a$ and maximum deceleration $b$. It starts and ends at rest.

   (i)   Show that, if there is a speed limit of $v$ m/s, the time taken to complete the journey is given by $\frac{v}{2a} + \frac{v}{2b} + \frac{s}{v}$

   (ii)  Show that if there is no speed limit, the time is given by

   $$\sqrt{2s \frac{(a+b)}{ab}}$$

6. (a) A particle travels, starting with initial speed $u$, with uniform acceleration $a$.
   Show that the distance travelled during the $n^{th}$ second is $u + an - \frac{1}{2}a$

   (b) If the particle travels 17 m in the $2^{nd}$ second of motion and 47 m in the $7^{th}$ second of motion, how far will it go:
   (i)   in the $10^{th}$ second of motion?
   (ii)  in the $n^{th}$ second of motion?

   (c) During which two consecutive seconds will it cover 256 m?

7. A train accelerates from rest to a speed $v$ m/s. It continues at this constant speed for a certain time and then decelerates uniformly to rest. If the average speed for the whole journey is $\frac{5v}{6}$, show that $\frac{4}{5}$ of the whole distance is covered at a constant speed.

8. A lift starts from rest and travels with constant acceleration 4 m/s$^2$. It then travels with uniform speed and finally comes to rest with constant retardation 4 m/s$^2$. The total distance travelled is $d$ and the total time taken is $t$.
   (i)   Draw a time–speed graph representing the motion of the lift
   (ii)  Show that the time spent travelling at a constant speed is $\sqrt{t^2 - d}$

# Summary of important points

$$v = u + a t$$
$$s = \frac{(u + v)}{2} t$$
$$s = u t + \frac{1}{2} a t^2$$
$$v^2 = u^2 + 2 a s$$

1. The area under a time–velocity graph represents the distance travelled.
2. The greatest gap between two particles occurs when their speeds are equal.
3. Overtaking occurs when the displacements of two particles from a certain point are equal.

4. If particles $P$ and $Q$ set off together and later overtake each other, then overtaking will occur when $S_p = S_q$. If, however, $P$ was 80 metres behind $Q$ at the start, then when overtaking occurs, $S_p = S_q + 80$

5. If $P$ and $Q$ are a distance $l$ apart and move towards each other, they will meet when $S_p + S_q = l$

6. The greatest gap between particles $P$ and $Q$ occurs when $v_p = v_q$ (because if their speeds are unequal then the gap is either increasing or decreasing)

7. If particle $A$ sets out and, three second later, particle $B$ sets out in pursuit, then let $t$ = the time which $A$ spends on the road and $t - 3 =$ the time which $B$ spends on the road. Students will often put $t + 3$ instead of $t - 3$.

## DOs and DON'Ts for the exam

### Do
- Do know where the formulae are in the *Formulae and Tables*
- Do know when you can and can't apply those formulae
- Do define your terms clearly: "Let $u$ = the speed of the first particle as it passes $P$."
- Do draw clear velocity - time graphs on graph paper. But they don't have to be too accurate.
- Do give the units in all answers: "The speed = 5 m/s."

### Don't
- Don't assume the particle starts from rest unless the question says so
- Don't let $u$ represent the speed at two different points
- Don't dive into the question without thinking about it for a bit
- Don't answer this question first simply because it is first on the paper.

# Projectiles on a horizontal plane

"Our scientific power has outrun our spiritual power. We have guided missiles and misguided men."

*Martin Luther King*

## Contents

## Learning outcomes

**In this chapter you will learn...**

- What a projectile is

- How to calculate the position of a projectile at any time

- How to calculate the velocity of a projectile at any time

- How to find the greatest height reached

- How to find the range of a projectile

## You will need to know...

- $\text{Sin } 2A = 2 \text{ Sin } A \text{ Cos } A$
- $\dfrac{1}{\text{Cos}^2 A} = \text{Sec}^2 A = 1 + \text{Tan}^2 A$

## *What is a projectile?*

A projectile is an object which is thrown from a point on the earth's surface. It usually flies through the air until gravity brings it back to earth.

### *Resolving a vector*

In Chapter 1 we saw how two vectors could be added to give one resultant vector. Conversely, we can split, or resolve, a vector into two vectors (called component vectors).

For example, a vector $\vec{v}$ has magnitude 10 units and direction 30° North of East.

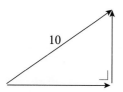

Fig. 3.1

$$\text{Adjacent} = \text{Hypotenuse} \times \cos 30°$$
$$= 10 \times \frac{\sqrt{3}}{2}$$
$$= 5\sqrt{3}$$

$$\text{Opposite} = \text{Hypotenuse} \times \sin 30°$$
$$= 10 \times \frac{1}{2}$$
$$= 5$$

We can replace the vector $\vec{v}$ by two component vectors — one horizontal of magnitude $5\sqrt{3}$, one vertical with magnitude 5.

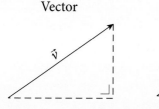

Fig. 3.2

A vertical vector will have no horizontal component. Why?

A horizontal vector will have no vertical component. Why?

It has been long accepted that all free objects at the earth's surface, under gravity, will accelerate towards the centre of the earth with an acceleration of approximately 9.8 m/s² — often called $g$.

Large and small objects all accelerate with this same acceleration. A feather falls to the ground more slowly than a stone only because it is more susceptible to air-resistance. In this course, we ignore air-resistance.

Let us consider a cannon-ball fired from a cannon. We call the ball a projectile because it moves freely under gravity. We will examine separately its distance and velocity in the *x*-direction (Horizontal) and *y*-direction (Vertical).

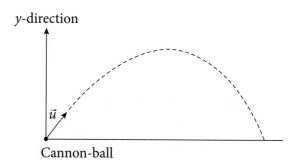

Fig. 3.3

We will call the initial speed in the *x*-direction $u_x$. We will call the final speed in the *x*-direction $v_x$, and the displacement in the *x*-direction $s_x$. What do you think will be understood by the three symbols $u_y$, $v_y$, and $s_y$?

Since gravity acts in the *y*-direction only, there will be no acceleration in the *x*-direction. But in the *y*-direction there is an adverse acceleration of –9.8 m/s² or –$g$.

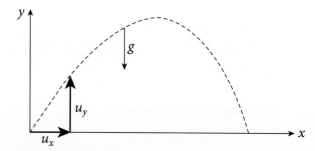

Fig. 3.4

We know that $v = u + at$ and that $s = ut + \frac{1}{2}at^2$. Our 4 equations will therefore be:

$$v_x = u_x$$
$$s_x = u_x t$$
$$v_y = u_y - g t$$
$$s_y = u_y t - \frac{1}{2} g t^2$$

**Note:**

1.  The velocity vector at any moment will be given by $\vec{v} = v_x \vec{i} + v_y \vec{j}$.

2.  The displacement vector or position vector (with reference to the point of projection) will be given by: $\vec{r} = s_x \vec{i} + s_y \vec{j}$.

---

### Worked Example 3.1

A particle is projected with initial velocity $14\vec{i} + 70\vec{j}$ from a point $p$ on a horizontal plane. Calculate:

  (i)   its height above the plane 4 seconds after it is projected.

  (ii)  its horizontal distance from $p$ 2 seconds after projection.

  (iii) the magnitude and direction of the velocity of the particle 5 seconds after projection.

  (iv)  its greatest height above the plane.

  (v)   the range of the particle.

**Solution:**

  (i)   Before we start we will find $v_x$, $s_x$, $v_y$ and $s_y$ in terms of $t$. (Remember: there is no acceleration in the $x$-direction.)

Velocity horiozontally $v_x$

$$v = u + a t$$
$$v_x = u + a t$$
$$= 14 + (0)\, t$$
$$v_x = 14$$

Displacement horizontally $s_x$

$$s_x = u t + \tfrac{1}{2} a t^2$$
$$= 14 t + \tfrac{1}{2}(0)\, t^2$$
$$\therefore s_x = 14 t$$

Velocity vertically

$$v_y = u + a t$$
$$= 70 - g t$$
$$\therefore v_y = 70 - 9.8 t$$

Displacement vertically $s_y$ after $t$ seconds

$$s_y = 70 t + \tfrac{1}{2} a t^2$$
$$= 70 t - \tfrac{1}{2}(9.8)\, t^2$$
$$\therefore s_y = 70 t - 4.9 t^2$$

The height is given by $s_y = 70 t - 4.9 t^2$

To get the height after 4 seconds let $t = 4$.

If $t = 4$ then
$$s_y = 70\,(4) - 4.9\,(4)^2$$
$$= 280 - 78.4$$
$$= 201.6 \text{ m}.$$

Answer: 201.6 m.

  (ii)  The horizontal displacement is given by:
$$s_x = 14\, t.$$

Let $t = 2$
$$s_x = 14\,(2)$$
$$= 28 \text{ m}.$$

Answer: 28 m.

  (iii) We will find $v_x$ and $v_y$ at $t = 5$.
$$v_x = 14$$
$$v_y = 70 - 9.8 t$$
$$= 70 - 9.8\,(5)$$
$$= 70 - 49$$
$$= 21$$
$$\therefore \vec{v} = 14\vec{i} + 21\vec{j}$$

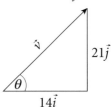

Fig. 3.5

To find its magnitude:
$$|\vec{v}| = \sqrt{v_x^2 + v_y^2}$$
$$|\vec{v}| = \sqrt{14^2 + 21^2}$$
$$= \sqrt{196 + 441}$$
$$= \sqrt{637}$$
$$= 25.24 \text{ m/s}$$

To find its direction:
$$\text{Tan } \theta = \frac{21}{14}$$
$$= \frac{3}{2}$$
$$= 1.5$$
$$\therefore \qquad \theta = 56°19' \text{ or E}56.31°\text{N}$$

Answer: Direction is 56°19′ N of E

  (iv)  When it reaches its greatest height, the projectile is neither ascending nor descending. So, its velocity in the $y$-direction must be zero, i.e. $v_y = 0$. We want to find its height, $s_y$, when $v_y = 0$. Let $h =$ the greatest height.

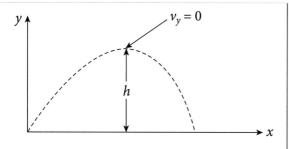

Fig. 3.6

We will write down the information on all variables in the $y$-direction at the moment when the particle reaches its greatest height:

Acceleration in $y$ direction $= a_y$
$$= -9.8$$

Velocity in $y$ direction
$$u_y = 70, \ v_y = 0.$$
$$s = h$$

Use the formula
$$v^2 = u^2 + 2\,a\,s$$
$$\therefore 0^2 = 70^2 + 2\,(-9.8)\,h$$
$$\therefore 0 = 4900 - 19.6\,h$$
$$\therefore \qquad 19.6\,h = 4900$$
$$\therefore \qquad h = 250$$

Answer: $h = 250$ m

(v)

Its range is the horizontal distance, $s_x$ covered when it hits the ground, i.e. its horizontal distance, $s_x$, when its height above the plane is zero, i.e. we want to find $s_x$ when $s_y = 0$.

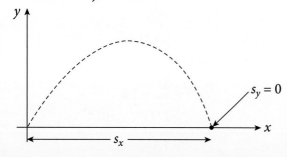

Fig. 3.7

**Step** 1: Find the time, $t$, when $s_y = 0$
$$s_y = 0 \qquad \Rightarrow 70\,t - 4.9\,t^2 = 0$$
$$\Rightarrow 700\,t - 49\,t^2 = 0$$
$$\Rightarrow 100\,t - 7\,t^2 = 0$$
$$\Rightarrow 7\,t^2 - 100\,t = 0$$
$$\Rightarrow t\,(7\,t - 100) = 0$$
$$\therefore \ t = 0 \ \text{or} \ t = \frac{100}{7}$$

Since $t = 0$ is at the moment of projection, $t = \frac{100}{7}$ must be the moment of landing.

**Step** 2: Find $s_x$ at $t = \frac{100}{7}$
$$s_x = 14\,t$$
$$= 14\left(\frac{100}{7}\right)$$
$$= 200 \text{ m.}$$

Answer: 200 m

### Worked Example 3.2

A particle is projected from a point on a horizontal plane, with initial speed 35 m/s at an angle $\alpha$ to the horizontal where $\tan \alpha = \frac{4}{3}$. Find

(i)   its initial velocity in terms of $\vec{i}$ and $\vec{j}$

(ii)  its displacement vector (or position vector) at $t = 3$.

(iii) the times when its height above the horizontal plane is 36.4 m.

### Solution:

(i)   Since $\tan \alpha = \frac{4}{3}$, we can calculate $\cos \alpha$, $\sin \alpha$ using a model triangle:

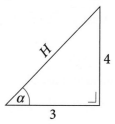

Fig. 3.8

$$\tan \alpha = \frac{4}{3} = \frac{\text{opposite}}{\text{adjacent}}$$

By Pythagoras
$$H^2 = 4^2 + 3^2$$
$$= 16 + 9$$
$$= 25$$
$$\therefore \qquad H = 5$$
$$\therefore \cos \alpha = \frac{\text{adjacent}}{\text{hypotenuse}} = \frac{3}{5}$$
$$\sin \alpha = \frac{\text{opposite}}{\text{hypotenuse}} = \frac{4}{5}$$

We can now calculate the initial velocity.

$$\text{Adjacent} = \text{Hypotenuse} \times \cos \alpha$$
$$= 35 \times \frac{3}{5}$$
$$= 21 \text{ m/s}$$

$$\text{Opposite} = \text{Hypotenuse} \times \sin \alpha$$
$$= 35 \times \frac{4}{5}$$
$$= 28 \text{ m/s.}$$

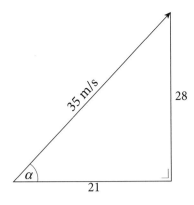

Fig. 3.9

∴ Initial velocity $\vec{u} = 21\,\vec{i} + 28\,\vec{j}$ m/s

(ii)   $s = u\,t + \frac{1}{2}a\,t^2$

∴      $s_x = 21\,t + \frac{1}{2}(0)\,t^2$

∴      $s_x = 21\,t$

$s_y = 28\,t - \frac{1}{2}g\,t^2$

$= 28\,t - 4.9\,t^2$

At $t = 3$, then

$s_x = 21\,(3)$

$= 63$ m.

$s_y = 28\,(3) - 4.9\,(3)^2$

$= 84 - 44.1$

$= 39.9$ m.

∴ The position vector is given by

$\vec{r} = 63\,\vec{i} + 39.9\,\vec{j}$ m.

(iii) We want to find $t$ when $s_y = 36.4$ m.

$s_y = 28\,t - 4.9\,t^2 = 36.4$

$280\,t - 49\,t^2 = 364$ (multiplying across by 10)

$49\,t^2 - 280\,t + 364 = 0$

$7\,t^2 - 40\,t + 52 = 0$        (dividing by 7)

$(7\,t - 26)(t - 2) = 0$

∴ Either $7\,t - 26 = 0$

∴ $t = \frac{26}{7}$  or  $t - 2 = 0$

$= 3\frac{5}{7}$      $t = 2$

Answer: $t = 3\frac{5}{7}$ or 2 seconds

## Worked Example 3.3

A golf-ball is hit with initial speed 12 m/s in a horizontal direction from the top of a vertical cliff, 490 m high, which overlooks the sea. How far from the foot of the cliff will it hit the sea?

**Solution:**

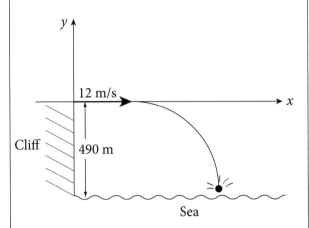

Fig. 3.10

We want to find $s_x$ when $s_y = -490$ m. We always let the point of projection be the origin. In this case, $s_y$ is negative since when it hits the sea, the golf-ball will be 490 m **below** the point of projection.

**Step** 1: Find $t$ when $s_y = -490$

**Note**: The initial velocity is $12\,\vec{i} + 0\,\vec{j}$, since the ball is struck horizontally.

$s_y = 0\,(t) - \frac{1}{2}g\,t^2$

$= -4.9\,t^2$

∴ $-490 = -4.9\,t^2$

∴ $100 = t^2$

∴ $t = 10$ s. ($t = -10$ is rejected)

**Step** 2: Find $s_x$ when $t = 10$

$s = u\,t + \frac{1}{2}a\,t^2$

$s_x = 12\,(t) + \frac{1}{2}(0)\,t^2$

$s_x = 12\,t$

At $t = 10$ s

$s_x = 12\,(10)$

$= 120$ m.

Answer: 120 m.

## Exercise 3 A

1.  A projectile is fired from a point on a horizontal plane with an initial velocity $21\,\vec{i} + 28\,\vec{j}$ m/s.
    Find:
    (i)   its height above the plane after 3 seconds
    (ii)  its greatest height above the plane
    (iii) its range.

2.  A projectile is fired from a point on a horizontal plane with initial velocity $56\,\vec{i} + 56\,\vec{j}$ m/s. Find:
    (i)   its greatest height above the plane
    (ii)  its range
    (iii) its velocity as a vector after 4 seconds.

3.  A particle is projected from a point on a horizontal plane with initial velocity $70\,\vec{i} + 105\,\vec{j}$ m/s. Find:
    (i)   the magnitude and direction of its velocity after 10 seconds
    (ii)  the range.

4.  A particle is projected from a point on a horizontal plane with velocity $14\,\vec{i} + 21\,\vec{j}$ m/s. Find:
    (i)   its height above the plane at $t = 1$
    (ii)  the two times when its height above the plane is 22.4 m

5.  A projectile is fired from a point on a horizontal plane with initial velocity $10\,\vec{i} + 49\,\vec{j}$ m/s. Find:
    (i)   its greatest height above the plane
    (ii)  its range
    (iii) its velocity as a vector after 6 seconds.

6.  A particle is projected from a point on a horizontal plane with initial velocity $70\,\vec{i} + 140\,\vec{j}$ m/s. Find:
    (i)   the magnitude and direction of its velocity after 5 seconds
    (ii)  the range.

7.  A particle is projected from a point on a horizontal plane with velocity $20\,\vec{i} + 28\,\vec{j}$ m/s. Find:
    (i)   its height above the plane at $t = 3$
    (ii)  its speed after 4 seconds of flight.

8.  A particle is projected from a point on a horizontal plane with initial speed $10\vec{i} + 35\,\vec{j}$ m/s. Find the times at which:

    (i)   it reaches its maximum height above the plane
    (ii)  its velocity is $10\,\vec{i} + 10.5\,\vec{j}$
    (iii) its velocity is $10\,\vec{i} - 10.5\,\vec{j}$
    (iv)  Show that the time in (i) is exactly half-way between the times in (ii) and (iii).

9.  A bullet is fired horizontally, with a speed of 200 m/s, from the top of a cliff, 490 m above sea-level. Show that it will strike the sea at a distance 2000 m from the foot of the cliff.

10. A particle is projected from a point on a horizontal plane with initial velocity $10\,\vec{i} + 98\,\vec{j}$ m/s. Find:
    (i)   the time when it reaches its maximum height above the plane.
    (ii)  its position vector at this time.

11. A particle is projected from a point on a horizontal plane with initial velocity $100\,\vec{i} + 98\,\vec{j}$ m/s. Find:
    (i)   the times when it reaches a height of 470.4 m above the plane.
    (ii)  its speed at these times to the nearest m/s.

12. A particle is fired from level ground with initial speed $8\,\vec{i} + 28\,\vec{j}$ m/s. Find the two times when its speed will be 10 m/s.

## Worked Example 3.4

A particle is fired with initial speed $u$. If it is fired at an angle $\alpha$ to the horizontal from a point on a horizontal plane, show that:

(i)   the greatest height it will reach is $\dfrac{u^2 \sin^2 \alpha}{2g}$

(ii)  the range is $\dfrac{u^2 \sin 2\alpha}{g}$

(iii) the range will be a maximum if $\alpha = 45°$.

**Solution:**

The initial velocity will be $u \cos\alpha\,\vec{i} + u \sin\alpha\,\vec{j}$

$$v_x = u_x$$
$$= u \cos \alpha$$
$$s_x = u_x t$$
$$= u \cos \alpha\, t$$
$$v_y = u_y - g t$$
$$= u \sin \alpha - g t$$
$$s_y = u_y t - \tfrac{1}{2} g t^2$$
$$= u \sin \alpha\, t - \tfrac{1}{2} g t^2$$

(i)   To find the greatest height, $H$:
$$u_y = u \sin \alpha,\ v_y = 0,\ a_y = -g,\ s_y = H$$

$$v^2 = u^2 + 2\,a\,s,$$

$$\therefore \quad (0)^2 = (u \sin \alpha)^2 + 2\,(-g)\,H$$

$$\therefore \quad 0 = u^2 \sin^2 \alpha - 2\,g\,H$$

$$\therefore \quad 2\,g\,H = u^2 \sin^2 \alpha$$

$$\therefore \quad H = \frac{u^2 \sin^2 \alpha}{2\,g} \quad \text{QED}$$

(ii)  To find the range, $R$: Find $s_x$ when $s_y = 0$.

$$u \sin \alpha \, t - \tfrac{1}{2} g\, t^2 = 0$$

$$\therefore t \left( u \sin \alpha - \tfrac{1}{2} g\, t \right) = 0$$

$$\therefore \quad t = 0 \text{ or } u \sin \alpha = \tfrac{1}{2} g\, t$$

$$\Rightarrow t = \frac{2\,u \sin \alpha}{g}$$

Therefore, the time of flight $= \dfrac{2\,u \sin \alpha}{g}$

At this time $\quad s_x = u \cos \alpha \, t$

$$= u \cos \alpha \left( \frac{2\,u \sin \alpha}{g} \right)$$

$$= \frac{2\,u^2 \sin \alpha \cos \alpha}{g}$$

$$= \frac{u^2 \sin 2\alpha}{g} \quad \text{(see note below).}$$

$$\therefore \quad R = \frac{u^2 \sin 2\alpha}{g} \quad \text{QED}$$

Note: from pg 14, Formulae & Tables we get
$$\sin 2\alpha = 2 \sin \alpha \cos \alpha$$

(iii)  The greatest value of $R$ occurs when $\sin 2\alpha$ attains its greatest value, which is 1.

$$\therefore \quad R_{\text{max}} = \frac{u^2\,(1)}{g} = \frac{u^2}{g}$$

This occurs when $\sin 2\alpha = 1$

$$\therefore \quad 2\alpha = \sin^{-1}(1) = 90°$$

$$\therefore \quad \alpha = 45° \quad \text{QED}$$

## Exercise 3 B

1.  A particle is projected with speed $7\sqrt{5}$ m/s at an angle $\alpha$, where $\tan \alpha = \frac{1}{2}$, from a point on a horizontal plane. Find:

    (i)  its initial velocity, in terms of $\vec{i}$ and $\vec{j}$

    (ii)  its horizontal range.

2.  A particle is projected with speed 35 m/s at an angle $\theta$ (where $\tan \theta = \frac{3}{4}$) to the horizontal plane from which it is fired. Write its initial velocity in the form $a\,\vec{i} + b\,\vec{j}$ and find its speed (i.e. the magnitude of its velocity) when it is 10 m off the ground, correct to 2 decimal places.

3.  Find the range, $R$, of a projectile whose initial velocity is $10\,\vec{i} + 7\,\vec{j}$ m/s. What is its height when its horizontal displacement is $\frac{3}{4} R$?

4.  A projectile is fired from a point $o$ on a horizontal plane with velocity $3\,\vec{i} + 4\,\vec{j}$ m/s.

    (i)  Find its vertical height off the ground when its horizontal displacement is one fifth of the range.

    (ii)  Find another time when its height is equal to this height.

5.  (a) Factorise $7\,t^2 - 20t - 500$.

    (b) A cannon fires a cannon-ball from the top of a cliff which is 350 m above sea-level with initial velocity $10\,\vec{i} + 14\,\vec{j}$ m/s. Find the distance from the foot of the cliff to the point where the ball hits the sea.

6.  A particle is fired from a point on a horizontal plane with initial velocity $50\,\vec{i} + 49\,\vec{j}$ m/s. Find its range.

7.  A particle is projected with initial speed $35\,\vec{i} + 14\,\vec{j}$ m/s from a point on a horizontal plane.

    (i)  Find the maximum height.

    (ii)  Find the times at which its height above the horizontal plane is $\frac{3}{4}$ of its maximum height.

8.  A particle is projected from the top of a vertical cliff 82.5 m above sea-level with initial speed $12\,\vec{i} + 8\,\vec{j}$ m/s. How far from the foot of the cliff will it hit the sea?

9.  A particle is projected horizontally from the top of a vertical cliff 78.4 m high with initial speed 98 m/s.

    (i)  How much time will pass before it hits the sea?

    (ii)  If the angle of projection is raised to 30° with the horizontal, find the time it will now take correct to 1 decimal place.

10.  A particle is projected with velocity 50 m/s at an angle $\theta$ to the horizontal. If $\vec{i}$ is along the horizontal and $\vec{j}$ is vertically upwards and if $\cos \theta = \frac{3}{5}$,

    (i)  express the position vector $\vec{r}$ of the particle after $t$ seconds in terms of $\vec{i}$ and $\vec{j}$

    (ii)  Find the magnitude, to the nearest m/s, and the direction, to the nearest degree, of the velocity of the particle when $t = 1$.

(iii) Calculate the horizontal range of the particle to the nearest metre.

11. A particle is projected with initial velocity $12\,\vec{i} + k\,\vec{j}$ m/s from a point on a horizontal plane. When its horizontal displacement is 30 m, it is 9.375 m above the plane. Find the value of $k$.

12. A particle is fired with initial speed $u$. If it is fired at an angle $\alpha$ to the horizontal from a point on a horizontal plane.

   (i) Show that the greatest height it will reach is $\dfrac{u^2 \sin^2 \alpha}{2g}$

   (ii) Show that the range is $\dfrac{2\,u^2 \sin\alpha \cos\alpha}{g}$

   (iii) If $u = 70$ m/s and if the greatest height is 125 m, find the value of $\alpha$ and find the range.

13. The maximum height and the range of a projectile are equal. Find the angle of projection to the nearest degree.

14. The maximum height of a projectile is double the range. Find the angle of projection to the nearest degree.

15. The greatest height reached by a particle above the horizontal plane from which it is fired is 3.6 m. Its range is 19.2 m.

   (i) Find the tan of the angle of projection and the initial speed $u$.

   (ii) What would the maximum range of this particle be if the angle of projection can be changed but the initial speed remains fixed?

16.
   (i) (i) If sin A = 0.5, find 2 values of A where $0° < A < 360°$.

   (ii) A particle is fired from a point on a horizontal plane with initial speed 28 m/s at an angle $\alpha$ to the plane. If its range is 40 m, find two possible angles of projection.

17. A particle is fired from a point on a horizontal plane with initial speed 10 m/s. If the greatest height reached above the plane is 2.5 m, find the sine of the angle of projection.

18. A particle is fired so as to have maximum possible range. Show that the angle of projection should be 45° and that the ratio of the greatest height to the range is 1:4.

19. A ball is kicked from a point $O$ on a horizontal plane with initial velocity $P\,\vec{i} + Q\,\vec{j}$ m/s. It lands at a point $R$, 60 m away. The greatest height above the ground is 5.625 m.

   (i) Find the value of $P$ and $Q$.

   (ii) A player runs at 7 m/s from the moment the ball is kicked and arrives to catch the ball as it lands. Find the greatest distance that this player could have been from the point $r$ when the ball was kicked.

20. A particle is fired from a point on a horizontal plane with initial speed $u$ m/s. The ratio of the greatest height to the range is 2:7. Find the angle of projection to the nearest degree.

## Target practice

When we are dealing with a projectile which hits a precise target, there are two important trigonometrical formulae (from page 14 of the *Formulae & Tables*):

1.  $\dfrac{\sin A}{\cos A} = \tan A$

2.  $\dfrac{1}{\cos^2 A} = 1 + \tan^2 A = \sec^2 A$

### Worked Example 3.5

A particle is projected from a point $o$ on horizontal ground at an angle $A$ to the horizontal. The initial speed is $\sqrt{6g}$ m/s. It hits a small target whose position vector relative to $o$ is $3\,\vec{i} + \dfrac{11}{12}\,\vec{j}$ metres. Find two values of $A$ to the nearest degree.

**Solution:**

$x$-direction:

$$u_x = \sqrt{6g}\cos A$$
$$a_x = 0$$
$$s_x = \sqrt{6g}\cos A\, t$$

$y$-direction:

$$u_y = \sqrt{6g}\sin A$$
$$a_y = -g$$
$$s_y = \sqrt{6g}\sin A\, t - \tfrac{1}{2}g t^2$$

At the moment when the particle hits the target,

$$S_x = 3 \text{ and } S_y = \tfrac{11}{12}$$

$$s_x = \sqrt{6g}\cos A\, t = 3$$

$\therefore \qquad t = \dfrac{3}{\sqrt{6g}\cos A}$

(we substitute $t$ into the second equation)

$$s_y = \sqrt{6g} \sin A\, t - \frac{1}{2} gt^2 = \frac{11}{12}$$

$$\sqrt{6g} \sin A\left(\frac{3}{\sqrt{6g}\cos A}\right) - \frac{1}{2} g\left(\frac{3}{\sqrt{6g}\cos A}\right)^2 = \frac{11}{12}$$

$$\therefore \left(\frac{3\sin A}{\cos A}\right) - \frac{1}{2} g\left(\frac{9}{6g\cos^2 A}\right) = \frac{11}{12}$$

Now, separate the numbers from the trigonometrical expressions:

$$\therefore 3\left(\frac{\sin A}{\cos A}\right) - \frac{3}{4}\left(\frac{1}{\cos^2 A}\right) = \frac{11}{12}$$

$$\therefore 3\tan A - \frac{3}{4}(1 + \tan^2 A) = \frac{11}{12}$$

(We will multiply across by 12)

$$\therefore 36\tan A - 9(1 + \tan^2 A) = 11$$

$$\therefore 36\tan A - 9 - 9\tan^2 A = 11$$

$$\therefore 9\tan^2 A - 36\tan A + 20 = 0$$

$$(3\tan A - 2)(3\tan A - 10) = 0$$

$$\therefore \tan A = \frac{2}{3} \quad \text{or} \quad \tan A = \frac{10}{3}$$

$$\therefore A = 34° \text{ or } A = 73°: \text{ Answer}$$

## Exercise 3 C

1. A particle is projected from a point $O$ on horizontal ground at an angle $A$ to the horizontal. The initial speed is $\sqrt{24g}$ m/s. It hits a small target whose position vector relative to $O$ is $16\,\vec{i} + \frac{11}{3}\,\vec{j}$ metres. Find two values of $A$ to the nearest degree.

2. A particle is projected from a point $O$ on horizontal ground at an angle $A$ to the horizontal. The initial speed is $\sqrt{g}$ m/s. It hits a small target whose position vector relative to $O$ is $\frac{1}{2}\,\vec{i} + \frac{1}{4}\,\vec{j}$ metres. Find two values of $A$ to the nearest degree.

3. A particle is projected from a point $O$ on horizontal ground at an angle $A$ to the horizontal. The initial speed is $4\sqrt{2g}$ m/s. It hits the top of a narrow wall which is 8 metres from $O$ and 14 m high.
   (i) Find two values of $A$ to the nearest degree.
   (ii) Find the time of flight in each case to one decimal place.

4. A particle is projected from a point $O$ on horizontal ground at an angle $A$ to the horizontal. The initial speed is $70\sqrt{5}$ m/s. It hits a small target whose position vector relative to $O$ is $700\,\vec{i} + 910\,\vec{j}$ metres.
   (i) Find two values of $A$ to the nearest degree.
   (ii) Find the time of flight in each case to two decimal places.
   (iii) Two particles are fired simultaneously from $O$ with speed $70\sqrt{5}$ m/s. Both hit the target at different times. Find the time which elapses between the two hits, to the nearest half-second.

5. (a) Given $\operatorname{Sin}^2 A + \operatorname{Cos}^2 A = 1$, show that $\operatorname{Sec}^2 A = 1 + \operatorname{Tan}^2 A$.

   (b) A projectile is projected from a point $P$ on a horizontal plane with initial speed $35\sqrt{5}$ m/s at an angle $\alpha$ to the plane. It strikes a small target which has displacement $350\,\vec{i} + 210\,\vec{j}$ metres from $P$. Find the two possible values of $\operatorname{Tan}\alpha$ and the time of flight in each case.

6. A jet-fighter is flying horizontally at a constant height of 210 m with constant speed 140 m/s. As it passes over a gun, the gunner fires a bullet with speed $70\sqrt{5}$ m/s at an angle $\tan^{-1}\frac{1}{2}$ to the horizontal. If the plane of the bullet's flight is also the plane of the fighter's flight, find when the bullet will strike the fighter.

7. A bird flies out of a tree exactly 5.6 m directly above a hunter's gun and flies at a constant speed of 28 m/s in a horizontal direction. If the speed of the bullets from the gun is 35 m/s and the gun is fired just as the bird is leaving the tree, show that:
   (i) the angle of projection must be $\tan^{-1}\frac{3}{4}$ if the bullet is to hit the bird
   (ii) the time taken for the bullet to reach the bird is $\frac{2}{7}$ sec.

8. A projectile is fired from a point $P$ on a horizontal plane with initial speed 35 m/s at an angle $A$ to the plane.
   (i) Show that if $x$ and $y$ are the horizontal and vertical distances of the particle from $P$, then
   $$250\,y = 250\,(\operatorname{Tan} A)\,x - (1 + \operatorname{Tan}^2 A)\,x^2.$$
   (ii) If the projectile strikes a small target whose horizontal and vertical distances from $P$ are 40 m and 20 m respectively, find 2 values for $\operatorname{Tan} A$ and the time taken to reach the target in each case.

9. A particle is projected from the ground with a velocity of 50.96 m/s at an angle $\tan^{-1}\frac{5}{12}$ to the horizontal. On its upward path it just passes over a wall 14.7 high. During its flight it also passes over a wall 18.375 high. Show that the second wall must not be less than 23.52 m and not more than 70.56 m from the first wall.

10. A ball is kicked from a point $P$ on level ground. It hits the ground for the first time 27 m from $P$ after 3 seconds. During its flight, the ball just passed over a vertical wall standing 5.4 m from $P$. Find
    (i)   the horizontal and vertical components of the initial velocity of the ball.
    (ii)  the height of the wall.
    (iii) the speed of the ball as it passed over the wall.

11. A dart player stands 2 metres from a dartboard. She throws the dart **horizontally** with speed $u$ m/s, from a height of 1.6 m above the ground. The dart strikes the board at a point 1.5 m above the ground. Find
    (i)   the time that the dart spends in flight
    (ii)  the initial speed of the dart ($u$)
    (iii) the speed of the dart when it hits the board.

12. A particle is projected with initial velocity $u\cos\alpha\,\vec{i} + u\sin\alpha\,\vec{j}$ m/s from a point 0 on a horizontal plane.
    (i)  Show that its range is given by: $\dfrac{2\,u^2\sin\alpha\cos\alpha}{g}$
    (ii) If this particle passes through two points whose displacements in metres from 0 are $3\vec{i}+\vec{j}$ and $\vec{i}+3\vec{j}$, show that the range is $\frac{13}{4}$ metres and that $\tan\alpha=\frac{13}{3}$.

13. A particle is fired at an angle $\theta$ to a horizontal plane, with initial speed $u$. It has to clear a fixed wall which is 90 m high and a distance 240 m away from the point of firing. If $\sin\theta=\frac{3}{5}$, find the minimum value of $u$ for it to clear the wall.

14. A bullet is fired from a gun fixed at a point $O$ with speed $v$ m/s at an angle $\theta$ to the horizontal. At the instant of firing, a moving target is 10 m vertically above $O$ and travelling with constant speed $42\sqrt{2}$ m/s at a constant angle 45° to the horizontal. The bullet and target move in the same plane.

(i)  If $v = 70$ m/s, show that if the bullet is to hit the target, then $\tan\theta=\frac{4}{3}$.
(ii) Find at what time after firing does the bullet strike the target and calculate the horizontal distance of the bullet from $O$.

# Summary of important points

1. For projectiles on a horizontal plane:
   $$v_x = u_x \qquad s_x = u_x t$$
   $$v_y = u_y - g t \qquad s_y = u_y t - \tfrac{1}{2}g t^2.$$

2. To find the **maximum height**, find $s_y$ when $v_y = 0$.

3. To find the **range**, find $s_x$ when $s_y = 0$.

4. The speed at any instant is given by $v = \sqrt{v_x^2 + v_y^2}$

## DOs and DON'Ts for the exam

**DO**
- When finding the maximum range, do use $\sin 2A = 2\sin A\cos A$
- When solving a problem about hitting a target, do use $\tan A = \dfrac{\sin A}{\cos A}$ and $\dfrac{1}{\cos^2 A} = 1 + \tan^2 A$ to get a quadratic in $\tan A$

**DON'T**
- Don't assume that 45° is the angle for maximum range: prove it using Maths!
- Don't forget that there is no acceleration in the $x$-direction
- Don't learn formulae for maximum range or maximum height above the ground by heart. You must **derive** these on paper in the exam. If you don't, you will lose most of the marks

# Relative velocity

"When a man sits with a pretty girl for an hour, it seems like a minute. But let him sit on a hot stove for a minute — and it's longer than any hour. That's relativity."

*Albert Einstein*

## Contents

## Learning outcomes

**In this chapter you will learn...**

- How to find the velocity of one particle relative to another

- How to determine if two particles are on collision course

- How to find the shortest distance between two particles

- How to find the time during which two particles are within a certain range of each other

- How to deal with problems involving rivers, currents and winds

- How to deal with the apparent velocity of the wind

- How to use the t-method to solve awkward problems

## You will need to know...

- How to find the magnitude and direction of a vector
- How to solve quadratic and simultaneous equations
- Basic trigonometry
- The sine rule and cosine rule
  (as on page 16 of *The Formulae & Tables*)

## The meaning of relative velocity

A car is travelling along a straight road at 20 m/s. It is overtaken by a bus which is travelling at 30 m/s in the same direction. The road is particularly smooth. Imagine that you are a fly inside the windscreen of the car. You can't hear the engine (flies are deaf)—so you don't know that you are moving. One second after the bus overtakes, it will be 10 metres ahead of you in the car. After 2 seconds it will be 20 metres ahead and after 3 seconds it will be 30 metres ahead. If you could talk, you would say: "I see a bus moving at 10 m/s". We, who can talk, say, "The velocity of the bus relative to the car is 10 m/s." By this we mean that an observer in the car will see the bus moving away from her (or him) at 10 m/s.

Here is the situation translated into vector notation (we will take $\vec{i}$ in the direction of the car's motion).

$$\boxed{\text{Car}} \xrightarrow{\ 20\vec{i}\ }$$

$$\boxed{\text{Bus}} \xrightarrow{\ 30\vec{i}\ }$$

Fig. 4.1

We write:

$\vec{v}_c = 20\,\vec{i}$ ("the velocity of the car is $20\,\vec{i}$ m/s")

$\vec{v}_b = 30\,\vec{i}$ ("the velocity of the bus is $30\,\vec{i}$ m/s")

$\vec{v}_{bc} = 10\,\vec{i}$ ("the velocity of the bus relative to the car is $10\,\vec{i}$ m/s")

As you can see, the relative velocity is found by subtraction.

In general: $\vec{v}_{ab} = \vec{v}_a - \vec{v}_b$

where $\vec{v}_a$ means $A$'s actual velocity, $\vec{v}_b$ means $B$'s actual velocity and $\vec{v}_{ab}$ means the velocity of $A$ relative to $B$, i.e. the rate at which an observer at $B$ will see $A$ moving away from $B$.

Let's take another example, this time in two dimensions:

A tanker and a liner leave New York Harbour simultaneously; the tanker ($T$) travels at $2\,\vec{i} + 3\,\vec{j}$ km/h. The liner ($L$) travels with velocity $\vec{i} - 2\,\vec{j}$ km/h. Here are their positions over the first 3 hours:

The left-hand column uses New York Harbour as its origin.

The right-hand column uses the liner's position as its origin, even though the liner's position changes.

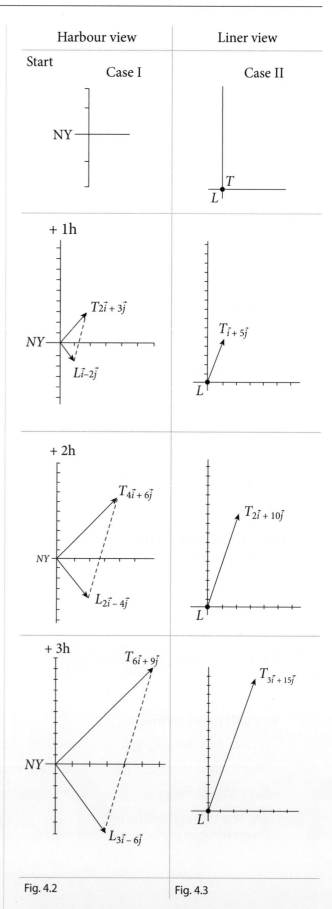

Fig. 4.2                    Fig. 4.3

If you were the lookout person on the liner you would see the tanker moving away from you. But at what rate and in what direction?

What we are asking is, "What is the velocity of the tanker relative to the liner?"

Using our formula:

$$\vec{V}_{TL} = \vec{V}_T - \vec{V}_L$$
$$= (2\vec{i} + 3\vec{j}) - (\vec{i} - 2\vec{j})$$
$$= \vec{i} + 5\vec{j} \text{ km/h.}$$

This is shown to be correct by the Case II illustration where we see that, relative to the liner, the tanker has position $\vec{i} + 5\vec{j}$ after 1 hour, $2\vec{i} + 10\vec{j}$ after 2 hours, etc. In other words, it is moving with velocity $\vec{i} + 5\vec{j}$ km/h away from the liner. We say, "The velocity of the trawler relative to the liner is $\vec{i} + 5\vec{j}$ km/h."

In general we can show the relative velocity by a diagram:

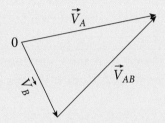

Fig. 4.4

### Worked Example 4.1

A destroyer is 500 km due West of a frigate. The destroyer is travelling at 10 km/h in a direction 30° North of East. The frigate is travelling at $5\sqrt{2}$ km/h in a NW direction.

(i)  Find the velocity of the frigate relative to the destroyer.

(ii)  Show that they are on collision course.

(iii)  When will they collide?

**Solution:**

(i)  $\vec{V}_d = 10\cos 30° \vec{i} + 10\sin 30° \vec{j}$
$$= 8.66\vec{i} + 5\vec{j}$$
$$\vec{V}_f = -5\sqrt{2}\cos 45° \vec{i} + 5\sqrt{2}\sin 45° \vec{j}$$
$$= -5\vec{i} + 5\vec{j}$$
$\therefore \quad \vec{V}_{fd} = \vec{V}_f - \vec{V}_d$
$$= \left(-5\vec{i} + 5\vec{j}\right) - \left(8.66\vec{i} + 5\vec{j}\right)$$
$$= -13.66\vec{i}$$

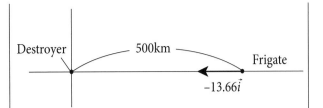

Fig. 4.5

(ii)  The position of the frigate relative to the destroyer is at $500\vec{i}$ km.
We write $\vec{r}_{fd} = 500\vec{i}$ km.
The velocity of the frigate relative to the destroyer is $\vec{v}_{fr} = -13.66\vec{i}$ km/h.
Since $\vec{v}_{fd} = -k\vec{r}_{fd}$ where $k$ is a positive constant, they must be on collision course.

(iii)  The time of the collision is given by:
$$t = \frac{\text{relative distance}}{\text{relative speed}}$$
$$= \frac{500}{13.66}$$
$$= 36.6$$
$$= 36 \text{ hrs and } 36 \text{ minutes later.}$$

## Relative displacement

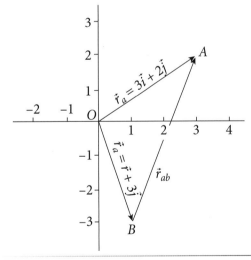

Fig. 4.6

Taking Oscar's house ($O$) as the origin, Antoinette ($A$) lives at $3\vec{i} + 2\vec{j}$ km as shown. That is to say that to get from Oscar's to Antoinette's house you have to travel across 3 km and up 2 km. Bernadine lives at $\vec{i} - 3\vec{j}$.

But how would you get from Bernadine's to Antoinette's house? What we are asking is: "What is the displacement of Antoinette's house relative to Bernadine's?"

The picture seems to suggest that you would have to go across two kilometers and up 5 kilometers – the vector
$2\vec{i} + 5\vec{j}$ km would then be the displacement of Antoinette to Bernadine.

Let $\vec{r}_a$ = the displacement of $A$ relative to the origin (i.e. the position vector of $A$).
Let $\vec{r}_b$ = the displacement of $B$ relative to the origin.
Let $\vec{r}_{ab}$ = the displacement of $A$ relative to $B$.
We find that, as for velocity, the relevant equation is:
$$\vec{r}_{ab} = \vec{r}_a - \vec{r}_b$$
In this case: $\vec{r}_a = 3\vec{i} + 2\vec{j}$
$$\vec{r}_b = \vec{i} - 3\vec{j}$$
$$\vec{r}_{ab} = \vec{r}_a - \vec{r}_b$$
$$= (3\vec{i} + 2\vec{j}) - (\vec{i} - 3\vec{j})$$
$$= 2\vec{i} + 5\vec{j} \text{ km.}$$

(as the picture suggested.)

## Exercise 4 A

1. An automobile is travelling along a straight road at 25 m/s. It is overtaken by a bus which is travelling at 30 m/s in the same direction.
   (i) Find the velocity of the bus relative to the automobile.
   (ii) Calculate how long will it take for them to be 1 km apart.

2. Alan and Betty start from the same point. They then cycle along a straight road in the same direction. Alan is cycling at 4 m/s, Betty at 7 m/s.
   (i) Find the velocity of Betty relative to Alan.
   (ii) How far apart will they be after 60 seconds?
   (iii) After how long will they be 600 m apart?

3. A cyclist is travelling along a straight road at 10 m/s. A lorry is travelling along the same road in the opposite direction at 15 m/s. Using $\vec{i}$ as the unit vector in the same direction as the cyclist is moving, write down
   (i) $\vec{v}_c$ the velocity of the cyclist
   (ii) $\vec{v}_{cl}$ the velocity of the cyclist relative to the lorry.
   (iii) How long after they pass will they be $\frac{1}{2}$ km apart?

4. A girl is walking along a straight path at 1.2 m/s. A boy is walking along the same path in the opposite direction at 1.3 m/s. Using $\vec{i}$ as the unit vector in the direction in which the girl is moving, write down
   (i) $\vec{v}_g$, the velocity of the girl
   (ii) $\vec{v}_{gb}$, the velocity of the girl relative to the boy.
   (iii) How long after they pass will they be $\frac{1}{4}$ km apart?

5. Two ships, $P$ and $Q$, leave a small harbour.
   (i) If $\vec{v}_P = 5\vec{i} + 2\vec{j}$ km/h and $\vec{v}_Q = 2\vec{i} - 2\vec{j}$ km/h, find $\vec{v}_{PQ}$ the velocity of $P$ relative to $Q$.
   (ii) Find also $|\vec{v}_{PQ}|$, the magnitude of $\vec{v}_{PQ}$.
   (iii) After how long will the two ships lose sight of each other if visibility is down to 20 km?

6. Three players $A$, $B$ and $C$ are running with velocities $\vec{V}_1$ m/s, $\vec{V}_2$ m/s, $\vec{V}_3$ m/s respectively, where
   $$\vec{V}_1 = 4\vec{i} - 3\vec{j}, \vec{V}_2 = 6\vec{i} - \vec{j}, \vec{V}_3 = 8\vec{i}.$$
   (i) Calculate (in surd form) the magnitude and direction of the relative velocity of $A$ with respect to $B$
   (ii) Calculate (in surd form) the magnitude and direction of the relative velocity of $C$ with respect to $B$.

7. Taking $O$ as the origin, the position vectors of $A$, $B$, and $C$ respectively are:
   $\vec{r}_A = 4\vec{i} + 2\vec{j}$,
   $\vec{r}_B = -3\vec{i} + 6\vec{j}$, and
   $\vec{r}_C = -4\vec{i} + 2\vec{j}$.
   Write, in terms of $\vec{i}$ and $\vec{j}$, $\vec{r}_{BA}$ the displacement of $B$ with respect to $A$ and also $\vec{r}_{CA}$ the displacement of $C$ relative to $A$. Which is further from $A$: $B$ or $C$? Justify your answer, mathematically.

8. With $O$ as the origin, the position vectors of $P$, $Q$, $S$ are
   $\vec{r}_P = \vec{i} - 2\vec{j}, \vec{r}_Q = -4\vec{i} + \vec{j}, \vec{r}_S = -3\vec{i} + 5\vec{j}$.
   (i) Find $\vec{r}_{QP}$, the displacement of $Q$ relative to $P$.
   (ii) Find in terms of $\vec{i}$ and $\vec{j}$ the position vector of $T$ if $\vec{r}_{TS} = \vec{r}_{QP}$.

9. A train is travelling on a straight track with velocity $30\vec{j}$ and a car, visible from the train, is travelling on a straight road with velocity $10\vec{i} + 6\vec{j}$ where speeds are measured in m/s. Calculate the magnitude and direction of the car's velocity as it appears to a person sitting on the train.

10. A particle $P$ is 100 m due West of another particle $Q$. The velocity of $P$ is $6\vec{i} + 2\vec{j}$ m/s, and the velocity of $Q$ is $-4\vec{i} + 2\vec{j}$ m/s. Show that $P$ and $Q$ are on collision course. How much time will pass before the collision occurs?

11. Two ships $A$ and $B$ are 40 km apart. $A$ is due west of $B$. The velocity of $A$ is $4\vec{i} + 3\vec{j}$ km/h. The velocity of $B$ is $-\vec{i} + 3\vec{j}$ km/h.
    (i) Find the velocity of $B$ relative to $A$.
    (ii) Show that they are on collision course.
    (iii) When will they collide?

12. Two ships $A$ and $B$ are 60 km apart. $A$ is due west of $B$. The velocity of $A$ is $12\vec{i} + 4\vec{j}$ km/h. The velocity of $B$ is $4\vec{j}$ km/h.
    (i) Find the velocity of $B$ relative to $A$.
    (ii) Show that they are on collision course.
    (iii) When will they collide?

13.
(a) If $\left|t\vec{i} + 3\vec{j}\right| = 5$, find the value of $t > 0$, $t \in R$.
   (b)
   (i) A ship $K$ is 60 km due West of another ship $M$ which is travelling with velocity $-2\vec{i} + 3\vec{j}$ km/h. If ship $K$ travels at 5 km/h, find in terms and $\vec{i}$ and $\vec{j}$ its velocity if it is to intercept $M$. (Hint: $K$ will have to travel with the same $\vec{j}$-speed as ship $M$ in order to keep on collision course.)
   (ii) When will $K$ intercept M?

14. A ship $P$ is 3.4 km due West of another ship $Q$. The ship $P$ is moving with speed $5\sqrt{2}$ m/s in a NE direction. $Q$ can travel at 13 m/s.
    (i) Write the velocity of $P$ in terms of $\vec{i}$ and $\vec{j}$
    (ii) If they are on collision course, find the velocity of $Q$ in terms and $\vec{i}$ and $\vec{j}$.
    (iii) When will the collision occur?

15. Ship $K$ is 3000 m to the west of ship $H$. Ship $K$ is travelling with velocity $12\vec{i} + 6\vec{j}$ m/s.

    (i) What is the minimum speed with which $H$ must travel if it is to intercept $K$?
    (ii) If, in fact, the speed of $H$ is 10 m/s, find the two directions in which $H$ may steer in order to intercept $K$ – and find the time of interception in each case.

16. Ship $X$ is 40 km due west of ship $Y$. Ship $Y$ is travelling north at 10 km/h. Ship $X$ can travel at 20 km/h. The captain of ship $X$ wishes to intercept ship $Y$.
    (i) Show that the captain must steer the ship in a direction 30° N of $E$.
    (ii) After how long will $X$ intercept Y?

17. At 10.00 hours, ship $A$ has position $2\vec{i} - 3\vec{j}$ km relative to fixed point $O$ and is travelling at $3\vec{i} + \vec{j}$ km/h. At the same time ship $B$ has position $37\vec{i} + 25\vec{j}$ km relative to a fixed point $O$ and is travelling at $-2\vec{i} - 3\vec{j}$ km/h.
    (i) Show that if they continue at these velocities they will collide.
    (ii) Find the time at which the collision will occur.

18. At midnight a ship $A$ has position $-8\vec{i} + 4\vec{j}$ km relative to a small island $O$. At the same time the position of a boat $B$ is $24\vec{i} - 12\vec{j}$ km relative to $O$. The velocities of $A$ and $B$ are $3\vec{i} + \vec{j}$ km/h and $\vec{i} + 2\vec{j}$ km/h, respectively.
    (i) Show that they are on collision course.
    (ii) When will they collide?

19. At 01.00 hours, ship $X$ has position $10\vec{i} - 4\vec{j}$ km relative to a fixed point $O$ and is travelling at $3\vec{i} + \vec{j}$ km/h. At the same time ship $Y$ has position $37\vec{i} + k\vec{j}$ km relative to a fixed point $O$ and is travelling at 1 km/h due South.
    (i) Given that they are on collision course, find the value of $k$.
    (ii) Find the time at which the collision will occur.

20. At midday a ship $P$ has position $-11\vec{i} + \vec{j}$ km relative to a lighthouse $O$. At the same time the position of a boat $Q$ is $4\vec{i} - 13\vec{j}$ km relative to $O$. The velocities of $P$ and $Q$ are $3\vec{i}$ km/h and $x\vec{j}$ km/h, respectively.
    (i) If they are on collision course, find the value of $x$.
    (ii) When will they collide?

## The shortest distance between particles

We often wish to find out how near a pair of ships (or a pair of cars) will get to one another. The easiest way (by far) is to use relative velocities.

### Worked Example 4.2

A cruiser is 50 km due west of a trawler at 12 noon. The velocity of the cruiser is $3\vec{i} + 5\vec{j}$ km/h. The velocity of the trawler is $-\vec{i} + 2\vec{j}$ km/h.

(i) Find the magnitude and direction of the velocity of the cruiser relative to the trawler.

(ii) Hence, find the shortest distance between the two ships in subsequent motion and the time at which this occurs.

(iii) For how long will the ships be within 34 km of one another?

**Solution:**

$$\vec{V}_C = 3\vec{i} + 5\vec{j}$$
$$\vec{V}_T = -\vec{i} + 2\vec{j}$$
$$\vec{V}_{CT} = \vec{V}_C - \vec{V}_T$$
$$= \left(3\vec{i} + 5\vec{j}\right) - \left(-\vec{i} + 2\vec{j}\right)$$
$$= 4\vec{i} + 3\vec{j} \text{ km/h}$$

(i) Magnitude? $\left|\vec{V}_{CT}\right| = \sqrt{4^2 + 3^2} = 5$ km/h.

Direction? The direction of $4\vec{i} + 3\vec{j}$, as before, is given by Tan $\theta = \frac{3}{4} = 0.7500$.

$$\therefore \theta = 36.87°$$

$\therefore$ Direction is 36.87° North of East.

(ii)

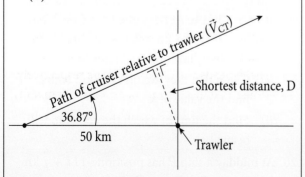

Fig. 4.7

$$\sin \theta = \frac{\text{opposite}}{\text{hypotenuse}}$$
$$\Rightarrow 0.6 = \frac{D}{50}$$
$$\Rightarrow D = 50 \times 0.6 = 30 \text{ km.}$$

(iii) To find the time taken, we will follow three steps:

**Step** 1: Find the distance which the cruiser has covered along the "relative path", using Pythagoras' Theorem:

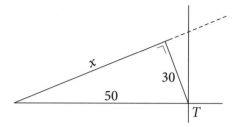

Fig. 4.8

$$x^2 + 30^2 = 50^2$$
$$\Rightarrow x^2 = 2500 - 900$$
$$\Rightarrow x^2 = 1600$$
$$\Rightarrow x = 40 \text{ km.}$$

**Step** 2: Its "relative speed" along this path, as we have already discovered, is 5 km/h.

**Step** 3: The time taken is given by

$$t = \frac{\text{relative distance}}{\text{relative speed}}$$
$$= \frac{40}{5}$$
$$= 8 \text{ h}$$

$\therefore$ The time at which this happens is at 20:00 hours.

(iv)

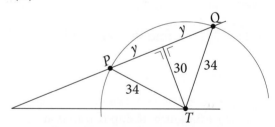

Fig. 4.9

Draw a circle of radius 34 km around $T$. Show the points $P$ and $Q$, where the path of $C$ relative to $T$ intersects this circle. We find the length of the line segment $[PQ]$ using Pythagoras' Theorem. The distance from $T$ to the relative path is 30 km.

Let $y = \frac{1}{2}|PQ|$

$$\therefore y^2 + 30^2 = 34^2$$
$$\therefore y = \sqrt{34^2 - 30^2}$$
$$= 16 \text{ km.}$$

But $|PQ| = 2y$

$$= 2 \times 16 = 32 \text{ km}$$

The time taken $= \frac{\text{Distance}}{\text{Speed}} = \frac{32}{5} = 6.4$ h: Answer

## Exercise 4 B

1.  $K$ is a particle which is 20 m due West of another particle $T$. Their velocities are $\vec{i} + 2\vec{j}$ m/s and $-2\vec{i} - 2\vec{j}$ m/s respectively.

    (i)   Find the velocity of $K$ relative to $T$.

    (ii)  Find the shortest distance between them in subsequent motion

2.  A particle $P$ is moving with velocity $-8\vec{i} + 12\vec{j}$ m/s while another particle $Q$ is moving with velocity $7\vec{i} + 4\vec{j}$ m/s. $P$ is originally 119 m east of $Q$.

    (i)   Find the velocity of $P$ relative to $Q$.

    (ii)  Show the positions of $P$ and $Q$ on a diagram and show the path of $P$ relative to $Q$.

    (iii) Calculate the least distance between $P$ and $Q$.

3.  $F$ is a frigate which is 5000 m due West of a tanker $T$. Their velocities are $2\vec{i} + 5\vec{j}$ m/s and $-4\vec{i} - 3\vec{j}$ m/s respectively.

    (i)   Find the velocity of $F$ relative to $T$.

    (ii)  Find the shortest distance between them in subsequent motion.

4.  Ship $T$ is 100 km due West of ship $Q$. $T$ is travelling at 10 km/h in a direction 30° South of East. $Q$ is travelling at 20 km/h in NW direction.

    (i)   Find in terms of $\vec{i}$ and $\vec{j}$ the velocity of $T$, the velocity of $Q$ and the velocity of $T$ relative to $Q$.

    (ii)  Find, also, the magnitude and direction of the velocity of $T$ relative to $Q$

    (iii) Hence find the shortest distance between them in the subsequent motion correct to one decimal place.

5.  Two straight roads cross at right angles at $O$. A person $X$ is running along one of the roads towards $O$ at 7 m/s. Another person is cycling along the other road at 24 m/s. When $X$ is 100 m from $O$, $Y$ is at $O$.

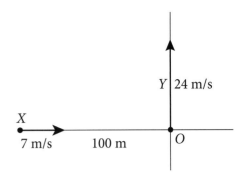

Fig. 4.10

    (i)   Find the velocity of $X$ relative to $Y$

    (ii)  Find the shortest distance between $X$ and $Y$ subsequently.

6.  $P$ is 350 km due east of $Q$. The velocity of $P$ is $-\vec{i} + \vec{j}$ km/h. The velocity of $Q$ is $3\vec{i} - 2\vec{j}$ km/h. Find

    (i)   the velocity of $Q$ relative to $P$

    (ii)  the magnitude and direction of the velocity of $Q$ relative to $P$

    (iii) the shortest distance between them in the subsequent motion.

    (iv)  If they can exchange signals while they are within 290 km of each other, for how long can they exchange signals?

7.  $A$ is 300 m due west of $B$. The velocity of $A$ is $2\vec{i} - \vec{j}$ m/s. The velocity of $B$ is $-2\vec{i} + 2\vec{j}$ m/s. Find

    (i)   the velocity of $A$ relative to $B$

    (ii)  the shortest distance between them in the subsequent motion

    (iii) the length of time they remain in vision of each other if visibility is 225 metres.

8.  Two cars $G$ and $H$ are moving along straight roads which are at right angles to each other. Their speeds are 6 m/s and 8 m/s respectively. When $H$ is at the crossroads, $G$ is 200 m away. Calculate

    (i)   the shortest distance between them subsequently

    (ii)  the time interval during which the cars are no more than 164 m apart.

9.  A ship $A$ is travelling in a direction 45° East of North at 16 m/s. A second ship $B$ is travelling in a direction 45° South of East at 20 m/s. Calculate:

    (i)   the velocity of $A$ relative to B

(ii) the shortest distance between the ships if $B$ is 10 km North of $A$ at a particular moment

(iii) the time interval during which the ships remain in visual contact if visibility is limited to 2 km.

10. A ship $A$ is 200 km West of another ship $B$. Ship $B$ is travelling due North at 10 km/h. Ship $A$ is travelling Northeast at 20 km/h. Find (correct to 2 decimal places)

   (i) the velocity of $A$ relative to B

   (ii) the shortest distance between them

   (iii) the distance between them 1 hour after they were nearest each other.

11. A speedboat is 100 km west of a trawler. The trawler is travelling south at 8 km/h. The speedboat is travelling at 20 km/h in a direction 30° South of East. Find (correct to 2 decimal places)

   (i) the velocity of the speedboat relative to the trawler, its magnitude and direction

   (ii) the nearest the two boats get to one another

   (iii) the distance between the boats 2 hours before they were closest to one another.

12. Adam is 100 m to the West of Barbara. Adam is cycling at 10 m/s in a direction 30° North of East. Barbara is running North at 3 m/s. Find

   (i) the velocity of Adam relative to Barbara

   (ii) the magnitude and direction (to the nearest degree) of the velocity of Adam relative to Barbara

   (iii) the shortest distance between them subsequently

   (iv) the time interval during which they are within 30 m of one another.

13. At 12 noon a ship $P$ is 75 km due West of a ship $Q$. Ship $P$ is travelling South-East at 50 km/h and ship $Q$ is travelling South at 30 km/h.

   (i) Calculate the velocity of $Q$ relative to $P$, its magnitude and direction.

   (ii) Find the shortest distance between them in subsequent motion.

(iii) If visibility is limited to 40 km, show that the ships will come into visibility at approximately 13:00 hours and calculate the time when they will lose sight of one another again.

## When the particles are at an awkward angle to one another

When the particles start in positions which are neither East-West nor North-South of one another, it can be difficult to find the shortest distance between them. But, there is a clever trick you can use: wait until the moment when they are East-West and then start the problem again. Here is such an example:

### Worked Example 4.3

Two straight roads run at right angles to one another and intersect at $P$. A car, which is 64 metres west of $P$, is travelling towards $P$ at 5 m/s. A bus, which is 60 m South of $P$, is travelling towards $P$ at 12 m/s. Find:

   (i) the velocity of the bus relative to the car

   (ii) the least distance between them in the subsequent motion

   (iii) the time at which they are closest.

**Solution:**

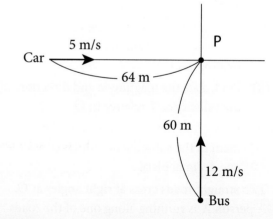

Fig. 4.11

   (i) $$\vec{v}_c = 5\,\vec{i}\ \text{m/s},$$

$$\vec{v}_b = 12\,\vec{j}\ \text{m/s},$$

$$\vec{v}_{bc} = \vec{v}_b - \vec{v}_c$$

$$= 12\,\vec{j} - 5\,\vec{i}$$

$$= -5\,\vec{i} + 12\,\vec{j}\ \text{m/s}.$$

$$\left|\vec{v}_{bc}\right| = \sqrt{(-5^2) + 12^2}$$

$$= 13 \text{ m/s}$$

The direction is $\tan^{-1}\left(\frac{12}{5}\right)$ North of West.

(ii)   It takes the bus $\frac{60}{12} = 5$ seconds to reach $P$. In this time the car will travel $5 \times (5) = 25$ m towards $P$. The car will be $64 - 25 = 39$ m from $P$ at this moment. Here, then, is the situation after 5 seconds:

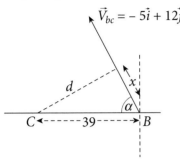

Fig. 4.12

The shortest distance between them, $d$, is given by $d = 39(\sin \alpha) = 39\left(\frac{12}{13}\right) = 36$ m

(iii)   The distance $x$ covered by the bus relative to the car is found using Pythagoras' Theorem:

$$x^2 + 36^2 = 39^2$$

$$\Rightarrow x = \sqrt{39^2 - 36^2}$$

$$\Rightarrow x = 15 \text{ m}$$

The relative speed is $\left|V_{bc}\right| = 13$ m/s. Therefore the time taken

$$= \frac{\text{Relative distance}}{\text{Relative speed}}$$

$$= \frac{15}{13}$$

$$= 1.15 \text{ s}$$

But this was all 5 seconds after the start.

Therefore, this occurs $(5 + 1.15) = 6.15$ seconds from the start: Answer

## Exercise 4 C

1.   Two cars $P$ and $Q$ travel towards a junction $O$ on roads, which are at right angles to one another. Car $P$ is travelling North at 12 m/s. Car $Q$ is travelling East at 5 m/s. At a certain instant $P$ is 60 m from $O$. At the same moment $Q$ is 51 m from $O$.

(i)   How long does it take $P$ to reach $O$?

(ii)   How far from $O$ will $Q$ be at this time?

(iii)   Find the velocity of $Q$ relative to $P$.

(iv)   Calculate the shortest distance between the cars in subsequent motion.

2.   Two cars $M$ and $N$ travel towards a junction $O$ on roads, which are at right angles to one another. Car $M$ is travelling East at 6 m/s. Car $N$ is travelling North at 8 m/s. At a certain instant $M$ is 65 m from $O$. At the same moment $N$ is 20 m from $O$.

(i)   How long does it take $N$ to reach $O$?

(ii)   How far from $O$ will $M$ be at this time?

(iii)   Find the velocity of $M$ relative to $N$.

(iv)   Calculate the shortest distance between the cars in subsequent motion.

3.   Two cars $A$ and $B$ travel towards a junction $O$ on roads, which are at right angles to one another. Car $A$ is travelling East at 21 m/s. Car $B$ is travelling South at 20 m/s. At a certain instant $A$ is 250 m from $O$. At the same instant $B$ is 100 m from $O$.

(i)   Find the velocity of $A$ relative to $B$.

(ii)   Calculate the shortest distance between the cars in subsequent motion.

(iii)   Find the time at which this occurs.

4.   Two straight roads intersect at a point $O$ and cross at an angle $\theta$ to one another, such that $\tan \theta = \frac{3}{4}$. Two cars, $A$ and $B$ are travelling towards $O$ on these roads, $A$ at 5 m/s and $B$ at 8 m/s.

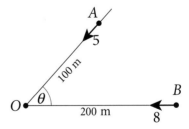

At a certain moment $A$ is 100 m from the junction and $B$, on the other road, is 200 m from the junction. Find

(i)   the time at which $A$ reaches $O$

(ii)   the distance between $A$ and $B$ at this time

(iii)   the magnitude and direction of the velocity of $A$ with respect to B

(iv)   the shortest distance between them

(v)   the time at which they are nearest to one another

(vi)   the time when they are equidistant from $O$.

5. Two straight roads intersect at a point $O$ and cross at an angle $\theta$ to one another, such that $\tan\theta = \frac{4}{3}$. Two cars, $A$ and $B$ are travelling towards $O$ on these roads, $A$ at 16 m/s and $B$ at $v$ m/s, where $v > 0$.

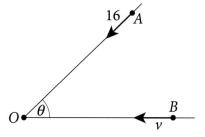

Fig. 4.13

If the magnitude of the velocity of $A$ relative to $B$ is 16 m/s, find the value of $v$.

If, at a given instant, $A$ is 96 m from the junction and $B$ on the other road is 38.4 m from the junction, find

(i) the shortest distance between the cars in subsequent motion

(ii) the distance, to the nearest metre, between the cars two seconds before the instant when they are nearest to each other.

6. Two straight roads intersect at a point $O$ and cross at an angle $\theta$ to one another, such that $\tan\theta = \frac{3}{4}$. Two cars, $A$ and $B$ are travelling towards $O$ on these roads, $A$ at 10 m/s and $B$ at 20 m/s.

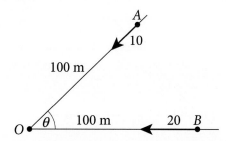

Fig. 4.14

If, at a given instant, $A$ and $B$ are both 100 m from the junction, find the shortest distance between the cars in subsequent motion.

7. Two straight roads cross at a point $O$ and cross at an angle 60° to one another. Cyclists $A$ and $B$ are travelling towards $O$ on these roads, $A$ at 30 km/h and $B$ at 40 km/h.

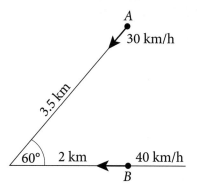

Fig. 4.15

If, at a given instant, $A$ is 3.5 km from the junction and $B$, on the other road, is 2 km from the junction, calculate (in kilometres, correct to two decimal places) the shortest distance between the cyclists in subsequent motion.

8. Two straight roads intersect at a point $O$ and cross at an angle 60° to one another. On one road car $A$ is travelling towards $O$ with uniform speed 16 m/s and on the other road, car $B$ is moving away from $O$ with uniform speed 20 m/s.

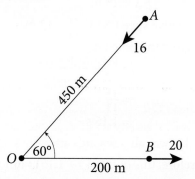

Fig. 4.16

(a) Calculate the velocity of $A$ relative to $B$.

(b) If, at a given instant, $A$ is 450 m from $O$ and $B$ is 200 m from $O$, calculate the time interval until the cars

(i) are nearest to each other

(ii) are equidistant from $O$.

## Rivers, currents and winds

Problems which involve crossing a river are best solved by using clear diagrams.

### Worked Example 4.4

A boat can travel at 13 m/s in still water. It has to travel across a stream which is 78 m wide and flowing at 5 m/s parallel to the straight banks. How long will the crossing take

(i) by the quickest route?

(ii) by the shortest route?

**Solution:**

So what's the difference?

In (i) time is a minimum, but in (ii) distance is a minimum.

If the boat puts all its force into going across (i.e. if it heads straight across) it will cross in the shortest time.

(i) In each second it will travel 13 m across and 5 m downstream.

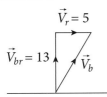

Fig. 4.17

The time taken will be given by:

$$\text{time} = \frac{\text{distance across}}{\text{speed across}} = \frac{78}{13} = 6 \ s.$$

(It is worth noting that the boat will land 6 × 5 = 30 m downstream.)

(ii) Since the boat can go faster than the stream, it will be able to go straight across — but how? It will have to head a bit upstream to counteract the current and end up going straight across.

Let's say the boat heads upstream at an angle $A$ to the bank at full speed, 13 m/s. The current will bring it back downstream at 5 m/s, so that the boat actually travels straight across the river at $x$ m/s.

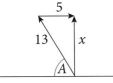

Fig. 4.18

By Pythagoras' Theorem,

$$x^2 + 5^2 = 13^2$$
$$\Rightarrow x = \sqrt{169 - 25}$$
$$\Rightarrow x = \sqrt{144}$$
$$\Rightarrow x = 12 \text{ m/s}.$$

Therefore the time taken will be given by :

$$\text{time} = \frac{\text{distance across}}{\text{speed across}}$$
$$= \frac{78}{12}$$
$$= 6.5 \ s.$$

### Worked Example 4.5

Ambrosia Island is 600 km due West of Beachcomber Island. A plane which can fly at $30\sqrt{5}$ km/h in still air has to travel from Ambrosia to Beachcomber. There is a wind blowing with velocity $20\vec{i} - 30\vec{j}$ km/h, where $\vec{i}$ is the unit vector along the line from Ambrosia to Beachcomber. Find the time taken.

**Solution:**

In order to counteract the wind, the plane will have to head north a bit, at an angle $\alpha$ to the line $AB$, at full speed $30\sqrt{5}$ km/h.

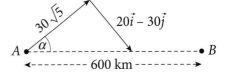

Fig. 4.19

In this case $\vec{V}_w$ will refer to the velocity of the wind.

$$\vec{V}_w = 20\vec{i} - 30\vec{j}$$
$$\vec{V}_{pw} = 30\sqrt{5}\cos\alpha \ \vec{i} + 30\sqrt{5}\sin\alpha \ \vec{j}$$
$$\therefore \vec{V}_p = \vec{V}_{pw} + \vec{V}_w$$
$$= \left(30\sqrt{5}\cos\alpha + 20\right)\vec{i} + \left(30\sqrt{5}\sin\alpha - 30\right)\vec{j}$$

But this must be along $AB$, so the $\vec{j}$ - component must be zero.

$$\therefore 30\sqrt{5}\sin\alpha - 30 = 0$$
$$\Rightarrow \sin\alpha = \frac{1}{\sqrt{5}} = \frac{\text{Opposite}}{\text{Hypotenuse}}$$

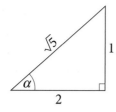

Fig. 4.20

Using Pythagoras' Theorem

$$x^2 + 1^2 = \left(\sqrt{5}\right)^2$$

$$x^2 + 1 = 5$$

$$\Rightarrow x = \sqrt{5 - 1}$$

$$\Rightarrow x = \sqrt{4} = 2$$

$$\therefore \cos \alpha = \frac{2}{\sqrt{5}}$$

$$\Rightarrow \vec{V_b} = \left(30\sqrt{5}\cos\alpha + 20\right)\vec{i} + \left(30\sqrt{5}\sin\alpha - 30\right)\vec{j}$$

$$\vec{V_b} = \left(30\sqrt{5}\left(\frac{2}{\sqrt{5}}\right) + 20\right)\vec{i} + \left(30\sqrt{5}\left(\frac{1}{\sqrt{5}}\right) - 30\right)\vec{j}$$

$$= (60 + 20)\vec{i} + (30 - 30)\vec{j}$$

$$= 80\vec{i} + 0\vec{j}$$

Time taken $= \dfrac{\text{distance}}{\text{speed}}$

$$= \frac{600}{80}$$

$$= 7\frac{1}{2}\,\text{h}$$

## Exercise 4 D

1. A straight river is flowing at 1 m/s, parallel to its banks. A boat heads straight across at 2 m/s. The river is 40 m wide.
   (i) How long will the boat take to cross?
   (ii) How far downstream will it land?

2. A river is 60 m wide and flows at 5 m/s parallel to its bank. A boat heads straight across at its maximum speed of 12 m/s. After how long and how far downstream will it land?

3. A river, 60 m wide, flows at 3 m/s parallel to its straight banks. A boat can go at 5 m/s in still water. Find the time which the boat will take to cross
   (i) by the quickest route
   (ii) by the shortest route.

4. A straight river is 39 m wide. It flows with speed 0.5 m/s. A boat can travel at 1.3 m/s in still water. Find the shortest time which the boat takes to cross the river
   (i) if it takes the quickest route
   (ii) if it takes the shortest route.

5. A straight river is 60 m wide. It flows with speed 0.7 m/s. A boat can travel at 2.5 m/s in still water. Find the time which the boat takes to cross the river
   (i) if it takes the quickest route
   (ii) if it takes the shortest route.

6. A straight river is 510 m wide. It flows with speed 0.8 m/s. A boat can travel at 1.7 m/s in still water. Find the time which the boat takes to cross the river
   (i) if it takes the quickest route
   (ii) if it takes the shortest route.

7. A straight river is 58 m wide. It flows with speed 2.1 m/s. A boat can travel at 2.9 m/s in still water.
   (i) If the boat crosses by the quickest route, how far downstream will it land?
   (ii) If it crosses by the shortest route, how long does the crossing take?

8. A straight river is 50 m wide. It flows with speed 0.3 m/s. A boat can travel at 0.5 m/s in still water. On one journey, the boat crosses by the quickest path, and on the next journey it crosses by the shortest path. Show that the crossing times differ by 25 seconds.

9. A straight river is 50 m wide. It flows with speed $\frac{5}{6}$ m/s. A boy can swim at $\frac{5}{9}$ m/s in still water. He crosses the river as quickly as possible. Calculate
   (i) the direction in which he should head
   (ii) the time taken to cross
   (iii) how far downstream he will land.

10. A plane heads due East at 100 km/h. A wind is blowing from the North at 10 km/h. Find the resultant speed and direction of the plane.

11. A stream flows at 3 m/s. A canoeist can row at 5 m/s in still water. How long would it take the canoeist to go 80 m upstream and back again? If the stream were a still lake would it take the same time to complete the same journey? Justify your answer.

12. A man has to row from $A$ to $B$ and back again, where $|AB| = 480$ m. He can row in still water at 8 m/s. Show that the journey takes less time in still water than if there is a current flowing from $A$ to $B$ at 2 m/s. What is the difference in these two times?

13. A boat crosses a river, 240 m wide, which flows parallel to the straight banks with velocity $\vec{v}_1 = 12\,\vec{i}$, while the velocity of the boat relative to the river is $\vec{v}_2 = 5\,\vec{j}$, where $\vec{v}_1$ and $\vec{v}_2$ are measured in m/s.
    (i) Find the magnitude of the actual velocity of the boat.
    (ii) Find how long it takes the boat to cross the river and the distance it has travelled downstream in doing so.

14. A ship is travelling at 15 m/s. A passenger on board runs across the deck at right angles to the direction of motion of the ship, at a speed of 8 m/s relative to the ship. Find the actual velocity of the passenger.

15. A river is 120 m wide and flows at 7 m/s parallel to its straight banks. A speed-boat can travel at 25 m/s in still water. If the speed-boat has to go straight across the river, find
    (i) the angle which its velocity relative to the river makes with the bank
    (ii) the time taken to cross the river.

16. A small aeroplane has to fly 189 km due East from Galway Airport to Dublin Airport. There is a wind blowing from the South at 60 km/h. The aeroplane can fly at 100 km/h in still air. Find the time taken for the journey. Is the time taken for the return journey the same? Give a reason for your answer.

17. A man can swim at twice the speed of the flow of a straight river. At what angle with the bank should he head upstream in order to end up going straight across the river? (i.e. what angle does his velocity relative to the river make with the bank?)

18. A swimmer is caught in a current which is flowing Southwards at 1 m/s. If the resultant velocity of the swimmer is 2 m/s in a South-East direction, find the speed of the swimmer relative to the current, correct to 2 decimal places.

19. An aeroplane which is flying at maximum speed is travelling due West at 100 km/h. It is partly helped by a wind blowing at 20 km/h in a direction 30° North of West. Find the maximum speed of the aeroplane in still air.

20. The maximum speed of an aeroplane is 200 km/h. Find the maximum speed with which it can travel due North if there is a North-East wind blowing at 50 km/h. (Note: A North-East wind is *from* the North-East.)

21.

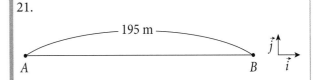

Fig. 4.21

A ship, which can sail at 10 m/s in still water, has to go from $A$ to $B$ and back again (see diagram). The current flows at $5\,\vec{i} - 6\,\vec{j}$ where $\vec{i}$ is along $AB$, as shown. If $|AB| = 195$ m, find the time taken to complete the whole journey. A faster ship can go from $A$ to $B$ in 13 seconds, how long will it take to go from $B$ to $A$?

22. A boat has to travel by the shortest route to the point $4.25\,\vec{j}$ km and then return immediately to its starting point at the origin. The velocity of the water is $8\sqrt{2}\,\vec{i} - 8\sqrt{2}\,\vec{j}$ km/h and the boat has a speed of 18 km/h in still water. If $a\,\vec{i} + b\,\vec{j}$ is the velocity of the boat on the outward journey, find $a$ and $b$ and the time taken for the outward journey, leaving your answer in surd form.
Find also, the time taken for the whole journey.

23. An aircraft flew due East from $P$ to $Q$ at $u_1$ km/h. Wind speed from the South West was $v$ km/h. On the return journey from $Q$ to $P$, due west, the aircraft's speed was $u_2$ km/h, the wind velocity being unchanged. If the speed of the aircraft in still air was $x$ km/h, $x > v$, show, by resolving along the perpendicular to $PQ$, or otherwise, that
    (i) $u_1 - u_2 = v\sqrt{2}$
    (ii) $u_1 u_2 = x^2 - v^2$
    If $|PQ| = d$, find in terms of $v$, $x$ and $d$, the time for the two journeys.

24. A woman wishes to cross a river 60 m wide in a boat. The river flows with a velocity of 13 m/s parallel to the straight banks, and the boat has maximum speed of 5 m/s relative to the water. If she heads at an angle $\alpha$ to the upstream direction, and her actual velocity is at an angle $\theta$ to the downstream direction, show that:

$$\tan\theta = \frac{5\sin\alpha}{13 - 5\cos\alpha}$$

Using calculus (or otherwise) prove that $\tan\theta$ has a maximum value when $\cos\alpha = \frac{5}{13}$. Deduce that the time taken for the woman to cross by the **shortest path** is 13 seconds.

25. A man wishes to swim across a river 36 m wide. The river flows with a velocity of 2 m/s parallel to the straight banks, and the man can swim at 1 m/s. If he heads at an angle $\alpha$ to the upstream direction, and his actual velocity is at an angle $\theta$ to the downstream direction, show that:

$$\tan\theta = \frac{\sin\alpha}{2 - \cos\alpha}$$

Prove that $\tan\theta$ has a maximum value when $\alpha = 60°$. Deduce that the time taken for the man to cross by the shortest path is $24\sqrt{3}$ seconds.

26. (a) Given that $\sin^2 A + \cos^2 A = 1$, write $\cos A$ in terms of $\sin A$.

   (b) The velocity of a boat relative to the water is $5\vec{i} - 2\vec{j}$ m/s. The current has a speed of 5 m/s. If the boat, as a result, moves in a NE direction find, two values of

   (i) the velocity of the current

   (ii) the resultant velocity of the boat.

## The apparent velocity of winds

There is a difference between the velocity of the wind and the **apparent velocity** of the wind. For example, a girl is running at 5 m/s. The wind is blowing in an opposite direction at 7 m/s. The **apparent velocity** of the wind (that is the velocity of the wind relative to the girl) is 12 m/s.

Mathematically, $\vec{v}_g = 5\vec{i}$

$$\vec{v}_w = -7\vec{i}$$

$$\Rightarrow \vec{v}_{wg} = \vec{v}_w - \vec{v}_g$$

$$= -7\vec{i} - 5\vec{i}$$

$$= -12\vec{i}\ \text{m/s}.$$

This means that the girl feels a wind of 12 m/s in her face.

The key thing to remember is that the apparent velocity of the wind means the velocity of the wind relative to the person.

## Directions of vectors

| Direction of $x\vec{i} + y\vec{j}$ | Conclusion 1 | Conclusion 2 |
|---|---|---|
| North-East | $x = y$ | $x$ & $y > 0$ |
| South | $x = 0$ | $y < 0$ |
| North West | $x = -y$ | $x < 0, y > 0$ |
| West | $y = 0$ | $x < 0$ |
| Fill in the missing boxes below yourself | | |
| South-East | | |
| North | | |
| East | | |
| South-West | | |

## Worked Example 4.6

When a boy runs north at 2 m/s, the wind appears to come from the south-west. When he runs east at 4 m/s, the same wind appears to come from the south. Find the actual velocity of the wind in terms of $\vec{i}$ and $\vec{j}$.

**Solution**

Let the actual velocity of the wind be $x\vec{i} + y\vec{j}$ m/s.

**Case 1:** $\qquad \vec{v}_b = 2\vec{j}$

$$\vec{v}_w = x\vec{i} + y\vec{j}$$

therefore $\vec{v}_{wb} = \vec{v}_w - \vec{v}_b$

$$= x\vec{i} + y\vec{j} - 2\vec{j}$$

$$= x\vec{i} + (y - 2)\vec{j}$$

We know that the vector $x\vec{i} + (y-2)\vec{j}$ has direction "from the south-west".

$$\text{Therefore, } x = y - 2 \qquad \text{equation I}$$

**Case 2:** $\qquad \vec{v}_b = 4\vec{i}$

$$\vec{v}_w = x\vec{i} + y\vec{j}$$

$$\Rightarrow \vec{v}_{wb} = \vec{v}_w - \vec{v}_b$$

$$= x\vec{i} + y\vec{j} - 4\vec{i}$$

$$= (x - 4)\vec{i} + y\vec{j}$$

We know that the vector $(x-4)\vec{i} + y\vec{j}$ has direction "from the south".

Therefore, $\quad x - 4 = 0$

$$\Rightarrow x = 4 \qquad \text{equation II}$$

Putting $x = 4$ into equation I,

we get $4 = y - 2$

$$\Rightarrow y = 6$$

Answer: The velocity of the wind is $4\vec{i} + 6\vec{j}$ m/s.

## Worked Example 4.7

A ship $P$ is travelling at $3\vec{i} + \vec{j}$ km/h. A second ship $Q$ is travelling at speed 10 km/h. To an observer on $P$, the ship $Q$ appears to be travelling in a north-easterly direction. Find the velocity of $Q$ in terms of $\vec{i}$ and $\vec{j}$.

### Solution

$$\text{Let } \vec{v}_Q = x\vec{i} + y\vec{j}$$

We know that $V_P = 3\vec{i} + 1\vec{j}$

$$\Rightarrow \vec{v}_{QP} = \vec{v}_Q - \vec{v}_P$$
$$= (x\vec{i} + y\vec{j}) - (3\vec{i} + 1\vec{j})$$
$$= (x-3)\vec{i} + (y-1)\vec{j}$$

We are told that the velocity of $Q$ relative to $P$ is "in a north-easterly direction".

Hence
$$x - 3 = y - 1$$
$$\Rightarrow x = y + 2 \ldots \text{equation 1}$$

The speed of $Q$ is 10 km/h.

$$\Rightarrow |x\vec{i} + y\vec{j}| = 10$$
$$\Rightarrow \sqrt{x^2 + y^2} = 10$$
$$\Rightarrow x^2 + y^2 = 100 \ldots \text{equation 2}$$

We solve these equations by "substitution".

Let $x = y + 2$ in equation 2:
$$\Rightarrow (y+2)^2 + y^2 = 100$$
$$\Rightarrow y^2 + 4y + 4 + y^2 = 100$$
$$\Rightarrow 2y^2 + 4y - 96 = 0$$
$$\Rightarrow y^2 + 2y - 48 = 0$$
$$\Rightarrow (y-6)(y+8) = 0$$
$$\therefore y = 6 \text{ or } y = -8$$

If $y = 6$, then $x = y + 2$
$$= 6 + 2$$
$$= 8$$

Hence $\vec{v}_Q = 8\vec{i} + 6\vec{j}$ km/h

If $y = -8$, then $x = y + 2$
$$= -8 + 2$$
$$= -6$$

Hence $\vec{v}_Q = -6\vec{i} - 8\vec{j}$ km/h

But which of these is the right answer? We'll check them out.

In the first case,
$$\vec{v}_{QP} = \vec{v}_Q - \vec{v}_P$$
$$= (8\vec{i} + 6\vec{j}) - (3\vec{i} + 1\vec{j})$$
$$= 5\vec{i} + 5\vec{j}$$

This is indeed from the south-west, and is, therefore, acceptable.

In the second case,
$$\vec{v}_{QP} = \vec{v}_Q - \vec{v}_P$$
$$= (-6\vec{i} - 8\vec{j}) - (3\vec{i} + 1\vec{j})$$
$$= -9\vec{i} - 9\vec{j}$$

This is **not** from the southwest (but rather to the southwest), and is, therefore, **not** acceptable.

The correct answer is $\vec{v}_Q = 8\vec{i} + 6\vec{j}$ km/h.

## Exercise 4 E

1. To a man, cycling east at 4 m/s, the wind appears to come from the north. To a woman walking south at 1 m/s, the same wind appears to come from the north-west.
   (i) Find the actual velocity of the wind.
   (ii) Find the speed and direction of the wind.
   (iii) If the man were to cycle north at 4 m/s, from what direction (to the nearest degree) would the wind appear to blow?

2. When a man walks due south at 1 m/s, the wind appears to come from the South-West. When he walks due North at 3 m/s, the wind appears to come from the North-West. Find the velocity of the wind in terms of $\vec{i}$ and $\vec{j}$.

3. To a woman who cycles at 2 m/s due south, the wind appears to blow from the North-West. When she speeds up to 14 m/s (without changing direction), the same wind appears to blow in a north-easterly direction.
   (i) Find the true velocity of the wind.
   (ii) Find the speed of the wind.

4. To a cyclist travelling North at 7 m/s the wind appears to blow from the North-West. To a pedestrian walking due West at 1 m/s the same wind appears to come from the South-West. Find the magnitude and direction of the true velocity of the wind.

5. To a boy running north at 1 m/s, the wind appears to come from the South West. When he cycles North at 5 m/s the same wind appears to come from the North-West. Find the true velocity of the wind.

6. When a cyclist's velocity is $3\vec{i} + 2\vec{j}$ m/s, the wind appears to come from the north-west. When the cyclist's velocity is $7\vec{i}$ m/s, the same wind appears to come from the north. Find the velocity of the wind.

7. When a cyclist travels north at 3 m/s, the wind appears to come from the south-west. She trebles her speed, without changing direction. The same wind now appears to her to come from the north-west.
   (i) Find the velocity of the wind.
   (ii) At what speed must the girl cycle north, so that the wind would appear to her to be blowing from the west?

8. The wind is blowing with speed 10 m/s. To a man who is running at 2 m/s in a southerly direction, this wind appears to be blowing from the North-West.
   (i) Find the true velocity of the wind.
   (ii) If the man reversed direction but continued to run at 2 m/s, from what direction would the wind appear to him to be blowing?

9. When a girl runs with speed 4 m/s in an easterly direction, the wind appears to blow from the North West. When she cycles north at 6 m/s, the same wind appears to have a speed of 10 m/s (i.e. its velocity is of magnitude 10).
   (i) Find the true velocity of the wind.
   (ii) At what speed should the girl cycle due west, so that the wind's speed would appear to be 8 m/s?

10. A speedboat is travelling at 20 m/s. A trawler is travelling east at 4 m/s. To an observer on the trawler, the speedboat appears to be travelling in a South-easterly direction. Find the velocity of the speedboat in terms of $\vec{i}$ and $\vec{j}$.

11. A ship $K$ is travelling at 25 km/h. Another ship $H$ is travelling east at 17 km/h. To an observer on ship $H$, ship $K$ appears to be travelling north-east.
    (i) Find the velocity of ship $K$.
    (ii) If $K$ is 41 km to the west of $H$ at a particular instant, find the shortest distance between the two ships in subsequent motion (to the nearest kilometre).
    (iii) For how long (to the nearest minute) are the ships within 30 km of one another?

## The t-method

When you steer your boat (or plane) at one angle in order to travel at another angle, the easiest way to solve the problem is to use the '$t$-method'. In such problems, we draw a diagram to show what happens over $t$ seconds. Usually, we use the Sine Rule (twice!) to get the answer. The Sine Rule appears on page 16 of *The Formulae & Tables*:

$$\frac{a}{\sin A} = \frac{b}{\sin B} = \frac{c}{\sin C}$$

### Worked Example 4.8

A girl wishes to cross a river, which is 20 m wide, in a boat. The river flows with speed 5 m/s. The boat can travel at 4 m/s in still water. The girl wishes to land on the opposite side at a point which is 21 m downstream. Find the time taken.

**Solution**

Let $t$ = the time taken to cross the river.

The boat will head upstream at 4 m/s, and would travel a distance $4t$.

Meanwhile the river carries the boat downstream a distance $5t$.

The boat lands 21 m downstream.

Here is a diagram of what happens:

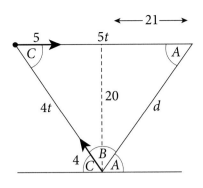

Fig. 4.22

$$\tan A = \frac{20}{21}$$
$$\Rightarrow A = 43.6°$$

By Pythagoras' Theorem,
$$d^2 = 21^2 + 20^2$$
$$= 441 + 400$$
$$= 841$$
$$\Rightarrow d = \sqrt{841} = 29 \text{ m}$$

Using the **Sine Rule**: $\dfrac{4t}{\sin 43.6°} = \dfrac{5t}{\sin B}$

$$\Rightarrow 4 \sin B = 5 \sin 43.6°$$
$$\Rightarrow \sin B = 0.8621$$
$$\Rightarrow B = 59.55° \text{ or } B = 120.45°$$

| **Case 1**: $B = 59.55°$ | **Case 2**: $B = 120.45°$ |
|---|---|
| $C = 180° - 59.55° - 43.6°$ | $C = 180° - 120.45° - 43.6°$ |
| $= 76.85°$ | $= 15.95°$ |

Using the Sine rule

| | |
|---|---|
| $\dfrac{4t}{\sin 43.6°} = \dfrac{29}{\sin 76.85°}$ | $\dfrac{4t}{\sin 43.6°} = \dfrac{29}{\sin 15.95°}$ |
| $\dfrac{4t}{0.6896} = \dfrac{29}{0.9738}$ | $\dfrac{4t}{0.6896} = \dfrac{29}{0.2748}$ |
| $3.8952\,t = 19.9984$ | $1.0992\,t = 19.9984$ |
| $t = 5.13 \text{ s}$ | $t = 18.19 \text{ s}$ |

Answer: the time taken could be 5.13 s or 18.19 s

## Exercise 4 F

1.  A boy wishes to cross a river, which is 100 m wide, in a boat. The river flows with speed 4 m/s. The boat can travel at 3 m/s in still water. The boy wishes to land on the opposite side at a point which is 105 m downstream. Show that there are two angles he can head in and find (to the nearest second) the time to get there in each case.

2.  A girl wishes to cross a river, which is 50 m wide, in a boat. The river flows with speed 2 m/s. The boat can travel at 1 m/s in still water. The girl wishes to land on the opposite side at a point which is 120 m downstream.
    (i)   Find the two directions in which the girl can steer the boat.
    (ii)  Find the two times of crossing (to the nearest second).

3.  A girl wishes to swim across a river, which is 60 m wide. The river flows with speed $q$ m/s parallel to the straight banks. The girl swims at a speed of $p$ m/s relative to the water. In crossing as quickly as possible, she takes 100 $s$ and is carried downstream 45 m.
    Find
    (i)   the values of $p$ and $q$.
    (ii)  how long (to the nearest second) it will take her to swim in a straight line back to the original starting point.

4.  The driver of a speedboat travelling in a straight line at 20 m/s wishes to intercept a yacht travelling at 5 m/s in a direction 50° North of East. Initially the speedboat is positioned 5 km South-East of the yacht.
    Find
    (i)   the direction the speedboat must take in order to intercept the yacht
    (ii)  how long the journey takes.

5.  A man wishes to row a boat across a river to reach a point that is 25 m downstream from his starting point. The man can row the boat at 3.2 m/s in still water. The river is 45 m wide and flows uniformly at 3.6 m/s.
    Find
    (i)   the two possible directions in which the man could steer the boat
    (ii)  the respective crossing times.

## Summary of important points

$$\vec{V}_{AB} = \vec{V}_A - \vec{V}_B \text{ where}$$

$\vec{V}_A$ = A's actual velocity

$\vec{V}_B$ = B's actual velocity

and

$\vec{V}_{AB}$ = velocity of A relative to B.

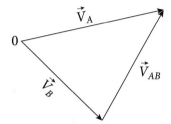

Fig. 4.23

## DOs and DON'Ts for the exam

### DO

- Do draw a large clear diagram showing the relative path
- Do remember that the shortest distance between the particles is the perpendicular distance from the 'stationary' particle to the relative path
- Do use Pythagoras' Theorem to find the time during which the particles are within a certain distance of one another
- Do delay the start until the particles are East-West of each other if the roads are at an awkward angle
- Do use large, clear diagrams on graph paper to solve problems of rivers and winds
- Do bring a Maths Set with you into the exam with a compass and ruler
- Do be careful with signs when converting a given vector into $\vec{i} - \vec{j}$ form

### DON'T

- Don't mix up the relative path with the real path
- Don't mix up the relative speed with the actual speed
- Don't mix up the actual angle of roads with the angle of the relative velocity
- Don't confuse the actual velocity of the wind with the apparent velocity of the wind
- Don't forget that if $\vec{v}_{ab} = -k \vec{r}_{ab}$ where $k$ is a positive constant, then $a$ and $b$ are on a collision course.

# Newton's laws and connected particles

"If I have seen a little farther than others, it is because I have stood on the shoulders of giants."

*Isaac Newton*

## Contents

### Learning outcomes

**In this chapter you will learn...**

- Definitions of force, mass and momentum

- Newton's laws of motion

- About forces such as weight, tension, normal reaction, friction

- How to use the equation $F = ma$ to solve problems

- How to solve problems involving two (or more) connected particles

- How to deal with particles on slopes

- How to deal with relative accelerations

- How to solve problems involving movable pulleys

- How to solve problems involving wedges

### You will need to know...

- How to solve simultaneous equations in two or three variables (or more!)

## Here are some important definitions

(i) A **force** is what causes an object to accelerate.

(ii) The **mass** of a body is the quantity of matter in it.

(iii) The **momentum** (or linear momentum) of an object is its mass multiplied by its velocity.

### Note on force

A leaf will sit motionless on your garage roof until the force of the wind moves it off. Its existing state of rest is changed by the force of the wind.

A puck (the "ball" in ice-hockey) will move along the ice at a constant speed in a straight line until it is hit by a stick. Its existing state of uniform motion in a straight line is changed by the force of the blow.

Force is a vector quantity since it has magnitude and direction. It is measured, as we shall see, in **newtons** (one newton is the force needed to accelerate a one kilogram mass at 1 metre per second squared).

### Note on mass

Mass is not the same as volume. The volume of the sugary bit of a candy-floss might be many times greater than the volume of the stick, but the stick might have more mass – more matter.

Again, mass is not the same as weight. Mass is a scalar quantity since it has magnitude but no direction. The weight of an object is the force (and therefore a vector) which pulls the object towards the centre of the earth.

If you bring a pot of jam to the moon, its weight will be less. But its mass – the quantity of the matter in it – is still the same. Mass is measured in kilograms but weight is measured in newtons.

### Note on momentum

Fig. 5.1

As a snowball rolls down a mountainside it "gathers momentum" in two ways. Momentum is the product of mass and velocity. The snowball will be increasing its mass and probably its velocity as well. It is becoming more and more difficult to stop. Indeed, momentum might be described as the **unstoppableness** of an object.

Momentum is a vector in the same direction as that of the velocity. For example, a ten-pin-bowling ball of mass 2 kg and velocity $1.5\,\vec{i}$ m/s has momentum given by

$$m\,\vec{v} = 2\left(1.5\,\vec{i}\right)$$
$$= 3\,\vec{i} \text{ kg m/s.}$$

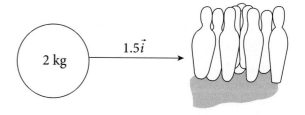

Fig. 5.2 (a)

A puck of mass 0.25 kg and velocity $3\,\vec{i} + 4\,\vec{j}$ has momentum

$$m\,\vec{v} = 0.25 \times \left(3\,\vec{i} + 4\,\vec{j}\right)$$
$$= 0.75\,\vec{i} + 1\,\vec{j} \text{ kg m/s}$$

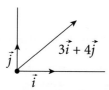

Fig. 5.3

Momentum has no special unit. It is measured in kg m/s.

## Newton's laws of motion

In 1687 Sir Isaac Newton published *Philosophiae Naturalis Principia Mathematica* (Mathematical Principles of Natural Philosophy). In this work, he produced three laws of motion. Since then, these laws have been the basis of a large part of all Applied Mathematics. It is hard to exaggerate how important these laws have been in the progress of mankind: they explain the relationship between the forces which act on a body and the consequent motion of the body.

Here are Newton's three historic laws:

1. **First Law:** A body will continue in a state of rest or of uniform motion in a straight line, unless it is impelled to change that state by an external force applied to it.

2. **Second Law:** The change in momentum per unit time is proportional to the applied force, and takes place along the straight line in which the force acts.

3. **Third Law:** To every action there is an equal and opposite reaction.

### Notes on Newton's First Law

(i) This law is, as you can see, not much more than our definition of force. It is hard to believe it, but a ball kicked in the air would travel forever in a straight line if it were not acted on by a force – namely its weight.

   **Weight** is the force due to gravity which pulls it back to earth again.

(ii) What is an external force?
   Imagine a leather football sitting motionless in your garden. There may be all sorts of internal forces at work: the ball may be held together by tensions in the threads; the air inside may be pushing at the leather from within, and the leather may be pushing the air back again; one stitch may be pulling at another. But these are **internal** forces because they are forces exerted by one part of the ball on another part. They will not make the ball move.

   **External** forces, unless perfectly balanced, will move the ball: for example, a strong wind blowing or a kick. These are external forces because they are exerted by agents other than the ball itself – namely, the air or a football-player.

### Notes on Newton's Second Law

(i) Let us imagine that an object of mass $m$ is travelling with velocity $u$. It is acted upon by a force, $F$, for $t$ seconds so that it ends up with increased velocity, $v$.

   (Note: $\propto$ means "is proportional to").

   According to Newton's Second Law,
   $F \propto$ the change in momentum per unit time.
   But the momentum before = $m\,u$, the

momentum after = $m\,v$, so the change in momentum is $m\,v - m\,u$. This change took $t$ seconds, so the change in momentum per unit time is $\dfrac{m\,v - m\,u}{t}$

$$\text{So, } F \propto \frac{m\,v - m\,u}{t}$$
$$\therefore F \propto m\left(\frac{v - u}{t}\right)$$

But $\dfrac{v - u}{t}$ is, by our earlier definition, the acceleration. We'll call it $a$.

$\therefore F \propto m\,a$

$\therefore F = k\,m\,a$, where $k$ is a constant.

In our system of units, the **m-k-s** system, when a force of 1 newton is applied to a particle of mass 1 kg, the acceleration is, according to the definition of the newton, $1$ m/s$^2$. Putting these into the equation above gives

$$1 = (k)(1)(1) \Rightarrow k = 1.$$
$$\therefore F = m\,a$$

This equation encapsulates Newton's Second Law mathematically.

(ii) Note that if $F = 0$, then $a = 0$. This is, in fact, the first law: that if no force is applied there will be no acceleration and therefore the existing state of rest or uniform velocity in a straight line is maintained.

(iii) We can now measure the force due to gravity (called **weight**). We know that free objects under gravity accelerate towards the centre of the earth with acceleration 9.8 m/s$^2$ (usually called $g$).

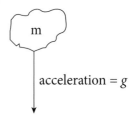

Fig. 5.4

If the mass of the object is $m$, then its weight, $W$, is given by $W = mg$.

So, an object of mass $m$, at the earth's surface will "feel" an external force pulling it towards the centre of the earth. This force is called its **weight** and has magnitude $mg$.

(iv) We know that $F = m\,a$. $F$ here represents the **resultant** (or sum) of all the forces acting on the object. Often many forces act at once.

## Note on Newton's Third Law

(i)  People who come home from a day's clay-pigeon shooting usually have a bruised shoulder. This is because if the gun fires the bullet by applying a force to it, the bullet applies the same force, but in the opposite direction, to the gun. So, the bullet goes forward but the gun recoils or jumps backwards, hurting the shooter's shoulder.

Fig. 5.5 "This hurts me equally but oppositely to how it hurts you."

(ii)  An ice-skater pushes the side wall with a force of magnitude $F$, the wall doesn't budge, because it is well secured. But the wall will push the skater with the same force $F$ in the opposite direction, and so the skater (who is not so well secured) starts moving.

Fig. 5.6

### Worked Example 5.1

A car has mass 1500 kg. Its engine produces a tractive force, $T$, (i.e. a pulling force) of magnitude 5000 N, but there is air resistance, $R$, of magnitude 2000 N. Ignoring friction, find the acceleration of the car.

**Solution:**

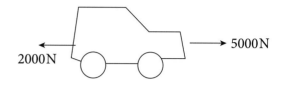

Fig. 5.7

Note that the resistance force, $R$, is in the opposite direction to motion.

$$T = 5000 \text{ newtons}$$
$$R = -2000 \text{ newtons}$$

$F$, the resultant force, is $5000 - 2000$
$$\therefore F = 3000 \text{ N}.$$
$$\text{But } F = ma$$
$$\therefore 3000 = (1500)\, a$$
$$\therefore a = 2$$

It will accelerate with acceleration 2 m/s$^2$: Answer

## Tension

Tension is a force exerted on objects by strings.

Fig. 5.8

This is a lamp hanging from the ceiling by a string. The string exerts an upward force on the lamp (otherwise the lamp would fall under the force of its weight).

So, the only external forces on the lamp are its weight $W$ and the tension $T$, in the string.

Tension acts along the line of the string, away from the object (always).

### *Worked Example 5.2*

An Inuit pulls a sled from rest. The sled and the luggage on it have total mass 800 kg. The Inuit pulls it by means of a horizontal light inextensible rope. There is no friction and the tension in the rope is 100 N in magnitude.

   (i)   Find the acceleration.

   (ii)   Find, also, the distance covered in the first 10 seconds of motion.

**Solution:**

   (i)

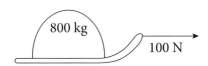

Fig. 5.9

$$F = ma$$
$$\therefore 100 = (800) \times a$$
$$\therefore a = \frac{1}{8} \text{ m/s}^2$$

   (ii)   We know $a = \frac{1}{8}$
$$t = 10$$
$$u = 0$$
$$s = ?$$

Use
$$s = u\,t + \frac{1}{2}a\,t^2$$
$$\therefore s = 0\,(10) + \frac{1}{2}\left(\frac{1}{8}\right)(100)$$
$$= \frac{100}{16}$$
$$= 6\frac{1}{4} \text{ m}$$

Answer: $a = \frac{1}{8}$ m/s$^2$; $s = 6\frac{1}{4}$ m.

### *Worked Example 5.3*

A bullet of mass 80 grams is travelling horizontally with velocity 100 m/s when it hits a tree. It stops when it has become embedded in the tree 50 cm from where it entered.

Find the resistance of the wood of the tree, assuming that it is uniform.

If the bullet had been of mass 100 grams, how far into the tree would it have gone if all other measurements remain the same?

**Solution:**

Our strategy here will be to find, firstly the acceleration, $a$, and then the resistance force, $R$, using $F = ma$.

$$u = 100$$
$$v = 0$$
$$s = \frac{1}{2}$$
$$a = ?$$

use $v^2 = u^2 + 2\,a\,s$
$$\therefore 0 = 10\,000 + 2\,a\left(\frac{1}{2}\right)$$
$$\therefore a = -10\,000 \text{ m/s}^2$$

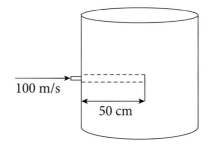

Fig. 5.10

The mass (in kilograms) is 0.080 kg

$$F = ma$$
$$\therefore R = (0.080)(-10\,000)$$
$$= -800 \text{ N: Answer}$$

The negative answer shows that it is indeed a resistance force in the opposite direction to motion. The force has magnitude 800 N.

In the second case we find the deceleration and then the distance travelled. The mass here is 0.1 kg.

$$F = m\,a$$
$$\therefore -800 = 0.1\,a$$
$$\therefore a = -8\,000 \text{ m/s}^2$$
$$u = 100$$
$$v = 0$$
$$a = -8\,000$$
$$s = ?$$

Use $v^2 = u^2 + 2\,a\,s$
$$\therefore 0 = 10\,000 + 2\,(-8\,000)\,s$$
$$\therefore s = \frac{5}{8} \text{ m} = 0.625 \text{ m}$$

Answer $= 62\frac{1}{2}$ cm

### Worked Example 5.4

A ball of mass 0.1 kg falls vertically and hits soft muddy ground whose resistance is 1.48 newtons. Show on a diagram the forces on the ball. If the ball's speed was 10 m/s on impact, find the depth to which it will penetrate the ground.

**Solution:**

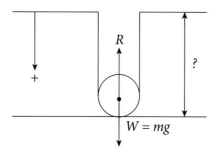

Fig. 5.11

$$W = m\,g$$
$$= (0.1)(9.8)$$
$$= 0.98 \text{ N}$$

Let the downward direction be our positive direction.

$$W = +\,0.98 \text{ N}$$
$$R = -1.48 \text{ N}$$

∴ the resultant force, $F$, will be given by

$$F = 0.98 - 1.48$$
$$= -0.5 \text{ N}$$

(The negative result means that the resultant force is a resistance force and will slow the ball down.)

$$F = m\,a$$
$$\therefore -0.5 = (0.1)\,a$$
$$\therefore a = -5 \text{ m/s}^2$$

The ball will decelerate at 5 m/s². How far will it travel before it comes to rest?

We know
$$u = 10$$
$$v = 0$$
$$a = -5$$
$$s = ?$$

Use
$$v^2 = u^2 + 2\,a\,s$$
$$0 = 100 + 2\,(-5)\,s$$
$$\therefore s = 10 \text{ m}$$

Answer: It will penetrate 10 m into the ground.

### Exercise 5 A

1. A car has mass 1000 kg. Its engine produces a tractive effort (or driving force) of 2500 N. There is a resistance to motion of magnitude 500 N. The car starts from rest.
   (i) Find the acceleration of the car.
   (ii) How far will it travel in the first 20 seconds?

2. A boat has mass 120 kg. A man pulls the boat in shallow water by means of a horizontal rope.

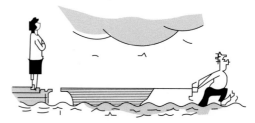

Fig. 5.12

   The resistance to motion is 40 N. The tension in the rope is 100 N. Find the acceleration of the boat.
   If the man's wife, who has mass 60 kg, gets into the boat, what will the acceleration become, assuming all forces remain the same?

3. A bicycle has mass 60 kg. Its rider has mass 90 kg. There is air-resistance to motion of magnitude 40 N. Find the driving force needed to accelerate the bicycle and rider with an acceleration of $\frac{1}{2}$ m/s². If the rider's mass was doubled, find the driving force needed for the same acceleration, assuming the resistance remains the same.

4. A go-cart and its occupant have total mass of 120 kg. A girl pulls the cart and occupant by means of a tight horizontal rope against a horizontal resistance force $R$. The tension in the rope is 40 N and the cart moves with acceleration $\frac{1}{8}$ m/s². Find the magnitude of $R$.

5. A bullet of mass 60 grams is fired horizontally so that it enters a block of solid wood at a speed of 150 m/s. If the resistance of the wood is uniform and of magnitude 900 N, how far into the wood will the bullet penetrate?

6. A cyclist covers 8 m from rest in 8 seconds. The mass of the bicycle and cyclist combined is 80 kg. If there is a resistance of 20 N find the constant driving force applied by the rider.

7. A car with its occupants has total mass 800 kg. The car is at rest when the engine is started and put into gear. The total resistance force is 350 N. If the car reaches a speed of 10 m/s after covering 50 m, find:
   (i) the acceleration
   (ii) the constant tractive effort of the engine.

8. A bullet of mass 50 grams is travelling horizontally at 200 m/s. It enters wood and travels a distance 1 m into the wood.
   Find the resistance of the wood, assuming it is uniform.
   If the bullet had been travelling at twice that speed — how far into the wood would it have penetrated?

9. A body of mass 10 kg falls from rest through the air. Air resistance is a constant 18 N. Show on a diagram the forces acting on the body.
   (a) Find the acceleration.
   (b) Find also, the distance covered in:
      (i) the first 10 seconds
      (ii) the next 10 seconds.

10. A bullet is fired horizontally at 300 m/s. It enters a fixed piece of wood which is 10 cm long and emerges at 200 m/s. If the resistance of the wood is 25 000 N, find the mass of the bullet in grams.

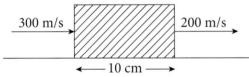

300 m/s    200 m/s

← 10 cm →

Fig. 5.13

   What is the shortest piece of the same wood which could have brought the bullet to rest?

11. A bullet of mass $m$ is fired with speed $u$ into a fixed block of wood and is brought to rest in a distance $s$. Find the resistance to motion assuming it to be constant.
   Another bullet, also of mass $m$, is then fired with speed $3u$ into another fixed block of thickness $5s$, which offers the same resistance as the first block. Find the speed with which the bullet emerges, and the time it takes to pass through the block.

12. A golf-ball of mass $\frac{1}{7}$ kg falls vertically and lands at a speed of 1.4 m/s on a marsh. If the resistance of the marsh to motion is of magnitude 2.1 N throughout, find the depth to which the ball will penetrate the marsh before coming to rest.

13. A particle of mass 10 grams falls from rest from a height of 2.5 m on to a soft material into which it sinks 0.35 m. Neglecting air resistance, calculate the constant resistance of the material.

14. A ball of mass $m$ falls vertically from rest at a height $4h$ onto marshy ground whose resistance is of magnitude $8mg$ newtons.
   (i) Find in terms of $h$ the depth to which it will penetrate the marsh.
   (ii) Would a ball of mass $4m$ dropped from a height $h$ penetrate the same distance? Justify your answer.

## Introducing two more kinds of force

### Normal reactions

A **reaction** is a force transmitted from one object to another by direct contact. The word 'normal' means 'perpendicular'. Hence, a **normal reaction** is one which is perpendicular to the surface of contact. For example, in the picture below we see that the ground supports the man by a normal reaction, $R$, upwards (that is, perpendicular to the ground).

$Mg$

$R$

Fig. 5.14

Let's take another example. A piece of wood is sliding along the top of a horizontal table, pulled by a horizontal string.

Fig. 5.15 (a)

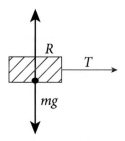

Fig. 5.15 (b)

If the table is smooth, then the only forces acting on the wood are:

(i)  the tension in the string,
(ii)  the weight $mg$,
(iii)  the reaction between the surface of the table and the piece of wood. Since this force is perpendicular to the table, it is often called the "normal reaction".

But if the table is not smooth then a force called **friction** takes effect and opposes motion. The force diagram looks like this:

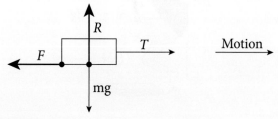

Fig. 5.16 (a)

Notice that the friction force $F$ is in the opposite direction to motion.

Now suppose that two different sized pieces of the same kind of wood are moving along this table, pulled by two strings

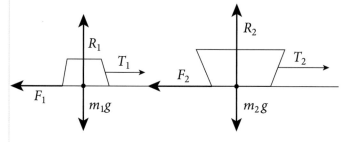

Fig. 5.17

The forces are as shown. Experiment has shown that $\dfrac{F_1}{R_1} = \dfrac{F_2}{R_2}$

This common ratio is called the **coefficient of friction** and is usually denoted by the Greek letter $\mu$ (pronounced "mew"). This coefficient depends on what the objects are made of and what the surface of the table is like but not on the shape or size of the objects.

So, when an object is moving across a surface, $\mu = \dfrac{F}{R}$ where $F$ is the magnitude of the friction force and $R$ is the magnitude of the normal reaction between the surface and the object. Hence, Friction $= \mu R$.

**How to calculate the friction force**

A piano is being dragged across a wooden floor. The mass of the piano is 100 kg and the coefficient of friction between the piano and the floor is 0.3. What is the amount of friction called into play?

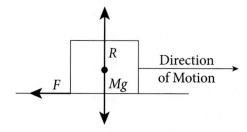

Fig. 5.18

Step 1: Since the piano does not move either up or down, the forces acting upward must equal the forces acting downward.

$$\therefore R = mg$$
$$= 100\,(9.8)$$
$$= 980 \text{ N}$$

Step 2:

$$\frac{F}{R} = \mu$$
$$\therefore F = \mu R$$
$$\therefore F = 0.3\,(980)$$
$$= 294 \text{ N}.$$

So, when the piano is moving, a friction force of magnitude 294 N opposes motion.

But what if the piano is not moving? Now imagine that your youngest brother Jimmy tries to push this piano across the floor. Jimmy can exert a force of magnitude 100 N and so the piano does not budge. Why? Because the piano resists Jimmy – not with a force of 294 N – but with a force of 100 N. There is no need for any more.

Case 1
Jimmy

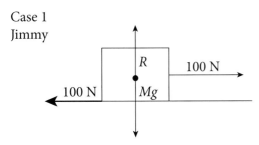

Fig. 5.19 (a)

The piano takes the lazy way out – it will call into play only enough friction to oppose the applied force.

Case 2
Kate

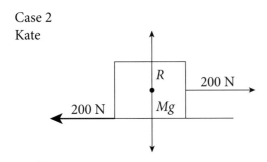

Fig. 5.19 (b)

Now your sister Kate has an attempt, applying a force of magnitude 200 N. Still, the piano does not budge, because it resists motion with a friction force of exactly 200 N – just enough to prevent motion.

Case 3
Jimmy and Kate

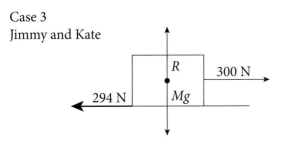

Fig. 5.20

Finally, the two push together. They can produce a total force of magnitude 300 N. The piano just begins to move, because there is a limit to the amount of friction which can be called into play. This limit is (as we saw) 294 N. A force of 300 N is greater than this, so the piano will move. We call the maximum

amount of friction which can be called into play the **limiting friction**. Limiting friction is called into play only when the object is moving or just on the point of moving. Otherwise, the amount of friction can be anything from zero up to the limiting friction.

## The laws of friction

1.  The direction of friction is opposite to the direction in which the body tends to move.

2.  The magnitude of the friction is, up to a certain point, equal to the magnitude of the force tending to produce motion.

3.  Only a certain amount of friction can be called into play. The maximum amount possible is called **limiting friction**.

4.  The ratio of the limiting friction to the normal reaction is a constant, $\mu$. This constant $\mu$ is called the **coefficient of friction** and depends on the nature of the two surfaces in contact, but not on their size nor their shape nor the area of surface in contact.

5.  When motion takes place, the limiting friction still opposes the motion and is independent of the velocity.

    (In truth, the amount of friction called into play when an object is moving is slightly less than when it is just on the point of moving – but we ignore this slight difference.)

### Worked Example 5.5

A sleigh and its occupants have total mass 500 kg. The coefficient of friction, $\mu$, between the sleigh and the snowy ground is $\frac{1}{10}$. If a husky dog can pull with a horizontal force of 100 N, find
  (i)   the limiting friction
  (ii)  the least number of dogs needed to get the sleigh going across horizontal ground.
  (iii) the acceleration if, in fact, six dogs are used.

**Solution:**

(i)

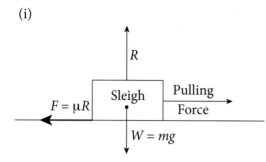

Fig. 5.21

Step 1: Since the sleigh neither rises nor falls, the force upwards = the force downwards.

Therefore, $R = m\,g$
$$= 500(9.8)$$
$$= 4900 \text{ N}$$

Step 2: The limiting friction, $F$
$$= \mu R$$
$$= \frac{1}{10}(4900)$$
$$= 490 \text{ N}$$

(ii) To move the sleigh, a driving force of at least 490 N is needed to overcome the limiting friction. So, 5 dogs will be needed (each producing 100 N of force).

(iii) If there are 6 dogs, the driving force, $D$, has magnitude 600 N. Here is the force diagram.

(iv)

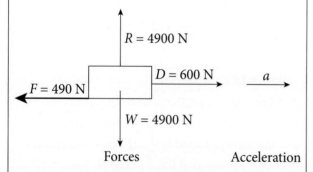

Fig. 5.22

The resultant force, is
$$600 - 490 = 110 \text{ N}$$
Since $F = m\,a$
$$\therefore 110 = 500\,(a)$$
$$\therefore a = 0.22 \text{ m/s}^2$$

Answer: (i) 490 N (ii) 5 dogs (iii) 0.22 m/s²

**Worked Example 5.6**

A 10 kg mass is pulled up a slope, inclined at an angle of 30° to the horizontal, by a force of magnitude 10$g$ newtons which is parallel with the slope. The slope is rough and the coefficient of friction between the mass and the sloped ground is $\frac{1}{2}$. Find, in terms of $g$, the acceleration of the mass.

**Solution:**

Here are the forces acting on the mass.

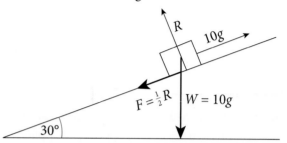

Fig. 5.23

The weight force can be resolved into two components – one along the slope, the other perpendicular to the slope.

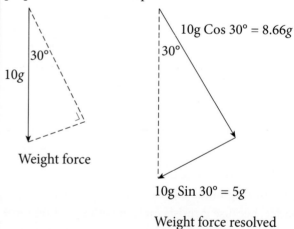

Weight force        Weight force resolved

Fig. 5.24        Fig. 5.25

The force diagram now looks like this:

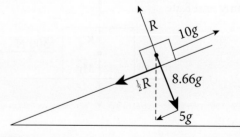

Fig. 5.26

Since there is no movement perpendicular to the slope, $R = 8.66g$.

The friction force $= \mu R$
$$= \frac{1}{2}(8.66g)$$
$$= 4.33g$$
Therefore, the total force up the plane
$$= 10g - 4.33g - 5g$$
$$= 0.67\,g\text{ N}.$$
But $F = m\,a$
$$\therefore 0.67\,g = 10\,a$$
$$a = 0.067\,g\text{ m/s}^2: \text{Answer}$$

---

## Worked Example 5.7

A man drags a particle of mass 100 kg over rough ground by means of a rope which makes an angle $A$ with the horizontal ground, where $\tan A = \frac{12}{5}$. The particle is just on the point of slipping when the tension in the rope is 260 N. Find the coefficient of friction between the particle and the ground.

### Solution:

Here are the forces acting on the particle:

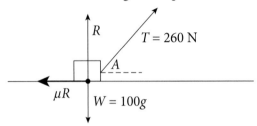

Fig. 5.27

The tension, $T$, can be resolved (since $\tan A = \frac{12}{5}$, $\cos A = \frac{5}{13}$ and $\sin A = \frac{12}{13}$). Here are the resolved forces:

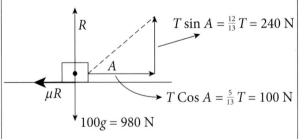

Fig. 5.28

In this case, the particle is not moving. Its acceleration is zero. By newton's second law, the force on the particle must also be zero. So, the total force upwards must equal the total force downwards; the force to the left must equal the force to the right.

1. (ups = downs)
$$R + 240 = 980$$
$$\therefore R = 740\text{ N}$$

2. (lefts = rights)
$$\mu R = 100$$

But $\quad R = 740$
Therefore, $\mu(740) = 100$
$$\Rightarrow \mu = \frac{100}{740}$$
$$= \frac{5}{37}: \text{Answer}.$$

---

## Exercise 5 B

1. A mule drags a felled tree of mass 500 kg by means of a horizontal rope across horizontal ground. The coefficient of friction between the tree and the ground is 0.4, and the tension in the rope is 3 kN (i.e. 3000 N). Find the acceleration of the tree.

2. A man pushes a desk of mass 50 kg across a floor by applying a horizontal force of 300 N. If the coefficient of friction between the desk and the floor is 0.6, find the acceleration of the desk.

3. A barwoman slides a pint glass of beer along the counter, so that it leaves her hand with a speed of 3.5 m/s. The mass of the full glass is 1 kg and the coefficient of friction between the glass and the counter is $\frac{1}{7}$.
   Find
   (i) the friction force
   (ii) the deceleration of the glass
   (iii) the distance which the glass will travel before coming to rest.

4. Slaves building a pyramid are ordered to drag a stone of mass 1 tonne (i.e. 1000 kg) across horizontal ground. The coefficient of friction between the stone and the ground is $\frac{1}{4}$. If each slave can pull with a horizontal force of 250 N, find
   (i) the limiting friction between the stone and the ground
   (ii) the least number of slaves needed to move the stone
   (iii) the acceleration of the stone, if this minimum number of slaves do the job.

5. A sleigh and its occupants have total mass 800 kg. The coefficient of friction, $\mu$, between the sleigh and the snowy ground is $\frac{1}{8}$. If a husky dog can pull with a horizontal force of 200 N, find
   (i) the limiting friction
   (ii) the least number of dogs needed to get the sleigh going across horizontal ground
   (iii) the acceleration if, in fact, the least number of dogs is used.

6. (a) Define momentum.
   (b) Define a newton.
   (c) State Newton's second law of motion.
   (d) A lift, of mass 1440 kg and carrying 8 people each of mass 70 kg, is being hoisted vertically upwards by a rope in which the tension is 24 kN.
   (i) Calculate the acceleration of the lift.
   (ii) Determine the reaction between the floor of the lift and each person.

7. A smooth plane has a slope of 1 in 7 (i.e. of angle $\sin^{-1}\frac{1}{7}$). A particle is placed on it and released from rest. Find the acceleration of the particle and how long it takes to reach a speed of 7 m/s. How far has it travelled by this time?

8. A particle of weight $W$ is pulled with constant velocity over rough horizontal ground. The pulling force has magnitude $\frac{1}{5}W$ and makes an angle $A$ with the ground, where $\text{Tan } A = \frac{5}{12}$ Find the coefficient of friction between the particle and the ground.
   (Note: There is no acceleration, so the resultant force is zero.)

9. A particle of mass 10 kg is pulled over horizontal ground. The pulling force has magnitude 100 N and makes an angle $A$ with the horizontal, where $\text{Tan } A = \frac{3}{4}$. Find the normal reaction and the acceleration
   (i) if the ground is smooth
   (ii) if the ground is rough and the coefficient of friction between the particle and the ground is $\frac{1}{2}$.

10. A particle of mass 10 kg is placed on a plane inclined at an angle $A$ to the horizontal, where $\text{Tan } A = \frac{3}{4}$. The particle is pulled up the plane by means of a string which makes an angle $B$ with the plane, where $\text{Tan } B = \frac{5}{12}$. The tension in the string is 130 N. Find the acceleration of the particle
   (i) if the plane is smooth
   (ii) if the plane is rough, having a coefficient of friction $\frac{1}{4}$ with the particle.

11. A particle of mass 2 kg is allowed to slip down a smooth slope which is inclined at an angle $A$ to the horizontal, where $\text{Sin } A = \frac{1}{5}$. Show that the acceleration of the particle is $\frac{1}{5}g$ and that the normal reaction between the particle and the sloped ground is of magnitude $\frac{4\sqrt{6}g}{5}$ N.

## Systems of connected particles

### Worked Example 5.8

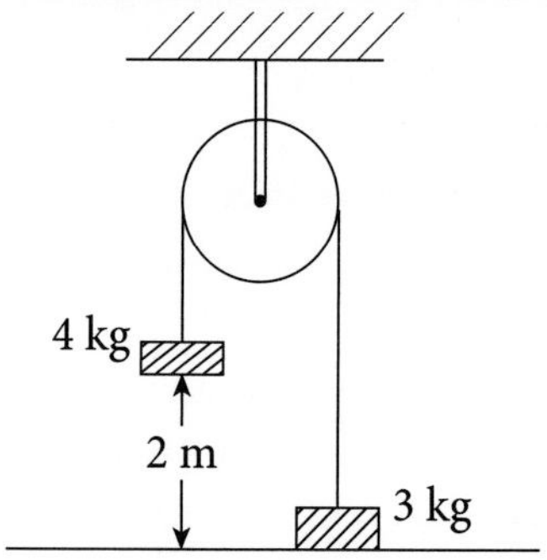

Fig. 5.29

Two particles of masses 4 kg and 3 kg are linked by a taut inelastic string which passes over a fixed smooth pulley above a table as shown. The system is released from rest when the 4 kg mass is 2 m above the table and the 3 kg is on the table.
Find:
   (i) the common acceleration of the particles
   (ii) the tension in the string
   (iii) the speed with which the 4 kg mass will hit the table
   (iv) how much further will the 3 kg mass rise after the 4 kg mass hits the table?

**Solution:**

(i) This diagram shows the forces on the moving parts at any time.

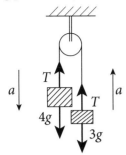

Fig. 5.30

We examine separately the forces (and accelerations) on the two particles.

**Note 1:** The tension, $T$, in the string is the same throughout because it's the same string and the pulley is smooth.

**Note 2:** The tension acts along the string, away from each object.

**Note 3:** The acceleration, $a$, is the same for both particles.

**Note 4:** It would be wrong to say that "the 4 kg mass pulls the 3 kg mass". The only external forces acting directly on the 3 kg mass are the tension ($T$) in the string and its own weight $3g$.

**The 3 kg mass**

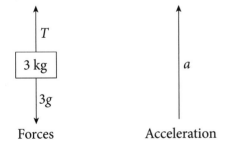

Fig. 5.31

Since    $F = ma$ (from Newton's Second Law)

$T - 3g = 3a$ ......Equation A.

**Important note:**

The "positive" direction is determined by the acceleration. The acceleration ($a$) is upward. Therefore, our "positive" direction is the upward direction. $T$, being upward, is positive; $3g$, being downward, is negative. The resultant force is therefore, $T - 3g$.

**The 4 kg mass**

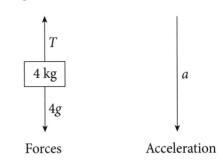

Fig. 5.32

$$F = m\,a$$

$$4g - T = 4a \ldots\ldots\text{Equation B}$$

Since the acceleration ($a$) is downward in this case, we will let the downward direction be our positive direction. $4g$ is positive, since it is downward. $T$ is negative since it is upward. The resultant force is, therefore, $4g - T$. Adding equations A and $B$ we get:

$$g = 7a$$

$$\therefore a = \frac{1}{7}g$$

$$= \frac{1}{7}(9.8)$$

$$= 1.4 \text{ m/s}^2$$

(ii) Equation A:

$$T - 3g = 3a$$

$$\therefore T = 3\,a + 3\,g$$

$$= 3\,(1.4) + 3\,(9.8)$$

$$= 33.6 \text{ N.}$$

(iii) The 4 kg mass starts from rest, moves a distance 2 m with acceleration 1.4 m/s$^2$. What will its final speed be?

We know          $u = 0$

$s = 2$

$a = 1.4$

$v = ?$

Using          $v^2 = u^2 + 2\,a\,s$

$$v^2 = 0 + 2\,(1.4)\,2$$

$$v^2 = 5.6$$

$$v = \sqrt{5.6} \text{ m/s}$$

(iv) When the 4 kg mass hits the ground, the string becomes loose and the 3 kg mass is now a projectile, flying vertically upwards freely under gravity. Its initial speed is $\sqrt{5.6}$ m/s; when it reaches its highest point its speed will be 0 m/s; it has deceleration 9.8 m/s² due to gravity slowing it down; we require the distance covered.

| We know | $u = \sqrt{5.6}$ |
| --- | --- |
| | $v = 0$ |
| | $a = -9.8$ |
| | $s = ?$ |

| Using | $v^2 = u^2 + 2\,a\,s$ |
| --- | --- |
| | $0 = 5.6 + 2\,(-9.8)\,s$ |
| | $\therefore s = \dfrac{5.6}{19.6} = \dfrac{56}{196} = \dfrac{2}{7}$ m. |

Answers:

$a = 1.4$ m/s² ; $T = 33.6$ N ; $v = \sqrt{5.6}$ m/s ; $s = \dfrac{2}{7}$ m

## Worked Example 5.9

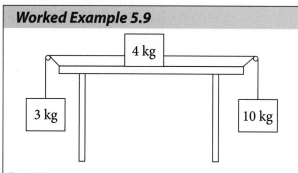

Fig. 5.33

A 4 kg block of wood is on a rough horizontal table. The coefficient of friction, $\mu$, between the block and the table is $\dfrac{3}{4}$. It is attached by two separate horizontal strings which pass over smooth pulleys to two hanging blocks of masses 3 kg and 10 kg, as shown. Find the common acceleration in terms of $g$, the acceleration due to gravity.

**Solution:**

There are two separate strings, so the tensions will more than likely be different. We will call them $T$ and $S$ respectively. Here are the forces on the moving parts:

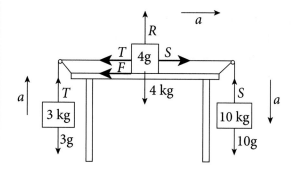

Fig. 5.34

Again, we take each moving mass separately, showing the forces acting on it and its acceleration (which, for all of them, is "$a$" ).

1. The 3 kg mass:

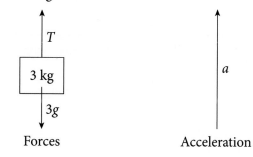

Forces                              Acceleration

Fig. 5.35

$$F = ma$$
$$T - 3g = 3a\ldots\ldots\ldots\text{Equation A}$$

2. The 4 kg mass:

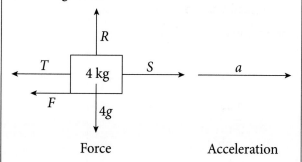

Force                              Acceleration

Fig. 5.36

To calculate the friction force, $F$, (which opposes motion).

**Step 1:**     $R = 4g$, since the block moves neither up nor down.

**Step 2:**     $F = \mu R$
$$= \frac{3}{4}\,(4g)$$
$$= 3g.$$

**Step 3:** The equation of motion is:
$$S - T - F = 4a$$
$$\therefore S - T - 3g = 4a \ldots.\ \text{Equation B.}$$

($R$ and $4g$ are perpendicular to the direction of motion, they are excluded from the equation because they have no component along the direction of the acceleration, $a$).

3. The 10 kg mass:

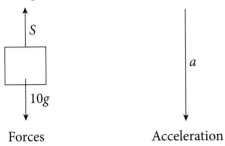

Fig. 5.37

$$10g - S = 10a \quad ..... \text{ Equation } C.$$

We want to find "$a$" in terms of $g$. It happens that if we add the three equations $A$, $B$ and $C$:

$$T - 3g = 3a .........\text{Equation } A$$
$$S - T - 3g = 4a .........\text{Equation } B.$$
$$\underline{10g - S = 10a} .......\text{Equation } C.$$

we get
$$4g = 17a$$
$$\therefore a = \frac{4g}{17} : \text{Answer}$$

### Exercise 5 C (using $g = 9.8$ m/s$^2$)

1. A fixed smooth pulley has masses of 3 kg and 11 kg hanging freely from either side by means of a light inextensible string.
   Find
   (i) the common acceleration of the two masses
   (ii) the tension in the string.

2. A fixed smooth pulley has masses of 1 kg and 13 kg hanging freely from either side by means of a light inextensible string. The system is released from rest.
   (i) Find the common acceleration of the two masses.
   (ii) Find the common speed of the masses after 3 seconds.

3. A fixed smooth pulley has masses of 5 kg and 9 kg hanging freely from either side by means of a light inextensible string. The system is released from rest.
   (i) Find the common acceleration of the two masses.
   (ii) Find the distance travelled by each particle in the first 3 seconds.

4. A fixed smooth pulley has masses of 2 kg and 5 kg hanging freely from either side by means of a light inextensible string. The system is released when the 2 kg mass is on a horizontal floor and the 5 kg mass is 2 m above the floor.
   (i) Find the common acceleration of the two masses.
   (ii) Find their common speed just as the 5 kg mass hits the floor.
   (iii) How much further will the 2 kg mass then rise?

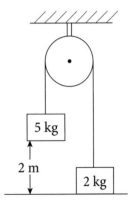

Fig. 5.38

5. A fixed smooth pulley has masses of 6 kg and 1 kg hanging from either side by means of a light inextensible string. The system is released from rest. After 1 second the 6 kg mass is suddenly held.
   Find
   (i) the common acceleration of the two masses
   (ii) their common speed when the 6 kg mass is held
   (iii) the further distance through which the 1 kg mass will then rise.

6. The diagram shows a horizontal table on which a 2 kg mass is placed. A 4 kg mass and a 1 kg mass hang freely over the sides. The coefficient of friction betwen the 2 kg mass and the table is $\frac{1}{2}$.
   Find
   (i) the common acceleration of the three masses.
   (ii) Find, also, the tension in each string.

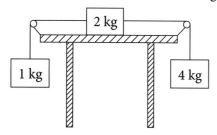

Fig. 5.39

7. The diagram shows a horizontal table on which a mass of 4 kg is placed. Masses of 10 kg and 1 kg hang over the sides by means of strings, which pass over smooth pulleys. Find, in terms of $g$, the common acceleration of the masses
   (i) if the table is smooth,
   (ii) if the table is rough with $\mu = \frac{1}{2}$.

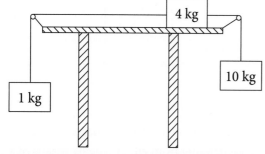

Fig. 5.40

8. Two particles of masses 5 kg and 4 kg respectively are connected by a light inextensible string passing over a smooth, light, fixed pulley. The particles are released from rest.
   Calculate (in terms of $g$)
   (i) the acceleration of the particles
   (ii) the tension in the string.
   If after two seconds the larger mass is caught and held, how much farther will the lighter mass rise?

9. A mass of 12 kg rests on a rough horizontal table and is attached by two horizontal inelastic strings to masses 10 kg and 4 kg, which hang over smooth pulleys at opposite edges of the table. The coefficient of friction between the 12 kg mass and the table is $\mu$.
   Show that if $\mu = \frac{1}{4}$, the common acceleration of the particles will be $\frac{3}{26} g$.
   What is the least value of $\mu$ for which the particles will not move?

10. The diagram shows particles of mass 2 kg and 3 kg, respectively, lying on a horizontal table in a straight line perpendicular to the edge of the table. They are connected by a taut, light, inextensible string. A second such string, passing over a fixed, light pulley at the edge of the table connects the 3 kg particle to another of mass 3 kg hanging freely under gravity. The contact between the particles and the table is rough with coefficient of friction $\frac{1}{4}$.

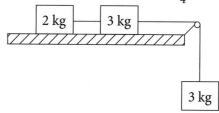

Fig. 5.41

   Show in separate diagrams the forces acting on the particles when the system is released from rest.
   Calculate (in terms of $g$)
   (i) the common acceleration
   (ii) the tension in each string.

11. A particle of mass 7 kg is placed on a smooth horizontal table, 3.3075 metres high, at a distance 6.615 m from the edge of the table and is connected by a light inextensible string of length 6.615 m to a particle of mass 3 kg at the edge of the table. If the 3 kg mass is pushed gently over the edge, find
    (i) how long the 3 kg takes to reach the ground
    (ii) how much longer the 7 kg takes to reach the edge of the table.

12. A mass of $M$ kg rests on a smooth horizontal table and is attached by two horizontal inelastic strings to masses $m$ and $m_1$ kg (where $m_1 > m$), which hang over smooth pulleys at opposite edges of the table. Show that the common acceleration of the system is given by

$$a = \left( \frac{m_1 - m}{m_1 + m + M} \right) g$$

## Movable pulleys

### Worked Example 5.10

A light inextensible string is fastened at one end to a point on the ceiling. It then passes under a smooth movable pulley $P$ of mass 8 kg, then over a smooth, light fixed pulley. A second particle $Q$, of mass 6 kg, hangs freely from the other end of the string. All parts of the string which are not in contact with the pulleys are vertical. Find the acceleration of the 8 kg mass.

**Solution**

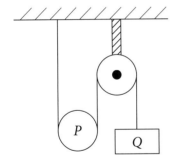

Fig. 5.42

To decide whether $P$ will go up or down, we perform the following test: Since the 8 kg pulley is pulled upwards by **two** strings and the 6 kg is pulled by **one** string, we ask, "Which is greater: 8/2 or 6/1?" Whichever is the greater indicates which mass will move **down**. In this case the 6 kg mass will move down since 6/1 > 8/2.

Now, if $P$ moves up 1 metre, $Q$ will move down 2 metres, since there will be 2 metres more string available. Hence, if $P$ moves up $x$ metres while $Q$ moves down $y$ metres, it follows that $y = 2x$. Hence, the velocity and acceleration of $Q$ will be twice those of $P$. We will let the acceleration of $P$ be $a$. Therefore, the acceleration of $Q$ will be $2a$.

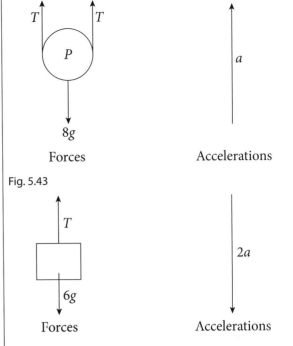

Fig. 5.43

Fig. 5.44

The equation of motion for $P$ is

$$2T - 8g = 8a$$

$$\therefore T - 4g = 4a \ldots \text{Equation 1}$$

The equation of motion for $Q$ is

$$6g - T = 6(2a)$$

$$\therefore 6g - T = 12a \ldots \text{Equation 2}$$

Adding equations 1 and 2 gives:

$$2g = 16a$$

$$\therefore a = \frac{1}{8}g: \text{Answer}$$

### Worked Example 5.11

The diagram shows particles of mass 1 kg and 2 kg at the ends of a piece of light inextensible string. The string goes up and over two fixed pulleys to a third movable pulley of mass 10 kg.

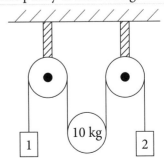

Fig. 5.45

Find
    (i)   the tension $T$ in the string
    (ii)  the acceleration of each particle
    (iii) the acceleration of the movable pulley

## Solution

Let us suppose that the 1 kg mass moved up 11 cm while the 2 kg mass moved up 3 cm. The movable pulley would move down a distance $\frac{11 + 3}{2} = 7$ cm.

Now, let us suppose that the 1 kg mass moved up a distance $x$ while the 2 kg mass moved up $y$. The movable pulley would move down a distance $\frac{x + y}{2}$. Their velocities and accelerations will be in these proportions, too.

In our solution, we will let the acceleration upwards of the 1 kg mass be $a$ m/s². We will let the acceleration upwards of the 2 kg mass be $b$ m/s² Consequently, the acceleration downwards of the movable pulley will be $\frac{a + b}{2}$ m/s².

Here are the force diagrams and equations for each moving part:

### The 1 kg mass

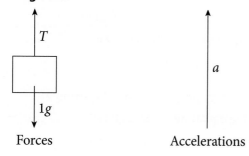

Forces              Accelerations

Fig. 5.46

Equation of Motion

$$T - g = 1\,a$$

$$\therefore a = T - g \ldots \text{Equation 1}$$

### The 2 kg mass

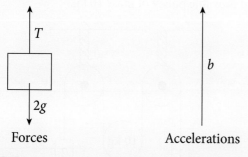

Forces              Accelerations

Fig. 5.47

Equation of Motion

$$T - 2g = 2b$$

$$\therefore b = \frac{1}{2}T - g \ldots \text{Equation 2}$$

### The movable pulley

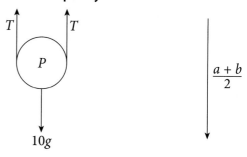

Forces              Accelerations

Fig. 5.48

Equation of Motion

$$10\,g - 2\,T = 10\left(\frac{a + b}{2}\right)$$

$$\therefore 10\,g - 2\,T = 5\,a + 5\,b \ldots \text{Equation 3}$$

Substituting for $a$ and $b$ in equation 3, we get

$$10\,g - 2\,T = 5\,(T - g) + 5\left(\frac{1}{2}\,T - g\right)$$

$$\Rightarrow 10\,g - 2\,T = 5\,T - 5\,g + 2.5\,T - 5\,g$$

$$\Rightarrow 20\,g = 9.5\,T$$

$$\Rightarrow 40\,g = 19\,T$$

$$\Rightarrow T = \frac{40}{19}\,g \text{ newtons}$$

(ii)
$$a = T - g$$
$$= \frac{40}{19}\,g - g$$
$$= \frac{21}{19}\,g$$

and $b = \frac{1}{2}\,T - g$
$$= \frac{20g}{19} - g$$
$$= \frac{1}{19}\,g$$

(iii) The acceleration of the movable pulley
$$= \frac{a + b}{2}$$
$$= \frac{\frac{21}{19}\,g + \frac{1}{19}\,g}{2}$$
$$= \frac{11}{19}\,g: \text{Answer}$$

**Exercise 5 D**

1. A light inextensible string has one end fastened to a point on the ceiling. It then passes under a smooth movable pulley $A$ of mass 10 kg, then over a smooth, light, fixed pulley. A second particle, $B$, also of mass 10 kg, hangs freely from the other end of the string. All parts of the string which are not in contact with the pulleys are vertical.
   (i) Find the acceleration of $A$ in terms of $g$.
   (ii) Find, also, the tension in the string in terms of $g$.

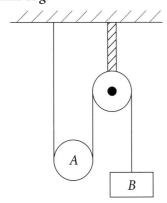

Fig. 5.49

2. A light inextensible string has one end fastened to a point on the ceiling. It then passes under a smooth movable pulley $A$ of mass 13 kg, then over a smooth, light, fixed pulley. A second particle $B$, of mass 9 kg, hangs freely from the other end of the string. All parts of the string which are not in contact with the pulleys are vertical. Show that
   (i) the acceleration of A is 1 m/s$^2$
   (ii) the acceleration of $B$ is 2 m/s$^2$
   (iii) the tension in the string is 70.2 N.

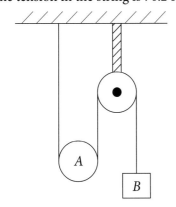

Fig. 5.50

3. A light inextensible string has one end fastened to a point on the ceiling. It then passes under a smooth movable pulley $A$ of mass 18 kg, then over a smooth, light, fixed pulley. A second particle $B$, of mass 20 kg, hangs freely from the other end of the string. All parts of the string which are not in contact with the pulleys are vertical.

   Show that the acceleration of $A$ is 2.2 m/s$^2$. Show that the tension in the string is 108 N.

4. A light inextensible string has one end fastened to a point on the ceiling. It then passes under a smooth movable pulley $A$ of mass 8 kg, then over a smooth, light, fixed pulley. A second particle $B$, of mass 22.5 kg, hangs freely from the other end of the string. All parts of the string which are not in contact with the pulleys are vertical.

   Show that
   (i) the acceleration of A is 3.7 m/s$^2$
   (ii) the acceleration of $B$ is 7.4 m/s$^2$
   (iii) the tension in the string is 54 N.

5. A light inextensible string has one end fastened to a point on the ceiling. It then passes under a smooth movable pulley $A$ of mass $m$, then over a smooth, light, fixed pulley. A second particle, $B$, also of mass $m$, hangs freely from the other end of the string. All parts of the string which are not in contact with the pulleys are vertical.

   Show that if the acceleration of $A$ is $a$, then the acceleration of $B$ is $2a$.
   (i) Find $a$ in terms of $g$.
   (ii) Find, also, the tension in the string in terms of $g$ and $m$.

6.

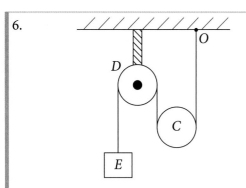

Fig. 5.51

The diagram shows a light inextensible string having one end fixed at $O$, passing under a smooth movable pulley $C$ of mass $km$ kg and then over a fixed smooth light pulley $D$. The other end of the string is attached to a particle $E$ of mass $m$ kg.
(i)   Show on separate diagrams the forces acting on each mass.
(ii)  Show that the upward acceleration of $C$ is $\dfrac{(2-k)g}{4+k}$
(iii) If $k = 0.5$, find the tension in the string.

7.   One end of a light inextensible string is attached to a mass of 4 kg which rests on a rough horizontal table. The coefficient of friction between the mass and the table is $\frac{1}{4}$. The string passes over a smooth fixed pulley at the edge. It then passes under a smooth movable pulley of mass 20 kg and over a smooth fixed pulley. A mass of 5 kg is attached to its other end.
Show on separate diagrams the forces acting on each mass.
Calculate the acceleration of the 20 kg pulley in terms of $g$.

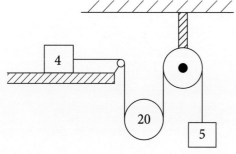

Fig. 5.52

8.   A particle of mass 10 kg rests on a horizontal table and another particle of mass 6 kg rests on another horizontal table, as shown.

The particles are connected by a light inextensible string, which passes under a movable pulley of mass 20 kg. The coefficient of friction between each particle and its table is $\frac{1}{2}$.

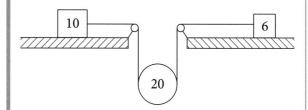

Fig. 5.53

Find the tension in the string and the acceleration of the particles and the pulley.

9.   Two particles of masses 6 kg and 8 kg rest on two horizontal tables. The coefficient of friction between both particles and their respective tables is $\frac{1}{2}$. The particles are connected by a smooth inextensible string which passes over smooth pulleys and under a smooth movable pulley of mass $M$ kg (as shown).

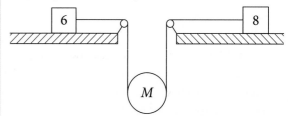

Fig. 5.54

Show that none of the particles will move if $M \le 6$. If $M = 12$, find the accelerations of the particles and of the movable pulley (in terms of $g$).

10.

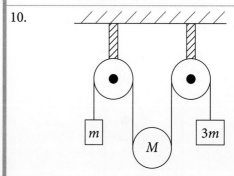

Fig. 5.55

A light inextensible string passes over a fixed pulley $A$, under a movable pulley $B$, of mass $M$, and then over a second fixed pulley $C$.

A mass $m$ is attached to one end of the string and a mass $3m$ is attached to the other end. The system is released from rest.

(i) Show in separate diagrams the forces acting on each of the three masses.

(ii) Prove that the tension $T$ in the string is given by the equation $T\left(\dfrac{1}{M} + \dfrac{1}{3m}\right) = g$

(iii) Show that if $M = 3m$ then pulley $B$ will remain at rest while the other two masses are in motion.

## Particles on slopes

When particles are on slopes, we resolve forces so that they are along and perpendicular to the slope.

### Worked Example 5.12

A particle of mass $m$ is held at rest on a smooth plane, which is inclined at an angle $A$, where $\text{Tan}\,A = \dfrac{3}{4}$, to the horizontal. A light inelastic string connects this particle, over a smooth pulley at the top of the plane, to a second particle of mass $2m$, hanging freely. The part of the string on the plane lies along the line of greatest slope and the other part is vertical. Find the common acceleration of the particles and the tension in the string, in terms of $g$, after the system is released from rest.

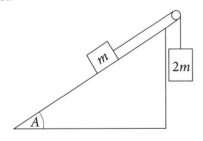

Fig. 5.56

**Solution:**

Let $T$ = the tension in the string. Here are the forces acting on the particles:

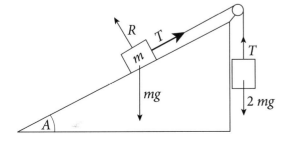

Fig. 5.57

The weight of the smaller mass is resolved into components parallel to and perpendicular to the line of greatest slope.

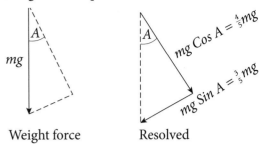

Weight force      Resolved

Fig. 5.58

We now examine separately the resolved forces on the particles.

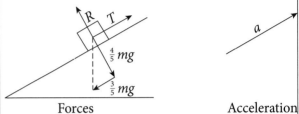

Forces      Acceleration

Fig. 5.59

1. There is no motion perpendicular to the plane.
$$\therefore R = \frac{4}{5} M g \qquad \text{Equation 1}$$

2. $$F = M a$$
$$\therefore T - \frac{3}{5} m g = m a \qquad \text{Equation 2}$$

3. The 2m mass::

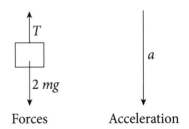

Forces      Acceleration

Fig. 5.60

$$F = M a$$
$$\therefore 2 m g - T = 2 m a \qquad \text{Equation 3}$$

Adding equations 2 and 3, we get
$$\frac{7}{5} m g = 3 m a$$

$$\therefore \qquad a = \frac{7}{15} g : \text{Answer}$$

But $$T = ma + \frac{3}{5} mg \quad \text{(from Eq 2)}$$

$$= \frac{7}{15} mg + \frac{3}{5} mg$$

$$= \frac{16}{15} mg$$

Answer $$= \frac{16}{15} mg$$

## Exercise 5 E

1.  (a) A block of mass 100 kg is dragged up a smooth slope which makes an angle $A$ with the horizontal, where $\text{Tan } A = \frac{4}{3}$. If the pulling force is of magnitude 984 N and is parallel with the line of greatest slope, find the acceleration of the block.

    (b) If, in part (a), the slope was rough and the coefficient of friction between the block and the slope was $\frac{1}{3}$, find the new acceleration.

2.  A particle of mass 3 kg is held on a smooth plane which is inclined with a slope of 1 in 3 (i.e. $\text{Sin } A = \frac{1}{3}$). It is connected, by means of a light, inextensible string passing over a smooth pulley at the top of the plane, to a particle of mass 10 kg, which hangs freely. Find the common acceleration of the particles and the tension in the string, after the system is released from rest, in terms of $g$.

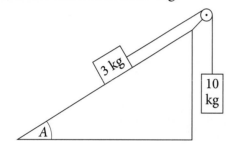

Fig. 5.61

3.  A particle of mass 20 kg is held on a smooth plane which is inclined at an angle $A$ to the horizontal, where $\text{Tan } A = \frac{4}{3}$. The particle is connected to another particle of mass 15 kg by means of a light inextensible string passing over a smooth pulley at the top of the plane.
    (i)  Find the common acceleration of the two particles, correct to two decimal places.
    (ii) Does the 15 kg mass rise or fall?

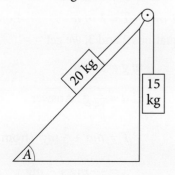

Fig. 5.62

4.

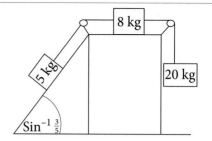

Fig. 5.63

The diagram shows a 5 kg particle on a slope of 3 in 5 (that is, $\sin^{-1}\left(\frac{3}{5}\right)$), an 8 kg particle on a horizontal table and a 20 kg particle hanging freely. They are all connected by two light inextensible strings passing over smooth pulleys. Find the common acceleration of the masses, in terms of $g$.
(i)  if the surfaces are all smooth
(ii) if the surfaces are all rough with coefficient of friction $\frac{1}{4}$.

5.  The diagram shows a 6 kg particle connected to a 12 kg particle by means of a light inextensible string, passing over a smooth pulley. The particles are both on sloped rough surfaces. The angle of slope in both cases is $\tan^{-1}\left(\frac{4}{3}\right)$.

    The coefficient of friction in both cases is $\frac{1}{6}$. Find the common acceleration of the particles and the tension in the string, in terms of $g$.

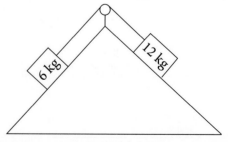

Fig. 5.64

6.  The diagram (next page) shows two particles, of masses 20 kg and 13 kg connected by means of a light inextensible string, passing over a smooth pulley. The angles with the horizontal are given by $\text{Tan } A = \frac{4}{3}$ and $\text{Tan } B = \frac{5}{12}$.

    Find the acceleration of the particles and the tension in the string
    (i)  if both surfaces are smooth
    (ii) if both surfaces are rough, having coefficient of friction $\frac{1}{4}$ with the particles.

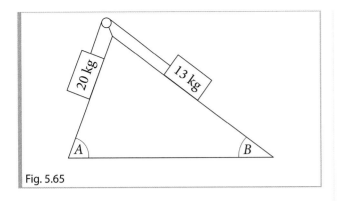

Fig. 5.65

## Relative acceleration

If you run down an escalator (the right way) you travel with the sum of your speed and the speed of the escalator. If you run up the same escalator, you will travel with your own speed minus the speed of the escalator. Something similar happens in the following examples – but with accelerations rather than velocities.

### Worked Example 5.13

The diagram shows a light inelastic string, passing over a fixed light pulley $B$, connecting a particle of mass $5m$ to a light movable pulley $C$. Over pulley $C$ passes a second light inelastic string connecting particles $D$ and $E$ of masses $m$ and $3m$, respectively. Find the common acceleration, $a$, of $A$ and $C$. Find, also, the common acceleration, $b$, of $D$ and $E$ relative to $C$.

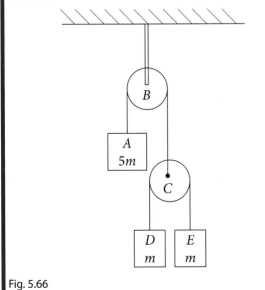

Fig. 5.66

**Solution:**

Here are the forces and accelerations of the system:

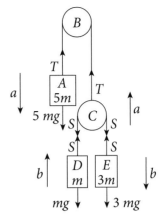

Fig. 5.67

We now examine separately the forces and accelerations of each moving part.

1. The particle A:

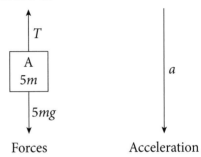

Fig. 5.68

    Since $F = ma$,

    $5mg - T = 5ma$ ...equation 1.

2. The movable light pulley $C$. The word "light" means that is of negligible mass. In such cases, we write its mass as zero.

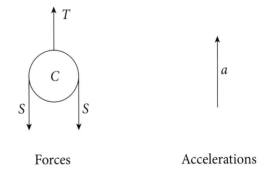

Fig. 5.69

    Since $F = ma$,

    $T - 2S = 0(a)$

    $\therefore T = 2S$ ....equation 2.

3. The particle $D$.

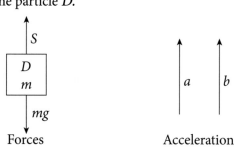

Forces                              Acceleration

Fig. 5.70

Note: $D$ moves upwards with acceleration $b$ relative to $C$. But $C$ is already moving upwards with acceleration $a$. The actual acceleration of $D$ is the sum of these two (i.e. $a + b$).

Therefore,

$$S - mg = m(a + b)$$

$$\therefore S - mg = ma + mb \text{ ...equation 3.}$$

4. The particle $E$.

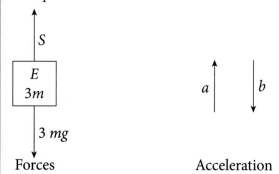

Forces                              Acceleration

Fig. 5.71

$E$ is moving downwards with acceleration $b$ relative to $C$. But $C$ is already moving upwards with acceleration $a$. The actual downward acceleration of $E$ is $(b - a)$.

Therefore,

$$3mg - S = 3m(b - a)$$

$$\therefore 3mg - S = 3mb - 3ma \text{ ...equation 4.}$$

We have four equations with four unknowns:

1.         $5mg - T = 5ma$
2.              $T = 2S$
3.         $S - mg = ma + mb$
4.         $3mg - S = 3mb - 3ma$

Since $T = 2S$, equation 1 reads

$$5mg - 2S = 5ma$$

$$\therefore S = \frac{5}{2}mg - \frac{5}{2}ma \text{ ...equation 5.}$$

Substituting this result into equation 3, we get

$$\frac{5}{2}mg - \frac{5}{2}ma - mg = ma + mb$$

$$\therefore 5g - 5a - 2g = 2a + 2b$$

$$\therefore 7a + 2b = 3g \text{ ...equation 6.}$$

Substituting the result of equation 5 into equation 4, we get

$$3mg - \frac{5}{2}mg + \frac{5}{2}mg = 3mb - 3ma$$

$$\therefore 6g - 5g + 5a = 6b - 6a$$

$$\therefore 11a - 6b = -g \text{ ..equation 7.}$$

Solving the simultaneous equations 6 and 7 gives

$3 \times$ Eqn 6:   $21a + 6b = 9g$

Eqn 7:       $\underline{11a - 6b = -g}$

Adding           $32a = 8g$

$$\therefore a = \frac{1}{4}g \text{ and } b = \frac{5}{8}g : \text{Answer}$$

## Exercise 5 F

1.  The diagram shows a light, inelastic string passing over a fixed smooth pulley $B$. The string connects a particle $A$ of mass 6 kg to a light movable pulley $C$. Over this pulley passes a second string which connects a particle $D$ of mass 4 kg to a particle $E$ of mass 3 kg. Find the common acceleration, $a$, of $A$ and $C$. Find also the common acceleration, $f$, of $D$ and $E$ relative to $C$.

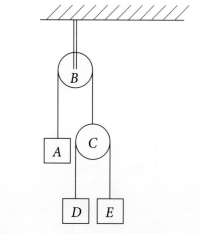

Fig. 5.72

2. A particle $A$ of mass $4\,m$ rests on a rough horizontal table. The coefficient of friction between the particle and the table is $\frac{1}{2}$. The particle is connected by means of a light, inelastic string passing over a smooth light pulley at the table's edge to a second smooth pulley $B$ of mass $3\,m$, hanging freely. A second string passes over pulley $B$, connecting particles $C$ and $D$, of mass $m$ and $2\,m$, respectively. Find the common acceleration of $A$ and $B$. Find, also, the common acceleration of $C$ and $D$ relative to $B$. What is the actual acceleration of particle $D$?

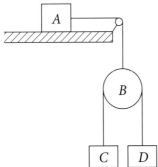

Fig. 5.73

3. The diagram shows a light, inelastic string passing over a fixed smooth pulley $B$. The string connects a particle $A$ of mass $2\,M$ to a second smooth pulley $C$ of mass $M$. Over pulley $C$ passes a second such string, connecting particles $D$ and $E$ of mass $M$ and $2\,M$, respectively. Find the common acceleration of $A$ and $C$. Find, also, the common acceleration of $D$ and $E$ relative to $C$. Calculate the magnitude and direction of the actual accelerations of $D$ and $E$.

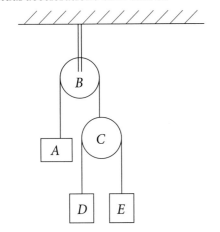

Fig. 5.74

4. The diagram shows a light inextensible string having one end fixed at 0, passing under a movable pulley $A$ of mass 8 kg and then over a fixed light pulley $B$. The other end of the string is attached to a light pulley $C$, of negligible mass. Over pulley $C$, a second light inextensible string is passed, having particles of mass 2 and 4 kg respectively, attached. All pulleys are smooth.

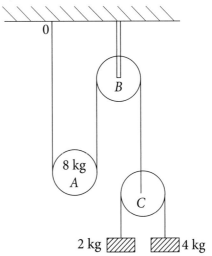

Fig. 5.75

(i) Show in the diagram the forces acting on each pulley when the system is released from rest.

(ii) Find the acceleration of

pulley A

pulley C

each particle.

5.  A body of mass 7*m* lies on a smooth horizontal table.

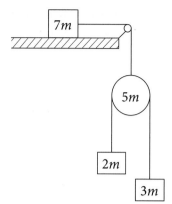

Fig. 5.76

It is connected by means of a light inextensible string passing over a smooth light pulley at the edge of the table to a second smooth pulley of mass 5*m* hanging freely. Over this second pulley passes another light inextensible string carrying masses of 2*m* and 3*m*.

Show in separate diagrams the forces acting on each of the masses and the pulley.

Show that the acceleration of the 7*m* mass is $\frac{7}{12}g$.

6.  A particle of mass 8 kg lies on a rough plane which is inclined at 30° to the horizontal.

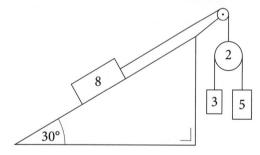

Fig. 5.77

The coefficient of friction between the particle and the plane is $\frac{1}{\sqrt{3}}$. The 8 kg mass is connected by a light inextensible string passing over a smooth light pulley at the top of the plane to a pulley of mass 2 kg hanging freely. Over this pulley (which is also smooth) a second light inextensible string is passed having particles of mass 3 kg and 5 kg attached. Show in separate diagrams the forces acting on each of the masses when the system is released from rest.

Show that the acceleration of the 8 kg mass is $\frac{3}{35}g$.

# Wedges

A wedge is an object in a triangular shape (like a piece of cheese). It is **not** the same as an inclined plane, because a wedge is free to move – unlike an inclined plane which is fixed.

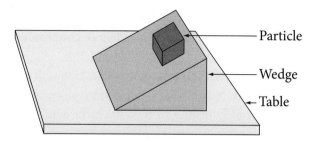

Fig. 5.78

## Worked Example 5.14

A wedge of mass 3*m* rests on a smooth horizontal table with one of its plane faces inclined at an angle 30° to the horizontal. A particle of mass *m* is placed on this face which is smooth and the system is released from rest. Show on separate diagrams the forces acting on the particle and the wedge. By considering the forces and accelerations of the particle in two directions: the first along the plane and the other perpendicular to the plane, find the acceleration, *a*, of the wedge and the acceleration, *f*, of the particle relative to the wedge.

### Solution:

Since the particle moves to the left, the wedge will move to the right. This is because no force, external to the system, acts along the horizontal direction. According to Newton's Second Law, it follows that the momentum in the horizontal direction will remain unchanged. So, as the particle moves to the left, the wedge will begin to move to the right, leaving the total momentum in the horizontal direction unchanged.

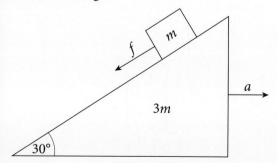

Fig. 5.79

Here are the forces acting on the particle and the wedge, separately, with their accelerations.

**Particle**

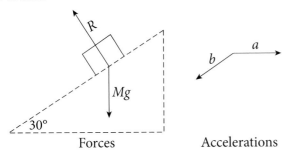

Fig. 5.80

**Wedge**

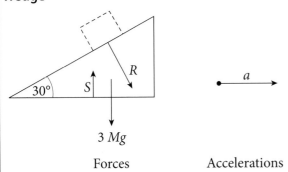

Fig. 5.81

Consider the forces and accelerations of the particle, resolved into components parallel to and perpendicular to the plane.

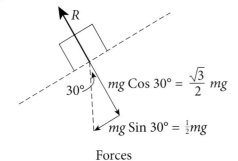

Fig. 5.82

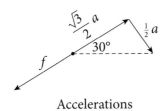

Fig. 5.83

Now consider the forces and accelerations parallel to the inclined plane.

$$F = m\,a$$
$$\therefore \tfrac{1}{2}\,m\,g = m\left(f - \tfrac{\sqrt{3}}{2}\,a\right)$$
$$\therefore m\,g = 2\,m\,f - \sqrt{3}\,m\,a$$
$$\therefore g = 2\,f - \sqrt{3}\,a \;...\text{equation 1.}$$

Next, consider the forces and accelerations perpendicular to the inclined plane. Taking down into the wedge as positive:

$$F = m\,a$$
$$\therefore \tfrac{\sqrt{3}}{2}\,m\,g - R = m\left(\tfrac{1}{2}\,a\right)$$
$$\therefore \sqrt{3}\,m\,g - 2\,R = m\,a \;...\text{equation 2.}$$

Finally, consider the forces and accelerations of the wedge, along the horizontal.

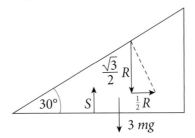

Fig. 5.84

$$F = m\,a$$
$$\therefore \tfrac{1}{2}\,R = 3\,m\,a$$
$$\therefore R = 6\,m\,a \;...\text{equation 3.}$$

Putting this result into equation 2 gives

$$\sqrt{3}\,m\,g - 2\,(6\,m\,a) = m\,a$$
$$\therefore \sqrt{3}\,m\,g = 13\,m\,a$$
$$\therefore a = \frac{\sqrt{3}}{13}\,g$$

Putting this result into equation 1 gives

$$g = 2\,f - \sqrt{3}\left(\frac{\sqrt{3}}{13}\,g\right)$$
$$\therefore g = 2\,f - \frac{3}{13}\,g$$
$$\therefore 2\,f = \frac{16}{13}\,g$$
$$\therefore f = \frac{8}{13}\,g$$

Answer: $\quad a = \frac{\sqrt{3}}{13}\,g \text{ and } f = \frac{8}{13}\,g$

## Exercise 5 G

1. A wedge of mass $2M$ rests on a smooth horizontal table. One of its faces, which is smooth, makes an angle of 30° with the horizontal. A particle of mass $M$ is placed on this face and the system is released from rest. Find the acceleration of the wedge and the acceleration of the particle relative to the wedge.

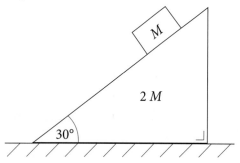

Fig. 5.85

2. A wedge of mass 7 kg rests on a smooth horizontal table. One of its faces, which is smooth, makes an angle of 45° with the horizontal. A particle of mass 1 kg is placed on this face and the system is released from rest. Find the acceleration of the wedge and the acceleration of the particle relative to the wedge. Find the speed of the wedge when the speed of the particle relative to the wedge is $\sqrt{2}$ m/s.

3. A wedge of mass 3 kg rests on a smooth horizontal table. One of its faces, which is smooth, makes an angle of 45° with the horizontal. A particle of mass 1 kg is placed on this face and the system is released from rest. Find the acceleration $a$ of the wedge and the acceleration $f$ of the particle relative to the wedge.
   By writing $a$ and $f$ in terms of $\vec{i}$ and $\vec{j}$, and then adding, show that the actual acceleration of the particle is of magnitude $\frac{5}{7} g$.

4. A wedge of mass $4m$ rests on a smooth horizontal table. One of its faces, which is smooth, makes an angle $A$ with the table, where $\tan A = \frac{3}{4}$. A particle of mass $m$ is placed on this face and the system is released from rest.
   Find the acceleration of the wedge.

5. The diagram shows a wedge, all of whose faces are smooth, resting on a smooth horizontal table. Its faces make angle $A$ and $B$ with the table, where $\tan A = \frac{4}{3}$ and $\tan B = \frac{3}{4}$. Particles, each of mass $m$ are placed on these faces. If the mass of the wedge is $2m$, show that the wedge will not move.

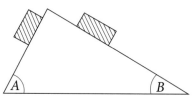

Fig. 5.86

6. The diagram shows a wedge of mass $m$ on a horizontal table. The angle of the wedge is $\tan^{-1} 2$. On the top of the wedge is placed a particle of mass $4m$. The particle is smooth but the surface between the wedge and the table is rough with $\mu = \frac{1}{3}$.
   (i) On separate diagrams show the forces on the particle and on the wedge.
   (ii) Show that the acceleration of the wedge is $\frac{3}{11} g$.

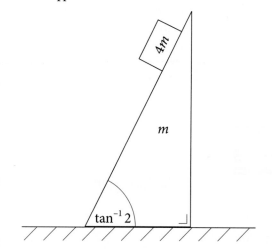

Fig. 5.87

7. The diagram shows a wedge, all of whose faces are smooth, resting on a horizontal table. The mass of the wedge is $3m$. The faces of the wedge both make angles of 45° with the table. Particles of masses $2m$ and $m$ are placed on these faces. Find the acceleration of the wedge after the system is released from rest.

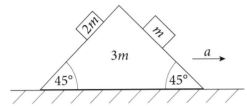

Fig. 5.88

8. A wedge of mass $m$ is placed on a rough horizontal table. The coefficient of friction between the wedge and the table is $\frac{1}{2}$. A particle of mass $5m$ is placed at rest on the plane face of the wedge, which is inclined at an angle $\tan^{-1}\frac{3}{4}$ to the horizontal.
   (i) Prove that the acceleration of the wedge is $\frac{3}{16}g$, while the acceleration of the particle relative to the wedge is $\frac{3}{4}g$.
   (ii) How far down the wedge will the particle travel in the time that it takes the wedge to travel 1 metre?

9. The diagram shows a wedge of mass 8 kg, all of whose faces are smooth, resting on a smooth horizontal table. One of the faces makes an angle $A$ with the table, where $\tan A = \frac{3}{4}$. The other free face is vertical. At the top of the wedge is attached a smooth light pulley. A light inextensible string passes over this pulley, connecting particles of masses 5 kg and 1 kg, as shown, with the 1 kg mass against the vertical face of the wedge.

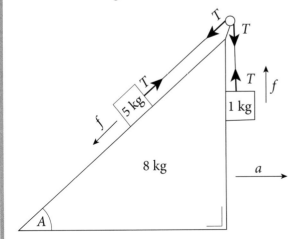

Fig. 5.89

When the system is released from rest, the 5 kg mass moves down the inclined face with acceleration $f$ relative to the wedge. The wedge moves to the right with acceleration $a$. Write down five equations of motion, answering the following descriptions:
(i) the 5 kg mass along the inclined face
(ii) the 5 kg mass perpendicular to the inclined face
(iii) the 1 kg mass along the vertical
(iv) the 1 kg mass along the horizontal
(v) the wedge along the horizontal.
(Note: There will be equal and opposite reactions between the wedge and the particle of mass 1 kg. The two tension forces will act, as external forces, on the wedge like a lasso around its neck.)

10. The diagram shows the same system as in question 6, but with the 5 kg and 1 kg particles in reversed places. After this system is released from rest, the 5 kg mass swings out, making an angle $\theta$ with the vertical, as shown. Write down the five equations of motion under the same headings as before.

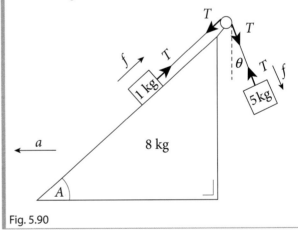

Fig. 5.90

## Summary of important points

1. Momentum $= m \vec{v}$.

2. Newton's laws:
   (i)   A body will continue in a state of rest or of uniform motion in a straight line, unless it is impelled to change that state by an external force applied to it.
   (ii)  The change in momentum per unit time is proportional to the applied force, and takes place along the straight line in which the force acts. ($F = ma$)
   (iii) To every action there is an equal and opposite reaction.

3. Weight, $W = mg$.

4. Limiting friction, $F = \mu R$.

5. When a friction force is involved, take three steps:
   (i)   Find the normal reaction
   (ii)  Then find the friction
   (iii) Then write down the equation of motion.

6. Take the direction in which the particle is moving as the positive direction

## DOs and DON'Ts for the exam

### DO
- Do draw **separate** diagrams for each particle and show all the forces
- Do put arrows at the end of all force vectors to show their directions
- Do  put the acceleration vector beside the particle
- In the equation of motion $F = ma$ do put forces on the left hand side of the equation and accelerations on the right
- Do remember that if a pulley is 'light' or 'of negligible mass', you must put its mass as zero

### DON'T
- Don't assume that the acceleration of each particle is $a$
- Don't mix up inclined planes with wedges.  They are different and require different treatment.
- Don't leave a force and its components in the same form on a diagram.  Put them in different colours, or draw one in dotted lines and the other in continuous lines.  You have to show that the original force has been **replaced** by the components.  It is even enough to put a bracket around the original force like this: ($mg$).  If you don't do this, you will lose marks.

# Work, power, energy and momentum

## Chapter 6

"I like work; it fascinates me. I can sit and look at it for hours."

*Jerome K. Jerome*

**Learning outcomes**

**In this chapter you will learn...**

- Definitions of work and power

- How to use the formula $P = Tv$

- The definitions of potential energy and kinetic energy

- The Principle of Conservation of Energy and its applications

- The Principle of Conservation of Momentum and its applications

## Contents

**You will need to know...**

- The formulae for uniform acceleration

- Basic trigonometry

- How to solve problems with pulleys

## Work and power

**Definition:** If a force is constant, then the work done by the force is the product of the component of the force in the direction of motion and the distance through which the point of application moves.
In short, work = force × distance. Work is a scalar quantity measured in joules. A joule is a newton-metre, the work done when a force of 1 newton is applied over a distance of 1 metre.
1000 joules = 1 kilojoule = 1 kJ

**Definition: Power** is the rate at which work is done. Power is the work done per unit time.
Power is a scalar quantity measured in watts.
1 watt = 1 joule per second.
1000 watts = 1 kilowatt = 1 kW

**Note 1:** A person drags a stone by means of a horizontal rope over rough horizontal ground. The force is 100 N. If the stone is dragged a distance of
20 m, then the work done is given by
$$\text{Work} = F \times s$$
$$= 100 \times 20$$
$$= 2000 \text{ Nm}$$
$$= 2000 \text{ joules.}$$

Fig. 6.1

But if the rope made an angle $A$ with the ground, where $\tan A = \frac{3}{4}$, how much work would be done in dragging the stone 20 m along the ground?
Since $\tan A = \frac{3}{4}$, $\sin A = \frac{3}{5}$ and $\cos A = \frac{4}{5}$, we resolve the force into horizontal and vertical components.

Fig. 6.2

The lifting force $F_y$ does no work. Why?
The component of the force in the direction of motion, $F_x$, does work. This work is given by

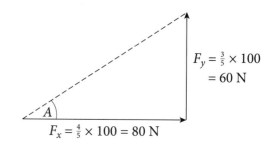

$$F_y = \tfrac{3}{5} \times 100 = 60 \text{ N}$$
$$F_x = \tfrac{4}{5} \times 100 = 80 \text{ N}$$

Fig. 6.3

$$\text{Work} = F \text{ (along motion)} \times s$$
$$= F_x \times s$$
$$= 80 \times 20$$
$$= 1600 \text{ joules.}$$

**Note 2:** A weak person could carry a $\frac{1}{4}$ tonne of coal to the top of a hill – if he does it one piece at a time. Only a powerful person could carry it up in one go. The difference between the two cases is not the work done on the coal (both do the same work) but the rate at which it is done. The work in each case is the same, the power is not.

**Note 3:** A woman drags a stone over rough horizontal ground by means of a horizontal rope. She drags the stone a distance of 100 m in 20 seconds, by applying a constant force of 300 N. What is her power output?
$$\text{Work done} = F \times s$$
$$= 300 \times 100$$
$$= 30\,000 \text{ J.}$$

$$\text{Power} = \text{work done per unit time}$$
$$= \frac{F \times s}{t} = \frac{30\,000 \text{ J}}{20 \text{ s}}$$
$$= 1500 \text{ J/s}$$
$$= 1500 \text{ watts.}$$

**Note 4:** Suppose that an object, like a car, moves at a constant speed $v$, driven by a constant tractive effort $T$. The power output is the rate at which work is done.
$$\text{Power} = \frac{T s}{t}$$
$$= T \times \frac{s}{t}$$
$$= T v$$
since the force is a constant.

Using calculus, (letting $P$ = power and $W$ = work) we would write

$$P = \frac{\mathrm{d}W}{\mathrm{d}t} = \frac{\mathrm{d}\,(Ts)}{\mathrm{d}t}$$
$$= T\left(\frac{\mathrm{d}s}{\mathrm{d}t}\right)$$
$$= T\,v \text{ (since } T \text{ is a constant)}$$

In the case of the woman in Note 3, she dragged the stone 100 m in 20 seconds. The speed of the stone, $v$, is therefore 5 m/s. The tractive effort is a constant 300 N.

$\therefore$ Power output = $T\,v$
$= 300\,(5)$
$= 1500$ watts.

This agrees with the previous result.

**Note 5:** It is true to say that at any moment the instantaneous power output is the product of the instantaneous force and the instantaneous velocity. When cars or trains are driven forward by the force of the engine, we call such a force **tractive effort** and we denote it by the letter $T$. The equation which relates the power output of an engine and the tractive effort it produces is $P = T\,v$.

### Worked Example 6.1

A block of wood of mass 50 kg is dragged across a rough horizontal surface by means of a string which makes an angle $A$, where $\tan A = \frac{3}{4}$, with the ground. The coefficient of friction between the block and the ground is $\frac{1}{4}$. The tension in the string is 150 N.

(i) Show the forces acting on the block.
(ii) Find the magnitude of the normal reaction at the ground.
(iii) Find the magnitude of the friction force.
(iv) Find the work done in moving the block a distance of 2 m.
(v) Find the acceleration of the block.

**Solution:**

(i) Here are the forces acting on the block:

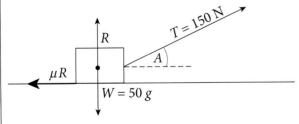

Fig. 6.4

(ii) Resolve the tension force.
$\cos A = \frac{4}{5}$; $\sin A = \frac{3}{5}$; $T = 150$ N.

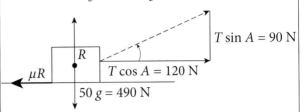

Fig. 6.5

There is no motion perpendicular to the plane. Therefore, forces up = forces down.
$90 + R = 490 \Rightarrow R = 400$ N.

(iii) Friction force = $\mu R = \frac{1}{4}(400) = 100$ N

(iv) The pulling force, along the line of motion, is 120 N.

Work done = $F$ (along motion) $\times s$
$= 120 \times 2$
$= 240$ joules.

(v) The resultant force = $120 - 100 = 20$ N
But $\qquad\qquad F = m\,a$
$\therefore 20 = 50\,a$
$\therefore a = 0.4 \text{ m/s}^2.$

### Worked Example 6.2

A train of weight 100 kN moves up a hill of incline one in fifty. The resistance to motion is 20 kN and the maximum power output of the engine is 440 kilowatts. Find the maximum uniform speed of the train.

**Solution:**

An incline of one in fifty means $\sin A = \frac{1}{50}$ where $A$ is the angle of inclination of the hill. Let $T =$ the tractive effort of the train (i.e. the pulling force). Here are the forces acting on the train:

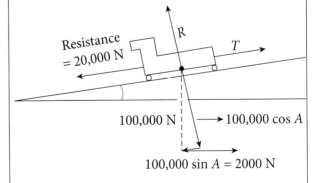

Fig. 6.6

Since the train is moving with uniform speed, say $v$, there is no acceleration. Consequently, the forces in any line must be zero.

$$\therefore T = 20\,000 + 2\,000$$

$$= 22\,000 \text{ N.}$$

But $\qquad P = T\,v.$

$$\therefore 440\,000 = 22\,000\,v$$

$$\therefore v = 20 \text{ m/s: Answer}$$

## Exercise 6 A

1. A sleigh is pulled by a horizontal force of magnitude 80 N. The sleigh moves 30 m across horizontal ground.
   (i) Find the work done.
   (ii) If this took 10 seconds, find the power output.

2. A woman pushes a car by exerting a horizontal force of 200 N. She pushes the car a distance of 12 m.
   (i) Find the work done.
   (ii) If she took 8 seconds to do this, find the power output of the woman.

3. A sledge is pulled across horizontal ground by a pulling force of 130 N. The force makes an angle $A$, where $\tan A = \frac{5}{12}$, with the ground.
   (i) If the sledge moves a distance of 50 m, find the work done.
   (ii) If this took one minute, find the power output.

4. A car moves at a constant speed of 20 m/s, driven by a constant tractive effort of magnitude 600 N. The car is travelling on a straight horizontal road. Find the power output of the engine.

5. A trawler's engine has power output of 100 kW (kilowatts). If the trawler has constant speed of 5 m/s, find the constant tractive effort of the engine.

6. An Inuit loads some provisions on a toboggan. He then drags the toboggan across horizontal snowy ground, by means of a light rope. The loaded toboggan has a mass 20 kg. The coefficient of friction between the toboggan and the ground is $\frac{1}{7}$.

   The tension in the rope is 50 N and the rope makes an angle $A$, where $\tan A = \frac{7}{24}$ with the gound. If the toboggan moves a distance of 30 m, find

   (i) the magnitude of the normal reaction at the ground
   (ii) the magnitude of the friction force
   (iii) the work done by the tension force
   (iv) the acceleration
   (v) the power output of the man if all this took 20 seconds.

7. A car whose weight is 5000 N climbs a hill of incline one in twenty at a steady speed of 12 m/s. If the resistance to motion is 500 N, find the power output of the car's engine.

8. A train of mass 100 tonnes climbs a hill of incline one in fifty at a steady speed of 10 m/s. The total resistance to motion is 10 kN (i.e. 10 000 N). Find the power output of the train's engine.

9. A cyclist and his bicycle together have mass 50 kg. The cyclist is ascending a hill of incline 1 in 10 at a steady speed, against a resistance force of magnitude 21 N. If the power output of the cyclist is 350 watts, find his speed.

10. A car has weight 5000 N. The resistance to its motion is 800 N. On flat ground it can move at a steady speed of 50 m/s, when its engine produces maximum power.
    (i) Find the maximum power output of the engine.
    (ii) Find the car's maximum speed up a hill of incline 1 in 25.

11. A particle of mass 20 kg is pulled along a rough horizontal plane by a string which is inclined at 30° to the horizontal. If the tension in the string is 80 N and the coefficient of friction between the particle and the plane is $\frac{1}{3}$ calculate
    (i) the horizontal and vertical components of the tension
    (ii) the normal reaction between the particle and the plane
    (iii) the acceleration of the particle
    (iv) the total work done in moving the particle through a distance of 0.5 m.

12. The maximum power output of a train of mass 200 tonnes is 500 kW.

    (i) Find the maximum acceleration of the train on a level track at a speed of 10 m/s if the resistance to motion at this speed is 2 kN. (1 kW = 1000 W; 1 kN =1000 N.)

    (ii) Find the maximum acceleration of the same train on an incline of 1 in 196 at a speed of 20 m/s if the resistance to the motion at this speed is 9 kN.

13. A car of mass 750 kg attains a speed of 30 m/s when travelling down an incline of 1 in 25 with the engine switched off. It can attain a maximum speed of 20 m/s up the same incline when the engine is working. The resistance to motion $R$ is given by $R = k\,v^2$, when the speed is $v$ ($k$ being a constant).

    (i) Show that $k = \dfrac{g}{30}$

    (ii) Show that the maximum power output of the engine is $\dfrac{2600\,g}{3}$ watts

    (iii) Show that the maximum speed of the car on level ground is 29.625 m/s (assuming that the power output remains the same).

## Energy

**Definition:** The **energy** of a body is its capacity for doing work. Energy is measured in joules.

Some objects have energy due to their **position**. We call such energy **potential energy**.

For example, a stone held 10 m above the ground has potential energy. Due to its position, it can do work. It can crack open almonds or knock out a sabre-tooth tiger.

Other objects have energy due to their **speed**. We call such energy **kinetic energy**. For example, a car moving at 30 m/s, even freewheeling with the engine turned off, has kinetic energy. Because of its speed, it can do work. It can knock down a brick wall or drag along a sack of potatoes dropped in front of it. It could not do these things if it were not moving.

There are other kinds of energy, such as **heat** energy, **nuclear** energy and **chemical** energy, but these are not studied as part of this course.

**Definition:** The **potential energy** of a body is the energy it has due to its position. This energy is measured by the amount of work it can do in moving from its actual position to some standard position.

**Definition:** The **kinetic energy** of a body is the energy it has due to its motion. This energy is measured by the amount of work it can do in coming to rest.

1. **To measure potential energy of a body**

   What work can a body of mass $m$, at a height $h$ above the ground, do? The work it can do is equal to the work done on it in moving it to the ground, that is, the work done by the gravitational force which brings it down to the ground.

   Since work = Force × distance
   $$= F \times s = (m\,a)\,s,$$
   the work done by the gravitational force, $mg$, is given by $(mg)(h) = mgh$. It follows that the energy of the object is $mgh$.
   **Potential energy** = $mgh$.

2. **To measure the kinetic energy of a moving body**

   Take a body of mass $m$ moving with initial speed $u$. What kinetic energy does it have? What work can it do before coming to rest? Again, the work it can do is equal to the work done on it in bringing it to rest.

Let us say that the body's retardation is of magnitude $a$ and that it covers a distance $s$ before coming to rest.

| We know | $u = u$ |
|---------|---------|
|         | $v = 0$ |
|         | $a = -a$ |
|         | $s = s$ |

$$\text{Use } v^2 = u^2 + 2\,a\,s$$
$$\therefore 0 = u^2 - 2\,a\,s$$
$$\therefore as = \frac{1}{2}\,u^2$$

But work done
$$= F \times s$$
$$= m\,a\,s$$
$$= m\left(\frac{1}{2}\,u^2\right)$$
$$= \frac{1}{2}\,m\,u^2$$

Therefore, the energy of a body of mass $m$ moving with speed $u$ is $\frac{1}{2}mu^2$.

**Kinetic energy** $= \frac{1}{2}mv^2$, where $v$ is the velocity.

## Summary

$$\text{Potential energy} = mgh$$

$$\text{Kinetic energy} = \frac{1}{2}mv^2$$

## Conservation of energy

Take an object of mass $m$ at rest at a height $h$ above the ground. At this stage its potential energy is $mgh$ and its kinetic energy is zero, since it is not moving. Let the object fall under gravity. What is its speed when it hits the ground?

We know
$$u = 0$$
$$a = g$$
$$s = h$$
$$v = ?$$

Use $v^2 = u^2 + 2\,a\,s$
$$v^2 = 0 + 2\,g\,h$$
$$v = \sqrt{2\,g\,h}$$

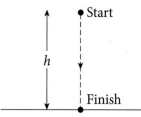

Fig. 6.7

When the object hits the ground, it has no potential energy but its kinetic energy is
$$\frac{1}{2}mv^2 = \frac{1}{2}m\,(2gh) = mgh.$$

It is interesting to note that at both points the total energy was $mgh$ joules. The energy was converted from potential energy at the start to kinetic energy at the end, but the amount of energy did not change. The energy was converted from one kind to another, but it did not disappear.

This is an example of the Principle of Conservation of Energy.

## Principle of Conservation of Energy

The total amount of energy of a closed system remains constant, though it may be converted from one form to another. (A closed system is one which does not share energy with its surrounding environment.)

Here is a specific case of this general principle:

If a body is acted upon by any number of forces in such a way that the gravitational forces are the only forces which do work on the body, then the sum of the potential and kinetic energy remains a constant at all points along its path. (Forces doing work on the body are forces which speed up or slow down the body – friction, for example.)

In short, $m\,g\,h + \frac{1}{2}m\,v^2 = \text{constant}$

### Worked Example 6.3

A spaceship of mass 2 tonnes fires rockets which speed it up from 500 m/s to 600 m/s. Find the work done.

**Solution:**

The work done is measured by the gain in energy, in this case kinetic energy.

| | |
|---|---|
| Energy before | $= \frac{1}{2}mu^2$ |
| | $= \frac{1}{2}(2000)(500)^2$ |
| | $= 250\ 000\ 000$ J |
| | $= 250\ 000$ kJ |
| Energy after | $= \frac{1}{2}mv^2$ |
| | $= \frac{1}{2}(2000)(600)^2$ |
| | $= 360\ 000\ 000$ J |
| | $= 360\ 000$ kJ |

$\therefore$ Energy gained $= 360\ 000 - 250\ 000$

$$= 110\ 000 \text{ kJ}.$$

$\therefore$ Work done $= 110\ 000$ kJ : Answer.

## Worked Example 6.4

A painter at the top of a vertical 10 m ladder pulls up a 2 kg pot of paint by means of a rope. Find the work done. Find, also, the power output if he takes 7 seconds to do it.

### Solution:

The work done equals the energy gained — in this case, potential energy.

$$\text{P.E.} = mgh = 2(9.8)(10) = 196 \text{ J.}$$

$$\text{Power} = \frac{\text{Work}}{\text{Time}} = \frac{196}{7} = 28 \text{ W}$$

## Worked Example 6.5

A projectile is fired from level ground at 200 m/s. Find its speed when it is 1000 m above the ground.

### Solution:

(This question could be solved using projectile equations—but we will use the Principle of Conservation of Energy.)

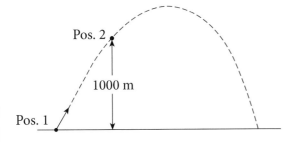

Fig. 6.8

Let $m$ be its mass and $v$ its velocity at position 2. The total energy at position 1 = the total energy at position 2.

$$m g h_1 + \frac{1}{2} m v_1^2 = m g h_2 + \frac{1}{2} m v_2^2$$

$$\therefore mg(0) + \frac{1}{2} m (200)^2 = m g (1000) + \frac{1}{2} m v^2$$

$$\therefore 20\,000\, m = 9800\, m + \frac{1}{2} m v^2$$

$$\therefore \frac{1}{2} v^2 = 10\,200$$

$$\therefore v = \sqrt{20\,400}$$

$$= 142.8 \text{ m/s}$$

## Worked Example 6.6

A swing, when at its lowest point, is 1 m above the ground. A girl sits on it. When at its highest point, the swing is 2 m above the ground.

   (i)   Find the speed when the swing is at its lowest point.

  (ii)  If, when she was at the highest point, the girl was pushed so that she starts with speed 2 m/s, find her greatest speed in subsequent motion.

### Solution:

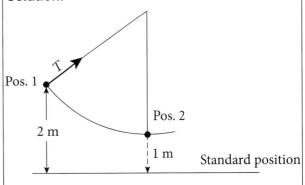

Fig. 6.9

   (i)   We may use the Principle of Conservation of Energy here because the gravitational force is the only force which does work. The tension, $T$, acts perpendicularly to the path of the swing and, therefore, does not speed it up or slow it down – it does no work.

Let $m$ = the mass of the swing and girl, together. At position 1, the speed is zero; let $v$ be the speed at position 2.

$$\text{K.E.}_1 + \text{P.E.}_1 = \text{K.E.}_2 + \text{P.E.}_2$$

$$\therefore \frac{1}{2} m\, 0^2 + m g (2) = \frac{1}{2} m v^2 + m g (1)$$

$$\therefore 0 + 2 m g = \frac{1}{2} m v^2 + 1\, m g$$

$$\therefore m g = \frac{1}{2} m v^2$$

$$\therefore v^2 = 2 g$$

$$\therefore v = \sqrt{2 g}$$

$$= \sqrt{19.6}$$

$$= 4.427 \text{ m/s: Answer}$$

  (ii)  In the second case, the greatest speed is reached at position 2, because the kinetic energy will be greatest when the potential energy is least.

The speed at position 1 is 2 m/s; let $v$ be the speed at position 2.

$$\text{K.E.}_1 + \text{P.E.}_1 = \text{K.E.}_2 + \text{P.E.}_2$$

$$\therefore \frac{1}{2} m (2)^2 + m g (2) = \frac{1}{2} m v^2 + m g (1)$$

$$\therefore 2 + 2 g = \frac{1}{2} v^2 + g$$

$$\therefore v^2 = 4 + 2\,g$$

$$= 4 + 19.6$$

$$= 23.6$$

$$\therefore v = \sqrt{23.6} = 4.858 \text{ m/s: Ans.}$$

## Worked Example 6.7

A weightless see-saw is at rest with a boy of mass $m$ sitting at the lower end at ground level. His father, of mass $3m$, sits at the other end, one metre off the ground, and then the system starts to move. Find the common speed of the boy and his father just before the father hits the ground.

**Solution:**

Position 1

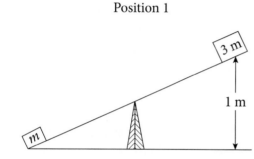

Fig. 6.10

Position 2

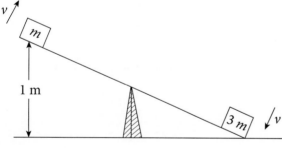

Fig. 6.11

The total energy of the system (**son** and **father**) before = total energy after.

$$\text{K.E.}_{1s} + \text{P.E.}_{1s} + \text{K.E.}_{1f} + \text{P.E.}_{1f}$$

$$= \text{K.E.}_{2s} + \text{P.E.}_{2s} + \text{K.E.}_{2f} + \text{P.E.}_{2f}$$

$$\tfrac{1}{2}m(0) + mg(0) + \tfrac{1}{2}(3m)(0) + 3\,mg\,(1)$$

$$= \tfrac{1}{2}\,mv^2 + mg\,(1) + \tfrac{1}{2}(3m)v^2 + (3m)g(0)$$

$$\therefore 2\,m\,g = 2\,m\,v^2$$

$$\therefore v = \sqrt{g} = \sqrt{9.8} = 3.13 \text{ m/s}$$

## Exercise 6 B

1. A projectile is fired from level ground at 20 m/s. Use the Principle of Conservation of Energy to find the speed of the projectile when it is 10 m above the ground.

2. A particle of mass $m$ swings at the end of a light string. Its speed is 2 m/s at its lowest point. Find the greatest vertical height to which it will rise in subsequent motion (to the nearest centimetre).

3. A pendulum is made of a mass at the end of a light string. The pendulum, which is 1 metre long, makes an angle 60° with the vertical when at its greatest height. Find its speed (in m/s) when at its lowest point, correct to 2 decimal places.

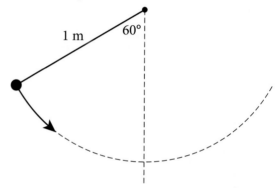

Fig. 6.11

4. A girl throws a rugby ball of mass 0.4 kg straight up into the air from a height of 1 metre off the ground. The initial speed of the ball is 7 m/s. Find the greatest height the ball will reach over the ground.

5. A pendulum, 1.3 m long, swings in a vertical plane so that its greatest angle with the vertical is $A$, where $\tan A = \frac{5}{12}$. Find, in terms of $g$, its greatest speed in subsequent motion.

6. A tennis ball is hit straight up in the air from a point 0.5 m above level ground. Its initial speed is 14 m/s.
   (i) Find the greatest height the ball will reach above ground level.
   (ii) Find the speed with which the ball hits the ground (correct to 2 decimal places).

7. A bobsleigh slides down a frictionless surface which is inclined at an angle of 30° to the horizontal. It starts from rest and travels a distance of 20 m. Why may the Principle of Conservation of Energy be used here?
Find its final speed.

8. A small ring is threaded on a smooth piece of wire, which is bent to form a circle of radius 5 m. The ring is projected with speed of 14 m/s from the lowest point on the wire circle, which is held in a vertical position.
   (i) Find the speed (to the nearest m/s) of the ring when its height is the same as the height of the centre of the circle.
   (ii) Show that the ring will just reach the highest point of the circle when it comes to rest.

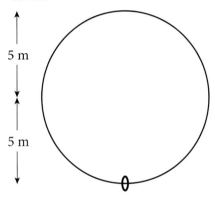

5 m

5 m

Fig. 6.12

9. State the principle of conservation of energy.
   A smooth circular wire, radius $a$, is fixed in a vertical plane. A small ring, mass $m$, threaded on the wire is projected from its lowest point with speed $u$ given by $u^2 = 2ga$. Calculate
   (i) the total energy at the instant of projection
   (ii) the greatest height reached by the ring
   (iii) the speed of the ring on reaching a height equal to half the greatest height.

10. Johnny, whose mass is $M$, sits at one end of a light see-saw at ground level. Margery, whose mass is $\frac{3}{2}M$, then sits on the other end which is $\frac{1}{2}$ a metre off the ground. Find their common speed when Margery hits the ground.

## Conservation of momentum

### The Principle of Conservation of Momentum
**Definition**: **Momentum** is the product of mass and velocity.

Momentum, as we saw before, is a vector quantity along the line of the velocity. It is measured in kg m/s (or kg m s$^{-1}$).

Newton's Second Law states that "the rate of change of momentum is proportional to the applied force and is along the line of action of the applied force". This implies that in the absence of external forces, the momentum of a system does not change. More specifically, if there is no external force acting in a certain direction, then the momentum of the system in that direction remains the same. We call this the **Principle of Conservation of Momentum**.

### Principle of Conservation of Momentum
In the absence of an external force in a certain direction, the total momentum of a system in that direction remains a constant.

### Impulse
We know that $\vec{F} = m\,\vec{a}$

$$\therefore \vec{F} = \frac{m(\vec{v} - \vec{u})}{t}$$
$$= \frac{m\vec{v} - m\vec{u}}{t}$$
$$\therefore \vec{F}t = m\vec{v} - m\vec{u}$$

= change in momentum.          Equation 1.

When a golfball is struck by a club, or a nail hit by a hammer, the force applied is very large but the time over which it is applied (when the two objects are in actual contact) is very small. It is hard to measure the force and harder still to measure the time taken. It is practical, instead, to measure the strength of the blow not by the force, nor by the time taken, but by their product. How?

Take a look at equation 1. It can be seen that the product $\vec{F}\,t$, which is called the **impulse** $(\vec{I})$, can be measured by calculating the change in momentum, $\vec{I} = m\vec{v} - m\vec{u}$.

**Definition**: The **impulse**, $\vec{I}$, imparted onto a body is the change in its momentum.
Mathematically, $\vec{I} = m\vec{v} - m\vec{u}$. Impulse is a vector quantity and is measured in newton-seconds, N s, since it is the product of force and time, as we saw.

### Worked Example 6.8

A golfball of mass 0.1 kg is hit from rest so that immediately after impact it moves horizontally at 60 m/s. Find the impulse imparted to it by the blow.

**Solution:**

Before

Fig. 6.13

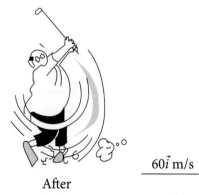

After

$60\vec{i}$ m/s

Fig. 6.14

$$\text{Momentum}_{before} = m\,\vec{u} = (0.1)\,(0)\,\vec{i} = 0\vec{i}$$

$$\text{Momentum}_{after} = m\,\vec{v} = (0.1)\,(60)\,\vec{i} = 6\vec{i}$$

$$\text{Impulse} = \vec{I}$$

$$= m\,\vec{v} - m\,\vec{u}$$

$$= 6\,\vec{i} - 0\,\vec{i} = 6\,\vec{i}\ \text{N s}$$

### Worked Example 6.9

A tennis ball, of mass 0.05 kg, moves horizontally at 8 m/s. A player hits it so that it leaves his racquet travelling at 18 m/s in the opposite direction. Find the impulse imparted to the ball by the stroke.

**Solution:**

Take $\vec{i}$ along the initial direction of the ball.

Before

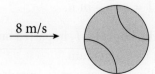

8 m/s

Fig. 6.15

After

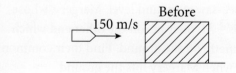

18 m/s

Fig. 6.16

$$\text{Momentum}_{before} = m\,\vec{u}$$

$$= (0.05)\,(8)\,\vec{i}$$

$$= 0.4\,\vec{i}$$

$$\text{Momentum}_{after} = m\,\vec{v}$$

$$= 0.05\,\left(-18\,\vec{i}\right)$$

$$= -0.9\,\vec{i}$$

$$\text{Impulse} = \vec{I} = m\,\vec{v} - m\,\vec{u}$$

$$= -0.9\,\vec{i} - 0.4\,\vec{i}$$

$$= -1.3\,\vec{i}\ \text{N s}$$

The impulse is, as expected, along the same line as the stroke of the racquet.

### Worked Example 6.10

A bullet of mass 0.1 kg travels horizontally with speed 150 m/s until it enters a block of wood, which rests on a smooth horizontal table. The bullet emerges from the other end of the block with speed 100 m/s. If the block has mass 2 kg, find the speed of the block after impact. Find, also, the impact imparted by the bullet onto the block and vice-versa.

**Solution:**

Before

150 m/s

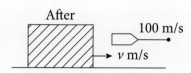

Fig. 6.17

After

100 m/s

$v$ m/s

Fig. 6.18

Since the forces are conservative (no external forces act on the bullet-block system), the total momentum before impact = the total momentum afterwards.

$$m_1 \vec{u}_1 + m_2 \vec{u}_2 = m_1 \vec{v}_1 + m_2 \vec{v}_2$$
$$\therefore (0.1)\left(150\,\vec{i}\right) + (2)(0) = (0.1)\left(100\,\vec{i}\right) + 2\,\vec{v}$$
$$\therefore 15\,\vec{i} = 10\,\vec{i} + 2\,\vec{v}$$
$$\therefore \vec{v} = 2.5\,\vec{i}\ \text{m/s}$$
$$\text{The speed} = |\vec{v}| = 2.5\ \text{m/s}.$$

The impulse imparted to the block = its change in momentum.

$$\therefore \vec{I} = m\,\vec{v} - m\,\vec{u}$$
$$= 2\left(2.5\,\vec{i}\right) - 2\left(\vec{0}\right)$$
$$= 5\,\vec{i}\ \text{N s}$$

The impulse imparted to the bullet is given by

$$\vec{I} = m\,\vec{v} - m\,\vec{u}$$
$$= (0.1)\left(100\,\vec{i}\right) - (0.1)\left(150\,\vec{i}\right)$$
$$= 10\,\vec{i} - 15\,\vec{i}$$
$$= -5\,\vec{i}\ \text{N s}$$

In what way is Newton's third law shown to hold true in this example?

## Exercise 6 C

1. A golfball of mass 0.125 kg leaves the tee at 40 m/s in a horizontal direction. Find the impulse imparted to it.

2. A hurling ball of mass $\frac{1}{4}$ kg comes towards a player at 40 m/s in a horizontal direction. The player hits it so that it leaves his hurley at 20 m/s in the opposite direction. Find the magnitude of the impulse imparted to the ball by the hurley.

3. A hammer of mass 4 kg is used to drive a 1 kg wooden stake into the ground. The hammer, immediately before impact, has a downward velocity of 2 m/s. Find the speed of the stake immediately after impact, when the hammer has come to rest.

   Find, also, the impulse imparted to

   (i) the stake

   (ii) the hammer.

4. A snowball of mass 0.1 kg is thrown at a wall at a speed of 8 m/s. The snowball comes to rest at the wall. Find the magnitude of the impulse imparted to the wall, assuming that it is equal and opposite to the impulse imparted to the snowball.

5. 2 kg of water is fired at a speed of 5 m/s against a wall. The water does not rebound at all, but comes to rest at the wall. Find the magnitude of the impulse imparted to the wall.

6. (i) A train consists of four carriages and is travelling at 12 m/s when it picks up a fifth carriage. Assuming each carriage has the same mass, find the new speed of the train.

   (ii) A train has five carriages and is travelling at 12 m/s when it picks up $n$ more carriages. Assuming each carriage has the same mass, and given that the new speed of the train is 7.5 m/s, find the value of $n$.

7. A bullet of mass 0.15 kg is fired horizontally with speed 200 m/s into a stationary block of wood. The block is of mass 3 kg and rests on a smooth horizontal surface. If the bullet emerges from the block with speed 100 m/s, find the speed of the block.

8. A bullet of mass 0.1 kg is fired at 400 m/s in a horizontal line. It strikes a stationary wooden target. The wooden target is of mass 3 kg and is on a smooth horizontal surface. If the bullet becomes embedded in the wood, find the speed of the compound body after impact.

9. A bullet of mass 0.1 kg is fired horizontally at 200 m/s. It immediately enters a block of wood which is at rest, and becomes embedded. If the velocity of the joint mass is then 10 m/s, find the mass of the block of wood.

10. A bullet of mass 50 grams is fired into a block of wood which is at rest. The bullet becomes embedded in the wood, whose mass is 1.45 kg. The velocity of the joint mass immediately after impact is 4 m/s.
    Find the original speed of the bullet.

11. A bullet of mass 0.1 kg is fired horizontally into a block of mass 2.9 kg, which hangs at the end of a light 20 m string. The bullet becomes embedded and the joint mass swings, finally coming to rest when the string makes an angle of 60° with the vertical.

    With what speed did the bullet enter the block?

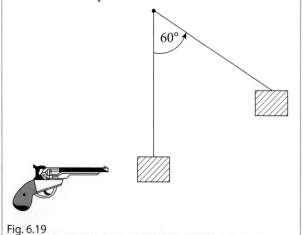

Fig. 6.19

## The Principle of Conservation of Momentum and strings

The Principle of Conservation of Momentum may be applied to bodies at the ends of a piece of string. We must regard the string-particle system as one body, like a long train going round a corner.

### Example 6.11

Two particles of masses 4 kg and 3 kg hand from a pulley at the ends of a light inextensible string. The system is released from rest. After 2 seconds, the 3 kg mass picks up a particle of mass 2 kg. How much further will the 4 kg mass move downward before it stops?

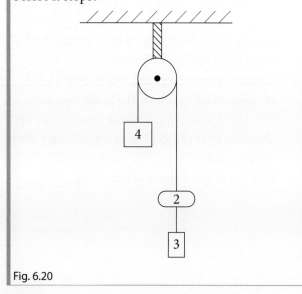

Fig. 6.20

## Solution

Let $a$ = the common acceleration of the particles during the first 2 seconds.

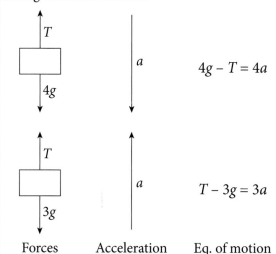

| Forces | Acceleration | Eq. of motion |

Fig. 6.21

Solve:
$$4g - T = 4a$$
$$T - 3g = 3a$$

Adding these gives $g = 7a$

$$\therefore a = \frac{1}{7}g$$

After 2 seconds the speed of each particle will be given by

$$v = u + at$$
$$= 0 + \left(\frac{1}{7}g\right)2$$
$$= \frac{2}{7}g \text{ m/s}$$

At this point the 3 kg mass picks up a 2 kg mass, to become a new mass of 5 kg. The system will immediately be jolted to a slower speed. This speed can be found by applying the Principle of Conservation to the particle-string system. The mass of this whole system was 7 kg before the jolt and 9 kg after the jolt. Let $v$ be the new speed.

**Principle of Conservation of Momentum:**

$$m_1 u = m_2 v$$
$$\therefore 7\left(\frac{2}{7}g\right) = 9v$$
$$\therefore 2g = 9v$$
$$\therefore v = \frac{2}{9}g \text{ m/s}$$

Let $b$ = the new common acceleration of the particles. We will continue to take *up* as the positive direction of the 5 kg mass and *down* as the positive direction for the 4 kg mass.

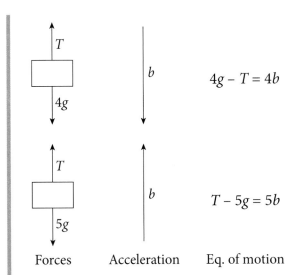

Forces     Acceleration     Eq. of motion

Fig. 6.22

$$4\,g - T = 4\,b$$
$$\underline{T - 5\,g = 5\,b}$$

Adding these gives $- g = 9\,b$

$$\therefore b = -\frac{1}{9}g$$

The fact that $b$ is negative is not surprising, as we would expect them to slow down. Their accelerations are in the opposite directions to their velocities.

Take the 4 kg mass, after the jolt:

We know
$$a = -\frac{1}{9}g$$
$$v = 0$$
$$s = s$$

Using $v^2 = u^2 + 2\,a\,s$

$$\therefore 0^2 = \left(\frac{2}{9}\,g\right)^2 + 2\left(-\frac{1}{9}g\right)s$$

$$\therefore 0 = \frac{4}{81}g^2 - \frac{2}{9}g\,s$$

$$\therefore \frac{2}{9}g\,s = \frac{4}{81}g^2$$

Answer: $s = \frac{2}{9}\,g$ metres

## Exercise 6 D

1. Two particles of masses 5 kg and 1 kg hang from a smooth pulley at the ends of a light inextensible string. The system is released from rest. After 1 second, the 1 kg mass picks up a particle of mass 2 kg.
   (i) What distance will the 5 kg particle fall in the first second?
   (ii) What distance will the 5 kg particle fall in the 2nd second?

2. Two particles of masses 5 kg and 2 kg hang from a smooth pulley at the ends of a light inextensible string. The system is released from rest. After 3 seconds, the 2 kg mass picks up a particle of mass 4 kg.
   How much further will the 5 kg mass move downward before it stops instantaneously?

3. Two particles of masses 10 kg and 3 kg hang from a smooth pulley at the ends of a light inextensible string. The system is released from rest. After 2 seconds, the 3 kg mass picks up a particle of mass 2 kg.
   (i) What distance will the 10 kg particle fall in the first 2-second period?
   (ii) What distance will the 10 kg particle fall in the next 2-second period?

4. Two masses of 5 kg and 1 kg hang from a smooth pulley at the ends of a light inextensible string. The system is released from rest. After 2 seconds, the 5 kg mass hits a horizontal table.
   (i) How much further will the 1 kg mass rise?
   (ii) The 1 kg mass then falls and the 5 kg mass is jolted off the table. With what speed will the 5 kg mass begin to rise?

5. Two masses of 6 kg and 2 kg are connected by a light inextensible string passing over a small smooth pulley. The 6 kg mass is at rest on a horizontal table. A third mass of 2 kg is let fall from a height of 1 metre. It then strikes the second mass of 2 kg and sticks on to it. Show that the 6 kg mass will rise to a height of 20 cm above the table.

6. Two particles of masses 1 kg and 2 kg are tied to the ends of a string 6 m long. The string passes over a smooth small peg. The peg is 3.5 metres above a horizontal table. The 2 kg mass rests on the table. The 1 kg mass is held next to the peg and released from rest. It falls 2.5 m before the string becomes taut.
   (i) Show that the 2 kg mass rises from the table with initial speed $\frac{7}{3}$ m/s.
   (ii) Investigate if the 1 kg mass will reach the table.

## Summary of important points

1. Work = $Fs$ (joules).

2. Power = rate of work = $Tv$ (watts).

3. Potential energy = $mgh$.

4. Kinetic energy = $\frac{1}{2} m v^2$

5. Principle of Conservation of Energy:
   If the only forces which do work on a body are gravitational forces, then
   $$mgh + \frac{1}{2} m v^2 = \text{constant}.$$

6. Principle of Conservation of Momentum:
   When two objects collide,
   $$m_1 u_1 + m_2 u_2 = m_1 v_1 + m_2 v_2$$

## DOs and DON'Ts for the exam

### DO

- Do remember the units for force (newtons), work (joules), energy (joules) and power (watts)
- Do remember that the Conservation of Momentum applies when two particles collide
- Do remember that the Conservation of Energy applies when the only forces which do work are gravitational forces

### DON'T

- Don't mix up conservation of energy and momentum
- Don't confuse force and power

## *Joule*

James Prescott Joule (1818–1889) was from Salford near Manchester where his family were wealthy brewers. He was educated at home with his brother Benjamin. Joule was fascinated by electricity. He and his brother experimented by giving electric shocks to each other and to the family's servants.

Joule became interested in the mechanical equivalent of heat. He designed clever experiments to measure the amount of mechanical energy needed to raise the temperature of water. His discoveries were not immediately accepted, perhaps because he was perceived as a brewer rather than a scholar. For example, when he gave a paper to the British Association for the Advancement of Science in Cork in 1843, his talk was 'met by silence'.

In 1847 Joule married Amelia Grimes and the couple went on honeymoon near Mont Blanc in France. While on this holiday, Joule met up with fellow physicist, Irishman William Thomson (the 1st Baron Kelvin, who gave his name to the Kelvin scale of temperature). The newlyweds arranged with Thomson to attempt an experiment a few days later. They planned to measure the difference in temperature at the top and bottom of the Cascade de Sallaches waterfall. The water at the bottom should be hotter, because the potential energy would be converted into heat. The experiment proved impractical, because too much of the cascading water was lost in spray.

Joule's work was gradually accepted. It helped to produce the discovery of the Principle of Conservation of Energy. The SI unit of energy is called the 'joule' in his honour.

# Impacts and collisions

"I do not know what I may appear to the world; but to myself I seem to have been only like a boy playing on the seashore and diverting myself in now and then finding a smoother pebble or a prettier shell than ordinary, whilst the great ocean of truth lay all undiscovered before me."

*Isaac Newton*

## Contents

## Learning outcomes

**In this chapter you will learn...**

- The meaning of coefficient of restitution

- How to solve problems of spheres impacting on a wall or floor

- Newton's Law of Restitution

- Solving problems of direct collisions of spheres

- Solving problems of oblique collisions of spheres

## You will need to know...

- Simultaneous equations
- Kinetic energy
- Principle of Conservation of Momentum

## Impacts

A ball hits the ground, when falling vertically with speed 20 m/s. It rebounds with speed 15 m/s. The ball has kept $\frac{3}{4}$ of its previous speed. We say that the **coefficient of restitution**, e, between the ball and the ground is $\frac{3}{4}$.

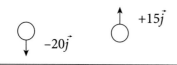

Fig. 7.1

If the same ball hit the same ground as it fell at a speed of 16 m/s, it would rebound with speed $\frac{3}{4}$ of 16, i.e. 12 m/s.

More exactly, the ball's velocity before impact was $-16\,\vec{j}$ m/s. The velocity after impact is $+12\,\vec{j}$ m/s.

The ratio $\quad \dfrac{12}{-16} = -\dfrac{3}{4} = -e$

In general, if a ball moves with speed $u\,\vec{j}$ m/s before impact and $v\,\vec{j}$ m/s after impact, then

$$\frac{\text{New Velocity}}{\text{Old Velocity}} = \frac{v}{u} = -e$$

If a collision is perfectly elastic, then $e = 1$. If it is perfectly inelastic, then $e = 0$. Always, $0 \le e \le 1$.

### Worked Example 7.1

A football of mass 2 kg is falling vertically towards horizontal ground. Immediately before impact its velocity is $-12\,\vec{j}$ m/s. If the coefficient of restitution, e, is $\frac{2}{3}$, find

(i) the velocity of the ball immediately after impact,

(ii) the impulse imparted to the ball by the impact,

(iii) the football's loss of kinetic energy.

**Solution:**

(i)

| Before | Mass | After |
|--------|------|-------|
| $-12\,\vec{j}$ | 2 kg | $p\vec{j}$ |

$$\frac{\text{New}}{\text{Old}} = -e$$

$$\Rightarrow \frac{p}{-12} = -e$$

$$\Rightarrow \frac{p}{-12} = -\frac{2}{3}$$

$$\Rightarrow p = 8$$

Therefore, the new velocity is $+8\,\vec{j}$ m/s.

(ii)
$$\vec{I} = m\,\vec{v} - m\,\vec{u}$$
$$= (2)\left(8\vec{j}\right) - (2)\left(-12\vec{j}\right)$$
$$= 16\,\vec{j} + 24\,\vec{j}$$
$$= 40\,\vec{j}\ \text{N s}$$

(iii) $\text{K.E.}_{before}$
$$= \tfrac{1}{2}\,m\,u^2$$
$$= \tfrac{1}{2}\,(2)\,(144)$$
$$= 144\ \text{joules}$$

$\text{K.E.}_{after}$
$$= \tfrac{1}{2}\,m\,v^2$$
$$= \tfrac{1}{2}\,(2)\,(64)$$
$$= 64\ \text{J}$$

Therefore, the loss in K.E.
$$= 144 - 64$$
$$= 80\ \text{J}$$

### Worked Example 7.2

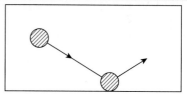

Fig. 7.2

A smooth snooker ball of mass 0.5 kg moves across a snooker table with velocity $6\vec{i} - 5\vec{j}$ m/s. It hits a smooth horizontal cushion and rebounds. The coefficient of restitution is $\frac{4}{5}$. Find

(i) the velocity of the ball after impact

(ii) the impulse imparted to the ball by the impact

(iii) the loss in kinetic energy.

**Solution:**

(i) Since the cushion hits the ball along the $\vec{j}$-direction only, the $\vec{i}$-component of the ball's velocity is unchanged by the impact. We will let the velocity of the ball after impact be $6\vec{i} + p\vec{j}$.

| Before | Mass | After |
|--------|------|-------|
| $6\,\vec{i} - 5\,\vec{j}$ | 0.5 kg | $6\vec{i} + p\,\vec{j}$ |

Again, the "bouncing" takes place along the $\vec{j}$-direction only. So, we ignore the $\vec{i}$-components of the velocities.

$$\frac{\text{New}}{\text{Old}} = -e$$

$$\Rightarrow \frac{p}{-5} = -\frac{4}{5}$$
$$\Rightarrow p = 4$$

The new velocity is $6\vec{i} + 4\vec{j}$ m/s.

(ii)
$$\vec{I} = m\vec{v} - m\vec{u}$$
$$= (0.5)\left(6\vec{i} + 4\vec{j}\right) - (0.5)\left(6\vec{i} - 5\vec{j}\right)$$
$$= 3\vec{i} + 2\vec{j} - 3\vec{i} + 2.5\vec{j}$$
$$= 4.5\vec{j} \text{ N s}$$

(iii) Initial velocity $\vec{u} = 6\vec{i} - 5\vec{j}$.
$$\therefore |\vec{u}| = \sqrt{36 + 25}$$
$$= \sqrt{61}$$
$$\therefore u^2 = 61$$

Final velocity $\vec{v} = 6\vec{i} - 4\vec{j}$
$$\therefore |\vec{v}| = \sqrt{36 + 16}$$
$$= \sqrt{52}$$
$$\therefore v^2 = 52$$

$$\text{K.E.}_{before} = \frac{1}{2}mu^2 = \frac{1}{2}(0.5)(61) = 15.25 \text{ J}$$
$$\text{K.E.}_{after} = \frac{1}{2}mv^2 = \frac{1}{2}(0.5)(52) = 13 \text{ J}$$

The loss in K.E. $= 15.25 - 13 = 2.25$ joules.

## Worked Example 7.3

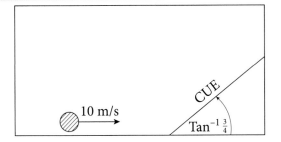

Fig. 7.3

A smooth snooker ball of mass 2 kg moves along one side of a snooker table at 10 m/s. Someone has left a cue on the table, as shown, making an angle $\text{Tan}^{-1}\left(\frac{3}{4}\right)$ with the line of motion of the ball. The coefficient of restitution between the ball and the cue is $\frac{1}{2}$. Find

(i) the speed of the ball after impact
(ii) the loss in kinetic energy
(iii) the magnitude of the impulse imparted to the ball by the impact.

### Solution:

(i) We make the line of the cue our $x$-axis. The picture now looks like this:

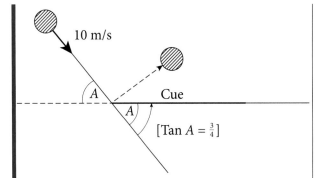

10 m/s

Cue

$A$    Cue

$A$

$[\text{Tan } A = \frac{3}{4}]$

Fig. 7.4

Since $\text{Tan } A = \frac{3}{4}$, $\text{Sin } A = \frac{3}{5}$ and $\text{Cos } A = \frac{4}{5}$

Therefore, the velocity of the ball before impact is given by

$$= 10 \text{ Cos } A \, \vec{i} - 10 \text{ Sin } A \, \vec{j}$$
$$= 10\left(\frac{4}{5}\right)\vec{i} - 10\left(\frac{3}{5}\right)\vec{j}$$
$$= 8\vec{i} - 6\vec{j} \text{ m/s}$$

| Before | Mass | After |
|--------|------|-------|
| $8\vec{i} - 6\vec{j}$ | 2 kg | $8\vec{i} + p\vec{j}$ |

Note: the "bounce" takes place along the $\vec{j}$-direction only, so the $\vec{i}$-velocity remains unchanged by the impact. We really ignore the $\vec{i}$-velocity.

$$\frac{\text{New}}{\text{Old}} = -e$$
$$\Rightarrow \left(\frac{p}{-6}\right) = -\left(\frac{1}{2}\right)$$
$$\Rightarrow p = 3$$

Therefore, the new velocity is $8\vec{i} + 3\vec{j}$ m/s, and the new speed $= \sqrt{64 + 9} = \sqrt{73}$ m/s.

(ii) Loss of Kinetic Energy
$$\text{K.E.}_{before} = \frac{1}{2}mu^2$$
$$= \frac{1}{2}(2)(8^2 + 6^2)$$
$$= 100 \text{ J}$$
$$\text{K.E.}_{after} = \frac{1}{2}mv^2$$
$$= \frac{1}{2}(2)(8^2 + 3^2)$$
$$= 73 \text{ J}$$

Therefore, loss in K.E.
$$= 100 - 73 = 27 \text{ joules.}$$

(iii) Impulse
$$\vec{I} = m\vec{v} - m\vec{u}$$
$$= (2)\left(8\vec{i} + 3\vec{j}\right) - (2)\left(8\vec{i} - 6\vec{j}\right)$$
$$= 16\vec{i} + 6\vec{j} - 16\vec{i} + 12\vec{j}$$
$$= 18\vec{j} \text{ N s}$$

The magnitude of the impulse is 18 N s.

**Exercise 7 A**

1. A ball of mass 2 kg falls vertically onto horizontal ground. Before impact its velocity is $-10\vec{j}$ m/s. If the coefficient of restitution $e$ is $\frac{3}{5}$ find
   (i) its velocity immediately after impact
   (ii) the impulse imparted to the ball
   (iii) the loss in kinetic energy.

2. A tennis ball of mass 0.2 kg falls vertically with speed 20 m/s. The coefficient of restitution is 0.5. Find
   (i) its speed immediately after impact
   (ii) the magnitude of the impulse due to the impact
   (iii) the loss in kinetic energy of the ball.

3. A ball of mass 1 kg is dropped from rest at a height 2.5 m above horizontal ground. If the coefficient of restitution is $\frac{4}{7}$, find
   (i) its speed just before impact
   (ii) its speed just after impact
   (iii) the impulse imparted to the ball
   (iv) the loss in kinetic energy.

4. A shot-putt of mass 6 kg falls to the ground from a height of 10 m. The coefficient of restitution is zero (i.e. the impact is perfectly inelastic, and the ball sticks to the ground). Find
   (i) the speed of the ball just before impact
   (ii) the impulse imparted to the ball
   (iii) the loss in kinetic energy.

5. A ball of mass 0.1 kg is dropped from rest at a height 22.5 m above horizontal ground. If the coefficient of restitution is $\frac{5}{7}$, find
   (i) its speed just before impact
   (ii) its speed just after impact
   (iii) the impulse imparted to the ball
   (iv) the loss in kinetic energy.

6. A ball of mass 2 kg is moving with velocity $5\vec{i} - 8\vec{j}$ when it hits a smooth barrier along the $\vec{i}$-axis. The coefficient of restitution is $\frac{3}{4}$. Find
   (i) the new velocity of the ball
   (ii) the loss in kinetic energy
   (iii) the impulse imparted to the ball by the impact.

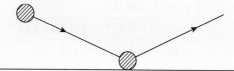

Fig. 7.5

7. A ball of mass 0.2 kg is moving with velocity $8\vec{i} - 15\vec{j}$ when it hits a smooth barrier along the $\vec{i}$-axis. The coefficient of restitution is $\frac{2}{5}$.
   (i) Find the new velocity of the ball.
   (ii) Show that the speed of the ball falls by 7 m/s on impact.
   (iii) Find the loss in kinetic energy.

8. A sphere of mass 4 kg hits a smooth barrier along the $\vec{i}$-axis. Before impact, its velocity was $8\vec{i} - 6\vec{j}$ m/s; after impact it is $8\vec{i} + 4\vec{j}$ m/s. Find
   (i) the coefficient of restitution
   (ii) the percentage loss in kinetic energy
   (iii) the ratio $\frac{\tan B}{\tan A}$, where $A$ and $B$ are the acute angles which the line of motion make with the $\vec{i}$-axis before and after impact, respectively.

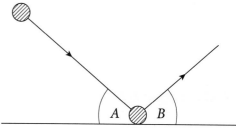

Fig. 7.6

9. A sphere of mass 0.2 kg hits a smooth barrier along the $\vec{j}$-axis. Before impact, its velocity was $4\vec{i} + 3\vec{j}$ m/s. The coefficient of restitution is 0.75. Find
   (i) the velocity after impact
   (ii) the percentage loss in kinetic energy.

10. A ball of mass 1 kg falls from a height of 40 m onto horizontal ground. The coefficient of restitution is $\frac{1}{2}$. Find
    (i) its speed on hitting the ground
    (ii) the speed with which it first rises from the ground
    (iii) the height it reaches after the first bounce

11. A ball of mass $m$ falls from a height of $h$ metres onto horizontal ground. The coefficient of restitution is $e$. Find (in terms of $g$, $h$ and $e$)
    (i) its speed on hitting the ground
    (ii) the speed with which it first rises from the ground
    (iii) the height it reaches after the first bounce.

12. A ball of mass $m$ moves with speed $u$ at an angle $A$ to the horizontal until it hits a smooth horizontal barrier. After impact, it moves with speed $v$ at an angle $B$ to the horizontal. Show that the coefficient of restitution, $e$, is given by

$$e = \frac{\tan B}{\tan A}$$

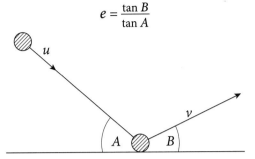

Fig. 7.7

13. A ball of mass $m$ moves horizontally with speed 20 m/s towards a smooth barrier $xy$ which makes an angle $\text{Tan}^{-1}\left(\frac{4}{3}\right)$ with the horizontal. The coefficient of restitution is $\frac{3}{4}$. Find

    (i)   the speed of the ball after impact

    (ii)  the magnitude of the impulse due to the impact

    (iii) the loss in kinetic energy

    (iv)  the tan of the angle between the ball's new path and the horizontal.

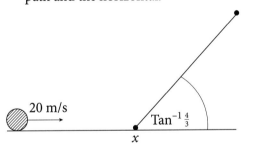

Fig. 7.8

14. A ball of mass 0.1 moves horizontally with speed 25 m/s towards a smooth barrier $xy$ which makes an angle $\tan^{-1}\left(\frac{7}{24}\right)$ with the horizontal.
    The coefficient of restitution is $\frac{3}{7}$. Find

    (i)   the speed of the ball after impact, correct to one decimal place

    (ii)  the magnitude of the impulse due to the impact

    (iii) the loss in kinetic energy, to the nearest joule.

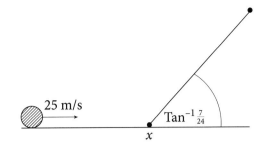

Fig. 7.9

15. A smooth metal sphere falls vertically and strikes a fixed smooth plane inclined at an angle of $\theta$ to the horizontal. If the coefficient of restitution is $\frac{2}{3}$ and the sphere rebounds horizontally, calculate the fraction of kinetic energy lost during impact.

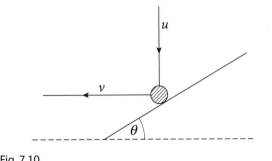

Fig. 7.10

## Direct collisions

Two smooth spheres have velocities of $10\,\vec{i}$ m/s and $2\,\vec{i}$ m/s before they collide. After the collision, their velocities are $3\,\vec{i}$ m/s and $9\,\vec{i}$ m/s respectively. What is the coefficient of restitution in this case?

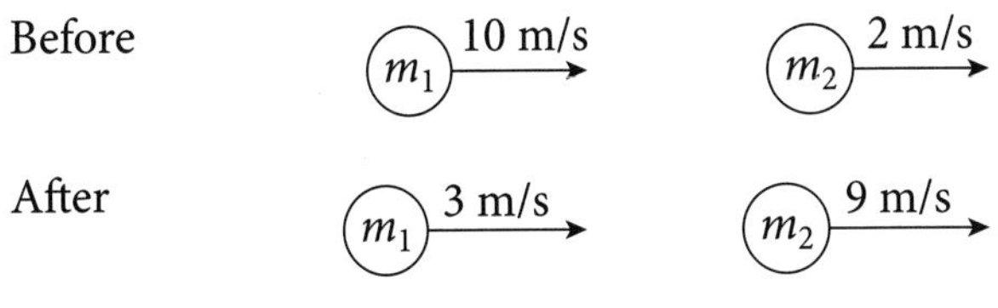

Before (m₁) 10 m/s → (m₂) 2 m/s →

After (m₁) 3 m/s → (m₂) 9 m/s →

Fig. 7.11

We know that $\left(\frac{\text{New}}{\text{Old}}\right) = -e$, but in this case we have two new velocities and two old ones. How can we evaluate $e$?

Imagine that you are a tiny bug living on the second sphere. You cannot feel that your "planet" is moving any more than a human living on the earth can. What do you see? You see another planet approaching yours—but with what velocity?

The answer is with the relative velocity of $+8\vec{i}$ m/s

(since $\vec{V}_{ab} = \vec{V}_a - \vec{V}_b = 10\vec{i} - 2\vec{i} = 8\vec{i}$ m/s)

After the impact you see the other planet moving away with velocity $-6\vec{i}$ since
$$\vec{V}_{ab} = \vec{V}_a - \vec{V}_b$$
$$= 3\vec{i} - 9\vec{i}$$
$$= -6\vec{i} \text{ m/s}$$

So, you saw a ball coming down onto your planet with velocity $+8\vec{i}$ m/s, then bouncing and then moving off with velocity $-6\vec{i}$ m/s.

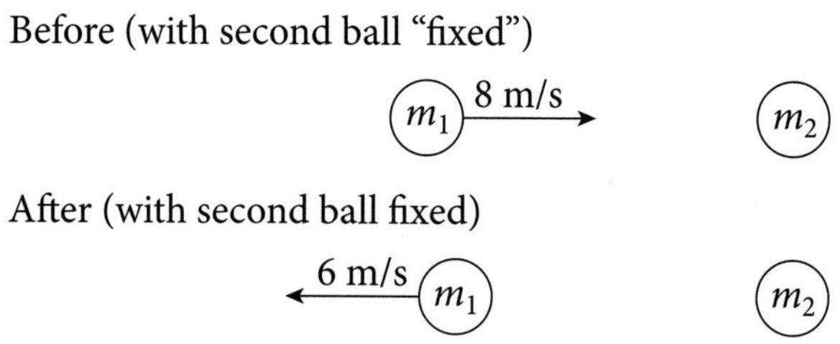

Before (with second ball "fixed")

$(m_1)\xrightarrow{8 \text{ m/s}}$ $(m_2)$

After (with second ball fixed)

$\xleftarrow{6 \text{ m/s}}(m_1)$ $(m_2)$

Fig. 7.12

$$\frac{\text{New}}{\text{Old}} = -e$$
$$\frac{-6}{8} = -e$$
$$\therefore \quad e = \frac{3}{4}$$

In general, if the balls have velocities $u_1\vec{i}, u_2\vec{i}$ before impact and $v_1\vec{i}, v_2\vec{i}$ after impact, then
$$\frac{v_1 - v_2}{u_1 - u_2} = -e$$

This result is called Newton's law of restitution. Here it is in plain language.

**Newton's law of restitution** : For two bodies impinging directly, their relative velocity after impact is equal to a constant ($e$) times their relative velocity before impact and in the opposite direction.

Secondly, since no external forces act on the system, the **Principle of Conservation of Momentum** applies. That is (if the masses of these two balls are $m_1$ and $m_2$ respectively) then
$$m_1u_1 + m_2u_2 = m_1v_1 + m_2v_2$$

**Summary**

The two equations which enable us to solve problems of direct collisions are:
$$\frac{v_1 - v_2}{u_1 - u_2} = -e$$
$$m_1u_1 + m_2u_2 = m_1v_1 + m_2v_2$$

**Worked Example 7.4**

A smooth snooker ball of mass 2 kg moving with velocity $10\vec{i}$ m/s collides directly with another ball of mass 3 kg which is moving with velocity $1\vec{i}$ m/s. The coefficient of restitution between the balls is $\frac{2}{3}$. Find

(i) the velocity of each ball after impact

(ii) the impulse imparted to each ball by the impact

(iii) the total loss of kinetic energy in the system.

**Solution:**

(i) We will let $p\vec{i}$ and $q\vec{i}$ be the velocities of the balls after impact.

| Before | Mass | After |
|---|---|---|
| $10\vec{i}$ | 2 kg | $p\vec{i}$ |
| $\vec{i}$ | 3 kg | $q\vec{i}$ |

**Conservation of Momentum**
$$m_1u_1 + m_2u_2 = m_1v_1 + m_2v_2$$
$$\therefore (2)(10) + (3)(1) = 2p+3q$$
$$\therefore 2p + 3q = 23 \qquad \text{Equation 1}$$

**Newton's Law of Restitution**
$$\frac{v_1 - v_2}{u_1 - u_2} = -e$$
$$\therefore \frac{p - q}{10 - 1} = -\frac{2}{3}$$
$$\therefore 3p - 3q = -18 \qquad \text{Equation 2}$$

Adding the simultaneous equations 1 and 2 gives $5p = 5$ which gives $p = 1$ and $q = 7$. Therefore the new velocities are $1\vec{i}$ and $7\vec{i}$ m/s respectively.

(ii) The impulse imparted to the first ball, $\vec{I}_1$ is given by
$$\vec{I}_1 = m_1\vec{v}_1 - m_1\vec{u}_1$$
$$= 2(1\vec{i}) - 2(10\vec{i})$$
$$= -18\vec{i} \text{ N s}$$

The impulse imparted to the second ball, $\vec{I}_2$ is given by

$$\vec{I}_2 = m_2\vec{v}_2 - m_2\vec{u}_2$$
$$= 3\left(7\vec{i}\right) - 3\left(1\vec{i}\right)$$
$$= +18\vec{i} \text{ N s}$$

We see that $\vec{I}_1$ and $\vec{I}_2$ are equal and opposite, as expected.

(iii)  Total .K.E.$_{before}$

$$= \frac{1}{2}m_1u_1^2 + \frac{1}{2}m_2u_2^2$$
$$= \frac{1}{2}(2)(100) + \frac{1}{2}(3)(1)$$
$$= 101\frac{1}{2} \text{ J}$$

Total K.E.$_{after}$

$$= \frac{1}{2}m_1v_1^2 + \frac{1}{2}m_2v_2^2$$
$$= \frac{1}{2}(2)(1) + \frac{1}{2}(3)(49)$$
$$= 74\frac{1}{2} \text{ J}$$

Therefore, the loss in K.E

$$= 101\frac{1}{2} - 74\frac{1}{2}$$
$$= 27 \text{ joules.}$$

## Worked Example 7.5

Two smooth spheres of masses $m$ and $3m$ have speeds $7u$ and $2u$ in opposite directions. They collide directly. The smaller mass is brought to rest by the collision. Find $e$, the coefficient of restitution.

**Solution:**

Before:

After:

Fig. 7.13

| Before | Mass | After |
|--------|------|-------|
| $7\,u\vec{i}$ | $m$ | $0\vec{i}$ |
| $-2\,u\vec{i}$ | $3m$ | $q\vec{i}$ |

1.     $m_1u_1 + m_2u_2 = m_1v_1 + m_2v_2$

$\therefore$   $m(7u) + 3m(-2u) = m(0) + 3m(q)$

$\therefore mu = 3mq$

$\therefore q = \frac{1}{3}u$

2.     $\dfrac{v_1 - v_2}{u_1 - u_2} = -e$

$\therefore \dfrac{0 - q}{7u + 2u} = -e$

$\therefore e = \dfrac{q}{9u}$

But      $q = \frac{1}{3}u,$

$\therefore e = \dfrac{\left(\frac{1}{3}u\right)}{9u}$

$= \dfrac{1}{27} : \text{Answer}$

## Exercise 7 B

1.  A smooth sphere of mass 2 kg collides directly with a smooth sphere of mass 1 kg. Their velocities before impact are $6\vec{i}$ and $4\vec{i}$, respectively. The coefficient of restitution is $\frac{1}{2}$. Find
    (i)   their velocities after impact
    (ii)  the total loss in kinetic energy.

2.  Two equal spheres, each of mass 1 kg, are travelling in opposite directions with speeds 2 m/s and 6 m/s when they collide directly. The coefficient of restitution is $\frac{3}{4}$. Find
    (i)    their speeds after impact
    (ii)   the magnitude of the impulse imparted to each sphere
    (iii)  the percentage loss in kinetic energy.

3.  A smooth sphere of mass 3 kg collides directly with a smooth sphere of mass 5 kg. Their velocities before impact were $10\vec{i}$ and $\vec{i}$ respectively. If the lesser mass is brought to rest by the impact, find
    (i)    the coefficient of restitution between the spheres
    (ii)   the velocity of the greater mass after the collision
    (iii)  the impulse imparted to each of the spheres.
    (iv)   If, after impact, the greater mass moves another 2 metres, find its deceleration.

4. Two smooth spheres $A$ and $B$ lie at rest on a smooth horizontal table. The sphere $A$ has mass 2 kg ; sphere $B$ has mass 1 kg. Sphere $A$ is projected towards $B$ with speed 5 m/s. They collide directly. After the impact $A$ moves with speed $v$ m/s and $B$ with speed $3v$ m/s.
   (i) Find the value of $v$.
   (ii) Find the coefficient of restitution between the two spheres.
   (iii) Find the percentage loss in kinetic energy due to the collision.

5. Two elastic spheres of mass 5 kg and 3 kg, travelling in opposite directions, collide directly. The speeds before collision are 6 m/s and 4 m/s respectively. If the coefficient of restitution between the spheres is $\frac{1}{3}$, calculate
   (i) the speed of each sphere after the collision
   (ii) the loss in kinetic energy due to the collision suffered by the 5 kg sphere
   (iii) the change in momentum of the 3 kg sphere.

6. A sphere $A$ of mass 2 kg moving at 10 m/s collides directly with a stationary sphere $B$ of mass 3 kg. The coefficient of restitution between the spheres is $\frac{1}{2}$.
   Calculate
   (i) the speed of each sphere after the collision
   (ii) the loss in kinetic energy due to the collision
   (iii) the power exerted by an agent which brings sphere $B$ to rest again after 2 seconds.

7. $A$, $B$ and $C$ are three equal spheres at rest in a straight line. $A$ is set in motion directly towards $B$ with speed 4 m/s. The coefficient of restitution between the spheres is $\frac{1}{2}$. Find the speed of $B$
   (i) after colliding with $A$
   (ii) after colliding with $C$.
   Will there be any more collisions? Justify your answer.

8. Two smooth spheres $A$ and $B$ lie on a smooth horizontal table. The sphere $A$ has mass 4 kg; sphere $B$ has mass 2 kg. The two spheres are projected towards each other with the same speed $v$. The coefficient of restitution is $e$. After the impact $A$ comes to rest.

   (i) Show that the speed of $B$ after the impact is the same as it was before impact.
   (ii) Find the value of $e$.
   (iii) Find the percentage loss in kinetic energy due to the collision.

9. Two smooth spheres, of equal mass, collide directly while moving with velocities $2\vec{i}$ and $\vec{i}$ m/s. After the collision they move in the same direction and the ratio of their speeds is 11:13. Find
   (i) their velocities after collision
   (ii) the coefficient of restitution.

10. Three equal spheres, $A$, $B$ and $C$, lie at rest in a straight line. $A$ is propelled towards $B$ with speed 6 m/s. If the coefficient of restitution between the spheres is $\frac{2}{3}$, find their speeds
    (i) after one collision
    (ii) after two collisions
    (iii) after three collisions.
    Why are there no further collisions?

11. A smooth sphere of mass 10 kg moving at 10 m/s impinges directly on another smooth sphere of mass 50 kg moving in the opposite direction at 5 m/s. If the coefficient of restitution is $\frac{1}{2}$, calculate the speeds after impact and the magnitude of the impulse during impact.

Fig. 7.14

12. (a) State
    (i) Newton's Law of Restitution (for direct collisions);
    (ii) the Law of Conservation of Momentum.
    (b) An elastic sphere, initially at rest 19.6 m above the ground, falls and bounces off the ground. If the coefficient of restitution is 0.8, find the greatest height attained after the first bounce.
    (c) A gun, of mass 2 kg, fires a bullet of mass 10 $g$ with a muzzle velocity of 300 m/s. Find the velocity of the recoil of the gun and the constant force required to stop the recoil in a distance of 50 mm.

13. Two smooth spheres of masses $m$ and $3m$ move with speeds $u$ and $v$ in opposite directions. The smaller mass is brought to rest.

    (i) Show that the coefficient of restitution, $e$, is given by
    $$e = \frac{u - 3v}{3u + 3v}$$

    (ii) Show that $u \geq 3v$.

14. Three spheres of mass 1 kg, 2 kg and 3 kg move in the same line with velocities $5\vec{i}$, $\vec{i}$ and $3\vec{i}$ respectively. The smaller masses are the first to collide. If only one collision takes place, find the maximum value for the coefficient of restitution between the smaller masses.

15. A smooth sphere of mass 3 kg and velocity $u_1$ collides directly with another smooth sphere of mass 4 kg and velocity $u_2$ both moving in the same direction. Show that

    $$7v_1 = u_1(3 - 4e) + 4u_2(1 + e)$$

    where $v_1$ is the velocity of the 3 kg sphere after the collision. Hence show that the impulse which each sphere receives is

    $$\frac{12}{7}(1 + e)(u_2 - u_1)$$

16. A smooth sphere $P$ of mass $3m$ and velocity $4u$ impinges directly on a smooth sphere $Q$ of mass $5m$ and velocity $2u$, moving in the same direction. The coefficient of restitution is $e$.

    (i) For what value of $e$ will the velocity of $P$ be halved by the impact?

    (ii) Show that whatever the value of $e$ in $0 \leq e \leq 1$, the velocity of $Q$ after impact will be at least $2.75u$.

17. A sphere of mass $4m$ travelling with speed $u$, strikes directly a stationary sphere of mass $2m$. The coefficient of restitution is $e$. Prove that

    (i) the speeds of the spheres after impact are $\frac{u}{3}(2 - e)$ and $\frac{2u}{3}(1 + e)$

    (ii) the loss in kinetic energy is $\frac{2mu^2}{3}(1 - e^2)$.

18. A small smooth sphere moves on a horizontal floor with speed $2u$. It strikes an identical sphere lying at rest on the floor, at a distance 1 metre from the vertical wall, the impact being along the line of centres and perpendicular to the wall. The coefficient of restitution for all collisions and impacts is $e$. Prove that

    (i) the speeds of the spheres after the first collision are $u(1 - e)$ and $u(1 + e)$

    (ii) when the second sphere hits the wall, the spheres are a distance $\frac{2e}{1 + e}$ apart

    (iii) the next collision takes place at a distance $\frac{2e^2}{1 + e^2}$ from the wall.

19. A sphere of mass 0.6 kg is attached to the end of a string, the other end being attached to a fixed point $O$. The string is 0.5 m long.

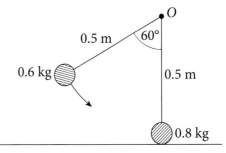

Fig. 7.15

    The sphere is released from rest when the string makes an angle of $60°$ with the vertical. The sphere then collides directly with another sphere, of mass 0.8 kg, which is hanging vertically at rest from $O$ by means of a string 0.5 m long. The coefficient of restitution between the spheres is $\frac{1}{11}$. Find (correct to one decimal place)

    (i) the speed of the 0.6 kg sphere just before the collision

    (ii) the speed of each sphere just after the collision.

20. A sphere, of mass $m$ and speed $u$, impinges directly on a stationary sphere of mass $3m$. The coefficient of restitution between the spheres is $e$.

    (i)   Find, in terms of $e$, the speed of each sphere after the collison

    (ii)  Show that the loss of kinetic energy due to the impact is $\dfrac{3mu^2}{8}(1 - e^2)$

    (iii) If $e = \frac{1}{4}$, find the percentage loss in kinetic energy to the nearest per cent.

    (iv)  Find the maximum possible percentage loss in kinetic energy for $0 \le e \le 1$

## Oblique collisions

When two smooth spheres collide obliquely it means that they collide when moving at an angle to one another.

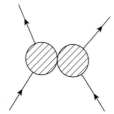

Fig. 7.16

We take the line joining their centres at the moment of impact as the $\vec{i}$ -axis. Because the spheres are smooth, the forces they exert on one another are along the $\vec{i}$ -axis, so the $\vec{j}$ -velocities remain unchanged by the impact. Furthermore, Newton's Law of Restitution applies only to the $\vec{i}$ -velocities, as the spheres collide along this line. Hence, the oblique collisions of two spheres is governed by three laws:

1. The Principle of Conservation of Momentum: The total momentum of the two spheres is conserved along the line of centres.

2. Newton's Law of Restitution: The relative velocity of the two spheres (in the line of centres at impact) is a constant ($e$) times the relative velocity before impact, but in the opposite direction.

3. If the $\vec{i}$ -axis is along the line of centres at impact, then the $\vec{j}$ -velocities remain unchanged by the impact.

   Assuming that this data has the usual meaning, we have four equations:

| Before | Mass | After |
|--------|------|-------|
| $a\vec{i} + c\vec{j}$ | $m_1$ | $p\vec{i} + s\vec{j}$ |
| $b\vec{i} + d\vec{j}$ | $m_2$ | $q\vec{i} + t\vec{j}$ |

1. $c = s$
   ($\vec{j}$ – velocity of the first sphere is unchanged)

2. $d = t$
   ($\vec{j}$ – velocity of the second sphere is unchanged)

3. $m_1 a + m_2 b = m_1 p + m_2 q$
   (momentum in the $\vec{i}$ -direction is conserved)

4. $\dfrac{p - q}{a - b} = -e$
   (Newton's Law of Restitution)

### Worked Example 7.6

Two smooth spheres of masses 2 kg and 1 kg collide obliquely when moving with velocities $2\vec{i} + 3\vec{j}$ and $-3\vec{i} + \vec{j}$ respectively, where $\vec{i}$ is along their line of centres at impact. If the coefficient of restitution is $\frac{4}{5}$, find

(i)   their velocities after impact

(ii)  the loss in kinetic energy

(iii) the impulse imparted to each sphere during the collision

(iv)  the angle through which the heavier sphere is deflected.

**Solution:**

| Before | Mass | After |
|--------|------|-------|
| $2\vec{i} + 3\vec{j}$ | 2 kg | $p\vec{i} + 3\vec{j}$ |
| $-3\vec{i} + \vec{j}$ | 1 kg | $q\vec{i} + \vec{j}$ |

(i) Momentum in the $\vec{i}$ -direction is conserved.

$2(2) + 1(-3) = 2(p) + 1(q)$

$\therefore 2p + q = 1$     Equation 1

From Newton's law

$\dfrac{p - q}{2 - (-3)} = -\dfrac{4}{5}$

$\therefore p - q = -4$     Equation 2

Adding equations 1 and 2, we get $3p = -3$, which gives $p = -1$, $q = 3$ Therefore the velocities after impact will be $-\vec{i} + 3\vec{j}$ and $3\vec{i} + \vec{j}$ m/s, respectively.

(ii) $\text{K.E.}_{before} = \dfrac{1}{2} m_1 u_1^{\,2} + \dfrac{1}{2} m_2 u_2^{\,2}$

$= \dfrac{1}{2}(2)(2^2 + 3^2) + \dfrac{1}{2}(1)((-3)^2 + 1^2)$

$= 13 + 5$

$= 18 \, \text{J}$

$\text{K.E.}_{after} = \dfrac{1}{2} \, m_1 \, v_1{}^2 + \dfrac{1}{2} \, m_2 \, v_2{}^2$

$\qquad = \dfrac{1}{2}(2)((-1)^2 + 3^2) + \dfrac{1}{2}(1)(3^2 + 1^2)$

$\qquad = 10 + 5$

$\qquad = 15 \, \text{J}$

Therefore, the loss in kinetic energy is

$\qquad 18 - 15 = 3$ joules.

(iii)  The impulse imparted to the heavier sphere is given by

Impulse $\vec{I}_1 = m\vec{v} - m\vec{u}$

$\qquad = (2)\left(-\vec{i} + 3\vec{j}\right) - (2)\left(2\vec{i} + 3\vec{j}\right)$

$\qquad = -2\vec{i} + 6\vec{j} - 4\vec{i} - 6\vec{j}$

$\qquad = -6\vec{i} \, \text{N s}$

The impulse imparted to the other sphere is given by

Impulse $\vec{I}_2 = m\vec{v} - m\vec{u}$

$\qquad = (1)\left(3\vec{i} + \vec{j}\right) - (1)\left(-3\vec{i} + \vec{j}\right)$

$\qquad = 3\vec{i} + \vec{j} + 3\vec{i} - \vec{j}$

$\qquad = 6\vec{i} \, \text{N s}$

(iv)  To find the angle of deflection, we need to find the angle between the vectors $\vec{u} = 2\vec{i} + 3\vec{j}$ and $\vec{v} = -\vec{i} + 3\vec{j}$.

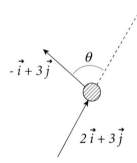

Fig. 7.17

The slope of $2\vec{i} + 3\vec{j} = \dfrac{\vec{j} \text{ component}}{\vec{i} \text{ component}} = \dfrac{3}{2} = 1.5 = m_1$

The slope of $-\vec{i} + 3\vec{j} = \dfrac{\vec{j} \text{ component}}{\vec{i} \text{ component}} = \dfrac{3}{-1} = -3 = m_2$

The tan of the angle between these is given by the formula

$\qquad \tan \theta = \pm \dfrac{m_1 - m_2}{1 + m_1 m_2} = \pm \dfrac{1.5 - (-3)}{-3.5} = \pm \dfrac{9}{7}$

Since $\theta$ is acute (see diagram), $\tan \theta = +\dfrac{9}{7}$

Therefore $\theta = \tan^{-1}\left(\dfrac{9}{7}\right) = 52.125°$

1.  Two smooth spheres, both of mass 2 kg, collide obliquely. Their velocities before impact are $4\vec{i} + 3\vec{j}$ and $\vec{i} + 2\vec{j}$, where $\vec{i}$ is along the line of centres at impact. The coefficient of restitution between the spheres is $\dfrac{1}{3}$, find

    (i)   the new velocities of the spheres

    (ii)  the loss in kinetic energy.

2.  Two smooth spheres of masses 2 kg and 3 kg collide obliquely. Their velocities before impact are $3\vec{i} + 4\vec{j}$ and $-4\vec{i} + 3\vec{j}$ respectively, where $\vec{i}$ is along the line of centres at impact. If the coefficient of restitution is $\dfrac{3}{7}$, find

    (i)    their velocities after impact

    (ii)   the loss in kinetic energy

    (iii)  the magnitude of the impulse imparted to each sphere.

3.  Two smooth spheres of masses $m$ and $2m$ collide obliquely. Their velocities before collision are $6\vec{i} + \vec{j}$ and $-2\vec{i} - 5\vec{j}$, respectively, where $\vec{i}$ is along their line of centres at impact. After the collision, the lighter sphere moves along the $\vec{j}$-axis. Find

    (i)   the velocity of the heavier sphere after impact

    (ii)  the coefficient of restitution.

4.  A sphere of mass $2m$, moving with velocity $5\vec{i} + 5\vec{j}$, collides obliquely with a sphere of mass $m$ which is at rest. $\vec{i}$ is along the line of their centres at impact. If the coefficient of restitution is $\dfrac{1}{2}$, find

    (i)    the velocities of each sphere after impact

    (ii)   the impulse imparted to each sphere during impact

    (iii)  the percentage loss in kinetic energy

    (iv)   the angle through which the heavier mass is deflected.

5.  Two smooth spheres of masses 2 kg and 3 kg have speeds 5 m/s and $4\sqrt{2}$ m/s respectively. They move towards each other, as shown, making angles $\tan^{-1}\left(\dfrac{3}{4}\right)$ and 45°, respectively, with the horizontal. The coefficient of restitution between the spheres is $\dfrac{7}{8}$. Find

(i)   their velocities before impact

(ii)   their velocities after impact

(iii)   the loss in kinetic energy.

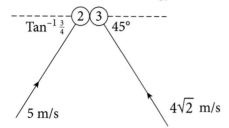

Fig. 7.18

6.   State the laws governing oblique collisions between two smooth elastic spheres. Two such spheres $A$ and $B$ of mass 5 and 10 kg respectively, collide obliquely. The coefficient of restitution is $\frac{1}{7}$. Immediately before collision the velocity of $A$ is $5\vec{i} + 4\vec{j}$ m/s and that of $B$ is $-2\vec{i} - 3\vec{j}$ m/s, where $\vec{i}$ and $\vec{j}$ are unit vectors along and perpendicular to the line of centres.

(i)   Find the velocity of $A$ and $B$ immediately after impact.

(ii)   Show that the loss of kinetic energy is 80 J.

(iii)   Calculate (to the nearest degree) the angle through which $B$ is deflected by the collision.

7.   A smooth sphere of mass 4 kg collides obliquely with another smooth sphere of mass $m$ which is at rest. After the impact the two spheres move at right angles to each other. If the coefficient of restitution was $\frac{4}{7}$, calculate the value of $m$.

8.   A smooth sphere of mass $m$ collides obliquely with a smooth sphere of mass $2m$ which is at rest. The velocity of the $m$ mass was $8\vec{i} + 4\vec{j}$ before impact, where $\vec{i}$ is along the line of centres at impact. The $m$ mass is then deflected through 90° by the impact. Find

(i)   its velocity immediately after impact

(ii)   the velocity of the $2m$ mass after impact

(iii)   the coefficient of restitution between the two spheres.

9.   Two smooth spheres of masses 4 kg and 2 kg impinge obliquely. The 2 kg mass is brought to rest by the impact. The coefficient of restitution is $\frac{1}{2}$.

(i)   Prove that before impact the spheres were moving in directions perpendicular to one another.

(ii)   Show that the kinetic energy gained by the 4 kg mass is equal to half that lost by the 2 kg mass.

10.   Two smooth spheres $P$ and $Q$ of equal radii have masses 4 kg and 8 kg, respectively. They lie at rest on a smooth horizontal floor so that the line joining their centres is perpendicular to the vertical wall.

$P$ is projected towards $Q$ with speed $12u$ and collides with $Q$. $Q$ then hits the wall, rebounds and collides with $P$ again. This final collision reduces $Q$ to rest. The coefficient of restitution between $P$ and $Q$ is $\frac{1}{4}$. The coefficient of restitution between $Q$ and the wall is $e$.

(i)   Show that $e = \frac{2}{7}$.

(ii)   Find the final velocity of $P$ in terms of $u$.

(iii)   Find the total loss in kinetic energy due to the three collisions.

## Harder Examples

### Worked Example 7.7

A smooth sphere of mass $m$ collides obliquely with a smooth sphere of mass $2m$, which is at rest. Before impact, the line of motion of the lighter sphere makes an angle $A$ with their line of centres at impact. After the collision, it makes an angle $B$ with that line. If $e$, the coefficient of restitution, is $\frac{1}{3}$ show that $\text{Tan } B = 9 \text{ Tan } A$.

**Solution:**

Let $u$ and $v$ be the speeds of the lighter sphere before and after the collision, respectively.

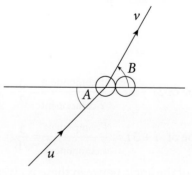

Fig. 7.19

| Before | Mass | After |
|---|---|---|
| $u\text{Cos}A\,\vec{i} + u\text{Sin}A\,\vec{j}$ | $m$ | $v\text{Cos}B\,\vec{i} + v\text{Sin}B\,\vec{j}$ |
| $0\,\vec{i} + 0\,\vec{j}$ | $2m$ | $p\,\vec{i} + 0\,\vec{j}$ |

1. The $\vec{j}$-velocity of the first mass remains unchanged.

$$\Rightarrow u \sin A = v \sin B \text{ ........ Equation 1}$$

2. Momentum in the $\vec{i}$-direction is conserved.

$$mu \cos A + 2m(0) = mv \cos B + 2mp$$

$$\Rightarrow p = \frac{1}{2} u \cos A - \frac{1}{2} v \cos B \text{ .... Eqn 2}$$

3. Newton's law of restitution.

$$\frac{v \cos B - p}{u \cos A - 0} = -\frac{1}{3}$$

$$\Rightarrow 3v \cos B - 3p = -u \cos A$$

$$\Rightarrow 3p = 3v \cos B + u \cos A$$

$$\Rightarrow p = v \cos B + \frac{1}{3} u \cos A \quad \text{Eq 3}$$

From equations 2 and 3, we get

$$\frac{1}{2} u \cos A - \frac{1}{2} v \cos B = v \cos B + \frac{1}{3} u \cos A$$

(multiplying across by 6)

$$\Rightarrow 3u \cos A - 3v \cos B = 6v \cos B + 2u \cos A$$

$$\Rightarrow u \cos A = 9 v \cos B \quad \text{Equation 4}$$

By dividing equation 1 by equation 4, we get

$$\frac{u \sin A}{u \cos A} = \frac{v \sin B}{9 v \cos B}$$

$$\Rightarrow \tan A = \frac{1}{9} \tan B$$

$$\therefore 9 \tan A = \tan B \qquad \text{Q.E.D.}$$

## Exercise 7 D

1.  A smooth sphere collides obliquely with an equal sphere which is at rest. Before the impact, the line of motion of the first sphere makes an angle $A$ with their line of centres; afterwards this angle is $B$. The coefficient of restitution between the spheres is $\frac{1}{4}$.
    Show that $8 \tan A = 3 \tan B$.

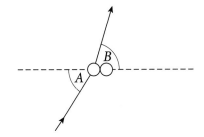

Fig. 7.20

2.  Two smooth spheres of mass $m$ and $2m$ collide obliquely, as shown. Before they collide, they move towards one another, one moving with speed $u$ along the $\vec{i}$-axis, the other moving with speed $2u$ at an angle $A$ to the $\vec{i}$-axis, which is the line of centres at impact. The lighter mass is brought to rest by the impact. The coefficient of restitution is $\frac{5}{118}$ if.

    (i)   Prove that $\cos A = \frac{9}{41}$

    (ii)  Show that the velocity of the greater mass after impact is $\frac{5u}{82}\left(-\vec{i} + 32\vec{j}\right)$ m/s

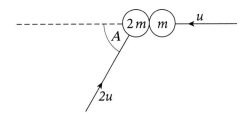

Fig. 7.21

3.  (i)   A sphere of mass $m$ is moving with speed $4u$ when it impinges directly with an equal sphere which is moving in the same direction with speed $2u$. Show that the loss in kinetic energy due to the impact is $mu^2(1 - e^2)$

    (ii)  If the second sphere had been at rest and the first sphere impinged with speed $4u$ obliquely, at an angle of $30°$ to the line of centres at impact, show that the loss in kinetic energy would be $3mu^2(1 - e^2)$.

4.  A smooth sphere $A$ impinges obliquely with an identical smooth sphere $B$ which is at rest. The direction of $A$ before and after impact makes angles $60°$ and $\theta$, respectively, with the line of centres at impact. The coefficient of restitution is $e$.

    (i)   Prove that $\tan \theta = \frac{2\sqrt{3}}{1 - e}$.

    (ii)  Show that if $e = 0$, then the percentage loss in kinetic energy is 12.5%.

    (iii) For what value of $e$ will the kinetic energies of $A$ and $B$ after impact be in the ratio $7 : 1$?

5. A smooth sphere $A$ of mass $m$, moving with speed 0.6 m/s, impinges at an angle $\theta$ on a smooth sphere $B$ of mass $2m$, which is at rest. After the collision $A$ is found to move with speed 0.2 m/s in a direction which is at right angles to its original direction.

   (i) Show that $\tan\theta = \frac{1}{3}$.
   (ii) Find the coefficient of restitution.
   (iii) Show that the loss in kinetic energy is 0.06m.

6. (a) Two vectors $a\,\vec{i} + b\,\vec{j}$ and $c\,\vec{i} + d\,\vec{j}$ are at right angles. Write down the condition satisfied by $a$, $b$, $c$ and $d$.

   (b) Two smooth spheres of masses $m$ and $2m$ and velocities $u$ and $v$, respectively, collide as shown on the diagram, where $\cos\theta = \frac{3}{7}$.

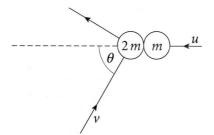

Fig. 7.22

The sphere of mass $2m$ is deflected through an angle of $90°$ by the collision. The coefficient of restitution is $\frac{3}{4}$. Prove that $v = \frac{7u}{25}$.

7. Two spheres of radius $r$ move horizontally in opposite directions. The first has mass $2m$ and speed $2u$, the second has mass $m$ and speed $4u$. The coefficient of restitution is $\frac{1}{\sqrt{3}}$. The centres of the two spheres lie on two parallel lines, a distance $r$ apart.

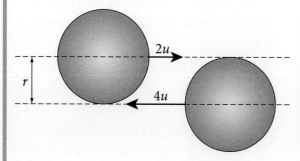

Fig. 7.23

   (i) Show that at the moment of impact, the line of centres of the spheres makes an angle of $30°$ with their previous lines of motion.
   (ii) Find the speeds of the spheres after impact.

8. Two equal spheres, each of mass $m$ and radius $r$ collide when moving on a smooth horizontal plane.

   Before impact, the spheres are moving with speeds $u$ and $2u$, their centres moving along parallel lines which are a distance $1.2r$ apart. The coefficient of restitution is 0.5. Show that

   (i) their speeds after impact are $\frac{\sqrt{61}}{5}u$ and $\frac{\sqrt{58}}{5}u$, respectively.

   (ii) the angle between their paths will be approximately $27°$ after impact.

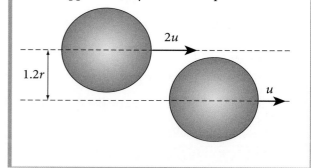

## Summary of important points

Impulse $\qquad \vec{I} = m\vec{v} - m\vec{u}$

Conservation of linear momentum:
$$m_1u_1 + m_2u_2 = m_1v_1 + m_2v_2$$

Newton's experimental law of restitution:
$$\frac{v_1 - v_2}{u_1 - u_2} = -e$$

## DOs and DON'Ts for the exam

### DO

- Do learn off by heart the statement of the two laws in English
- Do remember that in oblique collisions, the $\vec{j}$-velocity remains unchanged and hence a particle which is at rest will move along the $\vec{i}$-axis (so long as the $\vec{i}$-axis is along the line of centres at impact)

### DON'T

- Don't leave out the minus sign in front of $e$ in the equation $\frac{v_1 - v_2}{u_1 - u_2} = -e$
- Don't put $\vec{i}$'s or $\vec{j}$'s into the equations
- Don't forget that impulse is a vector quantity (measured in newton-seconds: Ns) but energy is a scalar quantity (measured in joules: J)

# Statics

δος μοι που στω και
κινω την γην

(Give me a place to stand
and I will move the earth.)

*Archimedes*

## Contents

## Learning outcomes

**In this chapter you will learn...**

- What a moment is

- The Principle of Moments

- How to calculate the magnitude and line of action of the resultant of a set of forces

- How to find the centre of gravity of a set of weights

- How to find the centre of gravity of certain laminae and symmetrical solids

- The Laws of Statics

- How to solve problems involving ladders, triangles, jointed rods, etc.

- How to solve three-force problems

## You will need to know...

- How to solve simultaneous equations in three variables

- What the median of a triangle is

- What the centroid of a triangle is

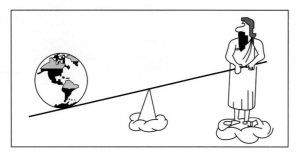

Fig. 8.1 Archimedes: "Give me a place to stand and I will move the earth."

## Moments

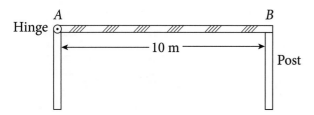

Fig. 8.2

A level crossing gate consists of a 10 m pole of mass 20 kg hinged at one end *A* and free at the other end *B*, where it rests on a post. The pole is horizontal. A man tries to lift the pole by applying an upward force of 110 N at a point 3 m from A. It does not budge.

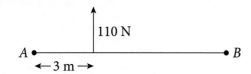

Fig. 8.3

He then moves to a point 6 m from *A* and applies the same upward force. Again, it does not budge.

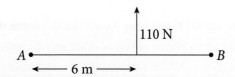

Fig. 8.4

He then moves to a point 9 m from *A* (1 m from *B*) and applies the same force. At last the pole turns on its hinge at A.

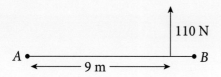

Fig. 8.5

But how can a force applied at one point do what the same force applied at another point cannot do? The answer is that the **turning effect** or **moment** about the hinge is not the same in each case.

**Definition:** The **moment** of a force about an axis is the product of the magnitude of the force and the perpendicular distance between its line of action and the axis.

In case 1, the moment of the force about the hinge's axis at *A* is given by

$$\text{Moment} = F \times d$$
$$= 110 \times 3$$
$$= 330 \ \text{newton-metres}$$

In case 2, the moment about the hinge is given by

$$\text{Moment} = F \times d$$
$$= 110 \times 6$$
$$= 660 \ \text{N m}$$

In case 3, the moment is given by

$$\text{Moment} = F \times d$$
$$= 110 \times 9$$
$$= 990 \ \text{N m}$$

Why is a moment of magnitude 990 N m able to turn the pole, while a moment of magnitude 660 Nm is not? It is because the pole is being turned in the other direction by another force – namely its weight.

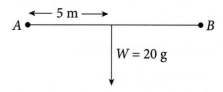

Fig. 8.6

The moment in the other direction is given by
Moment = $F \times d = 20 \, g \times 5 = 100 \, g = 980$ N m.

When the man produces a moment greater than this, but in the other direction, the pole will then turn in that other direction.

**Note 1**: By convention, an anti-clockwise moment is said to be positive; a clockwise moment is said to be negative. In the above case, the moment due to the man's push is anti-clockwise and therefore positive. It is +990 N m. The moment due to the weight force is clockwise and therefore negative. It is – 980 N m. The sum of the moments is, therefore, +10 N m. So, the pole turns in the positive (i.e. anti-clockwise) direction.

**Note 2:** Moment is sometimes called **torque**.

**Note 3:** Suppose that the man pushed the pole horizontally at $B$, with a force of 110 N towards the hinge at $A$.

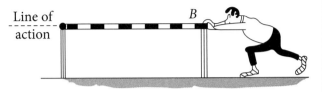

Fig. 8.7

Would this turn the pole? No, because the turning effect, or moment, is equal to $F \times d$ where $d$ is the distance of the line of action from the hinge at $A$. Since the line of action passes through $A$, $d = 0$. The moment $= F \times d = 110 \times 0 = 0$. There is no turning effect.

**Note 4:** Force has three properties:
(i)   its magnitude,
(ii)  its direction,
(iii) its line of action.

**Note 5:** The hinge is not a point. It may be a few centimetres long. Strictly speaking, the distance $d$ is the perpendicular distance from the line of action of the force to the line (or axis) of the hinge. In this case the line of the hinge is a line through $A$ coming out of the page.

---

### Worked Example 8.1

A light plank $AB$, 1 metre long, is subject to two forces $\vec{F}_1$ and $\vec{F}_2$, as shown. Their magnitudes are 1 N and 4 N respectively.

(i)   Find the magnitude of the resultant.

(ii)  How far from $A$ is the line of action of the resultant?

Fig. 8.8

---

**Solution:**

(i)   $\vec{F}_1 = 1\vec{j}$ ; $\vec{F}_2 = 4\vec{j}$
Therefore, the resultant, $\vec{R}$, is given by
$$\vec{R} = \vec{F}_1 + \vec{F}_2$$
$$= 1\vec{j} + 4\vec{j}$$
$$= 5\vec{j} \text{ N}$$

(ii)  But where is its line of action? It must be in such a place that its moment about any point is the same as the sum of the moments of $\vec{F}_1$, and $\vec{F}_2$ about that point. Let $x$ be the distance between the line of action of $\vec{R}$ and the point $A$. The system can be looked at in two ways:

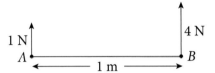

Fig. 8.9

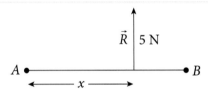

Fig. 8.10

The moment about $A$ must be the same in both cases.

It follows that
$$1\,(0) + 4\,(1) = 5\,(x)$$
$$5\,x = 4$$
$$x = 0.8 \text{ m}$$
$$= 80 \text{ cm}$$

The line of action of $\vec{R}$ is 80 cm from $A$.

(Note: Would the answer have been the same if we had taken moments about another point – say, $B$? Yes. Prove it for yourself if you don't believe it!)

## The Principle of Moments

In *Worked Example 8.1*, an assumption was used to find the line of action of the resultant force. This assumption is called the Principle of Moments – and here it is:

### The Principle of Moments

If any number of coplanar forces act on a rigid body, then the sum of their moments about any axis is equal to the moment of their resultant about that axis.

In short:

The sum of the moments of the forces about an axis = the moment of the sum (or resultant) of the forces about that axis.

Shorter still:

The sum of the moments = the moment of the sum.

### Worked Example 8.2

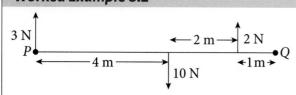

Fig. 8.11

A light plank, which is 7 m long, has three vertical forces acting on it, as shown. Find their resultant and the distance of its line of action from the endpoint *P*.

**Solution:**

(iii)  The resultant
$$\vec{R} = 3\vec{j} - 10\vec{j} + 2\vec{j}$$
$$= -5\vec{j}\,\text{N}$$

But where is the line of action of this resultant? Let $x$ be the distance between its line of action and the point *p*.

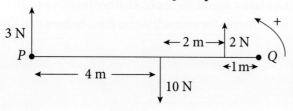

Fig. 8.12

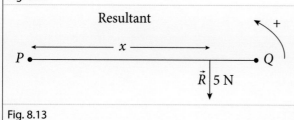

Fig. 8.13

Remember that anti-clockwise moment is positive, but clockwise moment is negative.

We will take moments about the point *P*. Imagine, if you like, that the plank is hinged at *P*. The forces which would turn the plank anti-clockwise (the 2 N force, for example) will have a positive moment. The forces which would turn the plank clockwise (the 10 N force, for example) will have a negative moment.

The sum of the moments = the moment of the sum.

$$\therefore 3\,(0) - 10\,(4) + 2\,(6) = -5\,(x)$$
$$\therefore -28 = -5\,x$$
$$\therefore x = 5.6 \text{ metres}$$

Answer: The resultant $\vec{R} = -5\vec{j}\,\text{N}$

Its line of action passes 5.6 m from *p*.

### Exercise 8 A

1.  Find in each case the resultant and its line of action.

(a)

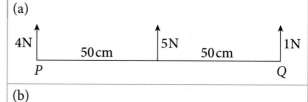

(b)

(c)

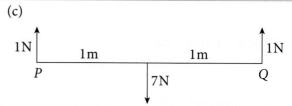

(d)

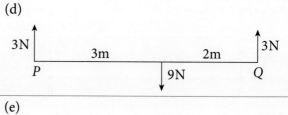

(e)

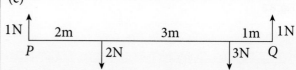

2. A uniform horizontal plank of weight $W$ and length 6 m has masses of weights $2W$ and $3W$ at each end. Find the resultant of the three weight forces. How far from each end is the line of action of the resultant?

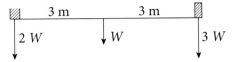

Fig. 8.14

3. A light (no weight) horizontal beam of length 1 m has masses of weight $7W$ and $3W$ placed at its endpoints. Find the resultant of the weight forces and how far its line of action is from the greater mass.

4. Masses of weights $w$ and $x$ are placed at the ends of a light plank. Show that the line of action of the resultant divides the plank into two pieces whose lengths are in the ratio $x{:}w$.

Fig. 8.15

5. Three forces of magnitude $4W$, $W$ and $kW$ act on a beam $PQ$, as shown.

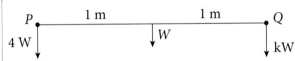

Fig. 8.16

Find the value of $k$ if the line of action of the resultant passes

(i) $\frac{7}{8}$ m from $P$

(ii) $\frac{9}{10}$ m from $Q$.

## Centre of gravity

**Definition:** The centre of gravity of an object is the point through which the resultant gravitational force acts, no matter what position the object is in.

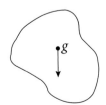

Fig. 8.17

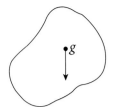

Fig. 8.18

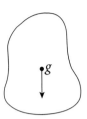

Fig. 8.19

The object is held in three positions and the line of action of the resultant gravitational force is shown in each case. These lines of action all pass through one point. This point is the centre of gravity of the object.

### Worked Example 8.3

(i) Particles of weights 4 N, 2 N and 1 N are placed in the same horizontal plane at positions $(-1, 2)$, $(2, 3)$ and $(7, 0)$ respectively. Where is the centre of gravity of the system?

(ii) Where should another particle of weight 3 N be placed so that the centre of gravity of this system would be at $(2\frac{1}{2}, \frac{1}{2})$.

**Solution:**

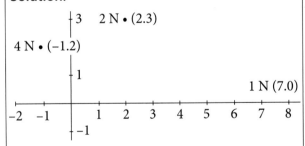

Fig. 8.20

(i) Imagine that you are looking down on the system from above, like a camera looking down on a snooker table.

The resultant $R = 4 + 2 + 1 = 7$ N

| Weight | 4 | 2 | 1 | = | 7 |
|---|---|---|---|---|---|
| Position | $(-1, 2)$ | $(2, 3)$ | $(7, 0)$ | | $(x, y)$ |

Let $(x, y)$ be the position of the centre of gravity. This means that the resultant force 7 N acts through $(x, y)$.

$$\left.\begin{array}{l} 4 \text{ N at } (-1, 2) \\ 2 \text{ N at } (2, 3) \\ 1 \text{ N at } (7, 0) \end{array}\right\} = 7 \text{ N at } (x, y)$$

Taking moments about the $y$-axis: the sum of the moments = the moment of the sum.

$$4(-1) + 2(2) + 1(7) = 7\,x$$
$$\therefore 7 = 7\,x$$
$$\therefore x = 1$$

Taking moments about the $x$-axis,

$$4(2) + 2(3) + 1(0) = 7\,y$$
$$\therefore 14 = 7\,y$$
$$\therefore y = 2$$

Therefore, the centre of gravity of the system is at $(1, 2)$.

(ii)  Let the 3 N weight be placed at the point $(x, y)$.

The resultant $R = 4 + 2 + 1 + 3$
$$= 10 \text{ N}$$

This 10 N force acts through $(2\frac{1}{2}, \frac{1}{2})$.

$$\left.\begin{array}{l} 4 \text{ N at } (-1, 2) \\ 2 \text{ N at } (2, 3) \\ 1 \text{ N at } (7, 0) \\ 3 \text{ N at } (x, y) \end{array}\right\} = 10 \text{ N at } (2\tfrac{1}{2}, \tfrac{1}{2}).$$

| Weight | 4 | 2 | 1 | 3 | = | 10 |
|--------|-----|-----|-----|-----|---|-----|
| Position | (−1, 2) | (2, 3) | (7, 0) | (x, y) | | $(2\frac{1}{2}, \frac{1}{2})$ |

Taking moments about the $y$-axis,

$$4(-1) + 2(2) + 1(7) + 3(x) = 10\left(2\tfrac{1}{2}\right)$$
$$\therefore 3x + 7 = 25$$
$$\therefore x = 6$$

Taking moments about the $x$-axis,

$$4(2) + 2(3) + 1(0) + 3(y) = 10\left(\tfrac{1}{2}\right)$$
$$\therefore 14 + 3y = 5$$
$$\therefore y = -3$$

The 3 N should be placed at the point $(6, -3)$.

1. Particles of weights 3 N, 2 N and 1 N are placed at $(2, 1)$, $(4, 3)$ and $(10, 9)$ respectively on a horizontal surface.
   Find the position of the centre of gravity.

2. Particles of weights 1 N, 2 N, 3 N and 4 N are placed at $(1, 1)$, $(1, 7)$, $(3, 1)$ and $(2, 3)$ respectively.
   Find the position of the centre of gravity.

3. Find the position of the centre of gravity of two particles whose weights are 3 N and 2 N and whose positions are $(4, 1)$ and $(9, -9)$ respectively. A third particle of weight 1 N is added to the system. The centre of gravity of this new system is at $(6, -2)$.
   Where was the 1 N weight placed?

4. Particles of weights $W$ and $2W$ are placed at $P\,(3, 1)$ and $Q\,(12, 19)$ on a horizontal plane.
   Find the position of the centre of gravity $G$.
   Show that $|PG| : |GQ| = 2{:}1$

5. Three points $P$, $Q$ and $R$ are determined by position vectors $\vec{i} + 2\vec{j}$, $\vec{i} + 7\vec{j}$, and $5\vec{i} - \vec{j}$ respectively. Particles of weights 2 N, 3 N and 5 N are placed at $P$, $Q$ and $R$, respectively. Find the position vector of the centre of gravity of this system. Where should an extra particle of weight 2 N be placed so that the centre of gravity of this new system would be at $4\vec{i} + \vec{j}$ ?

6. Particles of weights 1 N, 2 N and 3 N are placed at $(4, 1)$, $(1, h)$ and $(k, 1)$ respectively. The centre of gravity of the system is at $(2\frac{1}{2}, 4)$.
   Find the values of $h$ and $k$.

7. Three particles of equal mass are placed at $P(2,1)$, $Q(5, 3)$ and $R(3, -1)$. Show that the centre of gravity is at the point $\left(\frac{10}{3}, 1\right)$.
   A fourth particle, whose mass is double that of each of the others, is added to the system. Where should it be placed so that the centre of gravity of this system will be at $P(2, 1)$?

8. (i) Find the centre of gravity of the following system of weights: $W$ at $(6, 5)$, $2W$ at $(7, -1)$, $3W$ at $(2, 11)$ and $4W$ at $(6, 1)$.
   (ii) The $4W$ mass is replaced by a particle of weight $kW$. The centre of gravity is at $(11, y)$.
   Find the value of $k$ and the value of $y$.

9. A system of three particles is positioned as follows:

2 N at $(x, 5)$

3 N at $(11, y)$

5 N at $(5, -6)$

If the co-ordinates of the centre of gravity are $(6, -5)$, find the values of $x$ and $y$.

10. A system of four particles is positioned as follows:

1 N at $(7, 8)$

4 N at $(1, y)$

$x$ N at $(5, 2)$

2 N at $(6, -3)$

If the co-ordinates of the centre of gravity are $(4, 2)$, find the values of $x$ and $y$.

11. A uniform rectangular tray has length 60 cm and width 40 cm. Its weight is $3W$. On the tray is a packet of biscuits of weight $2W$ at $(20, 10)$, and a lump of cheese of weight $5W$ at $(50, 20)$, where co-ordinates are in reference to the origin $O$, as shown.

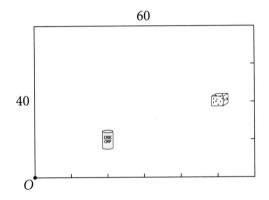

Fig. 8.21

Find the centre of gravity of the tray with the objects on it.

12. Particles weighing 3, 4, 5 and 6 newtons are placed on a horizontal plane at points $(-2\frac{1}{3}, 2)$, $(1, 7)$, $(3, 7)$ and $(4, -4)$ respectively. Calculate the co-ordinates of the centre of gravity of the four-particle system.

13. Particles of 5, 8, 3, 2 units of mass are placed at points the co-ordinates of which are $(3, -1)$, $(4, 2)$, $(-1, 5)$, $(2, -6)$ respectively. Calculate the co-ordinates of the centre of gravity of the system.

# Centroid of a triangle

Take any triangle. A line from a vertex to the midpoint of the opposite side is called a **median**. It can be proven that the three medians of a triangle are concurrent (i.e. they meet at one point). The point at which they meet is called the **centroid** and is usually denoted by the letter **G**. We will need to prove Theorem 8.1 first.

### Theorem 8.1

The centre of gravity of two particles at $P$ and $Q$ is on the line $PQ$.

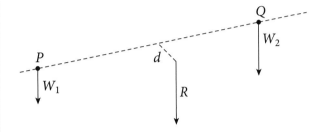

Fig. 8.22

The centre of gravity of two particles at $P$ and $Q$ is on the line $PQ$.

**Proof:** Let $W_1$ = the weight of the object at $P$.

Let $W_2$ = the weight of the object at $Q$.

The resultant $R = W_1 + W_2$.

Let $d$ = the distance of the line of action of $R$ from the line $PQ$. (We will prove that $d = 0$.)

Taking moments about $PQ$; the sum of the moments = the moment of the sum.

$$W_1(0) + W_2(0) = R(d)$$
$$\therefore d = 0$$

Therefore, the line of action of the resultant is always on the line $PQ$. This means that the centre of gravity is on the line $PQ$. Q.E.D.

### Theorem 8.2

The centre of gravity of a triangular lamina is at its centroid.

**Proof:** Let $ABC$ be the triangular lamina. Let $M$, $N$, $P$ be the midpoints of $[BC]$, $[AB]$, $[AC]$ respectively. So, $AM$, $CN$, $BP$ are the medians of triangle $ABC$.

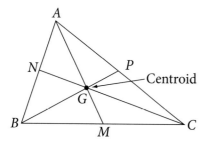

Fig. 8.23

Divide the triangle into infinitesimally thin strips parallel to $BC$. The centre of gravity of each strip is at its midpoint. So, the resultant of all the gravitational forces is somewhere along the line $AM$, as a consequence of *Theorem 8.1*. In other words, the centre of gravity of the lamina is on the median $AM$.

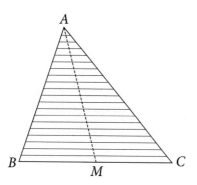

Fig. 8.24

Next, divide the triangle into thin strips parallel to $AB$. This will lead to the conclusion that the centre of gravity of the lamina is somewhere along the median $CN$.

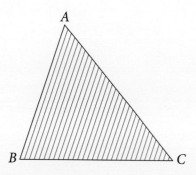

Fig. 8.25

It follows that the centre of gravity must be where the medians meet — that is, at the centroid. Q.E.D.

**Note 1:** If $(x_1, y_1)$, $(x_2, y_2)$ and $(x_3, y_3)$ are the co-ordinates of the vertices of a triangle, then the co-ordinates of the centroid, $g$, are

$$\left( \frac{x_1 + x_2 + x_3}{3}, \frac{y_1 + y_2 + y_3}{3} \right)$$

**Note 2:** The centroid divides each median in the ratio 2:1.

For example, in the proof of *Theorem 8.2*
$$|AG| : |GM| = 2 : 1$$
and
$$|CG| : |GN| = 2 : 1$$

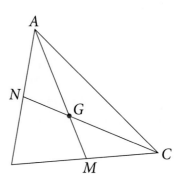

Fig. 8.26

### Theorem 8.3

The centre of gravity of three equal particles placed at points $A$, $B$ and $C$ on a horizontal plane is at the centroid of triangle $ABC$.

**Proof:** Let $W$ = the weight of each particle.
Let $A = (x_1, y_1)$, let $B = (x_2, y_2)$ and let $C = (x_3, y_3)$. Let $(x, y)$ be the position of the centre of gravity. The resultant

$$\begin{aligned} R &= W + W + W \\ &= 3\,W \end{aligned}$$

$$\left. \begin{array}{l} W \text{ at } (x_1, y_1) \\ W \text{ at } (x_2, y_2) \\ W \text{ at } (x_3, y_3) \end{array} \right\} = 3\,W \text{ at } (x, y)$$

Taking moments about the $y$-axis,

$$W(x_1) + W(x_2) + W(x_3) = 3\,W(x)$$
$$\therefore x = \frac{x_1 + x_2 + x_3}{3}$$

Taking moments about the $x$-axis,

$$W(y_1) + W(y_2) + W(y_3) = 3\,W(y)$$
$$\therefore y = \frac{y_1 + y_2 + y_3}{3}$$

Therefore the centre of gravity is at

$$\left( \frac{x_1 + x_2 + x_3}{3}, \frac{y_1 + y_2 + y_3}{3} \right)$$

which is the centroid of triangle $ABC$.   QED

## *Worked Example 8.4*

This giant letter $F$ is cut out of thin, uniform sheet metal.

(i)   Find its centre of gravity.

(ii)  If the $F$ is suspended freely from the point $p$, find the angle which the side $[pq]$ will make with the vertical when it is in equilibrium.

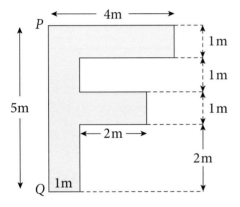

8.18 201/55

**Solution:**

(i)

**Step 1**: Fix the $F$ onto the $x$-$y$ plane.

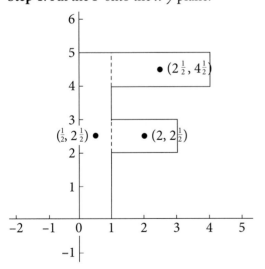

8.19 201/65

**Step 2**: Divide the $F$ into regularly shaped pieces and identify the centre of gravity of each piece.

**Step 3**: Let each square unit area have weight 1 unit (this unit is not necessarily a newton). We have three pieces of weights 5 units, 3 units and 2 units, as shown. The resultant weight = $5 + 3 + 2 = 10$ units.

Let its position be $(x, y)$.

| Weight | 5 | 3 | 2 | = | 10 |
|---|---|---|---|---|---|
| Position | $\left(\frac{1}{2}, 2\frac{1}{2}\right)$ | $\left(2\frac{1}{2}, 4\frac{1}{2}\right)$ | $\left(2, 2\frac{1}{2}\right)$ | | $(x, y)$ |

Taking moments about the $y$-axis,

$$5\left(\frac{1}{2}\right) + 3\left(2\frac{1}{2}\right) + 2(2) = 10\,x$$

$$\therefore 14 = 10\,x$$

$$\therefore x = 1.4$$

Taking moments about the $x$-axis,

$$5\left(2\frac{1}{2}\right) + 3\left(4\frac{1}{2}\right) + 2\left(2\frac{1}{2}\right) = 10\,(y)$$

$$\therefore 31 = 10\,y$$

$$\therefore y = 3.1$$

The centre of gravity of the $F$ is at $(1.4, 3.1)$.

(ii)  The $F$ will hang so that the centre of gravity is directly below the point of hanging, $p$.

Let $A$ be the angle between $[pq]$ and the vertical.

$$\tan A = \frac{1.4}{1.9} = 0.7368$$

$$\therefore A = 36.38° \quad \text{Answer.}$$

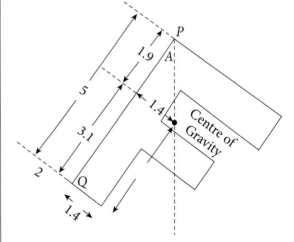

Fig. 8.27

### Worked Example 8.5

Find the centre of gravity of this lamina.

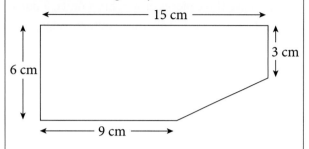

Fig. 8.28

### Solution:

Two methods of solving this problem will be shown.

**Method 1**: As before, the lamina is fixed onto the $x - y$ plane and divided into regular pieces.

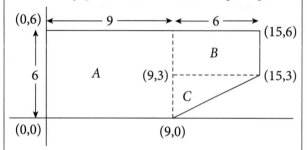

Fig. 8.29

| Piece | Area | CoG |
|-------|------|-----|
| A | $6 \times 9 = 54$ | $\left(4\frac{1}{2}, 3\right)$ |
| B | $6 \times 3 = 18$ | $\left(12, 4\frac{1}{2}\right)$ |
| C | $\frac{1}{2} \times 6 \times 3 = 9$ | see below |

Centre of gravity of Part C is at the centroid of the triangle whose vertices are
$(9, 0)$, $(15, 3)$ and $(9, 3)$. The centroid is at
$$\left(\frac{9 + 15 + 9}{3}, \frac{0 + 3 + 3}{3}\right) = (11, 2)$$

Let each unit area have 1 unit weight. The resultant weight = $54 + 18 + 9 = 81$ units.

| | A | B | C | | Resultant |
|--|---|---|---|--|-----------|
| Weight | 54 | 18 | 9 | = | 81 |
| CoG | $\left(4\frac{1}{2}, 3\right)$ | $\left(12, 4\frac{1}{2}\right)$ | $(11, 2)$ | | $(x, y)$ |

Taking moments about the $y$-axis,
$$54\left(4\frac{1}{2}\right) + 18(12) + 9(11) = 81(x)$$
$$\therefore 81\,x = 558$$
$$\therefore x = \frac{62}{9}$$

Taking moments about the $x$-axis,
$$54(3) + 18\left(4\frac{1}{2}\right) + 9(2) = 81(y)$$
$$\therefore 81\,y = 261$$
$$\therefore y = \frac{29}{9}$$

Answer: The centre of gravity is at $\left(\frac{62}{9}, \frac{29}{9}\right)$.

**Method 2**: The **"missing piece"** method.
The lamina is a rectangle with a triangle "missing" from the bottom right hand corner.

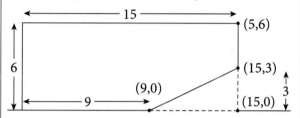

Fig. 8.30

1. The complete rectangle would have area = $15 \times 6 = 90$ square units. The centre of gravity would be at $\left(7\frac{1}{2}, 3\right)$.

2. The "missing piece" has area = $\frac{1}{2} \times 6 \times 3 = 9$ square units. Its centre of gravity is at the centroid of the triangle whose vertices are $(9, 0)$, $(15, 0)$ and $(15, 3)$. The centroid is at
$$\left(\frac{9 + 15 + 15}{3}, \frac{0 + 0 + 3}{3}\right) = (13, 1)$$

3. The remainder has area $(90 - 9) = 81$ square units. Let its centre of gravity be at $(x, y)$.
Now, the remainder together with the "missing piece" make up the complete rectangle. If each square unit has unit weight, we have:

| | Rectangle | Missing piece | | Resultant |
|--|-----------|---------------|--|-----------|
| Weight | 90 | 9 | = | 81 |
| CoG | $\left(7\frac{1}{2}, 3\right)$ | $(13, 1)$ | | $(x, y)$ |

Complete rectangle 90
at $(x, y)$
– Missing piece 9 at
$(13, 1)$ } = Resultant 81 at $(x, y)$

Taking moments about the $y$-axis,

$$90\left(7\tfrac{1}{2}\right) - 9(13) = 81\,(x)$$

$$\therefore 675 - 117 = 81\,x$$

$$\therefore x = \frac{62}{9}$$

Taking moments about the $x$-axis,

$$90(3) - 9(1) = 81\,(y)$$

$$\therefore 270 - 9 = 81\,y$$

$$\therefore y = \frac{29}{9}$$

The centre of gravity is at $\left(\frac{62}{9}, \frac{29}{9}\right)$ Answer.

## Exercise 8 C

1. Find the centres of gravity of these laminae. The answers should be given with reference to the origin $O$, taking the horizontal as the $x$-axis and the vertical as the $y$-axis. If each lamina were hung freely from $P$, find the angle which $OP$ would make with the vertical.

(i)
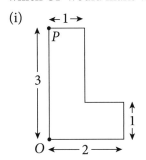

Fig. 8.31

(ii)
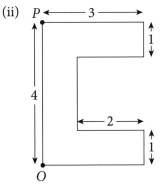

Fig. 8.32

(iii)
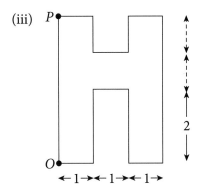

Fig. 8.33

(iv)
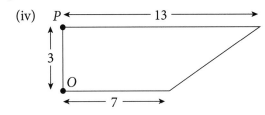

Fig. 8.34

2. A circle of radius 6 cm has a circle of radius 3 cm cut from it, as shown. How far from the centre of the greater circle is the centre of gravity of the remainder?

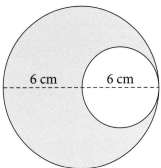

Fig. 8.35

3. A square lamina of side 4 m has a smaller square of side 1 m removed from a corner, as shown.

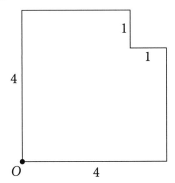

Fig. 8.36

Taking the bottom left as the origin, find the centre of gravity of the remainder.

4. Find the position of the centres of gravity of these shaded laminae.

(i)

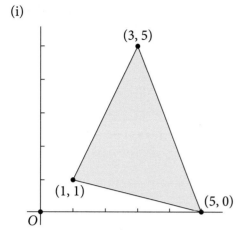

Fig. 8.37

(ii)

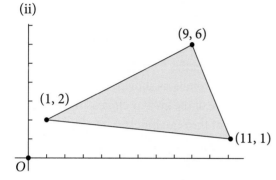

Fig. 8.38

(iii)

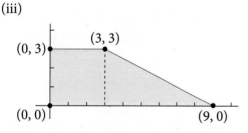

Fig. 8.39

(iv)

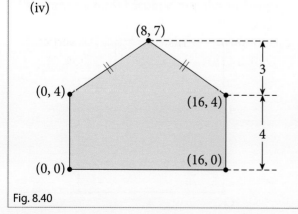

Fig. 8.40

5. *ABC* is an isosceles triangle. The midpoint of [*BC*] is *D*. *M* is the midpoint of [*AD*]. A circle of radius $\frac{7}{2}$ cm and centre *M* is cut from the triangle. How far from *D* is the centre of gravity of the remainder? (Take $\pi = \frac{22}{7}$.)

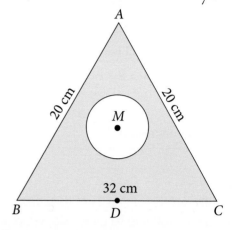

Fig. 8.41

6. A disc of centre *O* and radius 5 m has a smaller disc of radius 2 m removed, as shown. How far from *O* is the centre of gravity of the remainder? Give your answer to the nearest centimetre.

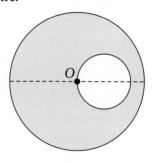

Fig. 8.42

7. *PQRS* is a rectangular lamina. |*PQ*| = 6 cm and |*PS*| = 10 cm. Two pieces (both shaded), one rectangular and one triangular, are cut off as shown in the diagram. Calculate the co-ordinates of the centre of gravity of the remaining portion, taking *Q* as the origin.

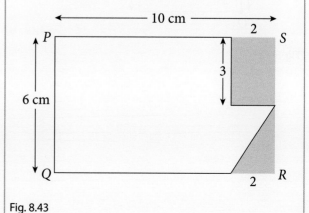

Fig. 8.43

8.  (a)  Particles of weights 4N, 5N, 1N and 3N
        are placed on a horizontal plane at points
        (2, 3), ($x$, 4), (5 , $y$) and (1, 7) respectively.
        If the centre of gravity of the four-particle
        system is at (2, 4), calculate $x$ and $y$.

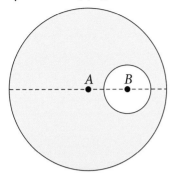

    (b)

Fig. 8.44

        A hole of radius $r$ and centre $b$ is punched
        in a circular lamina of radius $4r$ and
        centre $A$. The line joining the centres $A$
        and $B$ is horizontal. If $|AB| = 2r$, calculate
        the co-ordinates of the centre of gravity
        of the remaining portion, taking $A$ as the
        origin.

9.  A uniform lamina is in the shape of a square
    $ABCD$, $|AB| = 100$ mm. A circular portion of
    radius 20 mm is removed.
    Find, correct to the nearest mm, the
    $x$-coordinate of the centre of gravity of the
    remainder, if $AB$ and $AD$ are taken as the $x$
    and $y$ axes, respectively. (Assume $\pi = \frac{22}{7}$.)

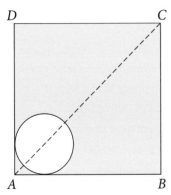

Fig. 8.45

10. (i)  Find the distance, from the bottom edge
        [$AB$], of the centre of gravity of a uniform
        rectangular sheet of plywood 90 cm by
        115 cm (see diagram).

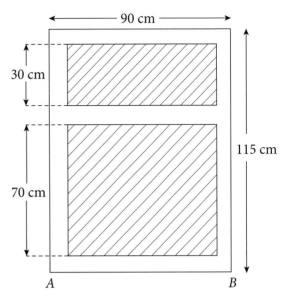

Fig. 8.46

    (ii)  The shaded sections were cut out to leave
         a frame 5 cm wide surrounding the cut
         out areas. Calculate the distance of the
         centre of gravity of the frame from the
         bottom edge [$AB$], correct to one place of
         decimals.

11. A uniform quadrilateral lamina has vertices
    $O(0, 0)$, $P(0, 12)$, $Q(18, 18)$ and $R(30, 0)$.
    (i)   Find the areas of $\triangle\,OPQ$ and $\triangle\,OQR$
    (ii)  Write down the centres of gravity of
          $\triangle\,OPQ$ and $\triangle\,OQR$
    (iii) Find (correct to two decimal places) the
          co-ordinates of the centre of gravity of the
          lamina $OPQR$.

12. A uniform quadrilateral lamina has vertices
    $O\,(0, 0)$, $P(-6, 6)$, $Q(18, 18)$ and $R(36, 0)$.
    (i)   Show that the areas of $\triangle\,OPQ$ and
          $\triangle\,OQR$ are in the ratio 1 : 3.
    (ii)  Write down the centres of gravity of
          $\triangle\,OPQ$ and $\triangle\,OQR$.
    (iii) Find the centre of gravity of the lamina
          $OPQR$.

## Centre of gravity of symmetrical solids

### Solid cylinder

The centre of gravity of a solid cylinder of height $h$ is (obviously!) half way up the central axis, at a height $\frac{1}{2}h$ above the base, as shown.

The volume of a cylinder is $\pi r^2 h$.

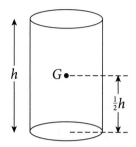

Fig. 8.47

### Solid cone

The centre of gravity of a solid cone of height $h$ is one-quarter of the way up the central axis, at a height $\frac{1}{4}h$ above the base, as shown.

The volume of a cone is $\frac{1}{3}\pi r^2 h$.

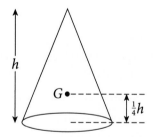

Fig. 8.48

### Solid hemisphere

The centre of gravity of a solid hemisphere is three-eighths of the way up the central axis, at a height $\frac{3}{8}r$ above the base, as shown.

The volume of a hemisphere is $\frac{2}{3}\pi r^3$.

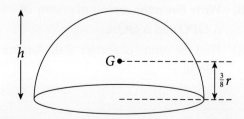

Fig. 8.49

### Hemispherical shell

The centre of gravity of a hemispherical shell is half of the way up the central axis, at a height $\frac{1}{2}r$ above the base, as shown.

The curved surface area of a hemisphere is $2\pi r^2$.

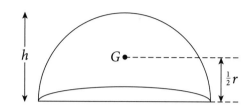

Fig. 8.50

### *Worked Example 8.6*

A solid cylinder, a solid cone, a solid hemisphere and a hemispherical shell are all of height 12 cm. They stand on a table. How high above the table is the centre of gravity of each?

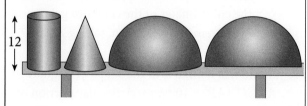

Fig. 8.51

**Solution:**

(i) The centre of gravity of the cylinder is at a height $\frac{1}{2}h = \frac{1}{2}(12) = 6$ cm above the table.

(ii) The centre of gravity of the cone is at a height $\frac{1}{4}h = \frac{1}{4}(12) = 3$ cm above the table.

(iii) The radius of the hemisphere is 12. Therefore, the centre of gravity of the hemisphere is at a height $\frac{3}{8}r = \frac{3}{8}(12)$ $= 4.5$ cm above the table.

(iv) The centre of gravity of the hemispherical shell is at a height $\frac{1}{2}h = \frac{1}{2}(12) = 6$ cm above the table.

### Worked Example 8.7

A solid wooden toy consists of a solid cone on a hemisphere.

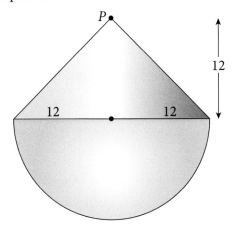

Fig. 8.52

(i) The radius of both is 12 cm. The height of the cone is also 12 cm. Prove that the volume of the hemisphere is twice the volume of the cone. (See Formulae & Tables.)

(ii) Assuming that the wood throughout has the same density, find the distance from apex $P$ to the centre of gravity of the toy.

**Solution:**

(i)

$$V_{cone} = \frac{1}{3}\pi r^2 h$$
$$= \frac{1}{3}\pi (12)^2 (12)$$
$$= 576\pi$$
$$V_{hemisphere} = \frac{2}{3}\pi r^3$$
$$= \frac{2}{3}\pi (12)^3$$
$$= 1152\pi$$
$$= 2(576\pi)$$

Therefore, the volume of the hemisphere is twice the volume of the cone.

(ii) Always imagine the object placed on its side, as shown:

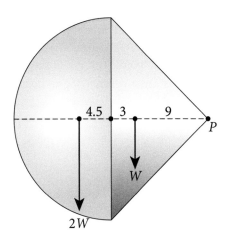

Fig. 8.53

Let $W$ be the weight of the cone. Therefore $2W$ is the weight of the hemisphere. $W$ acts through a point $\frac{3}{8}r = \frac{3}{8}(12) = 4.5$ cm from the base of the cone. $2W$ acts through a point $\frac{1}{4}h = \frac{1}{4}(12) = 3$ cm from the base of the hemisphere.

Here, then, is the diagram of forces. The total weight of the toy is $3W$ which acts through a point which is $x$ cm from $P$.

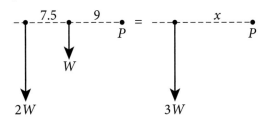

Fig. 8.54

By the Principle of Moments,
$$W(9) + 2W(16.5) = 3W(x)$$
$$\therefore 9W + 33W = 3xW$$
$$\therefore 42W = 3xW$$

Answer: $\qquad \therefore x = 14$ cm from $P$

### Exercise 8 D

1. A solid cylinder, a solid cone, a solid hemisphere and a hemispherical shell are all of height 24 cm. They stand on a horizontal table, as shown. How high above the table is the centre of gravity of each?

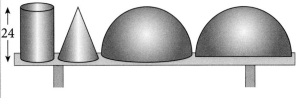

Fig. 8.55

2. A solid hemisphere and a hemispherical shell both have radius 16 cm. They stand, as shown, on a horizontal table. Find the difference in the heights of their centres of gravity above the table.

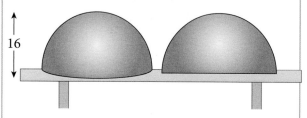

16

Fig. 8.56

3. A solid cone has radius 3 cm and height $h$ cm. The centre of gravity of the cone is 5 cm from the base. Find
   (i) the value of $h$
   (ii) the volume of the cone in terms of $\pi$.

4. A solid hemisphere has radius $r$. The centre of gravity of the sphere is 3 cm from the base. Find
   (i) the value of $r$
   (ii) the volume of the hemisphere in terms of $\pi$.

5. A hemispherical shell has radius $r$. The centre of gravity of the sphere is 3 cm from the base. Find
   (i) the value of $r$
   (ii) the curved surface area of the hemispherical shell in terms of $\pi$.

6. A solid cylinder has radius 8 cm and height 10 cm. Its weight is $3W$. It is attached, as shown, to a solid hemisphere, also of radius 8 cm, whose weight is $W$. How far from the base of the cylinder is the centre of gravity of the compound body?

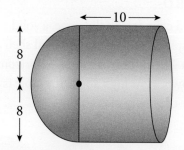

10

8

8

Fig. 8.57

7. A solid cylinder has radius 5 cm and height 14 cm. Its weight is $2W$. It is attached, as shown, to a solid cone, of radius 5 cm, and height 8 cm, whose weight is $W$.
How far from the base of the cylinder is the centre of gravity of the compound body?

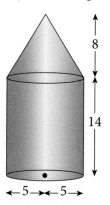

8

14

←5→←5→

Fig. 8.58

8. A solid cylinder has radius 24 mm and height 30 mm. Its weight is $5W$. It is attached, as shown, to a solid hemisphere, also of radius 24 mm, whose weight is $W$. How far from the base of the cylinder is the centre of gravity of the compound body?

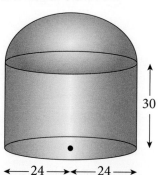

30

← 24 →←  24 →

Fig. 8.59

9. A test-tube consists of a cylindrical shell of radius 6 mm and height 10 mm attached, as shown, to a hemispherical shell of radius 6 mm. The cylindrical part has weight $3W$; the spherical part has weight $W$. How far from the base of the cylindrical part is the centre of gravity of the test-tube?

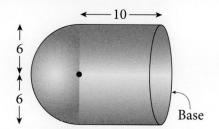

10

6

6

Base

Fig. 8.60

10. A solid hemisphere of radius 8 cm is attached, as shown, to a solid cone, of radius 8 cm, and height 12 cm. The weights of the hemisphere and the cone are equal. Show that the centre of gravity of the compound body is at the plane where their bases meet.

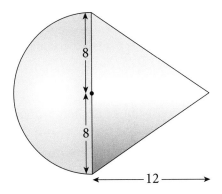

Fig. 8.61

11. A solid cylinder has radius 12 cm and height 40 cm. It is attached, as shown, to a solid cone, of radius 12 cm, and height 40 cm. Both are made out of the same wood of the same density.
    (i)  By finding their volumes, show that the weight of the cylinder is three times that of the cone.
    (ii) How far from the base of the cylinder is the centre of gravity of the compound body?

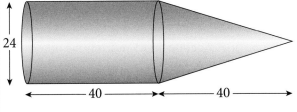

Fig. 8.62

12. A solid cylinder has radius 18 cm and height 24 cm. It is attached, as shown, to a solid hemisphere, of radius 18 cm. Both are made out of the same material of the same density.
    (i)  By finding their volumes, show that the weight of the cylinder and the hemisphere are in the ratio 2:1.
    (ii) How far from the base of the cylinder is the centre of gravity of the compound body?

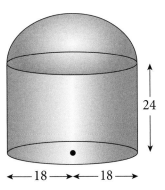

Fig. 8.63

13. A solid cylinder has radius 8 cm and height 20 cm. It is attached, at one end, to a solid hemisphere, of radius 8 cm and at the other end to a solid cone of radius 8 cm and height 16 cm. The mass of the cone is $m$ and the mass of the hemisphere is also $m$. But the mass of the cylinder is $3m$.
    How far from point $O$ (at the centre of the base of the hemisphere) is the centre of gravity of the compound body?

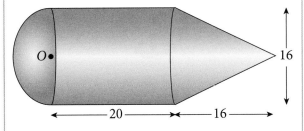

Fig. 8.64

14. A cylindrical shell has radius $r$ and height $4r$. It is attached, as shown, to a hemispherical shell, of radius $r$. Both are made of the same material of the same thickness.
    (i) By finding their curved surface areas, show that the weight of the cylindrical shell is 4 times that of the hemispherical shell.
    (ii) How far from the base of the cylinder is the centre of gravity of the compound body?

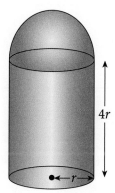

Fig. 8.65

## Couples

When you turn a steering wheel or screw the top off a bottle of lemonade, you apply two equal but opposite forces.

Fig. 8.66

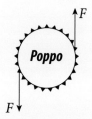

Fig. 8.67

The resultant of these forces is zero. But there is a turning effect. The steering wheel stays where it is but it turns on its axis. In these cases the Principle of Moments fails, because it is impossible to replace the forces by a resultant (since the resultant is zero). We will have to give such "double" forces special treatment. They have a special name. They are called **couples**.

**Definition:** A **couple** is a set of two equal and opposite forces which are displaced from one another.

Take a couple, consisting of two forces of magnitude 10 N each, a distance 4 m apart. What is the moment of this couple about a point $P$, 2 m from each line of action?

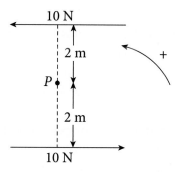

Fig. 8.68

The moments are both anti-clockwise and, therefore, both positive. The total moment about $P = 10(2) + 10(2) = 40$ N m.

Now, let's find the moment about $Q$, which is 3 m from one line of action and 1 m from the other.

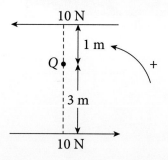

Fig. 8.69

The total moment about $Q = 10(3) + 10(1) = 40$ N m. Same as for about $P$!

It can be proved that in all cases the moment of any couple about a point is the same for all points in its plane.

## Worked Example 8.8

*abcd* is a square of side 1 metre. Forces of magnitude 1 N, 1 N, 2 N and 3 N act along $\overrightarrow{AB}, \overrightarrow{CB}, \overrightarrow{DC}$ and $\overrightarrow{DA}$ respectively. Find

(i)   the magnitude of the resultant

(ii)  the distance of its line of action from *A*

(iii) the ratio into which the line of action divides the line segment [*AB*].

**Solution:**

(i) Let $\vec{i}$ be the unit vector along *AB*.

Let $\vec{j}$ be the unit vector along *AD*.

Let $\vec{R}$ be the resultant.

$$\vec{R} = \vec{i} - \vec{j} + 2\vec{i} - 3\vec{j}$$
$$= 3\vec{i} - 4\vec{j}$$
$$\therefore |\vec{R}| = \sqrt{3^2 + (-4)^2} = 5 \text{ N}$$

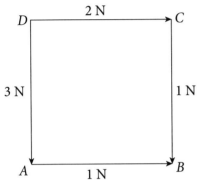

Fig. 8.70

(ii) Let *D* be the distance of the line of action of $\vec{R}$ from the point *A*. Taking moments about *A*, (the sum of the moments = the moment of the sum)

$$1(0) - 1(1) - 2(1) + 3(0) = -5(d)$$
$$\therefore d = 0.6 \text{ m}$$
$$= 60 \text{ cm.}$$

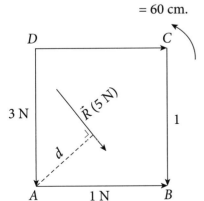

Fig. 8.71

(iii) Let *p* be the point where the line of action of $\vec{R}$ cuts the line *AB*, and let $|AP| = x$. Taking moments about *P*.

$$1(0) - 1(1-x) - 2(1) + 3(x) = -5(0)$$
$$\therefore -1 + x - 2 + 3x = 0$$
$$\therefore 4x = 3$$
$$\therefore x = \frac{3}{4}$$

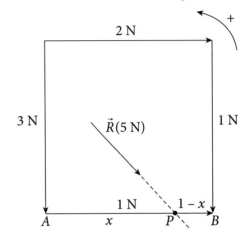

Fig. 8.72

Therefore, the line of action divides [*AB*] in the ratio $\frac{3}{4} : \frac{1}{4} = 3:1$

## Worked Example 8.9

*PQRS* is a square of side 1 m, as shown. Forces of magnitude 1 N, 2 N, 4 N and 6 N act along $\overrightarrow{PQ}, \overrightarrow{QR}, \overrightarrow{RS}$ and $\overrightarrow{SP}$ respectively. There is also a couple of anti-clockwise moment 4 N m. Find the resultant and the distance of its line of action from *p*.

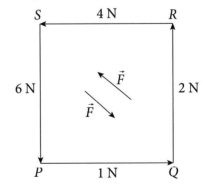

Fig. 8.73

**Solution:**

The system consists of forces $\vec{i}, 2\vec{j}, -4\vec{i}, -6\vec{j}$ and a couple which is made up from two equal and opposite forces. The resultant, $\vec{R}$, is given by

$$\vec{R} = \vec{i} + 2\vec{j} - 4\vec{i} - 6\vec{j}$$
$$= -3\vec{i} - 4\vec{j}$$
$$\therefore |\vec{R}| = \sqrt{(-3)^2 + (-4)^2}$$
$$= 5 \text{ N}$$

Let $d$ = the distance of the line of action of $\vec{R}$ from $P$. The moment of $\vec{R}$ about $P$ must equal the sum of the moments of the other forces, including the couple, about $P$.

$$5(d) = 1(0) + 2(1) + 4(1) + 6(0) + 4$$
$$\therefore 5d = 10$$
$$\therefore d = 2$$

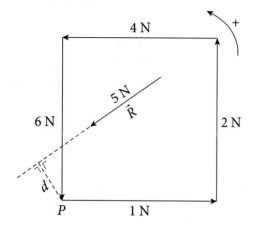

Fig. 8.74

This means that the entire system could be replaced by the force $-3\vec{i} - 4\vec{j}$ N, acting along a line 2 m from the point $P$.

---

### Exercise 8 E

1. Forces of magnitude 1 N, 2 N, 3 N, 4 N act along the sides $\overrightarrow{AB}, \overrightarrow{BC}, \overrightarrow{CD}, \overrightarrow{DA}$ of a square of side 1 metre. Find the magnitude of the resultant.
   If a further force of magnitude $3\sqrt{2}$ N along $\overrightarrow{DB}$ were added to the system, what would the magnitude of the resultant become?

2. A square $ABCD$ of side 1 m has forces of magnitude 3 N, 2 N, 5 N and 4 N acting along $\overrightarrow{AB}, \overrightarrow{CB}, \overrightarrow{DC}$ and $\overrightarrow{DA}$ respectively. Find the magnitude of the resultant and the distance of its line of action from $A$ Where does the line of action of the resultant intersect the line $AB$?

3. $ABCD$ is a square of side 1 m. Forces of magnitude 2, 4, 7 and 16 newtons act along the four sides $\overrightarrow{AB}, \overrightarrow{BC}, \overrightarrow{CD}$ and $\overrightarrow{DA}$ respectively. Find
   (i) the resultant, in terms of $\vec{i}$ and $\vec{j}$, if $\vec{i}$ is along $AB$
   (ii) the magnitude of the resultant
   (iii) the distance of its line of action from $a$.

4. $ABCD$ is a rectangle such that $|AB| = |CD| = 4$ m and $|BC| = |AD| = 3$ m. Forces of magnitude 2, 2, 2, 1 and 10 newtons act along $\overrightarrow{AB}, \overrightarrow{BC}, \overrightarrow{DC}, \overrightarrow{DA}$ and $\overrightarrow{DB}$ respectively.
   (i) Find the magnitude of the resultant.
   (ii) How far is its line of action from $D$?
   (iii) If a couple of anti-clockwise moment 12 N m were added to the system, find the distance of the line of action of the new resultant from $D$.

5. $ABC$ is an isosceles triangle such that $|AB| = 8$ m and $|BC| = |AC| = 5$ m. Forces of magnitude 16, 10 and 20 newtons act along $\overrightarrow{AB}, \overrightarrow{BC}$ and $\overrightarrow{CA}$ respectively. Find the magnitude of the resultant and the distance of its line of action from $C$.

6. $ABC$ is an equilateral triangle of side $l$. Forces of 8 N, 8 N, and 4 N act in the directions $AB$, $BC$ and $AC$ respectively. Calculate
   (i) the magnitude of the resultant
   (ii) the distance from $A$ to the line of action of the resultant.
   If instead of reducing the forces to a single force they were reduced to a force at $A$ and a couple of moment $M$, calculate $M$.

## Systems in equilibrium

If a rigid body is not accelerating, then the forces acting on it in any one line must equal zero. Otherwise, according to Newton's second law, the body would accelerate in that line. The resultant force is zero and hence its moment about any axis is zero. Therefore, the sum of the moments of the forces about any axis must be zero, in accordance with the Principle of Moments.

In most examples we will examine the forces along the horizontal and along the vertical lines. We will also examine the moments of the forces about some axis, usually through an extreme point. We have three equations:

1. The forces up = the forces down.

2. The forces to the left = the forces to the right.

3. Sum of the anti-clockwise moments about some axis = the sum of the clockwise moments about that axis.

## Worked Example 8.10

A uniform beam of weight $W$ and length 6 m carries weights $2W$ and $3W$ at points 1 m from $P$ and $Q$ respectively. The beam is supported in a horizontal position by two vertical strings at $P$ and $Q$. Find the tension in each string.

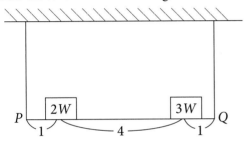

Fig. 8.75

### Solution:

Here are the forces acting on the beam, including its weight force, $W$, acting through its midpoint.

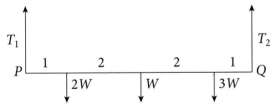

Fig. 8.76

1. Forces up = forces down
$$\Rightarrow T_1 + T_2 = 2W + W + 3W$$
$$\Rightarrow T_1 + T_2 = 6W \qquad \text{Equation 1}$$

2. Forces left = forces right: None.

3. Take moments about $P$. Strictly speaking this is taking moments about an axis through $P$ coming out of the page.

Anti-clockwise moments = clockwise moments.
$$T_1(0) + T_2(6) = 2W(1) + W(3) + 3W(5)$$
$$\therefore 6T_2 = 20W$$
$$\therefore T_2 = \frac{10}{3}W \text{ and } T_1 = \frac{8}{3}W, \text{ from Equation 1.}$$

## Worked Example 8.11

A uniform ladder of weight $W$ leans against a smooth, vertical wall so that it reaches 4 m up the wall. Its foot is 3 m from the foot of the wall. The ground is rough and the ladder is just on the point of slipping. Find the reaction forces at the wall and the ground in terms of $W$. Find also the coefficient of friction between the ladder and the ground.

### Solution:

The wall is smooth, so the only reaction force at the wall will be perpendicular to the wall, acting on the top of the ladder. There is no friction here. The ground is rough, so there is a reaction force and a friction force acting on the ladder at its foot. The ladder would tend to slip outwards, so the friction, which always opposes motion, acts inwards towards the wall. The weight of the ladder acts through its centre, since it is uniform. Here, then, is the force diagram:

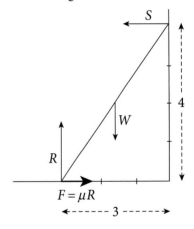

Fig. 8.77

Since the ladder is on the point of slipping, we know that the system is still in equilibrium, and the limiting friction is called into play.
That is, $F = \mu R$.

(i) Ups = downs: $R = W$      Eqn 1

(ii) Lefts = rights: $S = \mu R$      Eqn 2

(iii) Take moments about the foot of the ladder.

Anti-clockwise = clockwise.
$$S(4) + R(0) = W\left(1\tfrac{1}{2}\right) + \mu R(0)$$
$$\therefore 4S = \frac{3W}{2} \qquad \text{Eqn 3}$$

**Note:** The distances are the distances of the line of action of each force from the foot of the ladder.

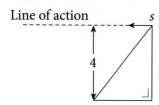

Fig. 8.78

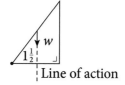

Fig. 8.79 0

Equation 3:    $4\,S = \frac{3}{2}\,W$

$\therefore 8\,S = 3\,W$

$\therefore S = \frac{3}{8}\,W$

Since $S = \frac{3}{8}\,W$ and $R = W$. Equation 2 reads:

$$\frac{3}{8}\,W = \mu\,W$$

$$\therefore \mu = \frac{3}{8}$$

Answer: $R = W$; $S = \frac{3}{8}\,W$, $\mu = \frac{3}{8}$.

---

### Exercise 8 F

1. A uniform rod $AB$, of weight $W$ and length 4 m, has a mass of weight $W$ attached to a point 1 m from $A$. The rod is held in a horizontal position by means of two vertical strings at $A$ and $B$. Find the tension in each of the strings.

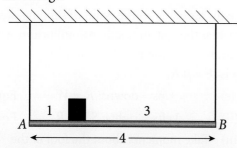

Fig. 8.80

2. $AB$ is a uniform plank of weight $W$, 8 m long. It is held in a horizontal position by means of two vertical strings at $A$ and $B$.

   A mass of weight $W$ is placed at a point 1 m from $B$. Find the tension in each string (see diagram top right).

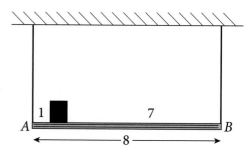

Fig. 8.81

3. A uniform rod $AB$ is 10 cm long and weighs 2 N. The rod is kept in a horizontal position by means of two vertical strings, one attached to it at $C$, the other at $D$, where $|AC| = 1$ cm and $|BD| = 2$ cm.

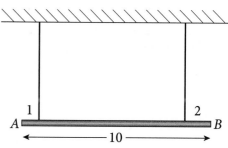

Fig. 8.82

   (i) Find the tension in each string.
   (ii) Where should a mass of weight 4 N be attached to the rod, so that the tension in the string at $C$ would be twice the tension in the string at $D$?

4. A uniform ladder rests on rough horizontal ground against a smooth vertical wall. The ladder begins to slip when it reaches 6 m up the wall and its foot is 4 m from the foot of the wall.

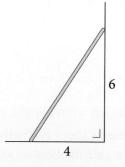

Fig. 8.83

   (i) Find the normal reactions at the wall and the ground.
   (ii) Find also the coefficient of friction between the ladder and the ground.

5. A uniform ladder rests on rough horizontal ground against a smooth vertical wall. The ladder begins to slip when it reaches 11 m up the wall and its foot is 10 m from the foot of the wall. Find the coefficient of friction between the ladder and the ground.

6. (a) Fill in the missing word/phrase in each of the following
   (i) "_____ is the force between two rough surfaces in contact which tends to oppose sliding".
   (ii) "The _____ is the measure of the turning effect of a force".

   (b) A uniform ladder of weight 250 N rests with one end against a smooth vertical wall and the other on rough horizontal ground, the coefficient of friction being 0.8. The ladder is just on the point of slipping when inclined at an angle $\alpha$ to the horizontal. Find the value of $\tan \alpha$.

7. A uniform ladder of weight $W$ rests on rough horizontal ground against a smooth vertical wall. The ladder begins to slip when it makes an angle $A$ with the ground. If the coefficient of friction between the ladder and the ground is $\frac{1}{2}$, find the value of $A$.

8. A uniform ladder of weight $W$ rests on rough horizontal ground against a rough vertical wall. The ladder begins to slip when it makes an angle $A$ with the ground. If the coefficient of friction between the ladder and the ground and between the ladder and the wall is $\frac{1}{2}$, find the value of $A$ to the nearest degree.

9. A uniform rod $AB$ of length 4 m and mass 20 kg stands with the end $B$ on a horizontal floor and the end $A$ against a vertical wall. The rod is in the plane perpendicular to the wall.
   The coefficient of friction, $\mu$, is the same at $A$ and $B$. If the rod is on the point of slipping when its inclination is 45°, show that $\mu = \sqrt{2} - 1$.

10. A 10 m uniform ladder of weight $W$ leans against a smooth vertical wall and on rough ground. The coefficient of friction between the ladder and the ground is $\frac{4}{5}$. The ladder makes an angle $A$ with the horizontal ground.
    (i) Show that slipping will begin to occur when $\tan A = \frac{5}{8}$.
    (ii) A man of weight $2W$ sets this ladder against the wall, fixing $\tan A = \frac{3}{4}$. How far up the ladder can the man go before slipping will occur?
    (iii) What is the least value of $\tan A$ for which the man will safely reach the top of the ladder?

## Triangular laminae

When dealing with triangles, remember that the centre of gravity lies at the centroid, $\frac{2}{3}$ of the way along each median. Each median runs from a vertex to the opposite midpoint.

### Worked Example 8.12

A uniform lamina is in the shape of an isosceles triangle $abc$ such that $|AB| = 10$ cm and $|AC| = |BC| = 13$. It stands in a vertical plane on rough ground against a rough wall in such a way that $AB$ is vertical. The coefficient of friction between the lamina and the wall is $\frac{1}{4}$. The coefficient of friction between the lamina and the ground is $\mu$. Find the least value of $\mu$ if slipping does not occur.

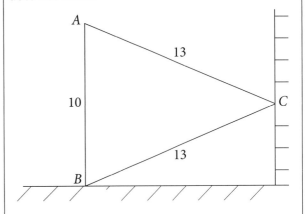

Fig. 8.84

**Solution:**

Let $m$ be the midpoint of $[AB]$.

By Pythagoras' Theorem,

$$|AM|^2 + |MC|^2 = |AC|^2$$
$$\therefore 25 + |MC|^2 = 169$$
$$\therefore |MC| = 12$$

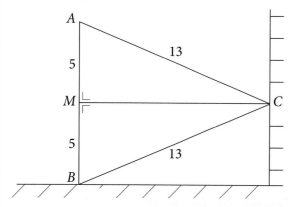

Fig. 8.85

The centre of gravity, $G$, of the lamina is at the centroid of $\triangle ABC$, which is one third of the way from $M$ to $C$. Therefore $G$ is 4 cm from $M$ and 8 cm from $C$. Here is the force diagram. We will assume that the triangle is on the point of slipping.

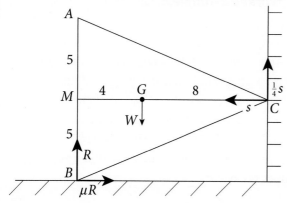

Fig. 8.86

Note that the point $C$ would slip down the wall, so the friction force at $C$ ($\frac{1}{4}S$) is in an upward direction. The point $B$ would slip to the left, so the friction at $B$ ($\mu R$) is to the right. Here are the three equations of equilibrium:

$$R + \frac{1}{4}S = W. \qquad \text{Eqn 1}$$
$$\mu R = S \qquad \text{Eqn 2}$$

(Taking moments about $b$):

$$S(5) + \left(\frac{1}{4}S\right)(12) = W(4)$$
$$\therefore 8S = 4W$$
$$\therefore S = \frac{1}{2}W \qquad \text{Eqn 3}$$

Equation 1: $R + \frac{1}{4}\left(\frac{1}{2}W\right) = W$

$$\therefore R = \frac{7}{8}W$$

Equation 2: $\quad \mu\left(\frac{7}{8}W\right) = \frac{1}{2}W$
$$\therefore \mu = \frac{4}{7}$$

If the lamina is on the point of slipping, then $\mu = \frac{4}{7}$. Therefore, if slipping does not occur, then $\mu \geq \frac{4}{7}$. The least possible value for $\mu$ is, therefore, $\frac{4}{7}$.

---

**Exercise 8 G**

1. A lamina is in the shape of an isosceles triangle $ABC$, such that $|AB| = 16$ cm and $|AC| = |BC| = 10$ cm. It stands in a vertical plane on rough ground against a smooth wall, with $[AB]$ vertical.
   (i) Show that the centre of gravity $G$ is 4 cm from $C$.
   (ii) Find the least value of the coefficient of friction between the lamina and the ground if slipping has not occurred.

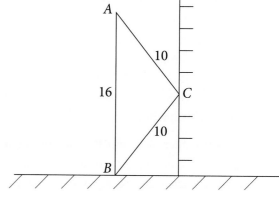

Fig. 8.87

2. A lamina is in the shape of an isosceles triangle $ABC$, such that $|AB| = 16$ cm and $|AC| = |BC| = 17$ cm. It stands in a vertical plane on rough ground against a smooth wall, with $[AB]$ vertical.
   (i) Show that the centre of gravity is 10 cm from $C$.
   (ii) Find the least value of the coefficient of friction between the lamina and the ground if slipping has not occurred.

3. A lamina is in the shape of an isosceles triangle $abc$, such that $|AB| = 40$ cm and $|AC| = |BC| = 29$ cm. It stands in a vertical plane on rough ground against a smooth wall, with $[AB]$ vertical.
   Find the least value of the coefficient of friction between the lamina and the ground if slipping has not occurred.

4.  A lamina of weight $W$ is in the shape of an isosceles triangle $ABC$, such that $|AB| = 14$ cm and $|AC| = |BC| = 25$ cm. It stands in limiting equilibrium in a vertical plane on rough ground against a rough wall, with $[AB]$ vertical. The coefficient of friction between the lamina and the wall is $\frac{1}{4}$.

    (i)  Find the normal reactions at the ground and the wall in terms of $W$.

    (ii) Find the least value of the coefficient of friction between the lamina and the ground if slipping has not occurred.

5.  (a)  Define
    (i)  limiting friction
    (ii) coefficient of friction.

    (b)  A lamina of weight $W$, in the shape of a thin equilateral triangle $PRQ$, is positioned vertically with the vertex $P$ against a smooth vertical wall, and $Q$ on a rough horizontal floor. $[QR]$ is parallel to the wall.

    (i)  Find, in terms of $W$, the friction force and the vertical reaction at $Q$.

    (ii) Find the least value of $\mu$, the coefficient of friction, so that slipping will not occur.

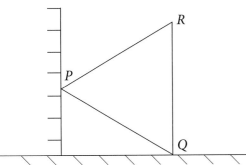

Fig. 8.88

6.  (a)  Prove that the centre of gravity of a uniform triangular lamina is at the point of intersection of its medians.

    (b)  A uniform triangular lamina $PQR$ has weight $W$ newtons. $|PQ| = 5$ cm, $|QR| = 4$ cm, $|PR| = 3$ cm and $\angle PRQ = 90°$.

    The lamina is suspended in a horizontal position by three inextensible, vertical strings, one at each vertex.

A particle of weight $\frac{4}{3}W$ newtons is positioned on the lamina 2 cm from $PR$ and 1 cm from $QR$. Calculate the tension in each string in terms of $W$.

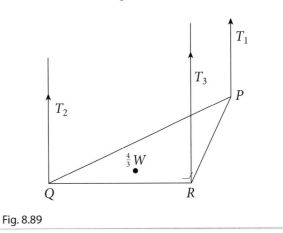

Fig. 8.89

## Angle of friction

**Definition:** The normal reaction, $R$, and the limiting friction, $F$, acting on a body which is either moving or on the point of moving, can be added to form a resultant. The angle between this resultant and the normal reaction is called the **angle of friction**. It is usually denoted by the Greek letter $\lambda$ (pronounced lambda).

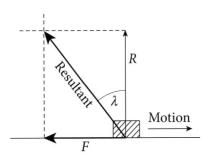

Fig. 8.90

From the diagram it is clear that

$$\tan \lambda = \frac{\text{opposite}}{\text{adjacent}}$$
$$= \frac{F}{R}$$
$$= \frac{\mu R}{R}$$
$$= \mu$$
$$\therefore \tan \lambda = \mu$$

### Worked Example 8.13

A rough plane is inclined at an angle $A$ to the horizontal, where $\tan A = \frac{1}{3}$. There is a wooden block of weight $W$ on the plane. The block is pushed by a horizontal force of magnitude $W$. If the block is on the point of moving up the plane, find the coefficient of friction between the block and the plane.

**Solution:**

Since the block is on the point of moving, we know two things:

1. The block is stationary and so the net force acting on it is zero.
2. The limiting friction, $\mu R$, is called into play.

Here are the forces acting on the block:

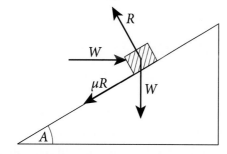

Fig. 8.91

The two $W$ forces must be resolved into components along and perpendicular to the slope. Since $\tan A = \frac{1}{3}$, $\cos A = \frac{3}{\sqrt{10}}$ and $\sin A = \frac{1}{\sqrt{10}}$

Weight force                        Resolved

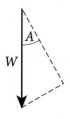   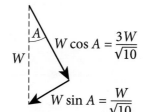

Fig. 8.92                          Fig. 8.93

Horizontal push

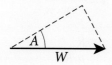

Fig. 8.94

Resolved

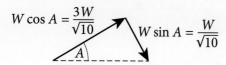

Fig. 8.95

Here are the resolved forces:

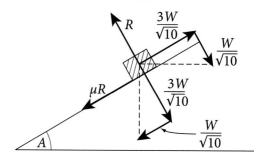

Fig. 8.96

1. Perpendicular to the plane: Ups = downs

$$W \cos A + W \sin A = R$$

$$\therefore R = \frac{3W}{\sqrt{10}} + \frac{W}{\sqrt{10}} = \frac{4W}{\sqrt{10}} \qquad \text{Eqn 1}$$

2. Parallel to the plane: Lefts = Rights

$$\mu R + \frac{W}{\sqrt{10}} = \frac{3W}{\sqrt{10}}$$

$$\therefore \mu R = \frac{2W}{\sqrt{10}} \qquad \text{Eqn 2}$$

Dividing equation 2 by equation 1, we get

$$\mu = \frac{\mu R}{R}$$
$$= \frac{2W/\sqrt{10}}{4W/\sqrt{10}}$$
$$= \frac{2W}{4W}$$
$$= \frac{1}{2}$$

Answer:　　　　　$\mu = \frac{1}{2}$

### Worked Example 8.14

A particle of weight $W$ is dragged across a rough horizontal surface by a force $F$ whose line of action makes an angle $\theta$ with the horizontal ground.

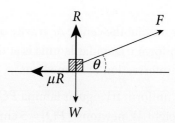

Fig. 8.97

(i) Prove that $F = \dfrac{W \tan \lambda}{\cos \theta + \tan \lambda \sin \theta}$

where $\lambda$ is the angle of friction.

(ii) Show that $F$ is a minimum when $\theta = \lambda$.

**Solution:**

(i) The forces acting on the particle are its weight $W$, the normal reaction $R$, the friction, and $F$.

Now, friction $= \mu R = (\tan\lambda) R$.

Here is the force diagram and a diagram of these forces (resolved)

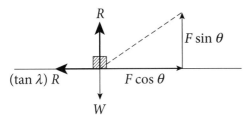

Fig. 8.98

I.         Ups = Downs: $R + F\sin\theta = W$

II.        Lefts = Rights: $(\tan\lambda) R = F\cos\theta$

From equation I we get $R = W - F\sin\theta$, which we 'substitute' into equation II.

$\therefore \tan\lambda (W - F\sin\theta) = F\cos\theta$

$\therefore W\tan\lambda - F\tan\lambda\sin\theta = F\cos\theta$

$\therefore W\tan\lambda = F\cos\theta + F\tan\lambda\sin\theta$

$\therefore W\tan\lambda = F(\cos\theta + \tan\lambda\sin\theta)$

$$\therefore F = \frac{W\tan\lambda}{\cos\theta + \tan\lambda\sin\theta}$$

(ii) To find a minimum for $F$ we solve $\dfrac{dF}{d\theta} = 0$

When differentiating it is essential to remember that $W$ and $\tan\lambda$ are constants and so their derivatives are both zero. Of course, we use the 'quotient rule'.

$$\frac{dF}{d\theta} = 0$$

$$\frac{(\cos\theta + \tan\lambda\sin\theta)(0) - W\tan\lambda(-\sin\theta + \tan\lambda\cos\theta)}{(\cos\theta + \tan\lambda\sin\theta)^2} = 0$$

$\therefore -\sin\theta + \tan\lambda\cos\theta = 0$

$\therefore \tan\lambda\cos\theta = \sin\theta$

$\therefore \tan\lambda = \tan\theta$ (dividing by $\cos\theta$)

$\therefore \lambda = \theta$                QED

**Exercise 8 H**

1. A particle of weight 50 N rests on a smooth inclined plane. The plane is inclined at an angle $\tan^{-1}\frac{4}{3}$ to the horizontal. The particle is just prevented from slipping down the plane by a force $F$ which acts up the plane. Find the magnitude of $F$.

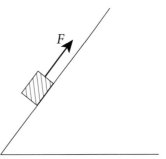

Fig. 8.99

2. A particle of weight 200 N rests on a rough inclined plane. The plane is inclined at an angle $\tan^{-1}\frac{3}{4}$ to the horizontal. The coefficient of friction between the particle and the plane is $\frac{1}{2}$. The particle is just prevented from slipping down the plane by a force $F$ which acts up the plane. Find the magnitude of $F$.

3. A particle of weight 100 N lies on a plane. The plane is inclined at 30° to the horizontal. A horizontal force $F$ is applied to the particle. The coefficient of friction between the particle and the inclined plane is $\frac{3}{5}$. Find the least value of $F$ that will move the particle up the plane.

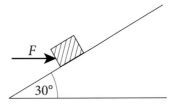

Fig. 8.100

4. Explain the terms

   (i) limiting friction

   (ii) coefficient of friction

   (iii) angle of friction.

   A rough plane is inclined at an angle $\alpha$ to the horizontal. Tan $\alpha = 2$. A body of weight $W$ on the plane is just prevented from slipping down along the plane by a horizontal force $W$. Calculate the coefficient of friction between the body and the plane.

5. A particle is placed on a rough plane inclined at an angle $\alpha$ to the horizontal. Show that the particle will slip down the plane if $\alpha > \lambda$, where $\lambda$ is the angle of friction between the particle and the plane.

6. A body of weight 14 N is kept at rest on a smooth plane of inclination $A$ by a horizontal force of 7 N together with a force of 7 N acting up along the line of greatest slope of the plane. Prove that $\cos A = \frac{3}{5}$.

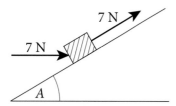

Fig. 8.101

7. A particle of mass 10 kg is placed on a rough inclined plane. The least force acting up along the plane which will prevent the particle slipping down the plane is 19.6 N. The least force acting up along the plane which will make the particle slip upwards is 98 N.
   (i) Find the angle of inclination of the plane.
   (ii) Show that the coefficient of friction is $\frac{1}{2}$.
   (iii) Find the least force required to move the particle. (The least force need not necessarily be parallel to the plane).

8. State the relationship between the coefficient of friction $\mu$ and the angle of friction $\lambda$.
   The diagram shows a particle of weight $W$ on a rough plane making an angle $\alpha$ with the horizontal. The particle is acted upon by a force $F$ whose line of action makes an angle $\theta$ with the line of greatest slope. The particle is just on the point of moving up the plane. Draw a diagram showing the forces acting on the particle and prove that
   $$F = \frac{W \sin(\alpha + \lambda)}{\cos(\theta - \lambda)}$$

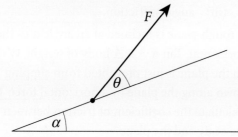

Fig. 8.102

If the particle is just on the point of moving up the plane, deduce
   (i) the force acting up along the plane that would achieve this
   (ii) the horizontal force that would achieve it
   (iii) the minimum force that would achieve it.

9. (i) Define angle of friction $\lambda$.
   (ii) One end of a uniform ladder rests on a rough horizontal floor and the other against a rough vertical wall. The angle of friction $\lambda$ is the same at both points of contact. The ladder makes an acute angle $\alpha$ with the wall.
   If the ladder is on the point of slipping, prove that $\alpha = 2\lambda$.

10. A uniform ladder of weight $W$ rests with one end against a smooth vertical wall and the other end on rough ground which slopes away from the wall at an angle $\alpha$ to the horizontal, as shown.

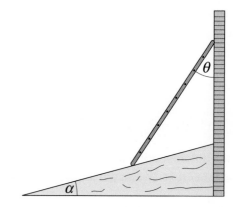

Fig. 8.103

The ladder makes and angle $\theta$ with the wall. The ladder is on the point of slipping, the angle of friction being $\lambda$.
Show that the reaction at the wall is $\frac{1}{2} W \tan \theta$
Prove that $\tan \theta = 2 \tan(\lambda - \alpha)$.

## Hinges and jointed rods

When two objects are freely joined together by a hinge, it will be possible to get nine equations: three for the first object, three for the second object and three for the entire system. Usually it is not necessary to use all nine.

## Worked Example 8.15

A uniform rod $PQ$ of length 3 m and weight $W$ is freely hinged at $p$ to a point on a vertical wall. The rod is kept in a horizontal position by means of a string of length 5 m, attached to the wall at a point 4 m above $P$. Find, in terms of $W$, the horizontal and vertical components of the reaction at the hinge and find the tension in the string.

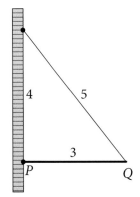

Fig. 8.104

**Solution:**

Since we do not know the direction of the reaction at the hinge, we break this force up into its horizontal ($X$) and vertical ($Y$) components. Here is the force diagram:

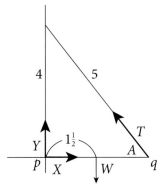

Fig. 8.105

The tension in the string can be resolved into vertical and horizontal components, too. Note that $\tan A = \frac{4}{3}$, $\sin A = \frac{4}{5}$ and $\cos A = \frac{3}{5}$.

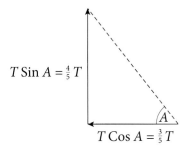

$$T \sin A = \tfrac{4}{5} T$$

$$T \cos A = \tfrac{3}{5} T$$

Tension resolved

Fig. 8.106

1.  $$Y + \tfrac{4}{5} T = W. \qquad\qquad \text{Eqn 1}$$
2.  $$X = \tfrac{3}{5} T. \qquad\qquad \text{Eqn 2}$$
3.  Take moments about $P$.
$$W\left(1\tfrac{1}{2}\right) = \tfrac{4}{5} T (3) \qquad \text{Eqn 3}$$
Other moments are zero.

Equation 3 $$\therefore \frac{3W}{2} = \frac{12T}{5}$$

$$\therefore 24 T = 15 W$$

$$\therefore T = \tfrac{5}{8} W$$

Equation 1 $$Y + \tfrac{4}{5}\left(\tfrac{5}{8} W\right) = W$$

$$\therefore Y + \tfrac{1}{2} W = W$$

$$\therefore Y = \tfrac{1}{2} W$$

Equation 2 $$X = \tfrac{3}{5}\left(\tfrac{5}{8} W\right)$$

$$= \tfrac{3}{8} W$$

Answer: The horizontal and vertical reactions at the hinge are $\frac{3}{8} W$ and $\frac{1}{2} W$. The tension in the string is $\frac{5}{8} W$.

## Worked Example 8.16

Two uniform rods $AB$ and $BC$, both of lengths $2a$, but of weight $W$ and $3W$ respectively, are freely jointed at $B$. They stand in a vertical plane on rough horizontal ground. Both rods make an angle $\theta$ with the ground.

(i)   Show the forces acting on the system.

(ii)  Find the normal reactions at $A$ and $C$.

(iii) The angle $\theta$ is increased until slipping occurs. Show that slipping will first occur at $A$.

(iv)  Show the external forces on the rods $AB$ and $BC$ separately.

(v)   If the coefficient of friction between both rods and the ground is $\frac{1}{2}$, show that slipping begins when $\tan \theta = \frac{4}{3}$.

(vi)  Find the magnitude of the reaction at $B$.

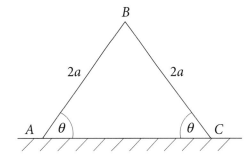

Fig. 8.107

**Solution:**

(i) Here is the force diagram for the system, including two inward friction forces, $F$ and $G$. They oppose motion, which would be outward.

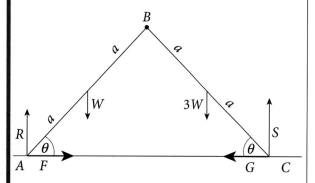

Fig. 8.108

(ii) $$R + S = 3W + W$$
$$\therefore R + S = 4W \qquad \text{Eqn 1}$$
$$F = G \qquad \text{Eqn 2}$$

Take moments about $A$.

$$S(4a\cos\theta) = W(a\cos\theta) + 3W(3a\cos\theta)$$
$$\therefore 4S = 10W$$
$$\therefore S = \frac{5}{2}W \qquad \text{Eqn 3}$$

Equation 1

$$R + \frac{5}{2}W = 4W$$
$$\therefore R = \frac{3}{2}W$$

The normal reactions are $\frac{3}{2}W$ and $\frac{5}{2}W$.

(iii) Since $R < S$, $\mu R < \mu S$.

This means that the limiting friction at $A$ is less than that at $C$. Therefore, slipping will occur at $A$ before it occurs at $C$.

(iv)

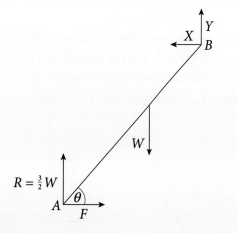

Fig. 8.109

The rod $AB$, independent of the rest of the system, now has an extra external force, namely the support it gets from the rod $BC$. We do not know the direction of this force, so we break it up into its horizontal ($X$) and vertical ($Y$) components.

(v)

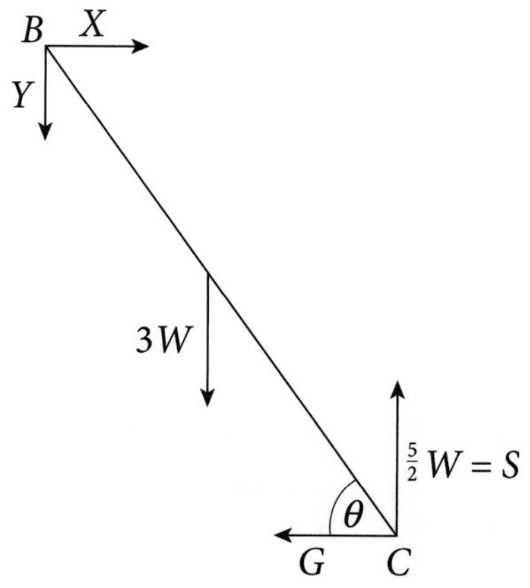

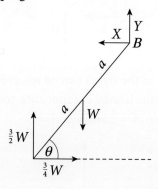

Fig. 8.110

It is important to note that the support forces for the rod $BC$ are equal but opposite to the support forces for the rod $AB$, in accordance with Newton's third law.

(vi) Slipping occurs at $A$. When the slipping begins, limiting friction is called into play — but only at $A$, not at $C$. So, $F = \mu R = \frac{1}{2}\left(\frac{3}{2}W\right) = \frac{3}{4}W$.

We examine the forces on the slipping rod $AB$ at the moment it is just on the point of slipping.

Fig. 8.111

1. $\frac{3}{2}W + Y = W$
$$\therefore Y = -\frac{1}{2}W \qquad \text{Eqn 4}$$

This means that vertical reaction at *B* has magnitude $\frac{1}{2}W$, but is in a downward direction.

2. $\frac{3}{4}W = X.$        Eqn 5

3. Take moments about *B,* to avoid more equations in *X* and *Y.*

$$\frac{3}{4}W(2a\sin\theta) + W(a\cos\theta) = \frac{3}{2}W(2a\cos\theta)$$

$$\frac{3}{2}W\sin\theta + W\cos\theta = 3W\cos\theta$$

$$\therefore \frac{3}{2}\sin\theta = 2\cos\theta \quad \text{Eqn 6}$$

Now, divide across by $\cos\theta$

$$\therefore \frac{3}{2}\tan\theta = 2$$

$$\therefore \tan\theta = \frac{4}{3} \quad \text{Q.E.D.}$$

(vii) The reaction $\vec{R} = X\vec{i} + Y\vec{j}$

Therefore, $\left|\vec{R}\right| = \sqrt{X^2 + Y^2}$

$$= \sqrt{\left(\frac{3}{4}W\right)^2 + \left(-\frac{1}{2}W\right)^2}$$

$$= \sqrt{\frac{9}{16}W^2 + \frac{1}{4}W^2}$$

$$= \sqrt{\frac{13}{16}W^2}$$

$$= \frac{\sqrt{13}}{4}W$$

## Exercise 8 I

1. A uniform rod *PQ* of length 4 m and weight *W* is freely hinged at *P* to a point on a vertical wall. The rod is kept in a horizontal position by means of a string of length 5 m, attached to the wall at a point 3 m above *P.* Find, in terms of *W,* the horizontal and vertical components of the reaction at the hinge and find the tension in the string.

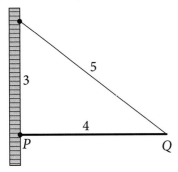

Fig. 8.112

2. A uniform rod *PQ* of length $2l$ and weight $5W$ is freely hinged at *P* to a point on a vertical wall. A force $2W$ is applied at *Q* to the rod. The force is perpendicular to the rod. The rod makes an angle *A* with the wall.

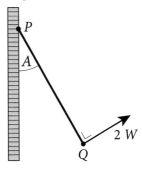

Fig. 8.113

(i) Find, in terms of *W,* the horizontal and vertical components of the reaction at the hinge.

(ii) Find *A* to the nearest degree.

3. A uniform rod *PQ* of weight $3W$ is freely hinged at *P* to a vertical wall. The rod is pulled aside by a force *W* applied at *Q* and at right angles to *PQ* (see diagram).

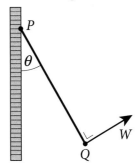

Fig. 8.114

(i) Draw a clear diagram showing all the forces acting on the rod.

(ii) Find $\theta$, the angle between the rod and the wall.

(iii) Calculate the horizontal and vertical components of the reaction at *P.*

4. A uniform beam $PQ$ of length 12 m and weight $W$ is freely hinged at $P$ to a vertical wall. It is held in a horizontal position by an inelastic string which is attached to $Q$ and to a point on the wall 5 m above $P$. Find

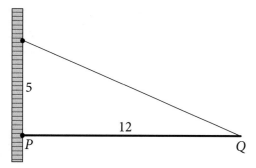

Fig. 8.115

  (i) the horizontal and vertical components of the reaction at $P$

  (ii) the tension in the string.

5. Two uniform rods $AB$ and $BC$ of lengths $2a$, but of weights $2W$ and $3W$ are freely hinged at $B$. They stand in a vertical plane on rough horizontal ground. Both rods make an angle $\theta$ with the ground.

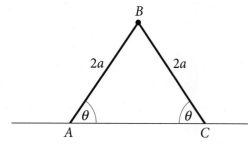

Fig. 8.116

  (i) Show in three separate diagrams the forces on the system $ABC$, the rod $AB$ and the rod $BC$.

  (ii) Find the normal reactions at $A$ and $C$.

  (iii) The angle at $B$ is opened out until slipping occurs. Show that slipping will first occur at $A$.

  (iv) If the coefficient of friction between each rod and the ground is $\frac{1}{3}$, find the value of $\theta$ when slipping begins to occur.

6. A double ladder consists of two uniform beams $AB$ and $BC$ freely hinged at $B$. Both have lengths 5 m but they weigh $W$ and $2W$ respectively. The ladder rests on smooth horizontal ground and is kept from slipping by means of a horizontal inextensible string attached to the midpoints of $AB$ and $BC$. If $|AC| = 6$ m, find the tension in the string and the reactions at the ground.

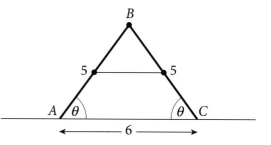

Fig. 8.117

7. Two uniform rods $AB$ and $BC$ both have length 10 m, but have weights $W$ and $2W$ respectively. They are freely hinged at $B$. They stand in a vertical plane, in limiting equilibrium (i.e. on the point of slipping), with $A$ on rough ground and $C$ against a smooth vertical wall, as shown. $AB$ makes an angle $\tan^{-1}\frac{4}{3}$ with the ground. $BC$ makes an angle $\theta$ with the horizontal.

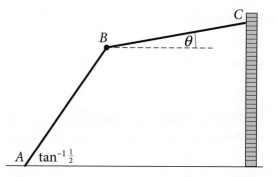

Fig. 8.118

Show on separate diagrams the forces on the rod $AB$ and on the rod $BC$. Show that the reaction at the wall is $\frac{15\,W}{8}$ and that the coefficient of friction between the rod $AB$ and the ground is $\frac{5}{8}$.

8. Two uniform rods $AB$ and $AC$ of equal length and of weights $2W$ and $W$ respectively are smoothly hinged together at $A$ and hinged at $B$ and $C$ to a horizontal beam. The rods are in a vertical plane with $A$ below $BC$. The rods make an angle $\beta$ with the horizontal.

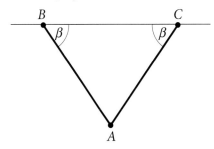

Fig. 8.119

Prove that

(i) the horizontal and vertical components of the reaction of the hinge at $A$ on the rod $AB$ are $\dfrac{3W}{4\tan\beta}$ and $\dfrac{W}{4}$ respectively.

(ii) If the total reactions at $B$ and $C$ are perpendicular to each other, then $\tan\beta = \dfrac{3}{\sqrt{35}}$

9. Two uniform rods $AB$ and $BC$ each of length $l$ and weight $W$ are smoothly jointed at $B$. The end $A$ is fixed by a smooth hinge to a rough vertical wall. The system rests in equilibrium in a vertical plane perpendicular to the wall with $C$ in contact with the wall and each rod inclined at an angle $\phi$ to the vertical.

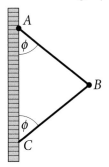

Fig. 8.120

(i) Find the frictional force and the normal reaction at $C$.

(ii) A force $W$, applied vertically downwards at $C$, is just sufficient to cause slipping. Show that the coefficient of friction between $C$ and the wall is $\dfrac{4}{\tan\phi}$.

10. Two uniform ladders $[AB]$ and $[AC]$, of equal length and equal weight $W$, are smoothly jointed at $A$ and stand with $B$ and $C$ in contact with a rough horizontal plane. The coefficient of friction at $B$ and $C$ is $\mu$. If a person of weight $W$ can stand anywhere on the ladders when $B$ and $C$ are a distance $2d$ apart, prove that

$$\mu \geq \frac{2d}{3\sqrt{l^2 - d^2}}$$

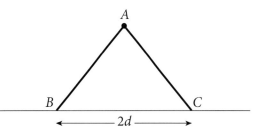

Fig. 8.121

11. A uniform rod $[AB]$ of weight $4W$ and length $2l$ is free to rotate smoothly about the fixed point $A$. A fixed wire $[AD]$ extends horizontally from $A$. The end $B$ of the rod is attached by a light inextensible string $[BC]$ of length $2l$ to a ring of weight $W$ and negligible diameter, which can slide on the wire. The coefficient of friction between the ring and the wire is $\mu$. The string makes and angle $\alpha$ with the horizontal when the system is in limiting equilibrium (that is, just on the point of slipping).

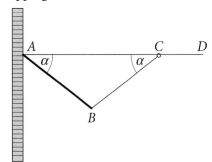

Fig. 8.122

(i) Show that $\tan\alpha = \dfrac{1}{2\mu}$.

(ii) Show that the tension in the string is $W\sqrt{1 + 4\mu^2}$

12. A uniform rod of length 3 m and weight 80 N is smoothly hinged at one end to a rough horizontal floor. The rod rests on the smooth curved surface of a hemisphere whose plane face is on the floor. The coefficient of friction between the plane surface and the floor is $\mu$. The rod and the centre of the hemisphere lie in the same vertical plane.

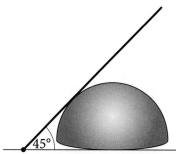

Fig. 8.123

The rod is in equilibrium inclined at an angle of 45° to the horizontal. The hemisphere, of radius 1 m and weight 40 N, is in limiting equilibrium (that is, on the point of slipping).

(i) Show, on separate diagrams, all the forces acting on the rod and the hemisphere.

(ii) Show that the reaction between the rod and the hemisphere is $60\sqrt{2}$ N.

(iii) Find the coefficient of friction $\mu$ between the hemisphere and the floor.

13. Two ladders, $[AB]$ and $[BC]$, each of weight $W$ and length $l$, are smoothly jointed at $B$. They rest in a vertical plane with $A$ and $C$ on rough horizontal ground.

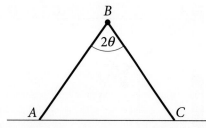

Fig. 8.124

The coefficient of friction at both $A$ and $C$ is $\mu$.
Let $|\angle ABC| = 2\theta$.
Show that $\mu \geq \frac{1}{2}\tan\theta$.

14. A uniform rod of mass 2 kg and length $6y$ metres leans against the smooth edge of a rectangular block of mass 6 kg and height $0.8y$ metres. The rod is smoothly hinged at $P$ to a rough horizontal floor and the block also rests on the floor (see diagram).

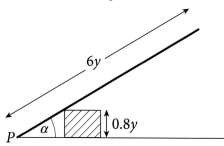

Fig. 8.125

The block is on the point of slipping when the rod makes an angle $\alpha$ with the horizontal, where $\tan\alpha = \frac{4}{3}$.

(i) Show that the distance from $P$ to where the block touches the rod is $y$.

(ii) Show in separate diagrams the forces acting on the rod and on the block.

(iii) Show that the coefficient of friction between the block and the floor is $\frac{6}{17}$.

(iv) Find, correct to the nearest newton, the magnitude of the reaction at the hinge.

## Three-force problems

### Theorem 8.4

If a body is in equilibrium when acted upon by three non-parallel forces, then their lines of action are concurrent.
**Proof:**

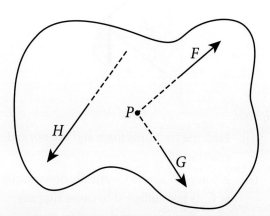

Fig. 8.126

Let the three forces be $F$, $G$ and $H$. Let $P$ be the point of intersection of the lines of action of forces $F$ and $G$.

Let $x$ be the distance of the line of action of $H$ from $P$. Take moments about $P$. Since the body is in equilibrium, the sum of the moments about $P$ must be zero.

$$\therefore F(0) + G(0) + H(x) = 0$$
$$\therefore x = 0$$

Therefore the line of action of $H$ must also pass through $P$ and so the three lines of action are concurrent.                                    Q.E.D.

**Note:** If the three forces were put "tip to tail" then they must form a triangle, since their sum is zero. Their magnitudes correspond to the lengths of the sides of this triangle.

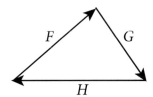

Fig. 8.127

---

### Worked Example 8.17

A sphere of weight $W$ and radius 50 cm hangs by a string 80 cm long which is attached at one end to a point on its surface and at the other end to a point on a smooth vertical wall. Find the tension $T$ in the string and the reaction $R$ at the wall in terms of $W$.

**Solution:**

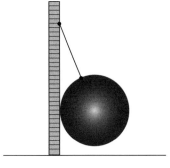

Fig. 8.128

Because $R$ and $W$ act through the centre of the sphere, the line of action of $T$ in the string must also act through the centre of the sphere in accordance with Theorem 8.4. The string is therefore in the same line as a diameter of the sphere, as shown.

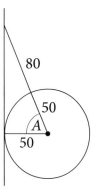

Fig. 8.129

If $A$ is the angle between the string and the horizontal, then

$$\cos A = \frac{50}{80+50} = \frac{50}{130} = \frac{5}{13}.$$

$$\therefore \sin A = \frac{12}{13}$$

The tension must be resolved into horizontal and vertical components:

Tension resolved

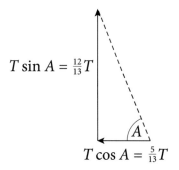

$$T \sin A = \tfrac{12}{13}T$$

$$T \cos A = \tfrac{5}{13}T$$

Fig. 8.130

Forces resolved

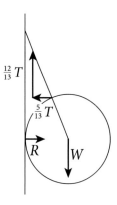

Fig. 8.131

Equation 1:     $$\frac{12}{13}T = W$$
$$\therefore T = \frac{13}{12}W$$

Equation 2:     $$R = \frac{5}{13}T$$
$$= \frac{5}{13}\left(\frac{13}{12}W\right)$$
$$= \frac{5}{12}W \quad \text{Answer}$$

## Exercise 8 J

1. A uniform sphere of weight $W$ and radius $r$ is suspended by a string of length $3r$, which has one end attached to a point on its surface. The other end is attached to a point on a smooth vertical wall. The sphere rests in equilibrium, leaning against the wall. Show that the angle which the string makes with the wall is $\sin^{-1}\frac{1}{4}$. Find the tension in the string and the reaction at the wall.

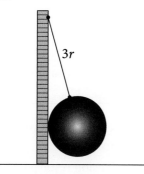

Fig. 8.132

2. A uniform rod $AB$ of weight 30 N and length 1 m is suspended by two light inelastic strings $AP$ and $PB$, each of length 1 m, from a fixed point $P$. Show in a diagram the forces acting on the rod. Find the tension in the strings.

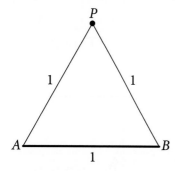

Fig. 8.133

3. (a) Complete the statement: "If a body is in equilibrium under the action of three non-parallel forces, the lines of action of these forces …"

   (b) A uniform rod $[AB]$, 2.5 m in length weighs 240 N. It is freely hinged to a vertical wall at $A$. A horizontal force $P$, acting at $B$, perpendicular to the wall, holds the rod so that $B$ is 1.5 m from the wall.

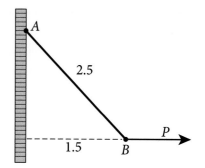

Fig. 8.134

   (i) Show on a diagram the lines of action and direction of all the forces acting on the rod.

   (ii) Calculate the magnitude of the force $P$.

   (iii) Calculate the resultant force at $A$ correct to the nearest newton.

4. A cylinder of weight $W$ and radius 5 m is being dragged over a thin obstacle of height 2 m by a horizontal force $F$, as shown.

   (i) Show the three forces acting on the cylinder on a diagram.

   (ii) Why does the reaction at the obstacle act through the centre, $C$, of the cylinder?

   (iii) Find, in terms of $W$, the reaction at the obstacle and the force $F$, when the cylinder just begins to leave the ground.

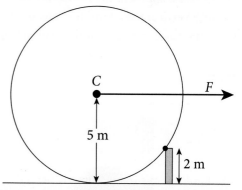

Fig. 8.135

5. A sphere of mass 3 kg and radius 150 mm is suspended by a string 100 mm long, the string joining a point on the surface with a point on a smooth vertical wall. Find the tension in the string in terms of $g$.

6. A heavy uniform rod of mass $m$ and length $2l$ is suspended from a point $O$ by two equal inelastic strings.

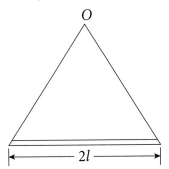

Fig. 8.136

Each string is fixed to $O$ and to an end point of the rod so that the rod hangs horizontally. If, then, a mass $\frac{1}{2}m$ is suspended half-way between the centre and one end of the rod, so that the rod is no longer horizontal, calculate the ratio $T_1:T_2$, where $T_1$ is the tension in one string and $T_2$ is the tension in the other.

7. A cylinder of weight $W$ and radius $r$ is being dragged over an obstacle of height $\frac{1}{5}r$ by a force $P$, which acts through the axis of the cylinder, making an angle $\theta$ with the horizontal.

   Let $A$ be the angle between the reaction at the obstacle and the horizontal.

   (i) Show on a diagram the forces acting on the cylinder at the instant when it is just leaving the ground.

   (ii) Show that $P = \dfrac{3W}{5\sin(A+\theta)}$

   (iii) Find the minimum *horizontal* force which will just lift the cylinder.

   (iv) Find the minimum force which will just lift the cylinder.

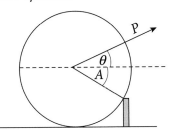

Fig. 8.137

8. A non-uniform rod $[PQ]$ of length 6 cm and weight $W$ rests inside a smooth sphere of radius 5 cm and centre $C$. The centre of gravity of the rod is at $G$, where $|AG| = 2$ cm and $|GQ| = 4$ cm.

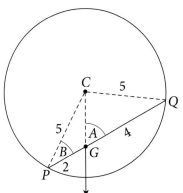

Fig. 8.138

   (i) Find $\sin A$ and $\sin B$, as in the diagram.

   (ii) Find the reactions at $P$ and $Q$ in terms of $W$.

9. Two smooth planes inclined at angles $\tan^{-1}\frac{1}{2}$ and $\tan^{-1}\frac{3}{4}$ to the horizontal, face each other with their line of intersection horizontal. A sphere of weight $W$ rests between them. Show that the reaction at the steeper plane is $\frac{1}{2}W$.

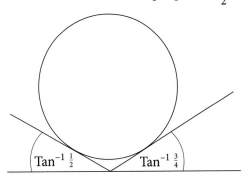

Fig. 8.139

## Summary of important points

1. **Moment** = Force × perpendicular distance from line of action of the force.

2. The **Principle of Moments**: If any number of coplanar forces act on a rigid body, then the sum of their moments about any point is equal to the moment of their resultant about that point.

1. The **centre of gravity** of an object is the point through which the resultant gravitational force acts, no matter what position the object is in.

2. The **moment of a couple** about a point is the same for all points in its plane.

3. The centre of gravity of a triangle is at the centroid where the medians meet.

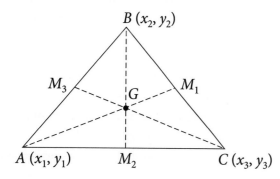

Fig. 8.140

$$G = \left( \frac{x_1 + x_2 + x_3}{3}, \; \frac{y_1 + y_2 + y_3}{3} \right)$$

$$|AG| : |GM_1| = |BG| : |GM_2| = |CG| : |GM_3| = 2 : 1$$

4. If a **body is in equilibrium** then

forces up = forces down

forces to the left = forces to the right

clockwise moments = anti-clockwise moments

(about any point)

5. If a body is in equilibrium when acted upon by three non-parallel forces, then their lines of action are concurrent.

6. **Limiting Friction** is the maximum amount of friction which can be called into play.

7. **Coefficient of Friction** μ is the ratio of the limiting friction to the normal reaction.

8. **Angle of Friction** is the angle between the resultant (of the limiting friction force and the normal reaction) and the normal reaction itself.

## DOs and DON'Ts for the exam

### DO

- Know the definition in English of Limiting Friction, Coefficient of Friction and Angle of Friction
- Do show clearly the forces with arrowed vectors in large diagrams on graph paper
- Do resolve all forces into horizontal and vertical directions
- Do write down the three equations
  - Forces up = forces down
  - Forces left = forces right
  - Clockwise moments = anti-clockwise moments
- Do solve the three equations to get the answers you need.
- Do give answers for forces in terms of $W$, the weight of the object.

### DON'T

- Don't forget that Centres of Gravity are more important for Ordinary Level students than for Higher Level students, as there is a whole question for them on this section
- Don't rush when you are creating the third equation (Clockwise Moments = anti-clockwise moments).  Don't mix up sines and cosines of angles.

# Hydrostatics

"ηυρηκα, ηυρηκα"
Eureka! I have discovered it.

*Archimedes*

## Contents

## Learning outcomes

**In this chapter you will learn...**

- The definitions of density and relative density

- How to solve problems of volume, density and weight

- How to solve problems of mixtures and alloys

- The meaning of pressure and thrust

- How to solve problems with U-tubes

- How to deal with thrust on horizontal surfaces

- Archimedes' Principle and its applications

- How to solve problems of rods and boards under liquid

## You will need to know...

- The volume of a cylinder, cone, sphere, rectangular solid and frustum
- The centroid of a triangle
- The laws of statics

## Density

**Definition:** The **density** of a substance is its mass per unit volume.

Density is a scalar quantity, usually measured in $kg/m^3$ but sometimes in $grams/cm^3$. The Greek letter $\rho$ (pronounced roe) is often used to denote density.

**Definition:** The **relative density** of a substance is the ratio of the density of the substance to the density of water.

Relative density is just a real number and is usually denoted by the letter $s$.

Since density = mass per unit volume, or $\rho = \frac{m}{V}$, it follows that $m = V\rho$.

Therefore, the **weight** of an object, $W$, is given by $W = m\,g = V\rho g$.

### Worked Example 9.1

(a) Given that 1 cm$^3$ of water has mass 1 gram, find the density of water in kg/m$^3$.

(b) A rectangular block of wood has height 0.5 m, length 0.4 m and breadth 0.3 m. It has mass 42 kg.
Find the density and the relative density of the wood.

**Solution:**

(a) $1 \text{ m}^3 = (100)^3 \text{ cm}^3 = 1\,000\,000 \text{ cm}^3$

1 cm$^3$ of water has mass 1 gram (1 g)

$\therefore$ 1 m$^3$ of water has mass of 1 000 000 grams = 1 000 kg.

$\therefore$ density of water = 1 000 kg/m$^3$

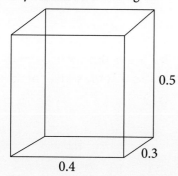

Fig. 9.1

(b) The volume of block = $l\,b\,h$

$\qquad = 0.5 \times 0.4 \times 0.3$

$\qquad = 0.06 \text{ m}^3$

The mass of the block = 42 kg.

$$\text{Density} = \frac{\text{Mass}}{\text{Volume}}$$

$$= \frac{42}{0.06}$$

$$= 700 \text{ kg/m}^3$$

$$\text{Relative Density} = \frac{\text{Density of the block}}{\text{Density of water}}$$

$$= \frac{700}{1000}$$

$$= 0.7$$

### Summary

1. Density $= \dfrac{\text{Mass}}{\text{Volume}}$  $\qquad \rho = \dfrac{m}{V}$

2. Relative density $= \dfrac{\text{Density of the substance}}{\text{Density of water}}$

3. The density of water = 1000 kg/m$^3$.

4. $W = V\rho g$

### Worked Example 9.2

100 millilitres (ml) of water are mixed with 20 ml of treacle of relative density 1.75. Find the relative density of the mixture.

**Solution:**

1. The total volume of the mixture

$\qquad = 100 + 20$

$\qquad = 120$ ml.

2. The density of the water = 1000 kg/m$^3$.

3. The density of the treacle

$\qquad = 1.75 \times 1000$

$\qquad = 1750$ kg/m$^3$

4. Mass = Volume × Density

$\qquad \therefore$ the total mass

$\qquad = $ mass of water + mass of treacle

$\qquad = 100 \times 1000 + 20 \times 1750$

$\qquad = 135\,000$ ml kg/m$^3$

5. The density of the mixture

$\qquad = \dfrac{\text{Mass}}{\text{Volume}}$

$\qquad = \dfrac{135\,000}{120}$

$\qquad = 1125$ kg/m$^3$

6. Relative Density

$\qquad = \dfrac{\text{Density of the mixture}}{\text{Density of water}}$

$\qquad = \dfrac{1125}{1000}$

$\qquad = 1.125$

**Quick method**

Like the weighted mean in statistics:

| Substance | $s$ | $v$ | $sv$ |
|---|---|---|---|
| Water | 1.00 | 100 | 100 |
| Treacle | 1.75 | 20 | 35 |
| | | 120 | 135 |

$$\bar{s} = \frac{\Sigma sv}{\Sigma s} = \frac{135}{120} = 1.125$$

---

### *Worked Example 9.3*

Find the weight of the water inside a bucket, 35 cm high, of smaller radius 5 cm and greater radius 8 cm.

**Solution:**

Volume of a frustrum

$$= \frac{1}{3}\pi h\,(R^2 + Rr + r^2)$$

$$= \frac{1}{3} \times \frac{22}{7} \times 35\,(64 + 40 + 25)$$

$$= 4\,730\text{ cm}^3$$

$$= 0.00473\text{ m}^3 \text{ (dividing by 1,000,000)}$$

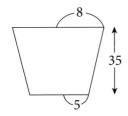

Fig. 9.2

Weight $= V\rho g$

$$= (0.00473)\,(1000)\,(9.8)$$

$$= 46.354\text{ newtons}$$

---

### **Exercise 9 A**

1. The relative density of an oil is 0.83. What is the density of the oil in kg/m³?

2. The density of balsa wood is 375 kg/m³. Find its relative density.

3. One cubic centimetre of mercury has mass 13.6 grams. Find
   (i) the density of mercury in kg/m³
   (ii) the relative density of mercury.

4. A rectangular lump of nickel has length 10 cm, breadth 6 cm and height 2 cm. It has mass 1.08 kg. Find the relative density and the density (in kg/m³) of the nickel.

5. A man has mass 70 kg. If the average relative density of his body is 0.98, find his volume. His exact image is carved out of stone of density 2450 kg/m³. Find the mass of the statue.

6. When 60 ml of water is mixed with 40 ml of alcohol of relative density 0.95, what is the relative density of the mixture?

7. Iron, of relative density 7, and nickel, of relative density 9, are mixed. Their volumes are in the ratio 10:1. Find the relative density of the alloy formed in this way correct to 3 places of decimals.

8. How much alcohol of relative density 0.9 should be mixed with 100 ml of water to form a mixture of relative density 0.9625?

9. Find the weight of the water inside a rectangular tank of length 40 cm, width 30 cm and height 20 cm in terms of $g$.

10. A cylindrical can contains oil of relative density 0.8. The can has radius 3 cm and height 10 cm. Find the weight of the oil, in terms of $\pi$ and $g$.

11. (i) A bucket of height 18 cm, smaller radius 6 cm and larger radius 9 cm is filled with water. Find the weight of the water in terms of $g$ and $\pi$.

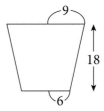

Fig. 9.3

   (ii) A bucket with the same dimensions is filled to one third of its height with alcohol, so that the surface of the alcohol is a circle with radius 7 cm. The relative density of the alcohol is 0.95. Find the weight of the alcohol.

   (iii) The liquids in (i) and (ii) are mixed. Find the relative density of the mixture.

## Pressure and thrust

**Definition:** The **pressure** on a surface is the force per unit area.

Pressure is a scalar quantity, measured in N/m², which are usually called Pascals (Pa).

In short, Pressure $= \dfrac{\text{Force}}{\text{Area}}$

When a man walks in snow, his task is made easier by wearing snow-shoes. This is because the snow-shoes have a large area and so the pressure on the snow is reduced. You should be able to answer the following questions:

• Why do elephants have big feet?
• Why does a sharp knife cut better than a blunt one?
• Why are stiletto heels bad for cork-tiled floors?
• Why do ducks, who have webbed feet, find marshy ground manageable, while birds with clawed feet do not?

### Theorem 9.1

The pressure at a point in a liquid is proportional to the depth at that point. (Air pressure is ignored.)

**Proof:** Take a tank filled with liquid. Let $\rho$ be the density of the liquid and $h$ the depth at the point $z$. Imagine a cylinder of radius $r$ and height $h$ with a circle, centre $P$, as its base. This cylinder is to be made out of the *liquid itself*.

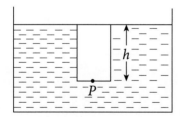

Fig. 9.4

The only force acting on the disc around $P$ is the weight of the liquid directly above it.

1.  Force = Weight of the liquid
    $$V \rho g = (\pi r^2 h) \rho g$$

2.  The area of the disc $= \pi r^2$

3.  The pressure at the disc is given by

$$\text{Pressure} = \frac{\text{Force}}{\text{Area}}$$
$$= \frac{(\pi r^2 h) \rho g}{\pi r^2}$$
$$= h \rho g$$

Since the radius $r$ can be made as small as we like, it is clear that the pressure at the point $P$, as $r \to 0$, must be equal to $h \rho g$. Therefore, the pressure at a point in a liquid is proportional to the depth $h$. Q.E.D.

**Note 1:** This proof tells us that the pressure at any two points in the SAME liquid at the SAME depth must be equal.

**Note 2:** Since Pressure $= \dfrac{\text{Force}}{\text{Area}}$, it follows that the force on a horizontal surface where the pressure is a constant is given by **Force = Pressure × Area**. This kind of a force is called **Thrust**.

### Summary

1.  Pressure $= \dfrac{\text{Force}}{\text{Area}}$.

2.  Pressure at a point in a liquid at a depth $h$ is given by $P = h \rho g$.

3.  Thrust = Pressure × Area

### Worked Example 9.4

A frustum has its axis vertical and its smaller end uppermost. Its dimensions are: $h = 3$ m, $r = 1$ m, $R = 2$ m. If it is filled with water, find, in terms of $\pi$ and $g$,

   (i)   the pressure at a point on the base
  (ii)  the thrust on the base
 (iii)  the ratio of the thrust on the base to the weight of the water.

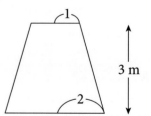

Fig. 9.5

**Solution:**

(i)   Pressure $= h \rho g$
$$= 3 (1\,000) g$$
$$= 3\,000\, g \text{ Pa}$$

(ii)  Thrust = Pressure × Area
$$= (3\,000 g) \times (\pi r^2)$$
$$= (3\,000 g) (4\pi)$$
$$= 12\,000\, \pi g \text{ newtons}$$

(iii)  Weight $= V \rho g$
$$= \frac{1}{3} \pi h (R^2 + Rr + r^2) (1\,000) g$$

$$= \frac{1}{3}\pi(3)(2^2 + 2(1) + 1^2)(1\,000)g$$

$$= 7\,000\,g \text{ newtons.}$$

(iv)  The ratio of thrust: weight

$$= 12\,000\,\pi\,g : 7\,000\,\pi\,g$$

$$= 12:7$$

### *Worked Example 9.5*

(a) A U-tube contains some water. A 10 cm column of heavy oil of relative density 0.9 is poured into one branch. Find the difference in the heights of liquid in the two branches.

(b) Light oil of relative density 0.8 is then poured into the other branch until the two levels are equal. Find the height of the column of light oil.

### Solution:

(a) The pressure at the **same** level of the **same** liquid must be the same. Take $Z$ as a point just under the heavy oil and $W$ at the same level in the other branch, as shown. The pressure at $Z$ and at $W$ must be equal. Let $x$ = the height of the column of water above $q$ in cm. The density of the heavy oil is $(0.9)(1\,000) = 900 \text{ kg/m}^3$.

$$\text{Pressure at } Z = h\,\rho\,g$$
$$= (10)(900)\,g$$
$$= 9\,000\,g$$
$$\text{Pressure at } W = h\,\rho\,g$$
$$= x(1\,000)\,g$$
$$= 1\,000\,x\,g$$
$$\therefore 1\,000\,x\,g = 9\,000\,g$$
$$\therefore x = 9 \text{ cm}$$

Therefore, the difference in heights

$$= 10 - 9$$
$$= 1 \text{ cm.}$$

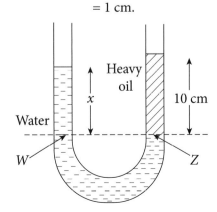

Fig. 9.6

(b) Take $Z$ and $W$ as before. Since $Z$ and $W$ are both at the **same** level in the **same** liquid, the pressures at $Z$ and at $W$ must be equal.

Let $y$ = the height of the column of light oil.

$\therefore 10 - y$ = the height of the column of water between $W$ and the oil.

$$\text{Pressure at } Z = h\,\rho\,g$$
$$= (10)(900)\,g$$
$$= 9\,000\,g$$
$$\text{Pressure at } W = (h\,\rho\,g)_{\text{oil}} + (h\,\rho\,g)_{\text{water}}$$
$$= y(800)\,g + (10 - y)(1\,000)\,g$$
$$= 800\,y\,g + 10\,000\,g - 1\,000\,y\,g$$
$$= 10\,000\,g - 200\,y\,g$$

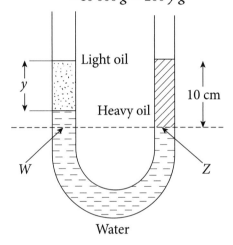

Fig. 9.7

But pressure at $Z$ = pressure at $W$.

$$\therefore 9000\,g = 10\,000\,g - 200\,y\,g$$
$$\therefore 200\,y = 1000$$
$$\therefore y = 5 \text{ cm.}$$

Answer: (a) 1 cm; (b) 5 cm.

### *Worked Example 9.6*

(a) A tank is in the shape of a cube of side 4 m. It is half full of water and stands with its base horizontal. Find the thrust on the base.

(b) If a cubic stone block of side 1 m is lowered into the tank by means of a thin wire until it is immersed. Find the thrust on the base now.

### Solution:

(a) The depth      = 2 m.

The pressure at the base $= h\,\rho\,g$

$$= 2 \times 1000 \times 9.8$$
$$= 19\,600 \text{ Pa.}$$

The thrust = Pressure × Area

$$= 19\,600 \times 16$$

$$= 313\,600 \text{ N}$$

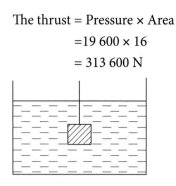

Fig. 9.8

(b) What will the depth be now?

The volume of all the matter under the surface

$$= (4 \times 4 \times 2) + (1 \times 1 \times 1)$$

$$= 33 \text{ m}^3$$

Let the depth be $h$; the length is 4 m; the breadth is 4 m.

Now, volume $= 4 \times 4 \times h = 33$

$$\therefore h = \frac{33}{16}$$

The pressure at the base depends only on the depth and the density of the liquid.

Pressure at the base $= h \rho g$

$$= \left(\frac{33}{16}\right)(1000)\,9.8$$

$$= 20\,212.5 \text{ N/m}^2$$

Thrust on the base $=$ Pressure × area

$$= 20\,212.5 \times 16$$

$$= 323\,400 \text{ N}$$

## Exercise 9 B

1. A tank is in the shape of a cube of side 2 m. It is filled with water.
   (i) Find the pressure at a point on the base of the tank.
   (ii) Show that the thrust on the base is equal to the weight of the water.

2. An upright cylindrical can has height 11 cm and diameter 10 cm. It is filled with oil of relative density 0.85. Find, in terms of $\pi$ and $g$
   (i) the pressure at a point on the base
   (ii) the thrust on the base
   (iii) the weight of the oil.

3. A bucket in the shape of a frustum has height 10 cm, smaller diameter 4 cm and greater diameter 10 cm. The axis is vertical with the larger end uppermost. If this bucket is filled with a liquid, find the ratio of the thrust on the base: the weight of the liquid. (Let $\rho =$ the density of the liquid.)

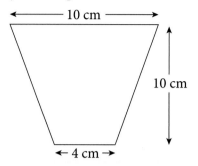

Fig. 9.9

4. (a) A U-tube contains some water. An 8 cm column of oil of relative density 0.85 is poured into one branch, as shown. Find the difference in the heights of the liquids in the two branches.

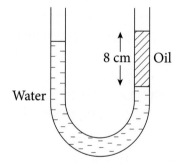

Fig. 9.10

(b) If a column of black oil of relative density 0.95 is poured into the other branch so that the water in both branches reaches equal levels, find the height of the column of black oil added.

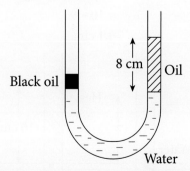

Fig. 9.11

5. (a) A U-tube contains mercury of relative density 13.6.
A 17 cm column of water is poured into one branch, as shown. Find the difference in the heights reached in the two branches.
(b) Oil of relative density 0.85 is poured into the other side until the liquid in each branch reaches the same level. Find the height of the column of oil.

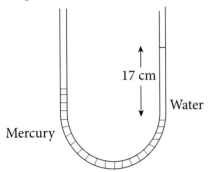

17 cm

Water

Mercury

Fig. 9.12

6. A rectangular tank has a horizontal base, 2 m long and 2 m wide. The tank contains water to a depth of 3 m. Find the pressure at a point on the base. Find also the thrust on the base. A stone block in the shape of a cube of side 1 m is lowered into the water by means of a thin wire. If the block is totally submerged, find
(i) the increase in the depth of the water
(ii) the increase in the pressure at the base
(iii) the increase in the thrust on the base.

7. A cylindrical tank of radius 4 cm is partly filled with water. A solid metal sphere of radius 3 cm is lowered into the water by means of a thin wire until it is totally immersed. Find the increase in
(i) the depth
(ii) the pressure at a point on the base
(iii) the thrust on the base (in terms of $\pi$).

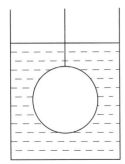

Fig. 9.13

8. A cylindrical vessel of diameter 12 cm is partly filled with oil of relative density 0.9. A sphere of diameter 6 cm is totally immersed in the oil. Find the increase in
(i) the depth
(ii) the pressure at a point on the base
(iii) the thrust on the base (in terms of $\pi$).

9. Given that 1 newton = $10^5$ dynes, write 1 dyne/cm$^2$ in terms of Pa.

10. A large cylindrical vat has internal diameter of length 2.8 m. It contains liquid of relative density 1.25 to a depth of 2 m.
(i) If $\pi = \frac{22}{7}$, calculate in kilonewtons, the thrust due to the liquid on the horizontal base of the vat.
(ii) If a solid body of mass 750 kg and relative density 2.5 is lowered by means of a fine wire into the liquid until it hangs fully immersed what, in kilonewtons, is the consequent increase in the thrust on the base? (Density of water = 1 000 kg/m$^3$).

## Archimedes' Principle

The **Principle of Archimedes** is as follows:

> If a body is wholly or partly immersed in a liquid, it suffers an upthrust (or buoyancy) which is equal in magnitude to the weight of the liquid displaced.

Take a tank containing some liquid. Now take any shape you like, consisting of some of the liquid itself. Imagine that this part of the liquid is surrounded by a dotted line, as shown.

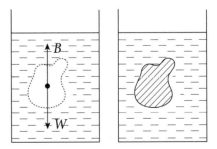

Fig. 9.14

This shape is at rest, in equilibrium. So the forces on it must be zero. The only downward force on it is the weight of the liquid ($W$) inside the dotted line. Therefore, there must be an upward force ($B$) equal to the weight of the liquid. This force is the buoyancy force.

Now, imagine that the liquid inside the dotted line is replaced by a solid object of exactly the same shape. The surrounding water will give the solid object the same support force which it gave to the liquid inside the dotted line. Why shouldn't it?

So, the object suffers a buoyancy force equal to the weight of the displaced liquid. Eureka!

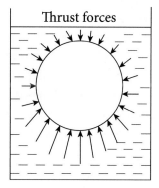

Fig. 9.15

Where does this buoyancy force come from? It is not magical. It appears because, when an object is immersed in a liquid, the thrust on the deeper parts is greater than the thrust on the more shallow parts. The resultant of these unequal forces is an upward buoyancy force.

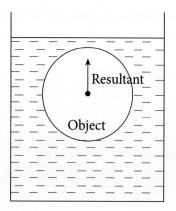

Fig. 9.16

---

### Worked Example 9.7

A solid cylinder of radius $r$ and height 3 m is held under water with its axis vertical so that its upper face is 2 m below the surface of the water. Find the thrusts on the upper and lower faces. Show that these are consistent with Archimedes' principle.

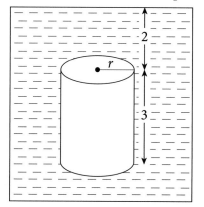

Fig. 9.17

**Solution:**

The pressure at the upper face
$$= h \rho g$$
$$= 2(1000) g$$
$$= 2000\, g \text{ N/m}^2$$

The thrust on the upper face
$$= \text{Pressure} \times \text{Area}$$
$$= 2000\, g \times \pi r^2$$
$$= 2000\, \pi r^2 g \text{ N}.$$

The pressure at the lower face
$$= h \rho g$$
$$= 5(1000) g$$
$$= 5000\, g \text{ N/m}^2$$

The thrust on the lower face
$$= \text{Pressure} \times \text{Area}$$
$$= 5000\, g \times \pi r^2$$
$$= 5000\, \pi r^2 g \text{ N}.$$

The resultant of these two forces is an upthrust, or buoyancy, of magnitude $3000\, \pi r^2 g$ N.

According to the principle of Archimedes, this buoyancy force should be equal to the weight of the water displaced.

The weight of the water $= V \rho g$
$$= (\pi r^2 (3))(1000) g$$
$$= 3000\, \pi r^2 g$$

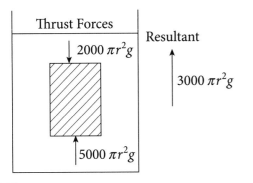

Fig. 9.18

Since the buoyancy force is equal in magnitude to the weight of the liquid displaced, Archimedes' Principle is seen to hold true in this case.

**Theorem 9.2**

If an object of weight $W$ and relative density $s$ is immersed in water, then the buoyancy force, $B$, is given by

$$B = \frac{W}{s}$$

**Proof:**

Let $V$ = the volume of the object and let
$\rho$ = its density
$W$ = The weight of the object
$= V \rho g$
$B$ = The buoyancy
= the weight of the water displaced
$= V(1000)g$.

$$\frac{W}{B} = \frac{V \rho g}{V(1000)g}$$

$$= \frac{\rho}{1000}$$

$$= \frac{\text{density of the object}}{\text{density of water}}$$

$$= s, \qquad \text{by definition}$$

$$\therefore W = s\,B$$

$$\therefore B = \frac{W}{s} \qquad \text{Q.E.D.}$$

**Theorem 9.3**

An object of weight $W$ is immersed in water and then in a liquid of relative density $s_l$. If $s_o$ = the relative density of the object and $B_l$ = the buoyancy in the liquid, then

$$B_l = \frac{s_l\,W}{s_o}$$

**Proof:** Let $V$ = the volume of the object and $\rho$ = the density of the liquid. Let $B_w$ = the buoyancy this object would suffer in water. $B_w$ = the weight of the water displaced

$$= V(1000)\,g = 1000\,V g$$

$B_l$ = the weight of the liquid displaced = $V \rho g$

$$\therefore \frac{B_l}{B_w} = \frac{V \rho g}{1000\,V g}$$

$$= \frac{\rho}{1000}$$

$$= \frac{\text{density of the liquid}}{\text{density of water}}$$

$$= s_l$$

$$B_l = s_l\,B_w$$

But $B_w = \dfrac{w}{s_o}$, from Theorem 9.2

$$\therefore B_l = \frac{s_l\,w}{s_o} \qquad \text{Q.E.D.}$$

**Worked Example 9.8**

A stone weighs 20 N in air, 12 N in water and 13 N in oil. Find

(i)  the relative density of the stone

(ii) the relative density of the oil.

**Solution:**

Apparent weight = Actual weight − buoyancy.

$\therefore$ Buoyancy
    = Actual weight − Apparent weight,

(i)  The buoyancy in water = 20 − 12 = 8 N

$$\text{But, } B = \frac{W}{s}$$

$$\therefore 8 = \frac{20}{s}$$

$$\therefore 8s = 20$$

$$\therefore s = 2.5$$

(ii) The buoyancy in the liquid,

$$B_L = 20 - 13 = 7\ \text{N}$$

$$B_L = \frac{s_L\,W}{s_o}$$

$$7 = \frac{s_L\,(20)}{2.5}$$

$$s_L = \frac{7\,(2.5)}{20}$$

$$= 0.875$$

Answer: (i) 2.5 (ii) 0.875

## Exercise 9 C

1. A piece of rock weighs 12 N in air and 8 N in water. Find the relative density of the rock.

2. A piece of wood floats in water with 65% of its volume under water. Find the relative density of the wood.

3. If $\frac{1}{10}$ of a floating block of ice is visible above the water, what is the relative density of the ice?

4. A piece of metal weighs 18 N in air and 15 N in water. Find the relative density of the metal. The metal weighs 16 N when weighed in a light oil.
   Find the relative density of the oil.

5. A piece of metal of relative density 6 weighs 30 N in air. What will it weigh
   (i) in water
   (ii) in an oil of relative density 0.9?

6. A gold bar, of relative density 17, weighs 200 N in air. Find its weight in mercury, which has relative density 13.6.

7. A stone weighs 50 N in air, 45 N in water and 46 N in an oil.
   (i) Find the relative density of the stone
   (ii) Find the relative density of the oil
   (iii) What would the stone appear to weigh if it were immersed in a liquid of relative density 0.75?

8. A body weighs 80 N in air, 60 N in water and 64 N in an oil. Find the relative density of the oil.

9. A solid sphere has radius 0.3 m. It is made of stone of relative density 2.5. Find (in terms of $\pi$ and $g$):
   (i) its volume
   (ii) its weight
   (iii) its apparent weight in water.

10. A solid cone has radius 0.3 m and height 0.7 m. It is made of metal of relative density 8. Find (taking $\pi = \frac{22}{7}$ and $g = 9.8$ m/s$^2$):
    (i) its volume
    (ii) its weight
    (iii) its apparent weight in water.

11. A body is weighed in water and in each of two liquids of relative density 0.8 and 0.75. If the resulting weights, in order, are $w_1$, $w_2$ and $w_3$, verify that $w_1 = 5\,w_2 - 4\,w_3$.

## Solving problems of immersed bodies

### Worked Example 9.9

A cubic block of wood of relative density 0.6 has sides of length $\frac{1}{2}$ m. The block is immersed in a tank which contains liquid of relative density 0.8, the block being attached to the floor of the tank by means of a vertical string. Find the tension in the string in terms of $g$.

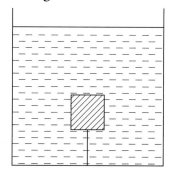

Fig. 9.19

**Solution:**

The volume (V) of the block $= \frac{1}{2} \times \frac{1}{2} \times \frac{1}{2} = \frac{1}{8}$ m$^3$
There are three forces acting on the block:

(i) Its weight $\quad W = V \rho g$
$$= \frac{1}{8}(600)\,g$$
$$= 75\,g \text{ N}.$$

(ii) The buoyancy $B$ = the weight of the liquid displaced
$$= V \rho g$$
$$= \frac{1}{8}(800)\,g$$
$$= 100\,g \text{ N}.$$

(iii) The tension in the string $T$.
But $B = W + T$, since the block is in equilibrium.
$$100\,g = 75\,g + T$$
$$\therefore T = 25\,g \text{ newtons: Answer}$$

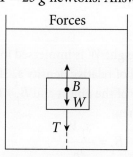

Fig. 9.20

## Worked Example 9.10

(i) A rectangular block of wood of mass 12 kg floats in water with $\frac{4}{5}$ of its mass under the water. Find the relative density of the wood.

(ii) A piece of metal is placed on top of the block so that all the wood is under water but the piece of metal is still just above the surface of the water. Find the mass of the metal.

### Solution:

(i) There are two forces acting on the block: its weight $W$ and the buoyancy force $B$.

Let $V$ = the volume of the block.

$\therefore \frac{4}{5} V$ = the volume of the water displaced.

Let $\rho$ = the density of the wood.

$$W = V \rho g$$

$B$ = the weight of the water displaced

$$= \left(\frac{4}{5} V\right)(1000) g$$

$$= 800 \, V g$$

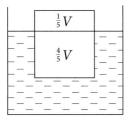

Fig. 9.21

Now, the block is in equilibrium,

so $W = B$

$\therefore V \rho g = 800 \, V g$

$\therefore \rho = 800$

The relative density of the wood

$$= \frac{800}{1000}$$

$$= 0.8 \qquad \text{Answer.}$$

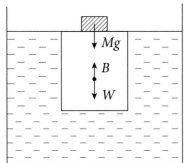

Fig. 9.22

(ii) Let $M$ = the mass of the metal.

Therefore, $Mg$ = the weight of the metal. The system is in equilibrium under these forces:

(i) the weight of the metal = $Mg$

(ii) the weight of the wood $W = 12 g$

(iii) the buoyancy $B = \frac{W}{s} = \frac{12 g}{0.8} = 15 g$

(Note: The formula, $B = \frac{W}{s}$ can be used because the wood is totally immersed in water.)

Since the system is in equilibrium,

$$W + M g = B$$

$$\therefore 12 g + M g = 15 g$$

$$\therefore M = 3 \text{ kg. Answer.}$$

## Worked Example 9.11

A solid hemisphere is held under water with its flat face uppermost and horizontal, 1 metre below the surface of the water. The radius of the hemisphere is 3 m. Find, in terms of $\pi$ and g,

(i) the buoyancy $B$,

(ii) the total thrust on the flat face of the hemisphere, $F_d$ ($d$ for downward),

(iii) the total thrust on the curved surface of the hemisphere, $F_u$ ($u$ for upward).

### Solution:

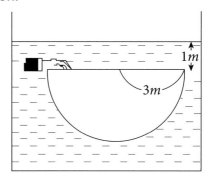

Fig. 9.23

(i) The volume of the hemisphere is given by

$$V = \frac{1}{2}\left(\frac{4}{3}\pi r^3\right) = \frac{2}{3}\pi (3)^3$$
$$= 18 \pi \text{ m}^3$$

The buoyancy $B$ = the weight of the displaced water

$$= V \rho g$$
$$= (18\pi)(1000)g$$
$$= 18,000 \, \pi \, g \text{ Newtons}$$

(ii)   The pressure at a point on the flat surface
$$= h \rho g = (1)(1000)g$$
$$= 1000 \, g.$$
The trust on the flat surface (a circle)
$$= \text{Pressure} \times \text{Area}$$
$$= 1000 \, g \times (\pi(3)^2)$$
$$= 9000 \, \pi \, g$$
$$\therefore F_d = 9000 \, \pi \, g \text{ Newtons}$$

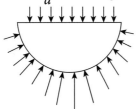

Fig. 9.24 (a)

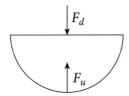

Fig. 9.29 (b)

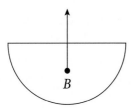

Fig. 9.29 (c)

(iii)   The buoyancy is the resultant of the upward and downward thrusts.
$$\therefore B = F_u - F_d$$
$$\text{But } B = 18,000 \, \pi \, g \text{ and}$$
$$F_d = 9000 \, \pi \, g$$
$$\therefore 18,000 \, \pi \, g = F_u - 9000 \, \pi \, g$$
$$\therefore F_u = 27,000 \, \pi \, g \text{ Newtons}$$

This upward force $F_u$ is the resultant of all the thrust forces on the curved surface of the hemisphere. It is in an upward direction and has magnitude $27,000 \, \pi \, g$ Newtons. This upward force of magnitude $27,000 \, \pi \, g$, combined with the downward force of magnitude $9000 \, \pi \, g$ gives the buoyancy force of magnitude $18,000 \, \pi \, g$ Newtons.

**Exercise 9 D**

1.   A piece of wood has volume 0.1 m³. It floats in water with $\frac{3}{4}$ of its mass under the surface of the water. Find the relative density and the weight of the wood.
     This piece of wood is then held downwards, totally submerged in water by means of a vertical string. Find the tension in the string.

2.   When floating in water, a body has 20% of its mass above the surface. What percentage of its mass would be above the surface if it were floating in a liquid of relative density 1.2?

3.   An iceberg, when floating in salt water, has 0.9 of its mass below the surface. If the relative density of salt water is 1.1, find
     (i)   the relative density of the iceberg
     (ii)   what fraction of its mass would be below the surface if it were floating in fresh water of relative density 1.

4.   A block of wood of mass 20 kg floats in water with $\frac{3}{4}$ of its mass under the surface. It is then put into an oil of relative density 0.8 and a piece of glass is placed on top of it. It floats in such a way that the wood is totally submerged but the glass remains just above the surface. Find the mass of the glass.

5.   Archimedes is asked whether a crown is made of gold or of lead, with gold plate. The king who owns the crown will not allow Archimedes to scratch it. Archimedes knows that the relative density of gold is about 18, but that of lead is about 12. He weighs the crown in air and in water, finding weights of 360 and 330 respectively. Is the crown made of gold or, for the most part, lead? Justify your answer.

6.   Assuming the relative density of ice is 0.9 and that of sea-water is 1.03, find what percentage of the volume of a block of ice floats under sea-water, correct to the nearest percent.

7.   A uniform rectangular block of metal 0.8 m × 0.6 m × 0.4 m rests on the bottom of a tank of water so that it is completely submerged. If the relative density of the metal is 2.5, find the reaction of the bottom of the tank on the block in Newtons.

8. An object of mass 12.5 kg and of relative density 2.5 is lowered by means of a fine wire into a liquid of relative density 0.8, until it hangs fully immersed.

   Calculate

   (i) the volume of the object

   (ii) the mass of the liquid displaced

   (iii) the tension in the wire.

9. A uniform rectangular block of wood 20 cm × 10 cm × 8 cm and of mass 1 kg floats in water with its longest edge vertical.

   Calculate

   (i) the volume of water displaced by the block,

   (ii) the depth (in cm) to which the block sinks in the water.

10. A solid piece of steel weighs 40 N in air and 35 N in water. Find the relative density of the steel.

11. An open rectangular tank is constructed from 5 sheets of steel: one sheet for the base 80 cm × 60 cm, two sheets for the front and back—each 80 cm by 40 cm and two sheets for the ends—each 60 cm by 40 cm. The thickness of each sheet is 0.15 cm and the density of the steel is 8 g/cm$^3$.

   Calculate the total area of the sheet metal used and hence the mass of the tank. If the tank is allowed to float in a lake, find the depth of the base below the surface of the lake. Take the density of the lake water to be 1 g/cm$^3$ and assume the external and internal dimensions of the tank to be the same.

12. A tank contains water. Oil of relative density 0.9 is poured into the tank until it reaches a depth of 5 cm. Show that the pressure at a depth of 9.5 cm is twice the pressure at a depth of 5 cm. At what depth will the pressure be five times the pressure at a depth of 3 cm?

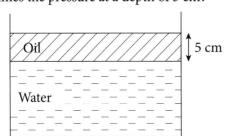

Fig. 9.25

13. If the pressure 14 m below the surface of a fresh water lake is twice the pressure 2 m below the surface, calculate the atmospheric pressure in newtons per square metre. (Density of fresh water = 1 000 kg/m$^3$.)

14. A hemisphere of radius 1 m is held immersed in water so that its flat surface is horizontal and lowermost, at a depth of 2 m below the surface of the water.

    Find

    (i) the buoyancy

    (ii) the upward thrust on the flat surface

    (iii) the downward thrust on the curved surface.

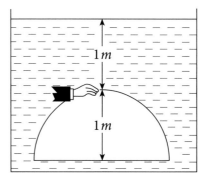

Fig. 9.26

15. A cone of diameter 4 m and height 6 m is held immersed in oil with its axis vertical and its vertex uppermost, 1 m below the surface. The relative density of the oil is 0.9. Find the magnitude of

    (i) the buoyancy force

    (ii) the thrust on the flat surface

    (iii) the thrust on the curved surface.

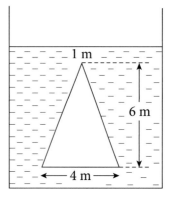

Fig. 9.27

16. A vessel is in the form of a frustum of a right circular cone. It contains liquid to a depth $h$ and at that depth the area of the free surface of the liquid is $\frac{1}{4}$ of the area of the base. Find in simplest form the ratio of the thrust on the base due to the liquid, to the weight of the liquid.

Fig. 9.28

17. A bucket has the form of a frustum of a right circular cone. When it is completely filled with water, find
    (i)   the pressure at a point on the base
    (ii)  the thrust, $T$, on the base
    (iii) the ratio of the weight of the water to the thrust on the base.

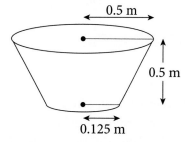

Fig. 9.29

18. A cubic block of wood of mass 50 kg floats in water with three quarters of its volume immersed.

    In oil, when a mass of 10 kg is placed on the same block, it floats just totally immersed, the 10 kg mass being above the oil. Find the relative density of the oil.

19. (i)   Given that the relative density of mercury is 13.6, find the mass (in tonnes) of half a cubic metre of mercury.

    (ii)  Mercury occupies the curved portion of a fixed upright U-tube of uniform cross-section. Water is poured into one arm and alcohol into the other, until both free surfaces are at the same level. The lengths of water and alcohol columns are 40.64 cm and 40.01 cm respectively. Calculate the density of the alcohol.

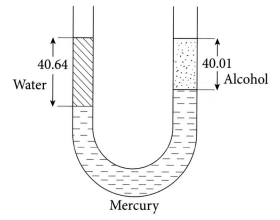

Fig. 9.30

    (iii) More alcohol is then poured in until the two mercury surfaces are at the same level. Find the new length of the alcohol column to the nearest mm.

20. A right circular cone of base radius $r$ and vertical height $3r$ is held with its vertex downwards in a liquid of density $\rho$. Its plane is horizontal and is at a distance $r$ below the surface. Calculate the forces exerted by the liquid on
    (i)   the base
    (ii)  the curved surface of the cone.

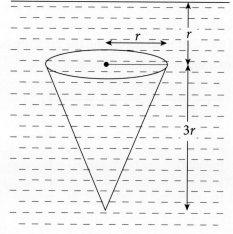

Fig. 9.31

21. A piece of steel floats on mercury in a dish. Water is added until the steel is just covered. If the volume of the steel in water is $v_1$ and the volume of steel under mercury is $v_2$ and the relative densities of steel and mercury are 7.8 and 13.6 respectively, calculate the ratio

$$\frac{v_1}{v_2}$$

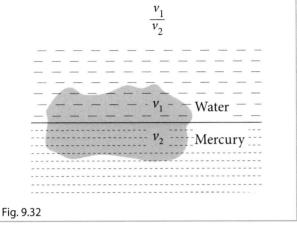

Fig. 9.32

## Immersed rods and boards

When rods on boards are partially submerged, we split the object into two parts: the wet and the dry. The centre of gravity of the submerged part is sometimes called "the centre of bouyancy". The bouyancy acts through this point.

### Worked Example 9.12

A uniform rod has weight $W$ and length 2 metres. It is in equilibrium when inclined to the horizontal with $\frac{1}{2}$ of its length immersed in water. It is supported at its upper end by a vertical force $F$. Find

   (i)   the relative density of the rod

   (ii)  the magnitude of $F$ in terms of $W$.

**Solution:**

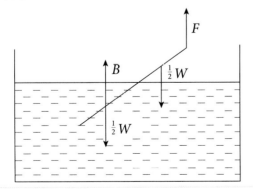

Fig. 9.33

Let $s$ = the relative density of the rod.

We split up the rod into "wet" and "dry" parts; each has weight $\frac{1}{2}W$. The buoyancy force, $B$, applies to the "wet" part only. Therefore,

$$B = \frac{\frac{1}{2}W}{s} = \frac{W}{2s}$$

Here, then, is the force diagram with 4 "unit" lengths shown. These are not metres but they certainly represent four equal lengths. They suit this kind of question where all forces are vertical.

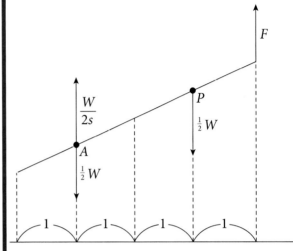

Fig. 9.34

1. ↑↓       $\dfrac{W}{2s} + F = \dfrac{1}{2}W + \dfrac{1}{2}W$

    ∴ $\dfrac{W}{2s} + F = W$          Eqn 1

2. ⇆          None

3. (Taking moments about $A$)

      $\dfrac{1}{2}W(2) = F(3)$

         ∴ $F = \dfrac{1}{3}W$        Eqn 2

Putting this result into equation 1, we get

$$\frac{W}{2s} + \frac{1}{3}W = W$$

$$\therefore \frac{W}{2s} = \frac{2}{3}W$$

$$\therefore 4s = 3$$

$$\therefore s = \frac{3}{4}$$

## Worked Example 9.13

A uniform rectangular board $ABCD$ such that $|AB| \neq |AD|$ hangs by means of a vertical string attached to the point $D$. The lower half of the board is immersed in an oil of relative density 0.8, so that the diagonal $[AC]$ is along the surface. Find

(i) the tension in the string in terms of $W$, the weight of the board

(ii) the relative density of the board.

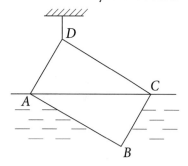

Fig. 9.35

### Solution:

Here is a force diagram:

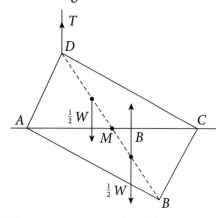

9.31 250/55

The centre of gravity of the dry part is at the centroid of triangle $ACD$. This point is $\frac{2}{3}$ of the way from $D$ to $M$, where $M$ is the midpoint of both diagonals.

Similarly, the centre of gravity of the wet part is $\frac{2}{3}$ of the way from $B$ to $M$. To calculate the buoyancy

$$B_L = s_L \, B_w$$

$$= s_L \left( \frac{W}{s} \right)$$

where $W$ refers to the weight of the immersed part.

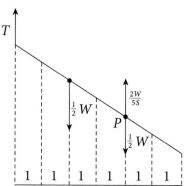

$$B = (0.8)\left( \frac{\frac{1}{2} W}{s} \right)$$

$$= \frac{2 \, W}{5s}$$

Here is the force diagram with six equal "unit" lengths.

Fig. 9.36

1. $\updownarrow$ $\qquad T + \dfrac{2W}{5s} = W$ $\qquad$ Eqn 1

2. $\leftrightarrow$ $\qquad$ None.

3. Taking moments about $P$

$$\frac{1}{2} W (2) = T (4)$$

$$\therefore T = \frac{1}{4} W \qquad \text{Eqn 2}$$

Putting this result into equation 1, we get

$$\frac{1}{4} W + \frac{2W}{5s} = W$$

$$\therefore \frac{2W}{5s} = \frac{3}{4} W$$

$$\therefore 15 \, s = 8$$

$$\therefore s = \frac{8}{15}$$

Answer: $T = \dfrac{1}{4} W; \; s = \dfrac{8}{15}$

## Exercise 9 E

1. A uniform rod of weight $W$ rests in equilibrium in an inclined position. It is supported at its upper end by a vertical force $F$, while the lower third of its length is under water. Find
   (i) $F$ in terms of $W$
   (ii) the relative density of the rod.

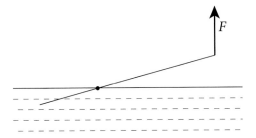

Fig. 9.37

2. A uniform rectangular board $PQRS$, $|PQ| \neq |PS|$, hangs vertically in fresh water with the diagonal $[QS]$ on the surface. The board is held in that position by a vertical string at $P$.
   (i) Show on a diagram all forces acting on the board.
   (ii) Calculate the tension $(T)$ in the string and the buoyancy force $(B)$ in terms of $W$, the weight of the board.
   (iii) Calculate the relative density of the board.

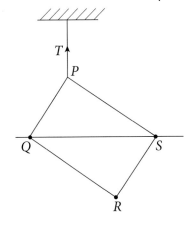

Fig. 9.38

3. A tank contains a layer of water and a layer of oil of relative density 0.9. A uniform rod of relative density $\frac{3}{4}$ is totally immersed with a quarter of its length in water and three quarters in oil. The rod rests in equilibrium, being kept in an inclined position by means of two vertical strings attached to the ends of the rod and to the bottom of the tank. Find the tension in each string in terms of $W$, the weight of the rod.

4. A uniform plank of length 1 metre and relative density 0.36 rests in equilibrium in an inclined position. It is supported at its upper end by means of vertical rope, while the other end dips into water. How much of its length is under water?

5. A uniform rod of relative density 6 is in equilibrium. It hangs by means of two vertical strings, one at each end. It is inclined with the lower half of its length immersed in water and the upper half in oil of relative density 0.8. Find the tension in each string in terms of $W$, the weight of the rod.

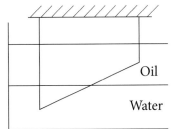

Fig. 9.39

6. A metre-stick rests on the edge of a fish-tank which contains water. 30 cm of the stick is under water and 20 cm is beyond the point of contact $P$ at the edge of the tank, as shown.

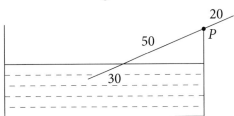

Fig. 9.40
   (i) Show why the reaction, $R$, at $P$ is vertical.
   (ii) Find the relative density of the metre stick.
   (iii) Find, also, the magnitude of $R$ in terms of $W$, the weight of the stick.

**177**

## Summary of important points

1. Density $= \dfrac{\text{Mass}}{\text{Volume}}$; $\rho = \dfrac{m}{V}$

2. Relative density $= \dfrac{\text{Density of substance}}{\text{density of water}}$.

3. Weight, $W = V \rho g$

4. Pressure $= \dfrac{\text{Force}}{\text{Area}}$.

5. Pressure at a point in a liquid $= h \rho g$.

6. Thrust on a horizontal surface = Pressure × Area.

7. Thrust on a vertical surface = Pressure at centre of gravity × Area.

8. Archimedes' Principle: When a body is wholly or partly immersed in a liquid, it suffers an upthrust, or buoyancy, which is equal in magnitude to the weight of the liquid displaced.

9. Apparent weight = Weight – Buoyancy.

10. $B_{\text{water}} = \dfrac{W}{s}$

11. $B_{\text{liquid}} = \dfrac{s_L W}{s_o}$

## DOs and DON'Ts for the exam

### DO

- Do remember that there are three ways of calculating buoyancy

1. Buoyancy $= V \rho g$ (where $V$ = the volume of liquid displaced and $\rho$ = the density of the liquid displaced).

2. Buoyancy in water $= \dfrac{W}{s_o}$, where $W$ is the weight of the immersed object and $s_o$ is its relative density.

3. Buoyancy in a liquid $= \dfrac{s_l W}{s_o}$, where W is the weight of the immersed object, $s_o$ is its relative and $s_l$ is the relative density of the liquid

### DON'T

- Don't mix up density and relative density. The density of water is 1000 kg/m$^3$ but its relative density is 1.
- Don't mix up pressure and thrust. Thrust is a force.
- Don't confuse weight and mass. Weight is a force.

# Projectiles on the inclined plane

## Higher Level only

"The miracle of the appropriateness of the language of mathematics for the formulation of the laws of physics is a wonderful gift, which we neither understand nor deserve."

*Eugene Wignen*

## Contents

## Learning outcomes

**In this chapter you will learn...**

- How to deal with inclined planes

- Range and maximum range on the inclined plane

- How to deal with the landing angle

- How to solve problems of projectiles which bounce

## You will need to know...

- Advanced trigonometry

- Formulae for compound angles: $\sin(A + B)$, $\cos(A + B)$, $\tan(A + B)$

- Coefficient of Restitution

## *The inclined plane*

Suppose a projectile is fired from the foot of an inclined plane, which is uniformly sloped at an angle $\theta$ to the horizontal, with initial speed $u$ at an angle $\alpha$ to the inclined plane and that the plane of the path of flight contains the line of greatest slope of the hill (i.e. the projectile is fired straight up the hill).

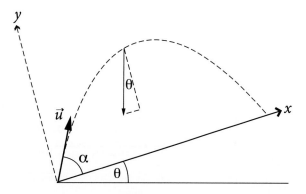

Fig. 10.1

The key strategy for success is this: we will let the line of greatest slope be our new $x$-axis (or $\vec{i}$ -axis). The $y$-axis will be the line through the point of projection, perpendicular to the $x$-axis. In each case of projectiles in the inclined plane we examine the initial velocity and acceleration due to gravity, resolving each into two components: the $x$-component and the $y$-component.

**Step 1.** $u$, the initial velocity makes an angle $\alpha$ with the $x$-axis.

$\therefore u_x = u \cos \alpha$ and $u_y = u \sin \alpha$

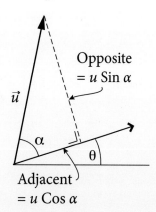

Fig. 10.2

**Step 2.** The acceleration due to gravity, $g$, makes an angle $\theta$ with the $y$-axis.

**Gravity**

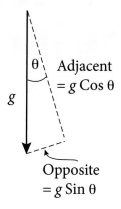

Fig. 10.3

**Resolved**

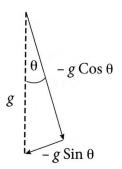

Fig. 10.4

$$a_x = - g \sin \theta$$
$$a_y = - g \cos \theta$$

The equations of motion are:

(a) Velocity : $\qquad v = u + a\,t$

$$\therefore v_x = u_x + a_x\,t$$
$$\text{while } v_y = u_y + a_y\,t$$
$$\therefore v_x = u \cos \alpha - g \sin \theta\, t$$
$$\text{and } v_y = u \sin \alpha - g \cos \theta\, t$$

The velocity vector $\vec{v}$ at time $t$ is

$$\vec{v} = \left( u\cos\alpha - g\sin\theta t \right)\vec{i} + \left( u\sin\alpha - g\cos\theta t \right)\vec{j}$$

(b) Displacement: $\quad s = u\,t + \frac{1}{2}a\,t^2$

$$\therefore s_x = u_x\,t + \frac{1}{2}a_x\,t^2$$
$$\text{while } s_y = u_y\,t + \frac{1}{2}a_y\,t^2$$
$$\therefore s_x = u \cos \alpha\, t - \frac{1}{2}g \sin \theta\, t^2$$
$$\text{and } s_y = u \sin \alpha\, t - \frac{1}{2}g \cos \theta\, t^2$$

The displacement vector $\vec{r}$ at time $t$ is

$$\vec{r} = \left( u\cos\alpha t - \frac{1}{2}g\sin\theta t^2 \right)\vec{i} + \left( u\sin\alpha t - \frac{1}{2}g\cos\theta t^2 \right)\vec{j}$$

**Note:** If a particle is projected **down** an inclined plane, the acceleration in the $x$-direction will be

$$a_x = + g \sin \theta.$$

Hence, the velocity vector $\vec{v}$ at time $t$ is

$$\vec{v} = \left( u \cos \alpha + g \sin \theta \, t \right) \vec{i} + \left( u \sin \alpha - g \cos \theta \, t \right) \vec{j}$$

and the displacement vector $\vec{r}$ at time $t$ is

$$\vec{r} = \left( u \cos \alpha t + \tfrac{1}{2} g \sin \theta \, t^2 \right) \vec{i} + \left( u \sin \alpha t - \tfrac{1}{2} g \cos \theta t^2 \right) \vec{j}$$

## Exercise 10 A

Write down $v_x$, $v_y$, $s_x$, $s_y$ in each of the examples below in terms of the time $t$.

1.  A particle is projected upwards with speed $u$ at an angle $\alpha$ to a hill which is itself inclined at an angle $\beta$ to the horizontal.

2.  A particle is projected with initial speed $u$ down a hill. The line of projection makes an angle $\alpha$ with the hill, and the hill is itself inclined at an angle $\beta$ with the horizontal.

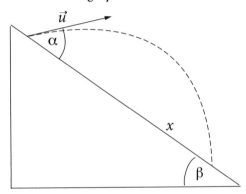

Fig. 10.5

3.  A particle is projected with initial speed $u$ down a hill which is inclined at an angle $\theta$ to the horizontal. The line of projection makes an angle $\alpha$ with the horizontal.

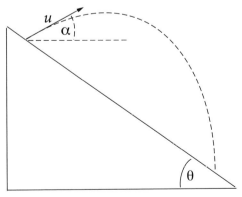

Fig. 10.6

4.  A projectile is fired up a hill with speed 10 m/s at an angle 75° to the horizontal. The hill is inclined at an angle 45° to the horizontal.

## Range and maximum height

To find the range, we find $s_x$ when $s_y = 0$ (as before). To find the greatest perpendicular height above the floor, find $s_y$ when $v_y = 0$ (as before)

### Worked Example 10.1

A particle is projected up a uniformly inclined plane with initial speed $u$, at an angle $\alpha$ to the horizontal. The plane is inclined at an angle $\theta$ with the horizontal. Prove that the range is given by:

$$R = \frac{u^2}{g \cos \theta} \left( \sin \left( 2\alpha - \theta \right) - \sin \theta \right)$$

and that the range is a maximum when the line of projection bisects the angle between the plane and the vertical, the range in this case being $\dfrac{u^2}{g \left( 1 + \sin \theta \right)}$

**Solution:**

We start by working out $v_x$, $v_y$, $s_x$, $s_y$ in each case in terms of the time t:

$$v_x = u \cos \left( \alpha - \theta \right) - g \sin \theta \, t$$

$$v_y = u \sin \left( \alpha - \theta \right) - g \cos \theta \, t$$

$$s_x = u \cos \left( \alpha - \theta \right) t - \tfrac{1}{2} g \sin \theta \, t^2$$

$$s_y = u \sin \left( \alpha - \theta \right) t - \tfrac{1}{2} g \sin \theta \, t^2$$

Range: Find $s_x$ when $s_y = 0$ (as before).

**Step 1:** To find $t$ when $s_y = 0$

$$\therefore u \sin \left( \alpha - \theta \right) t - \tfrac{1}{2} g \cos \theta \, t^2 = 0$$

$$\therefore 2 u \sin \left( \alpha - \theta \right) t - g \cos \theta \, t^2 = 0$$

$$\therefore t \left( 2 u \sin \left( \alpha - \theta \right) - g \cos \theta \, t \right) = 0$$

$$\therefore t = 0 \qquad \text{or} \qquad t = \frac{2 u \sin \left( \alpha - \theta \right)}{g \cos \theta}$$

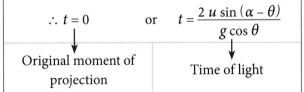

| Original moment of projection | Time of light |
|---|---|

**Step 2:** To find $s_x$ at $t = \dfrac{2 u \sin \left( \alpha - \theta \right)}{g \cos \theta}$

$$s_x = u \cos \left( \alpha - \theta \right) t - \tfrac{1}{2} g \sin \theta \, t^2$$

$$\therefore \text{ at } t = \frac{2 u \sin \left( \alpha - \theta \right)}{g \cos \theta}, \text{ the range } R \text{ is given by}$$

$$R = u \cos \left( \alpha - \theta \right) \left( \frac{2 u \sin \left( \alpha - \theta \right)}{g \cos \theta} \right)$$

$$- \tfrac{1}{2} g \sin \theta \left( \frac{4 u^2 \sin^2 \left( \alpha - \theta \right)}{g^2 \cos^2 \theta} \right)$$

$$R = \frac{2\,u^2 \cos\,(\alpha - \theta)\,\sin\,(\alpha - \theta)}{g \cos\theta}$$

$$- \frac{2\,u^2 \sin\theta\,\sin^2(\alpha - \theta)}{g \cos^2\theta}$$

$$R = \frac{2u^2\cos(\alpha-\theta)\sin(\alpha-\theta)\cos\theta - 2u^2\sin\theta\sin^2(\alpha-\theta)}{g\cos^2\theta}$$

$$= 2u^2\sin(\alpha-\theta)\,\frac{(\cos(\alpha-\theta)\cos\theta - \sin\theta\,\sin\,(\alpha-\theta))}{g\cos^2\theta}$$

But cos A cos B – sin A sin B = cos (A + B)

$$\therefore \cos\,(\alpha - \theta)\cos\theta - \sin\theta\,\sin\,(\alpha - \theta)$$

$$= \cos\,(\alpha - \theta + \theta)$$

$$= \cos\alpha$$

$$\therefore R = \frac{2\,u^2 \sin\,(\alpha - \theta)\cos\alpha}{g\cos^2\theta}$$

We now use another formula from the Formulae & Tables:

2 sin A cos B = sin (A + B) + sin (A – B)

$$R = \frac{2\,u^2 \sin\,(\alpha - \theta)\cos\alpha}{g\cos^2\theta}$$

$$= \frac{u^2}{g\cos^2\theta}(2\sin\,(\alpha - \theta)\cos\alpha)$$

$$= \frac{u^2}{g\cos^2\theta}(\sin\,(\alpha - \theta + \alpha) + \sin\,(\alpha - \theta - \alpha))$$

(by the above formula with A = $\alpha - \theta$ and B = $\alpha$)

$$= \frac{u^2}{g\cos^2\theta}(\sin\,(2\alpha - \theta) + \sin\,(-\theta))$$

$$\therefore R = \frac{u^2}{g\cos^2\theta}(\sin\,(2\alpha - \theta) - \sin\theta)$$

since sin (–A) = – sin A          Q.E.D.

To examine $R$, we must realise that $u$, $g$ and $\theta$ are all fixed. Only $\alpha$, the angle at which the projectile is fired, can vary.

The maximum value for the above expression is where sin $(2\alpha - \theta) = 1$, its maximum value (all other parts of the formula are fixed).

$$\sin\,(2\alpha - \theta) = 1$$

$$\therefore 2\alpha - \theta = 90°$$

$$\therefore 2\alpha = \theta + 90°$$

$$\therefore \alpha = \frac{\theta + 90°}{2}$$

∴ the line of projection is exactly half way between the hill and the vertical. Q.E.D.

If sin $(2\alpha - \theta) = 1$ then

$$R_{max} = \frac{u^2}{g\cos^2\theta}(1 - \sin\theta)$$

$$= \frac{u^2(1 - \sin\theta)}{g(1 - \sin^2\theta)}$$

[since $\cos^2\theta = 1 - \sin^2\theta$]

$$= \frac{u^2(1 - \sin\theta)}{g(1 - \sin\theta)(1 + \sin\theta)}$$

[since $1 - x^2 = (1 - x)(1 + x)$]

$$= \frac{u^2}{g(1 + \sin\theta)} \qquad \text{Q.E.D.}$$

## Exercise 10 B

1.  A particle is projected with speed $u$ up a hill at an angle $\alpha$ to the hill. The hill is uniformly inclined at an angle $\beta$ to the horizontal. Show
    (i)   the time of flight $= \dfrac{2\,u\sin\alpha}{g\cos\beta}$
    (ii)  the time taken to reach its highest perpendicular height above the hill is exactly half the time of flight.

2.  A particle is fired with initial speed $u$ from the foot of an inclined plane which makes an angle 30° with the horizontal. If the particle's line of projection makes an angle 75° with the horizontal, find the range and the maximum perpendicular height above the plane in terms of $u$ and $g$.

3.  A particle is projected with speed 10 m/s at an angle $\tan^{-1}\frac{3}{4}$ to an inclined plane, which makes an angle of $\tan^{-1}\frac{5}{12}$ with the horizontal. Find the range $R$ in terms of $g$.
    Show that after $\frac{2}{5}$ of the time of flight, the distance along the line of the inclined plane through which the particle has travelled is $\frac{28}{55}\,R$.

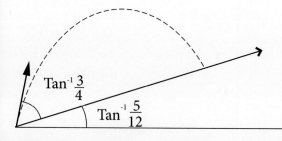

Fig. 10.7

4.  A particle is projected with a speed of 10 m/s from the foot of an inclined plane which makes an angle 30° with the horizontal. Find the range in the cases where $\alpha$, the angle which the line of projection makes with the horizontal, is

    (i)   75°         (ii)   60°

5.  A particle is projected with speed $7\sqrt{5}$ m/s at an angle $\tan^{-1} 2$ to the horizontal, up the line of greatest slope of an inclined plane of angle $\tan^{-1}\frac{1}{2}$. Show that the times taken for the particle to reach its greatest perpendicular height above the horizontal and above the plane are in the ratio 4:3.

6.  A particle is projected with speed 10 m/s at an angle $\tan^{-1}\frac{4}{3}$ to an inclined plane. If the plane makes an angle $\tan^{-1}\frac{5}{12}$ to the horizontal, find, in terms of $g$, the time at which the distance travelled parallel to the inclined plane is twice the perpendicular distance above the inclined plane.

7.  A particle is projected with speed $4\sqrt{5}$ m/s at an angle $\tan^{-1}\frac{1}{2}$ to an inclined plane. The plane makes an angle of 45° with the horizontal. The particle is projected along the line of greatest slope. Using speed $= |\vec{v}| = \sqrt{v^2{}_x + v^2{}_y}$ show that the speed of the particle when it lands is 4 m/s.

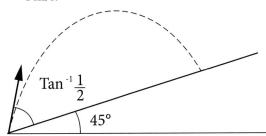

Fig. 10.8

8.  A particle is projected with speed $\sqrt{26}$ m/s up an inclined plane. The line of projection makes an angle $\alpha$ with the plane and the plane makes an angle $\beta$ with the horizontal where $\tan \beta = \frac{1}{5}$. Show that:

    (i)   the time of flight is $\dfrac{52 \sin \alpha}{5g}$

    (ii)  the range is $\dfrac{52\sqrt{26} \sin \alpha}{25\,g}(5 \cos \alpha - \sin \alpha)$

    (iii) if $\alpha = \beta$, then the range is $\dfrac{48\sqrt{26}}{25g}$

    (iv)  if $\alpha = 2\beta$, then the range is $\dfrac{44\sqrt{26}}{13g}$.

9.  A particle is projected down an inclined plane with speed $u$. If the line of projection makes an angle $\alpha$ with the plane, while the plane makes an angle $\beta$ with the horizontal, show that the range $R$ is given by
    $$R = \frac{u^2}{g \cos^2 \beta}[\sin(2\alpha - \beta) + \sin \beta]$$
    that the maximum range is given by:
    $$R_{\max} = \frac{u^2}{g(1 - \sin \beta)} \text{ when } \alpha = \frac{\beta + 90°}{2}$$

    (i)   If $\beta = 20°$, find the value of $\alpha$

    (ii)  If $\beta = 0°$, find the value of $\alpha$.

10. A plane is inclined at an angle $\alpha$ to the horizontal. A particle is projected up the plane with a velocity $u$ at an angle $\theta$ to the plane. The plane of projection is vertical and contains the line of greatest slope.

    (i)   Show that the time of flight is $\dfrac{2\,u \sin \theta}{g \cos \alpha}$.

    (ii)  Prove that the range is a maximum when $\theta = \frac{1}{2}\left(\frac{\pi}{2} - \alpha\right)$.

## Landing Angles

In the following examples we examine the angle at which the particle strikes the plane

### Worked Example 10.2

A particle is projected up an inclined plane with initial speed $u$. The line of projection makes an angle $\alpha$ with the plane, which is itself inclined at an angle $\beta$ with the horizontal. Prove that if the particle strikes the plane at right angles then
$$\tan \alpha \tan \beta = \frac{1}{2}.$$
If $\beta = 30°$, find $\tan \alpha$ and the time of flight in terms of $u$ and $g$.

**Solution:**

1. $u$: Resolve

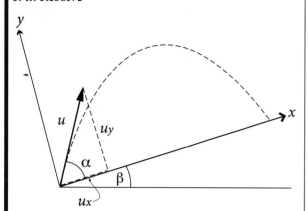

Fig. 10.9

$$u_x = u \cos \alpha$$
$$u_y = u \sin \alpha$$

2. $g$: Resolve

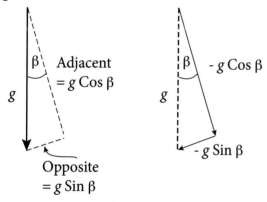

Fig. 10.10

| | |
|---|---|
| $a_x = -g \sin \beta$ | $a_y = -g \cos \beta$ |
| $v_x = u \cos \alpha - g \sin \beta\, t$ | $v_y = u \sin \alpha - g \cos \beta\, t$ |
| $s_x = (u \cos \alpha)\, t$ | $s_y = (u \sin \alpha)\, t$ |
| $\quad -\frac{1}{2}(g \sin \beta)\, t^2$ | $\quad -\frac{1}{2}(g \cos \beta)\, t^2$ |

If rain falls at right angles to the ground, its velocity is in the $y$-direction only, i.e. $v_x = 0$.
If this projectile lands at right angles to the plane, then $v_x = 0$ when it hits the plane.

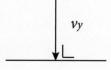

Fig. 10.11

i.e. $v_x = 0$ when $s_y = 0$

**Step 1:** Find $t$ when $s_y = 0$

$$\therefore u (\sin \alpha)\, t - \frac{1}{2} g (\cos \beta)\, t^2 = 0$$
$$\therefore 2 (u \sin \alpha)\, t - g (\cos \beta)\, t^2 = 0$$

$$\therefore t (2 u \sin \alpha - g (\cos \beta)\, t) = 0$$

| $\therefore t = 0$ **or** | $t = \dfrac{2 u \sin \alpha}{g \cos \beta}$ Equation 1 |
|---|---|
| Time of starting | Time of flight |

**Step 2:** $v_x = 0$ at $t = \dfrac{2 u \sin \alpha}{g \cos \beta}$

$$\therefore v_x = u \cos \alpha - g \sin \beta \left( \frac{2 u \sin \alpha}{g \cos \beta} \right) = 0$$

$$u \cos \alpha - 2 u \sin \alpha \frac{g \sin \beta}{g \cos \beta} = 0$$

$$\therefore u \cos \alpha - 2 u \sin \alpha \tan \beta = 0$$

$$\therefore u - 2 u \tan \beta \tan \alpha = 0 \text{ (dividing by } \cos \alpha)$$
$$\therefore 2 u \tan \beta \tan \alpha = u$$
$$\therefore \tan \beta \tan \alpha = \frac{1}{2} \text{ (dividing by } 2u)$$

Q.E.D.

If $\beta = 30°$ then

$$\tan \beta = \frac{1}{\sqrt{3}}, \cos \beta = \frac{\sqrt{3}}{2}, \sin \beta = \frac{1}{2}$$

$$\therefore \frac{1}{\sqrt{3}} \tan \alpha = \frac{1}{2}, \text{ from equation 2.}$$

$$\therefore \tan \alpha = \frac{\sqrt{3}}{2} \therefore \cos \alpha = \frac{2}{\sqrt{7}} \text{ and } \sin \alpha = \frac{\sqrt{3}}{\sqrt{7}}$$

The time of flight, given in Equation 1 is

$$t = \frac{2 u \sin \alpha}{g \cos \beta}$$

$$= \frac{2 u \frac{\sqrt{3}}{\sqrt{7}}}{g \frac{\sqrt{3}}{2}}$$

$$= 2 u \frac{\sqrt{3}}{\sqrt{7}} \times \frac{1}{g} \times \frac{2}{\sqrt{3}}$$

$$= \frac{4 u}{\sqrt{7}\, g}$$

Answer: $\dfrac{4 u}{\sqrt{7}\, g}$

### Worked Example 10.3

A particle is projected up an inclined plane with initial speed $u$. The line of projection makes an angle $\alpha$ with the plane, which itself makes an angle $\beta$ with the horizontal. Prove that if the particle lands while travelling horizontally then

$$2 \tan \alpha \tan^2 \beta = \tan \beta - \tan \alpha$$

and find $\tan \alpha$, if $\beta = 45°$.

**Solution:**

As in the last question

$$v_x = u \cos \alpha - g \sin \beta \, t$$
$$v_y = u \sin \alpha - g \cos \beta \, t$$
$$s_x = u \cos \alpha \, t - \frac{1}{2} g \sin \beta \, t^2$$
$$s_y = u \sin \alpha \, t - \frac{1}{2} g \cos \beta \, t^2$$

The angle at which a particle lands, $l$, is given by

$$\tan l = -\frac{v_y}{v_x}$$

at the moment when it lands (i.e. $s_y = 0$).

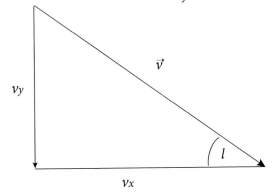

**Fig. 10.12**

This is because $\tan l = \dfrac{|v_y|}{|v_x|}$, as shown. But since $v_y$ is negative and $v_x$ is positive, at the moment of landing, $\tan l = -\dfrac{v_y}{v_x}$

In this case $l = \beta$, since the particle lands while travelling horizontally and therefore $l$ and $\beta$ are "alternate angles".

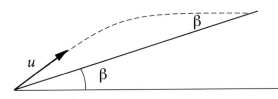

**Fig. 10.13**

$$\therefore \tan \beta = -\frac{v_y}{v_x} \text{ when } s_y = 0$$

**Step 1:** Find $t$ when $s_y = 0$

$$\therefore u (\sin \alpha) \, t - \frac{1}{2} g (\cos \beta) \, t^2 = 0$$

$$\therefore 2 u (\sin \alpha) \, t - g (\cos \beta) \, t^2 = 0$$

$$\therefore t \left( 2 u (\sin \alpha) - g (\cos \beta) \, t \right) = 0$$

| $\therefore t = 0$ **or** | $t = \dfrac{2u \sin \alpha}{g \cos \beta}$ |
|---|---|
| Time of projection | Time of flight |

**Step 2:** Find $v_y$ when $s_y = 0$.

$$v_y = u \sin \alpha - g \cos \beta \, t$$
$$= u \sin \alpha - g \cos \beta \left( \frac{2 u \sin \alpha}{g \cos \beta} \right)$$
$$= u \sin \alpha - 2 u \sin \alpha$$
$$= - u \sin \alpha$$
$$\therefore v_y = - u \sin \alpha$$

**Step 3:** Find $v_x$ when $s_y = 0$

$$v_x = u \cos \alpha - g \sin \beta \, t$$
$$= u \cos \alpha - g \sin \beta \left( \frac{2 u \sin \alpha}{g \cos \beta} \right)$$
$$= u \cos \alpha - \frac{2 u \sin \beta \sin \alpha}{\cos \beta}$$
$$\therefore v_x = u \cos \alpha - 2 u \tan \beta \sin \alpha$$

**Step 4:** But $\tan \beta = -\dfrac{v_y}{v_x}$

$$\therefore \tan \beta = \frac{u \sin \alpha}{u \cos \alpha - 2 u \tan \beta \sin \alpha}$$

$$\therefore \tan \beta = \frac{\sin \alpha}{\cos \alpha - 2 \tan \beta \sin \alpha}$$

$$\therefore \tan \beta (\cos \alpha - 2 \tan \beta \sin \alpha) = \sin \alpha$$

$$\therefore \tan \beta \cos \alpha - 2 \tan^2 \beta \sin \alpha = \sin \alpha$$

$$\therefore \tan \beta - 2 \tan^2 \beta \tan \alpha = \tan \alpha$$
(dividing by $\cos \alpha$)

$$\therefore \tan \beta - \tan \alpha = 2 \tan^2 \beta \tan \alpha \qquad \text{Q.E.D.}$$

If $\beta = 45°$, then $\tan \beta = 1$.

$$\therefore 1 - \tan \alpha = 2 \tan \alpha \text{ (from above)}$$
$$\therefore 3 \tan \alpha = 1$$
$$\therefore \tan \alpha = \frac{1}{3} \text{:Answer}$$

If $l$ is the landing angle then $\tan l = \dfrac{-V_y}{V_x}$ when $S_y = 0$.

**Exercise 10 C**

1. A projectile is fired with initial velocity $u$ at an angle $\alpha$ to the horizontal. A plane $P$ passes through the point of projection and makes an angle $\beta$ with the horizontal. If the particle strikes the plane $P$ at right angles to $P$ after time $t$ show that:

$$t = \frac{2\,u \sin(\alpha - \beta)}{g \cos \beta}$$

and deduce that $2 \tan(\alpha - \beta) \tan \beta = 1$

If $(\alpha - \beta) = \frac{\pi}{4}$, find in terms of $u$ and $g$ the range of the projectile along $P$.

2. From a point $P$ on a plane, inclined at 30° to the horizontal, a particle is projected with speed $u$ at 30° to the plane. The motion takes place in a vertical plane through the line of greatest slope up the plane from $P$. Show that the landing angle is 60°.

3. A particle is projected from the foot of an inclined plane which makes an angle of 45° with the horizontal. The initial velocity is $u$ at an angle $\alpha$ to the horizontal. If the angle at which the particle meets the plane on landing is $\beta$, show that
$$\tan \beta = \frac{\tan \alpha - 1}{3 - \tan \alpha}$$
Find the value of $\tan \alpha$ if:

   (i) the particle lands while travelling horizontally

   (ii) the particle lands perpendicularly to the plane

   (iii) the particle meets the plane at an angle $\tan^{-1} \frac{1}{3}$.

4. A particle is projected from the foot of an inclined plane which makes an angle $\alpha$ with the horizontal, such that $\tan \alpha = \frac{1}{\sqrt{2}}$. The initial velocity is $u$ at the same angle $\alpha$ to the plane.

   (i) Prove that the particle lands at right angles to the plane.

   (ii) Find the range up the plane.

   (iii) Show that the Principle of Conservation of Energy holds in this case: i.e. that the sum of the kinetic energy and potential energy of the particle is the same at the moment of take-off and of landing.

5. A particle is projected with initial speed $u$ at an angle $\tan^{-1} \frac{1}{2}$ to an inclined plane. The plane contains the point of projection and makes an angle $\tan^{-1} \frac{3}{4}$ with the horizontal. Show that the angle at which the particle strikes the plane is $\tan^{-1} 2$.

6. A plane is inclined at an angle $\tan^{-1}\left(\frac{1}{2}\right)$ to the horizontal. A particle is projected up the plane with velocity $u$ at an angle $\theta$ to the plane. (The plane of projection is vertical and contains the line of greatest slope.) The particle strikes the plane parallel to the horizontal. Express $t$, the time of flight in terms of $u$ and $\theta$. Hence, or otherwise, establish that: $\tan \theta = \frac{1}{3}$.
Calculate the range along the plane.

7. A particle is projected from point $P$ up an inclined plane with a speed of $4g\sqrt{2}$ m/s at an angle $\tan^{-1}\left(\frac{1}{3}\right)$ to the inclined plane. The plane is inclined at an angle $\theta$ to the horizontal. (The plane of projection is vertical and contains the line of greatest slope). The particle is moving horizontally when it strikes the plane at a point $Q$.

   (a) Find two possible values for $\theta$.

   (b) If $\tan \theta = 0.5$, then

      (i) find the magnitude of the velocity with which the particle strikes the inclined plane at $Q$.

      (ii) determine the total energy at $P$ and show that it is equal to the total energy at $Q$.

8. A plane is inclined at an angle $\alpha$ to the horizontal. A particle is projected up the plane with a velocity $u$ at an angle $\theta$ to the plane. The plane of projection is vertical and contains the line of greatest slope.
Prove that the particle will strike the plane horizontally if
$$\tan \theta = \frac{\sin \alpha \cos \alpha}{2 - \cos^2 \alpha}$$

9. A particle is projected from a point $o$ with initial velocity $u$ up a plane inclined at an angle 60° to the horizontal. The direction of projection makes an angle $\theta$ with the horizontal. The maximum perpendicular height above the plane is $H$.
Prove that $H = \frac{u^2 \sin^2 \theta}{g}$
Show that the time interval between the two instants when the perpendicular height above the plane is $H \sin^2 \theta$ is given by
$$\frac{2\,u \sin 2\theta}{g}.$$

## Projectiles which bounce

When a ball bounces on a smooth plane along the $\vec{i}$ direction, then its velocity in the $\vec{i}$ direction remains the same, but its velocity in the $\vec{j}$ direction will be multiplied by $-e$.

### Worked Example 10.4

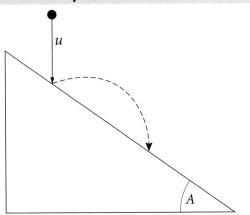

Fig. 10.14

A smooth sphere of mass $m$ is falling vertically under gravity with speed $u$ when it hits a plane inclined at an angle $A$ to the horizontal. The coefficient of restitution is $\frac{1}{2}$. Find the length of its first hop in terms of $u$, $g$ and $A$.

### Solution:

We will let the $\vec{i}$ direction be along the plane. The sphere's velocity on impact is
$$u \sin A \ \vec{i} - u \cos A \ \vec{j} .$$
After impact, its velocity in the $\vec{i}$ direction remains the same, but its velocity in the $\vec{j}$ direction will be multiplied by $-e$. So its velocity on take-off will be $u \sin A \ \vec{i} + e \, u \cos A \ \vec{j}$.

Furthermore, the accelerations due to gravity are:
$$a_x = + g \sin A \text{ and } a_y = - g \cos A.$$
After the sphere leaves the plane after the first bounce,
$$v_x = u \sin A + g (\sin A) t$$
$$\text{and } v_y = \tfrac{1}{2} u \cos A - g (\cos A) t$$
$$s_x = u (\sin A) t + \tfrac{1}{2} g (\sin A) t^2$$
$$\text{and } s_y = \tfrac{1}{2} u \cos A \, t - \tfrac{1}{2} g \cos A \, t^2$$
To find the length of the first hop is to find the range: i.e. find $s_x$ when $s_y = 0$.
$$s_y = 0$$
$$\therefore s_y = \tfrac{1}{2} u (\cos A) t - \tfrac{1}{2} g (\cos A) t^2 = 0$$
$$\therefore t \left( u \cos A - \tfrac{1}{2} g (\cos A) t \right) = 0$$
$$\therefore t = 0 \text{ or } t = \frac{u}{g}$$

At $t = \frac{u}{g}$,
$$s_x = u (\sin A) t + \tfrac{1}{2} g (\sin A) t^2$$
$$= u (\sin A) \left( \frac{u}{g} \right) + \tfrac{1}{2} g (\sin A) \left( \frac{u}{g} \right)^2$$
$$= \frac{u^2 \sin A}{g} + \frac{u^2 \sin A}{2 g}$$
$$= \frac{2 u^2 \sin A + u^2 \sin A}{2 g}$$
$$= \frac{3 u^2 \sin A}{2 g} : \text{Answer}$$

### Exercise 10 D

1. A ball is thrown vertically from ground level, so that it reaches a height $h$ above horizontal ground before it falls to the ground again. The coefficient of restitution is $\frac{3}{4}$.
   (i) Find the height it will reach after the first bounce.
   (ii) Using the formula for the sum to infinity of a geometric series, $S_\infty = \frac{a}{1 - r}$, find the distance travelled by the ball as the number of bounces tends towards infinity.

2. A ball falls vertically under gravity onto a smooth plane which is inclined at an angle $\tan^{-1} \frac{4}{3}$ to the horizontal. The speed of the ball at impact is 20 m/s. If the coefficient of restitution is $\frac{2}{3}$, find
   (i) the length of the first hop
   (ii) the landing angle after the first hop (to the nearest degree)

3. A ball is falling vertically with speed $u$ when it strikes a smooth plane inclined at an angle $A$ to the horizontal. If the coefficient of restitution is $\frac{1}{4}$, find the lengths of the first and second hops.

4. A particle is projected up an inclined plane with initial speed $13u$. The line of projection makes an angle $\tan^{-1} \left( \frac{5}{12} \right)$ with the plane. The plane is inclined at 45° to the horizontal. (The plane of projection is vertical and contains the line of greatest slope.) The particle next strikes the plane at a point $P$. If the coefficient of restitution between the ball and the inclined plane is $\frac{2}{5}$, show that the particle rises vertically from $P$.

5.  A particle is projected down an inclined plane with initial speed $u$. The plane is inclined at 30° to the horizontal. The line of projection makes an angle 60° with the inclined plane. The plane of projection is vertical and contains the line of greatest slope. The coefficient of restitution between the ball and the inclined plane is $e$.
    (i)   Find the range to the first hop in terms of $u$ and $e$.
    (ii)  For what value of $e$ is the range for the second hop double the range for the first hop?

6.  A ball is dropped from a height $h$ onto a smooth inclined plane. The ball strikes the plane at $P$ and rebounds. The plane is inclined at 30° to the horizontal. The coefficient of restitution between the ball and the inclined plane is $\frac{1}{2}$. Show that the ball's next impact will be a distance $\frac{3h}{2}$ from $P$.

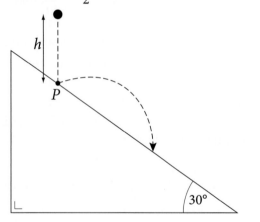

Fig. 10.15

# Summary of important points

1.  Suppose a particle is projected up an inclined plane with initial speed $u$. The line of projection makes an angle $\alpha$ with the plane, which is itself inclined at an angle $\beta$ with the horizontal.
    $$v_x = u \cos \alpha - g \sin \beta \, t$$
    $$v_y = \sin \alpha - g \cos \beta \, t$$
    $$s_x = u \cos \alpha \, t - \tfrac{1}{2} g \sin \beta \, t^2$$
    $$s_y = u \sin \alpha \, t - \tfrac{1}{2} g \cos \beta \, t^2$$

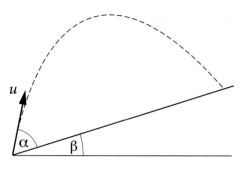

Fig. 10.16

2.  The landing angle is given by $\tan l = -\dfrac{v_y}{v_x}$ when $s_y = 0$.

3.  If a particle lands perpendicularly to the plane, then $v_x = 0$ when $s_y = 0$.

4.  If a particle lands while travelling horizontally then $\tan \beta = -\dfrac{v_y}{v_x}$ when $s_y = 0$, where $\beta$ = the angle of the inclined plane.

5.  When a ball bounces on a smooth plane along the $\vec{i}$ direction, then its velocity in the $\vec{i}$ direction remains the same, but its velocity in the $\vec{j}$ direction will be multiplied by $-e$.

## DOs and DON'Ts for the exam

### DO
*   Do be familiar with the trigonometrical formulae in the *Formulae and Tables*
*   Do start each question by getting the velocities and displacements along each axis, in terms of $t$:
    $$v_x = u \cos \alpha - g \sin \theta \, t$$
    $$v_y = u \sin \alpha - g \cos \theta \, t$$
    $$s_x = u \cos \alpha \, t - \tfrac{1}{2} g \sin \theta \, t^2$$
    $$s_y = u \sin \alpha \, t - \tfrac{1}{2} g \cos \theta \, t^2$$
*   Do read the question carefully: did the particle's initial speed make and angle $\theta$ with the plane or with the horizontal?

### DON'T
*   Don't mix up the inclined plane with the horizontal plane
*   Don't mix up the angle of the inclined plane with the angle of projection

# Motion in a circle

## Chapter 11

"My goal was to show that the celestial machine is not so much a divine organism but rather a clockwork"

*Johannes Kepler*

## Contents

## Learning outcomes

**In this chapter you will learn...**

- About radian measure and angular velocity

- The relationship between velocity and angular velocity

- That circular motion requires a force directed towards the centre of magnitude $\frac{mv^2}{r}$ or $m\omega^2 r$

- How to solve problems of motion in a horizontal circle

- How to solve problems of motion in a vertical circle, using the Principle of Conservation of Energy

## You will need to know...

- How to differentiate sin *kx* and cos *kx*
- Radians and degrees
- The Principle of Conservation of Energy

## Radian measure

**Definition:** If $C$ is a circle of radius $r$, the angle subtended at the centre of the circle by an arc of length $r$ is **one radian**.

It follows that
$$\text{angle (in radians)} = \frac{\text{length of arc}}{\text{length of radius}}$$

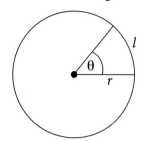

Fig. 11.1

If the arc has length $l$, when the angle is $\theta$, then $l = r\,\theta$.

This formula appears on page 9 of *Formulae and Tables*.

### Worked Example 11.1

A circle has radius 10 cm.

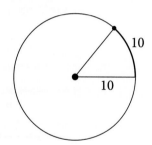

Fig. 11.2

(a) Find, in radians, the angle at the centre of the circle which is subtended by an arc of length (i) 10 cm (ii) 20 cm (iii) 17 cm.

(b) What is the length of the arc which subtends an angle of 2.5 radians?

**Solution:**

(a)

(i)   Angle $= \dfrac{\text{arc length}}{\text{radius}} = \dfrac{10}{10} = 1$ radian

(ii)  Angle $= \dfrac{20}{10} = 2$ radians

(iii) Angle $= \dfrac{17}{10} = 1.7$ radians

(b)
$$l = r\,\theta$$
$$= (2.5)(10)$$
$$= 25 \text{ cm}$$

**Note 1:** How many radians in a full circle? This is the same as asking how many times does the radius of a circle go into its circumference. But the circumference $C$ of a circle is given by $C = 2\pi r$. It follows that there are $2\pi$ radians in a full circle.

**Note 2:** How many degrees in 1 radian?

$$2\pi \text{ radians} = 360°$$

$$\therefore \quad 1 \text{ radian} = \frac{360}{2\pi} \text{ degrees}$$

$$= 57.3°$$

### Worked Example 11.2

A turntable turns through 12 radians per second. A speck of dust rests on the turntable, 5 cm from the centre. Find the speed of the speck of dust in cm/s.

**Solution:**

In 1 second the speck of dust travels along an arc of length $l = r\,\theta = (5)(12) = 60$ cm. Therefore, it travels at 60 cm/s.: Answer.

**Note 3:** 12 radians per second is called the **angular speed** of the speck of dust. Angular speed is usually denoted by the Greek letter $\omega$. It is the number of radians through which an object turns per second. In the last case we could say that $\omega = 12$ rad/s.

Supposing a particle is moving along the circumference of a circle of radius $r$ with angular speed $\omega$. What is the particle's speed?

Angular speed $= \omega$ rad/s

In one second the angle subtended is $\omega$.

In one second the particle travels a distance $v$.

Since $l = r\,\theta$, it follows that $v = r\,\omega$.

That is,

$$v = \omega\, r.$$

This is a frequently-used equation which links linear speed and angular speed.

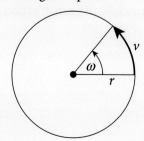

Fig. 11.3

## Worked Example 11.3

A merry-go-round has radius 5 metres. It completes 10 full turns every minute. A child is on a horse on the circumference of the merry-go-round. Find the speed of the child in m/s.

**Solution:**

In 60 seconds it completes 10 full turns.

In 1 second it completes $\frac{1}{6}$ of a full turn.

$$\frac{1}{6} \text{ of a full turn} = \frac{1}{6} \text{ of } 2\pi \text{ radians}$$

$$= \frac{1}{6}(2) \times 3.14 \text{ radians}$$

$$= 1.05 \text{ radians}$$

Therefore $\omega = 1.05$ rad/s

Now, $v = \omega\, r = (1.05)(5)$

$$= 5.25 \text{ m/s Answer}$$

## Exercise 11 A

1. A circle has radius 20 cm. Find, in radians, the angle subtended by arcs of length
   (i) 40 cm
   (ii) 100 cm
   (iii) 15 cm
   (iv) 11 cm.

2. A circle has radius 5 cm. Find the length of the arcs which subtend angles of magnitude
   (i) 3 radians
   (ii) 0.8 rad
   (iii) 1.2 rad
   (iv) 1.7 rad.

3. In a circle of radius $r$, an angle of 3.5 radians is subtended by an arc of length 14 cm. Find the value of $r$.

4. In a circle, an angle of 1.8 radians is subtended by an arc of length 2.07 cm. Find the radius of the circle.

5. A particle moves along the circumference of a circle of radius 10 cm. If the speed of the particle is 18 cm/s, find its angular speed.

6. A particle is moving in a circle with angular speed 4 rad/s. If the velocity of the particle is 7 cm/s, find the radius of the circle of motion.

7. A "single" vinyl record (from your grandfather's collection) completes 45 revolutions per minute. What is its angular speed correct to one decimal place?

8. A bicycle wheel is rotating with angular speed 10 rad/s. Find, to the nearest integer, the number of revolutions it completes per minute. If the radius of the wheels is 40 cm, find the speed of the bicycle.

9. When a CD is spinning at 200 rotations per minute, what is its angular speed in rad/s?

10. When a DVD is spinning at 570 revolutions per minute, what is the linear speed at a point 6 cm from the centre?
    Give your answer in m/s.

## Centripetal accelerations

Newton's first law states that an object will continue to be at rest or to move in a straight line unless it is acted on by some force. It follows that if a particle is moving in a circular path it must be acted on by some force. We will prove that this force, and hence the acceleration of the object, is towards the centre of the circle of motion.

For example, a ball being swung in a horizontal circle at the end of a string is being acted upon by the tension in the string. This tension is towards the centre of motion.

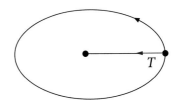

Fig. 11.4

Also, the moon travels in a circular orbit around the earth. The force acting on the moon is the gravitational attraction between the moon and the earth. Once more, this force is directed towards the centre of the circle of motion.

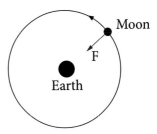

Fig. 11.5

It is hard to accept that the ball and the moon are accelerating, because their speeds are constant. But they are accelerating. This is because their velocity is changing, not in magnitude, but in direction. Any change in velocity is called an acceleration. Not only will we prove that this acceleration is directed towards the centre of the circle of motion, but also that its magnitude is

$$\omega^2 r \text{ or } \frac{v^2}{r}$$

where $\omega$ is the angular speed, $v$ is the speed of the particle and $r$ the radius of the circle of motion.

There will be two proofs given. The first uses trigonometry, the second differentiation. The second proof is for Higher Level students only.

## Proof of formulae

### Theorem 11.1

If a particle moves with constant speed $v$ along the circumference of a circle of radius $r$, then its acceleration is directed towards the centre of the circle and is of magnitude $\omega^2 r$ or $\frac{v^2}{r}$.

**Proof I:** The velocity vector at any instant is along the circumference of the circle, perpendicular to the radius. It is at a tangent to the circle.

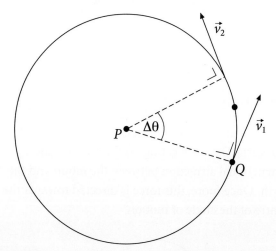

Fig. 11.6

Let $\vec{v}_1$ be the velocity vector at one moment, when the particle is at $Q$.

Let $\vec{v}_2$ be the velocity vector a small time $\Delta t$ later.

If we slide $\vec{v}_2$ over to $q$, as we can see that the small change in the velocity, $\Delta v$, is directed almost at a right angle to $\vec{v}_1$. We will call the small change in the angle $\Delta \theta$. Why is the angle $\Delta \theta$ in Diagram I the same as the angle $\Delta \theta$ in Diagram II?

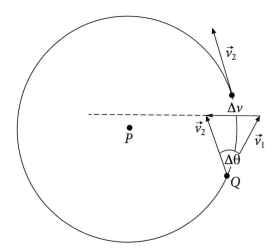

Fig. 11.7

If we made $\Delta t$ smaller, $\Delta v$ would be directed even more closely towards $p$, since it is almost perpendicular to $\vec{v}_1$ which is at a tangent to the circle. In the limit as $\Delta t \to 0$ the change in the velocity $\Delta v$ will be directed towards $p$. This means that at any moment the acceleration is directed towards the centre of the circle of motion, which is what we set out to prove.

Secondly, we can find the magnitude of this acceleration.

Draw a NEW circle around the point $q$ as its centre. Let the radius of this circle be $|\vec{v}_1| = |\vec{v}_2| = v$

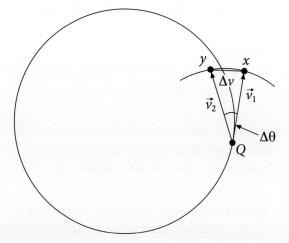

Fig. 11.8

If $\Delta \theta$ is small, the length of $\Delta v$ is almost the same as the length of the arc.

$$\Delta v \approx |\text{arc } xy|$$
$$= \text{radius} \times \text{angle (in radians)}$$
$$\therefore \Delta v \approx v \Delta \theta,$$

where $v$ = the speed of the particle

$$\therefore \frac{\Delta v}{\Delta t} \approx v \frac{\Delta \theta}{\Delta t}$$

If we let $\Delta t \to 0$ we get

$$a = v \omega$$

$$\text{since } \lim_{\Delta t \to 0} \frac{\Delta v}{\Delta t} = \frac{dv}{dt} = a$$

$$\text{and } \lim_{\Delta t \to 0} \frac{\Delta \theta}{\Delta t} = \frac{d\theta}{dt} = \omega$$

But $v = \omega r$.

Therefore, $a = v\omega$

$$= (\omega r)\omega$$

$$= \omega^2 r$$

But $\omega = \dfrac{v}{r}$

$$\therefore a = \omega^2 r$$

$$= \left(\frac{v}{r}\right)^2 r$$

$$= \frac{v^2 r}{r^2}$$

$$= \frac{v^2}{r} \quad \text{Q.E.D.}$$

---

**Proof II:** (For Higher Level students only.)

(Let $\omega$ be the angular speed of the particle; i.e. an angle of $\omega$ radians will be opened out every second. After $t$ seconds the angle subtended will be $\omega t$ radians.

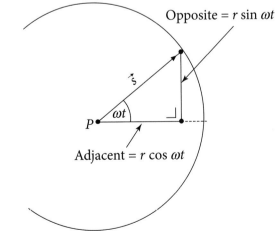

Opposite = $r \sin \omega t$

Adjacent = $r \cos \omega t$

Fig. 11.9

The displacement of the particle after time $t$ is given by

$$\vec{s} = r \cos \omega t \, \vec{i} + r \sin \omega t \, \vec{j} \qquad \text{Equation 1}$$

---

The velocity $\vec{v} = \dfrac{d\vec{s}}{dt}$ by definition.

By differentiating equation 1 with respect to $t$ we get,

$$\vec{v} = \frac{d\vec{s}}{dt}$$

$$= r(-\sin \omega t)\omega \, \vec{i} + r(\cos \omega t)\omega \, \vec{j}$$

$$\therefore \vec{v} = -\omega r \sin \omega t \, \vec{i} + \omega r \cos \omega t \, \vec{j} \qquad \text{Eq. 2}$$

The acceleration $\vec{a} = \dfrac{d\vec{v}}{dt}$ by definition.

By differentiating Equation 2 with respect to $t$ we get

$$\vec{a} = \frac{d\vec{v}}{dt}$$

$$= -\omega r(\cos \omega t)\omega \, \vec{i} + \omega r(-\sin \omega t)\omega \, \vec{j}$$

$$\therefore \vec{a} = -\omega^2 r \cos \omega t \, \vec{i} - \omega^2 r \sin \omega t \, \vec{j} \qquad \text{Eq. 3}$$

$$\vec{a} = -\omega^2 \left(r \cos \omega t \, \vec{i} + r \sin \omega t \, \vec{j}\right)$$

$$= -\omega^2 \vec{s}$$

from Equation 1.

Therefore, the acceleration is directed along $\vec{s}$ but in the opposite direction, that is towards the centre of the circle of motion. What is the magnitude of the acceleration $\vec{a}$?

$$\vec{a} = -\omega^2 r \cos \omega t \, \vec{i} - \omega^2 r \sin \omega t \, \vec{j} \text{ (equation 3)}$$

$$\therefore |\vec{a}| = \sqrt{\omega^4 r^2 \cos^2 \omega t + \omega^4 r^2 \sin \omega t}$$

$$= \sqrt{\omega^4 r^2} \sqrt{\cos^2 \omega t + \sin^2 \omega t}$$

$$= \omega^2 r (1)$$

$$= \omega^2 r$$

$$= \left(\frac{v}{r}\right)^2 r$$

$$= \frac{v^2}{r} \text{ Q.E.D.}$$

**Note 1:**

$$\vec{v} = -\omega r \sin \omega t \, \vec{i} + \omega r \cos \omega t \, \vec{j} \text{ (equation 2)}$$

$$\therefore |\vec{v}| = \sqrt{\omega^2 r^2 \sin^2 \omega t + \omega^2 r^2 \cos^2 \omega t}$$

$$= \sqrt{\omega^2 r^2} \sqrt{\sin^2 \omega t + \cos^2 \omega t}$$

$$= \omega r (1)$$

$$= \omega r$$

This is the expected result that the magnitude of the velocity, $v = \omega r$, and appears on page 51 of *Formulae and Tables*.

**Note 2:** We can prove that $\vec{v}$ is perpendicular to $\vec{s}$.

$$\vec{v}.\vec{s} = \left(-\omega r \sin \omega t \, \vec{i} + \omega r \cos \omega t \, \vec{j}\right).\left(r \cos \omega t \, \vec{i} + r \sin \omega t \, \vec{j}\right)$$

$$= -\omega r^2 \sin \omega t \cos \omega t + \omega r^2 \cos \omega t \sin \omega t$$

$$= 0$$

$$\therefore \vec{v} \text{ is perpendicular to } \vec{s}. \text{ Q.E.D.}$$

(Can be written as $\vec{v} \perp \vec{s}$)

# Motion in a horizontal circle

## Important Note For All Students

We have proved that, if a particle moves in a circle of radius $r$ and with constant speed $v$, then the acceleration has magnitude $\omega^2 r$ or $\frac{v^2}{r}$.
These formulae appear on page 51 of *Formulae and Tables*.

## Conclusion

A particle moving in a circle of radius $r$ with constant speed $v$ is, in fact, accelerating. This acceleration is directed towards the centre of the circle and is of magnitude $\omega^2 r$ or $\frac{v^2}{r}$. This kind of acceleration is called **centripetal acceleration**, because it is directed towards the centre of the circle of motion. Since $F = ma$, it follows that in the case of circular motion

$$F = m\,a = m\,\frac{v^2}{r} = m\,\omega^2 r$$

This means that if an object is to travel with constant speed $v$ in a circle of radius $r$, it requires a force directed towards the centre of the circle, and the magnitude of this force must be $m\,\omega^2 r$ or $\frac{mv^2}{r}$. Such a force is called a **centripetal force**, as it is directed towards the centre.

### Motion in a horizontal circle

When a particle moves in a horizontal circle there will be two equations:

1. $F_{up} = F_{down}$

2. $F_{centripetal} = m\,\omega^2 r$   or   $F_{centripetal} = \frac{mv^2}{r}$

## Worked Example 11.4

An inelastic light string is 3 m long. It is attached at one end to a fixed point $p$ on a horizontal smooth table and at the other end to a particle of mass 2 kg. If the particle is moving in a circle with constant speed 6 m/s, find the tension in the string which remains taut and horizontal.

**Solution:**

The particle is moving with constant speed in a circle. So, it must be acted upon by a force directed towards the centre of the circle. The force must have magnitude $\frac{mv^2}{r}$. In this case, the centripetal force is the tension $T$.

$$T = \frac{m\,v^2}{r} = \frac{2\,(36)}{3} = 24 \text{ N: Answer}$$

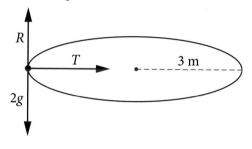

Fig. 11.10

(Note: the reaction $R$ and the weight $2g$ must be equal and opposite, since there is no vertical acceleration.)

## Worked Example 11.5

A light inextensible string of length 5 m is attached at one end to a fixed point $P$ which is 3 m above a smooth horizontal table. The other end is attached to a particle of mass 20 kg which moves in a circular path on the table with constant angular speed 1.2 rad/s. Find the tension in the string and the reaction at the table.

**Solution:**

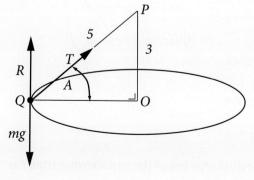

Fig. 11.11

$|OQ|^2 + |OP|^2 = |QP|^2$

$\therefore |OQ|^2 + 9 = 25$

$\therefore |OQ| = 4$

$\therefore \sin A = \dfrac{\text{opp}}{\text{hyp}} = \dfrac{3}{5}$

$\therefore \cos A = \dfrac{\text{adj}}{\text{hyp}} = \dfrac{4}{5}$

The forces on the particle are

(i)  its weight  $= mg$

$= 20(9.8)$

$= 196$ N

(ii)  the reaction at the table, $R$.

(iii)  the tension in the string, $T$

We resolve $T$ into horizontal and vertical components:

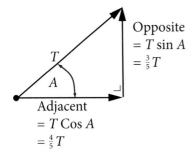

Opposite $= T \sin A = \frac{3}{5}T$

Adjacent $= T \cos A = \frac{4}{5}T$

Fig. 11.12

The forces on the particle can be illustrated thus:

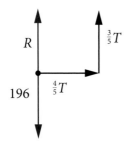

Fig. 11.13

Firstly, there is no vertical acceleration, so the forces up = the forces down:

$\therefore R + \dfrac{3}{5}T = 196$    Equation I.

Secondly, the force towards the centre of motion must be of magnitude $m\omega^2 r$. In this case, the centripetal force is $\frac{4}{5}T$.

$\therefore \dfrac{4}{5}T = m\omega^2 r$

$= (20)(1.2)^2(4)$

$\therefore T = \dfrac{(5)(20)(1.44)(4)}{4}$

$= 144$ N....    Equation II

From Equation 1, we get

$R + \dfrac{3}{5}T = 196$

$\therefore R + \dfrac{3}{5}(144) = 196$

$\therefore R = 109.6$ N.

Answer: $R = 109.6$ N; $T = 144$ N.

### Worked Example 11.6

A particle of mass $m$ moves along the inside surface of a sphere of radius 1.3 metres. It moves in a horizontal circle whose centre, $O$, is 1.2 metres below the centre of the sphere, $Q$. Show that the constant speed of the particle is given by

$$v = \sqrt{\dfrac{5g}{24}}.$$

**Solution:**

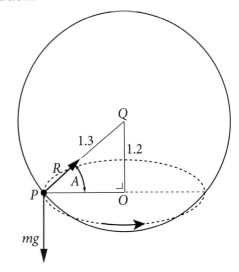

Fig. 11.14

By Pythagoras' Theorem,

$|OQ|^2 + |OP|^2 = |QP|^2$

$\therefore |OP|^2 + 1.44 = 1.69$

$\therefore |OP|^2 = 0.25$

$\therefore |OP| = 0.5$

$\therefore \sin A = \dfrac{1.2}{1.3} = \dfrac{12}{13}$ and

$\cos A = \dfrac{0.5}{1.3} = \dfrac{5}{13}.$

The forces on the particle are:

(i)  Its weight $= mg$.

(ii)  The reaction at the sphere, $R$. Since the sphere is smooth, $R$ is perpendicular to the surface and, so, directed towards $Q$.

We resolve $R$ into horizontal and vertical components:

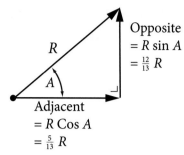

Opposite
$= R \sin A$
$= \frac{12}{13} R$

$R$

$A$

Adjacent
$= R \cos A$
$= \frac{5}{13} R$

Fig. 11.15

The resolved forces on the particle are:

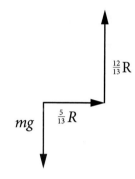

$\frac{12}{13}R$

$mg$  $\frac{5}{13}R$

Fig. 11.16

Firstly, there is no vertical acceleration, so the forces up = the forces down.

$$\therefore \frac{12}{13} R = mg$$

$$\therefore R = \frac{13\,m\,g}{12}$$

Secondly, the force towards the centre of motion must be of magnitude $\frac{mv^2}{r}$, where $r$ is the radius of the circle of motion ($\therefore r = 0.5$ in this case). This centripetal force in this case is $\frac{5}{13}$R.

$$\therefore \frac{5}{13} R = \frac{m\,v^2}{r} = \frac{m\,v^2}{0.5}$$

$$\text{But } R = \frac{13\,m\,g}{12}$$

$$\therefore \frac{5}{13}\left(\frac{13\,mg}{12}\right) = \frac{m\,v^2}{0.5}$$

$$\therefore \frac{5g}{12} = \frac{v^2}{0.5}$$

$$\therefore v^2 = \frac{2.5\,g}{12} = \frac{5\,g}{24}$$

$$\therefore v = \sqrt{\frac{5g}{24}} \qquad \text{Q.E.D.}$$

1.  A piece of light inextensible string is 2 m long. One end is fixed to a point on a smooth horizontal table. The other end is tied to a particle of mass 8 kg which moves in a circle on the table. If the speed of the particle is 5 m/s, find the tension in the string.

2.  A light inextensible string is $\frac{1}{8}$ metres long. One end is fixed to a point on a smooth horizontal table. The other end is attached to a particle of mass 7 kg. The particle moves in a circle on the table with uniform angular speed 4 rad/s. Calculate the tension in the string.

3.  A light inextensible string of length 5 m is attached at one end to a fixed point $P$ which is 4 m above a smooth horizontal table. The other end is attached to a particle of mass 5 kg which moves in a circle on the table. If the speed of the particle is 3 m/s, find

    (i)   the radius of the circle of motion

    (ii)   the tension in the string.

    (iii)   the reaction at the table.

4.  A light inextensible string of length $5\sqrt{2}$ m is attached at one end to a fixed point $P$, which is 5 m above a smooth horizontal table. The other end is attached to a particle of mass 10 kg which moves in a circle on the table with constant angular speed 1 rad/s. Find

    (i)   the angle which the string makes with the table

    (ii)   the tension in the string

    (iii)   the reaction at the table.

5.  A particle of mass $m$ is moving with constant speed in a horizontal circle which is on the inside surface of a smooth sphere of radius 13 m, so that the centre of the circle of motion is 5 m below the centre of the sphere. Show that the speed of the particle is 16.8 m/s.

6.  A conical pendulum consists of a particle of mass $m$ at the end of a piece of string, one metre long. The other end is fixed to a point on a ceiling. The particle is made to rotate in a horizontal circle, so that the string makes an angle of 30° with the vertical at all times.

    (i)   Find the tension in the string in terms of $m$ and $g$.

    (ii)   Find the constant angular speed, correct to three decimal places.

7. A marble of mass 10 kg is describing a horizontal circle on the smooth inside surface of a sphere.

   The radius of the sphere is 1.3 m and the centre of the circle of motion is 0.5 m below the centre of the sphere.

   (i) Find the radius of the circle of motion.

   (ii) Find the normal reaction between the marble and the sphere.

   (iii) Find the constant angular velocity $\omega$ of the marble.

8. A particle of mass 10 kg is describing a circle on a smooth horizontal table. It is connected by a light inelastic string of length 0.5 m to a point which is 0.4 m vertically above the centre of the circle. The reaction force at the table is 20 N.

   (i) Find the radius of the circle of motion.

   (ii) Find the tension in the string.

   (iii) Find the constant angular velocity ($\omega$) to one decimal place.

   (iv) If the angular speed is increased until the particle is on the point of taking off from the table, show that $\omega = \sqrt{24.5}$ rad/s.

9. A particle $P$ of mass 4 kg is on a smooth horizontal table. It is connected by a light, inextensible string which passes through a small hole in the table to a particle $Q$ of mass 2.5 kg. $P$ describes a circle of radius 0.5 m on the table, the centre of the circle being at the hole, and as a result $Q$ is kept hanging freely underneath the table at a height above the floor greater than 0.5 m. Find the angular speed of $P$.

   If $P$ is stopped, held and then released, show that the acceleration of $P$ is $\frac{49}{13}$ m/s$^2$ and show that its speed on reaching the hole is $\frac{7}{\sqrt{13}}$ m/s.

10. A particle of mass $m$ kg is connected by means of a light inextensible string of length $l$ metres to a fixed point $O$. The particle is describing a horizontal circle with angular speed $\omega$ rad/s. The centre of the circle is a distance $h$ below $O$.

    (i) Draw a clear diagram showing all the forces acting on the particle.

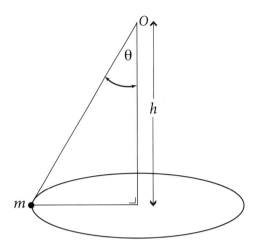

Fig. 11.17

    (ii) Write down the equations of motion.

    (iii) Show that $h = \dfrac{g}{\omega^2}$.

    (iv) If the horizontal circle must remain at least 0.25 metres below $O$, calculate, correct to one place of decimals, the maximum value of $\omega$.

11. A particle of mass 8 kg is describing a circle, with constant speed $v$, on a smooth horizontal table. It is connected by a light inextensible string of length 3 m to a point which is 1 m vertically above the centre of the circle.

    (i) Show that the tension in the string is given by $T = 3v^2$.

    (ii) Show that the particle will remain in contact with the table if $v < \sqrt{8g}$.

    (iii) If the speed of the particle is increased to $\sqrt{9.1g}$, calculate the height at which the particle rotates above the table.

## Harder Examples

### Worked Example 11.7

(a) A car goes around a roundabout which has radius 20 m at a speed of 10.5 m/s. Find the least possible value for the coefficient of friction between the tyres and the road if slipping does not occur.

(b) If, in wet weather, the coefficient of friction is $\frac{1}{4}$, find the maximum speed with which the car can safely go around the roundabout.

**Solution:**

Let $m$ = the mass of the car.

(a) The forces on the car are:

  (i)   its weight $mg$

  (ii)  the normal reaction at the road, $R$

  (iii) the friction force $F$. We assume that the car is on the point of slipping, so that $F = \mu R$. This friction force is inward because the car would tend to slip outward.

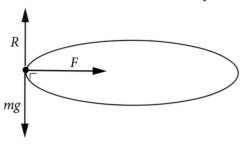

Fig. 11.18

Firstly, there is no vertical acceleration, so the forces up = the forces down.

$$R = mg$$
$$= 9.8\,m.$$

Secondly, the centripetal force must have magnitude $\dfrac{m v^2}{r}$. In this case the centripetal force is the friction force.

$$\therefore \mu R = \frac{m v^2}{r}$$
$$= \frac{m (10.5)^2}{20}$$

But $R = 9.8m$

$$\therefore \mu (9.8\, m) = \frac{m (10.5)^2}{20}$$
$$\therefore \mu = \frac{(10.5)^2}{(9.8)(20)}$$
$$= \frac{9}{16}$$

If $\mu \geq \dfrac{9}{16}$, the car will not slip.

(b) In this case $\mu = \dfrac{1}{4}$. The equations are still the same.

$$R = mg$$
$$= 9.8\,m;$$
$$\mu R = \frac{m v^2}{r}$$

Putting $R = 9.8m$ and $\mu = \dfrac{1}{4}$ into the second of these equations, we get

$$\frac{1}{4}(9.8\,m) = \frac{m v^2}{20}$$
$$\therefore v^2 = 49$$
$$\therefore v = 7 \text{ m/s}$$

If the car goes at 7 m/s, it will be on the point of slipping; if it goes faster it will slip.

---

**Worked Example 11.8**

A particle of mass 3 kg is attached to two strings, both of length 2 m. The other end of the first string is attached to a fixed point $P$ on a smooth vertical wire. The other end of the second string is tied to a ring of mass 3 kg through which the same vertical wire has been threaded so that the ring is below $P$ as shown. The wire and the strings turn in horizontal circular motion about the wire with a constant angular speed of 5 rad/s. Show the forces on the particle and the ring and hence find the tension in each string.

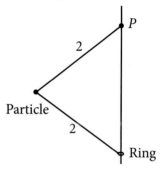

Fig. 11.19

**Solution:**

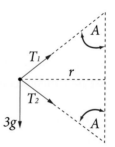

Fig. 11.20

Let $A$ be the angle between the strings and the vertical. (They are equal because the triangle is an isosceles triangle.)

The radius of the circle described by the particle is given by $r = 2 \sin A$.

The reaction between wire and the ring must be perpendicular to the wire (since the wire is smooth). Also, this reaction, which acts on the ring, must be to the right, in opposition to the tension in the lower string which is to the left.

The forces on the particle are shown here:

Forces

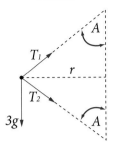

Fig. 11.21

Resolved forces

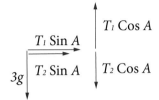

Fig. 11.22

The forces acting on the ring are shown here:

Forces                        Resolved forces

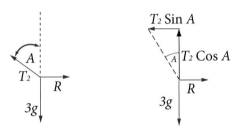

Fig. 11.23

**Step 1:** The particle has no vertical acceleration. Therefore the forces up = the forces down.

$$T_1 \cos A = 3g + T_2 \cos A \quad \text{Equation I}$$

**Step 2:** The resultant force towards the centre of the particle's circle of motion must be of magnitude $m\,\omega^2\,r$.

$$T_1 \sin A + T_2 \sin A = m\,\omega^2\,r$$
$$= (3)(5)^2\, 2 \sin A$$
$$\therefore T_1 \sin A + T_2 \sin A = 150 \sin A$$
$$\therefore T_1 + T_2 = 150 \quad \text{Equation II}$$

**Step 3:** The ring remains in equilibrium throughout. Therefore the forces up = the forces down. Also, the forces to the left = the forces to the right.

$$T_2 \cos A = 3g \qquad \text{Equation III}$$
$$T_2 \sin A = R \qquad \text{Equation IV}$$

Since $3g = T_2 \cos A$ (Equation III), Equation $I$ now reads

$$T_1 \cos A = T_2 \cos A + T_2 \cos A$$
$$\therefore T_1 = 2\,T_2 \qquad \text{Equation V}$$

Solving simultaneous equations II and $V$

we get $T_1 = 100$ N

$$T_2 = 50 \text{ N : Answer.}$$

## Exercise 11 C

1. A car of mass $m$ turns a corner on a horizontal road. The corner forms the arc of a circle of radius 50 m. Find the coefficient of friction if the car just begins to slip when it takes the corner at 21 m/s.

2. (i) A car turns around a bend on a horizontal road. The bend forms the arc of a circle of radius 24 m. If the coefficient of friction between the car's tyres and the road is $\frac{2}{3}$, find the maximum speed with which the car can safely take the bend.

   (ii) If, in wet weather, the maximum speed is 7 m/s, find the coefficient of friction between the tyres and the wet road.

3. A matchbox is placed upon a turntable, at a distance 10 cm from the centre. If the coefficient of friction between the box and the turntable is $\frac{1}{8}$, find the maximum angular speed with which the turntable can turn without the box falling off.
   (Note: convert to metres.)

4. A book rests on a horizontal shelf in the back window of a car. The coefficient of friction between the book and the shelf is $\frac{1}{2}$. The driver of the car takes every bend at 6 m/s. Find (to the nearest metre) the radius of the tightest horizontal bend which the car can take without the book slipping.

5. A corner on a level track has a radius of 20 m. Calculate the maximum speed with which a car can take the corner if the coefficient of friction is $\frac{1}{4}$.

6. An aeroplane of mass $m$ banks at an angle $\tan^{-1}\frac{1}{8}$ to the horizontal. It is travelling with speed 70 m/s and the lift force is perpendicular to the wings. Find the radius of the horizontal circle in which it is turning.

7. An aircraft of mass 50 tonnes described a horizontal and circular path of radius 4800 m. The sine of $\theta$, the angle of bank, is $\frac{5}{13}$.
$L$ represents the lifting force.
Taking $g = 10$ m/s$^2$, calculate the speed of the plane to the nearest m/s.

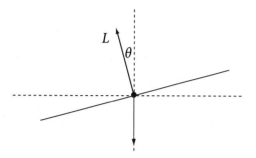

Fig. 11.24

8. A small ring is threaded on a piece of string 8 m long, the two ends of which are fixed at $P$ and $Q$, as shown. $Q$ is 4 m vertically below $P$. The ring describes a horizontal circle, centre $Q$, with angular speed $\omega$.
   (i) Find the radius of the circle of motion.
   (ii) Find $\omega$ in terms of $g$.

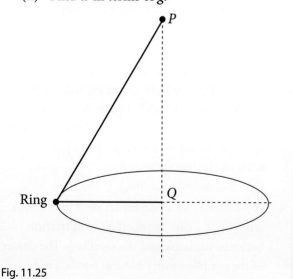

Fig. 11.25

9. A small ring is threaded on a piece of string which is 3.2 m long. The ends of the string are fixed at $A$ and $B$, as shown. $B$ is 2.4 m below $A$. The ring describes a horizontal circle (centre $B$) with angular speed $\omega$.

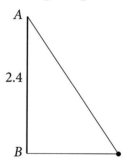

Fig. 11.26
   (i) Find the radius of the circle of motion
   (ii) Find $\omega$ in terms of $g$.

10. A hollow right circular cone of semi-vertical angle $\alpha$, where $\tan \alpha = \frac{3}{4}$, is fixed with its axis vertical and vertex downwards. The inner surface of the cone is rough with coefficient of friction $\frac{1}{2}$ and the cone rotates about its axis with uniform angular velocity 7 rad/s.

A particle of mass $m$ is placed on the inside surface and rotates with the cone at a vertical height $h$ above the vertex. Calculate the normal reaction of the particle with the inside surface and the height $h$ above the vertex if
   (i) the particle is about to slide down
   (ii) the particle is about to slide up.

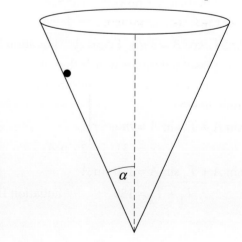

Fig. 11.27

11. Two particles of equal mass attached by a taut inextensible string of length $2y$ rests on a horizontal circular table. The particles are respectively $y$ and $3y$ from the centre so that the centre and the particles are collinear.

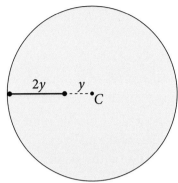

Fig. 11.28

The table rotates about its centre with angular velocity $\omega$ and the coefficient of friction is $\frac{y}{2}$. If both particles are on the point of slipping,

(i) show on separate diagrams all the forces on each particle;

(ii) calculate $\omega$.

12. A particle of mass 1 kg is attached to two strings, both of length 1 m. The other end of one string is attached to a fixed point $p$ on a smooth vertical wire. The other end of the second string is tied to a ring of mass 3 kg, through which the wire is threaded, so that the ring is vertically below $P$. The particle and strings turn in horizontal circular motion about the wire with constant angular speed 14 radians/second. Find the tension in each string and the angle which the strings make with the vertical, correct to the nearest degree.

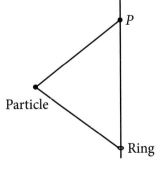

Fig. 11.29

## Motion in a vertical circle

In cases where the particle describes motion in a vertical circle we combine the usual equations with the energy equation, $mgh + \frac{1}{2}mv^2 = $ constant. We can do this so long as no work is done on the particle by forces other than gravitational forces.

### Worked Example 11.9

A chestnut hangs freely from a fixed point $o$ by a string of length $l$. The chestnut is struck so that it begins to move horizontally with initial speed $u$. Show that

(i) when the string makes an angle $\theta$ with the downward vertical, the tension $T$ in the string is given by

$$T = \frac{mu^2}{l} - 2mg + 3mg\cos\theta.$$

(ii) the chestnut will reach the point $P$ which is a distance $l$ vertically above $o$ if $u \geq \sqrt{5gl}$.

**Solution:**

(i) Here are the forces on the chestnut at an instant when the string makes an angle $\theta$ with the downward vertical. Let $v = $ the speed of the chestnut at this instant. Let $m = $ the mass of the chestnut.

Forces

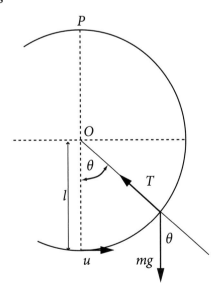

Fig. 11.30

Resolved forces. When the motion is vertical we resolve forces along and perpendicular to the radius.

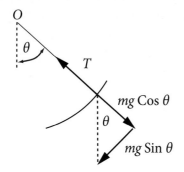

Fig. 11.31

Firstly, the resultant centripetal force must have magnitude $\frac{m v^2}{r}$; this force is $T - m\, g\cos\theta$.

$$T - m\, g\cos\theta = \frac{m v^2}{l} \qquad \text{Equation 1}$$

Secondly, we use the energy equation with the standard position as a tangent at the starting point.

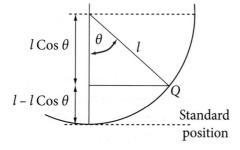

Fig. 11.32

$m\, g\, h_1 + \frac{1}{2} m\, v_1{}^2$ (at starting point)

$$= m\, g\, h_2 + \frac{1}{2} m\, v_2{}^2$$

(when the string makes an angle $\theta$ with the downward vertical)

$$\therefore m\, g\,(0) + \frac{1}{2} m\, u^2 = m\, g\,(l - l\cos\theta) + \frac{1}{2} m\, v^2$$

$$\therefore m\, u^2 = 2\, m\, g\, l\,(1 - \cos\theta) + m\, v^2$$

$$\therefore m\, v^2 = m\, u^2 - 2\, m\, g\, l\,(1 - \cos\theta)$$

Putting this into equation I, we get

$$T - m\, g\cos\theta = \frac{m\, u^2 - 2\, m\, g\, l\,(1 - \cos\theta)}{l}$$

$$\therefore T = \frac{m\, u^2}{l} - 2mg + 3mg\cos\theta \quad \text{Q.E.D.}$$

(ii) If, at worst, the string just slackens when $\theta = 180°$, then $T = 0$ when $\cos\theta = -1$.

$$\therefore 0 = \frac{m\, u^2}{l} - 2\, m\, g - 3\, m\, g$$

$$\therefore \frac{m\, u^2}{l} = 5\, m\, g$$

$$\therefore u^2 = 5\, g\, l$$

$$\therefore u = \sqrt{5\, g\, l}$$

If $u \ge \sqrt{5\, g\, l}$ then $T \ge 0$ throughout and the chestnut will reach $P$. \qquad Q.E.D.

## Worked Example 11.10

A marble $K$ is placed on the top of the outside surface of a smooth hemisphere of radius $r$ and centre $C$. It starts from rest and rolls down the outside of the hemisphere. Show that it will leave the hemisphere when $[CK]$ makes an angle $\cos^{-1}\frac{2}{3}$ with the vertical.

**Solution:**

We examine the forces on the marble when $[CK]$ makes an angle $\theta$ with the vertical.

Let $v$ = the speed of the marble at this point.
Let $m$ = the mass of the marble.
Let $R$ = the reaction at this point.

Forces

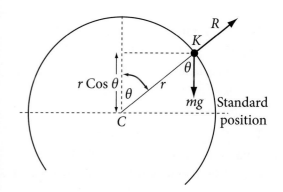

Fig. 11.33

Resolved forces along and perpendicular to the radius

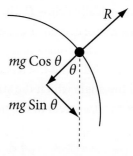

Fig. 11.34

Firstly, the centripetal force must have magnitude $\frac{m v^2}{r}$.

$$\therefore m\, g\cos\theta - R = \frac{m v^2}{r}$$

$$\therefore m\, g\, r\cos\theta - R\, r = m\, v^2 \qquad \text{Equation 1}$$

The energy equation is

$$m\, g\, h_1 + \frac{1}{2} m\, v_1{}^2 = m\, g\, h_2 + \frac{1}{2} m\, v_2{}^2$$

(at starting point) \qquad (at later point)

$$\therefore m\, g\, r + \frac{1}{2} m\,(0) = m\, g\, r\cos\theta + \frac{1}{2} m\, v^2$$

$$\therefore m\, v^2 = 2\, m\, g\, r\,(1 - \cos\theta)$$

Putting this result into equation I we get

$$m\, g\, r \cos \theta - R\, r = 2\, m\, g\, (r - r \cos \theta)$$

$$\therefore\ m\, g \cos \theta - R = 2\, m\, g - 2\, m\, g \cos \theta$$

$$\therefore\ R = 3\, m\, g \cos \theta - 2\, m\, g$$

At the moment when the marble leaves the sphere $R = 0$.

$$\therefore\ 0 = 3\, m\, g \cos \theta - 2\, m\, g$$

$$\therefore\ \cos \theta = \frac{2}{3}$$

$$\therefore\ \theta = \cos^{-1} \frac{2}{3} \qquad \text{Q.E.D.}$$

## Exercise 11 D

1. A particle $P$ hangs freely from a point $O$ by means of a light inextensible string of length $l$. The particle is projected horizontally with initial velocity $\sqrt{3\, g\, l}$. Show that the string will become slack when the line $[OP]$ makes an angle $\cos^{-1} \frac{1}{3}$ with the upward vertical.

2. A particle is at the top of the outside surface of a smooth sphere of radius $r$. The particle is projected horizontally with initial speed of $\sqrt{\frac{1}{2}\, g\, r}$. Find the angle which the normal to the sphere at the particle makes with the vertical when the particle leaves the sphere. Find also the speed of the particle when it leaves the sphere.

3. A ring $K$ of mass $m$ is threaded on a smooth circular wire, centre $C$ and of radius $a$, which is fixed in a vertical position. The ring is projected horizontally with initial speed $u$ from the lowest point on the wire. Show that the ring will just reach the uppermost point on the wire if $u = \sqrt{4\, g\, a}$.

   Find the magnitude of the reaction at the wire when the line $CK$ makes an angle $60°$ with the downward vertical from $C$, if $u = \sqrt{4\, g\, a}$.

4. A hollow sphere has centre $C$ and radius $r$. A small marble $Q$ rests at the lowest point inside the smooth sphere. The marble is then projected horizontally with initial speed $\sqrt{\frac{7}{2}\, g\, r}$. Find the angle which $[CQ]$ makes with the downward vertical at the moment when the marble moves away from the inside surface of the sphere. Through what vertical distance has the marble travelled at this point?

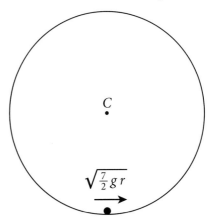

Fig. 11.35

5. A small bead of mass $m$ is threaded on a smooth circular wire of radius $a$, fixed with its plane vertical. The bead is projected from the lowest point of the wire with speed $u$. Show that the reaction between the bead and the wire, when the radius to the bead makes an angle of $60°$ with the downward vertical, is

$$m\left(\frac{u^2}{a} - \frac{g}{2}\right).$$

6. A particle of mass $m$ hangs freely from a point $O$ by means of a light inextensible string of length $l$. The particle performs a full circle in a vertical plane. The tension in the string when the particle is at its highest point of the orbit is $T_1$, and when at its lowest point it is $T_2$. Prove that $T_2 = T_1 + 6\, m\, g$.

## Summary of important points

1. Angle in radians $= \dfrac{\text{arc length}}{\text{radius}}$. Hence $l = r\,\theta$.

2. $v = \omega\, r$

3. Centripetal acceleration $= \dfrac{v^2}{r} = \omega^2\, r$

4. Centripetal force $= \dfrac{m\,v^2}{r} = m\,\omega^2\, r$

5. Principle of Conservation of Energy

$$PE_1 + KE_1 = PE_2 + KE_2$$

$$m\,g\,h_1 + \tfrac{1}{2}\,m\,v^2_1 = m\,g\,h_2 + \tfrac{1}{2}\,m\,v^2_2$$

## DOs and DON'Ts for the exam

### DO

- Do draw clear large diagrams on graph paper
- Do resolve the forces
- Do write down the two key equations

### DON'T

- Don't treat Circular Motion as if it is Statics: the equations are different here
- Don't mix up motion in a horizontal circle with motion in a vertical circle. They get very different treatments and use different equations

# Differential equations

## Chapter 12

*The whole of science is nothing more than a refinement of everyday thinking*

*Albert Einstein*

## Contents

## Learning outcomes

**In this chapter you will learn...**

- The laws of logs and their application

- How to integrate certain functions

- What a differential equation is

- How to find the general and the exact solution to first-order separable differential equations

- How to solve second-order differential equations

- How to solve real-life problems using differential equations

- How to solve problems which involve power

## You will need to know...

- The laws of logs
- Definite and indefinite integrals

## *Logarithms*

Firstly, here is a short review of log theory. These formulae appear on page 2 of *Formulae and Tables*.

(i)   $\log_e a + \log_e b = \log_e ab$

(ii)   $\log_e a - \log_e b = \log_e \dfrac{a}{b}$

(iii)   $n \log_e a = \log_e a^n$

(iv)   If $\log_e x = y$, then $x = e^y$

---

### *Worked Example 12.1*

Write as one log:

  (i)   $\log_e 7 + \log_e 3$

  (ii)   $\log_e 7 - \log_e 3$

  (iii)   $2 \log_e 7 - 3 \log_e 3$

  (iv)   $\frac{1}{2} \log_e 7 + 2 \log_e 3$

**Solution:**

  (i)   $\log_e 7 + \log_e 3 = \log_e 21$

  (ii)   $\log_e 7 - \log_e 3 = \log_e \dfrac{7}{3}$

  (iii)   $2 \log_e 7 - 3 \log_e 3 = \log_e 7^2 - \log_e 3^3$

$$= \log_e 49 - \log_e 27$$

$$= \log_e \dfrac{49}{27}$$

  (iv)   $\frac{1}{2} \log_e 7 + 2 \log_e 3 = \log_e 7^{\frac{1}{2}} + \log_e 3^2$

$$= \log_e \sqrt{7} + \log_e 9$$

$$= \log_e 9\sqrt{7}$$

---

### *Worked Example 12.2*

Solve for $x$:

  (i)   $\log_e \sqrt{e} = x$

  (ii)   $\log_e x = 0$

  (iii)   $2 \log_e x = \log_e 5$

  (iv)   $\log_e x = 2 + \log_e 3$

  (v)   $e^{\log_e x} = 7$

**Solution:**

  (i)   $\log_e \sqrt{e} = x$

$$\Rightarrow e^x = \sqrt{e}$$

$$\Rightarrow x = \frac{1}{2}$$

  (ii)   $\log_e x = 0$

$$\Rightarrow x = e^0$$

$$\Rightarrow x = 1$$

  (iii)   $2 \log_e x = \log_e 5$

$$\Rightarrow \log_e x^2 = \log_e 5$$

$$\Rightarrow x^2 = 5$$

$$\Rightarrow x = \sqrt{5}$$

  (iv)   $\log_e x = 2 + \log_e 3$

$$\Rightarrow \log_e x - \log_e 3 = 2$$

$$\Rightarrow \log_e \frac{x}{3} = 2$$

$$\Rightarrow \frac{x}{3} = e^2$$

$$\Rightarrow x = 3\,e^2$$

  (v)   $\log_e x$ and $e^x$ are inverse functions of each other. It follows that

$$e^{\log_e x} = x \text{ and } \log_e (e^x) = x$$

$$e^{\log_e x} = 7$$

$$\Rightarrow x = 7$$

---

### Exercise 12 A

1. Write as one log:

  (i)   $\log_e 4 + \log_e 3$

  (ii)   $\log_e 6 - \log_e 7$

  (iii)   $2 \log_e 3 + 3 \log_e 2$

  (iv)   $5 \log_e 2 - 2 \log_e 5$

  (v)   $\frac{1}{2} \log_e 4 + \frac{1}{3} \log_e 27$

  (vi)   $\frac{1}{2} \log_e 64 + \frac{1}{3} \log_e 64$

  (vii)   $2 \log_e 10 + \log_e 6 - 3 \log_e 4$

  (viii)   $\log_e x^2 + \log_e x$

  (ix)   $\frac{1}{2} \log_e x - \log_e 7 + \log_e 2$

2. Solve for $x$:

  (i)   $\log_e e = x$

  (ii)   $\log_e x = 2$

  (iii)   $\log_e \left(\frac{1}{e}\right) = x$

  (iv)   $\log_e \sqrt[3]{e} = x$

  (v)   $e^{\log_e x} = 8$

(vi) $\log_e (e^4) = x$

(vii) $e^{\log_e 2} = x$

(viii) $e^{\frac{1}{2}\log_e x} = 7$

(ix) $e^2 \log_e x = 9$

(x) $e^3 \log_e 4 = x$

(xi) $\log_e x = 1 + \log_e 2$

(xii) $\log_e x = 3 - \log_e 5$

(xiii) $2 \log_e x = 1 - \log_e 3$

(xiv) $\frac{1}{2}\log_e x + 1 = \frac{3}{2}\log_e 3$

## Rules of integration

Here are the main rules for integration – with constants of integration omitted:

1. $\displaystyle\int x^n \, dx = \frac{x^{n+1}}{n+1}$ for $n \neq -1$

2. $\displaystyle\int \frac{1}{x} \, dx = \log_e x$

   but $\displaystyle\int \frac{1}{ax+b} \, dx = \frac{1}{a}\log_e (ax+b)$

3. $\displaystyle\int e^x \, dx = e^x$

   but $\displaystyle\int e^{ax+b} \, dx = \frac{1}{a} e^{ax+b}$

4. $\displaystyle\int \cos x \, dx = \sin x$

   but $\displaystyle\int \cos (ax+b) \, dx = \frac{1}{a}\sin(ax+b)$

5. $\displaystyle\int \sin x \, dx = -\cos x$

   but $\displaystyle\int \sin (ax+b) \, dx = -\frac{1}{a}\cos (ax+b)$

6. $\displaystyle\int \frac{1}{\sqrt{a^2-x^2}} \, dx = \sin^{-1}\frac{x}{a}$

7. $\displaystyle\int \frac{1}{x^2+a^2} \, dx = \frac{1}{a}\tan^{-1}\frac{x}{a}$

## Indefinite integrals

### Worked Example 12.3

Integrate the following:

(i) $\displaystyle\int (5x^2 + x) \, dx$

(ii) $\displaystyle\int \int e^{2x} \, dx$

(iii) $\displaystyle\int \sin 5x \, dx$

(iv) $\displaystyle\int \frac{dx}{x^2+9}$

Solution:

(i) $\displaystyle\int (5x^2 + x) \, dx = \frac{5x^3}{3} + \frac{x^2}{2} + c$

(ii) $\displaystyle\int e^{2x} \, dx = \frac{e^{2x}}{2} + c$

(iii) $\displaystyle\int \sin 5x \, dx = \frac{-\cos 5x}{5} + c$

(iv) $\displaystyle\int \frac{dx}{x^2+9} = \int \frac{dx}{x^2+(3)^2}$

$= \frac{1}{3}\tan^{-1}\frac{x}{3} + c$

### Worked Example 12.4

Perform this integration:

$$\int \frac{1}{2x+1} \, dx$$

Solution:

$$\int \frac{1}{\text{linear function}}$$

will always result in an answer with logs.

In this case:

$\displaystyle\int \frac{1}{2x+1} \, dx = \frac{1}{2}\log_e(2x+1) + c$

$= \log_e(2x+1)^{1/2} + c$

$= \log_e \sqrt{2x+1} + c$

### Exercise 12 B

Perform the following integrations:

1. (i) $\displaystyle\int x^4 \, dx$     (ii) $\displaystyle\int 3x^4 \, dx$

2. (i) $\displaystyle\int \cos x \, dx$     (ii) $\displaystyle\int \cos 3x \, dx$

3. (i) $\displaystyle\int \sin x \, dx$     (ii) $\displaystyle\int \sin 4x \, dx$

4. (i) $\displaystyle\int \frac{1}{x} \, dx$     (ii) $\displaystyle\int \frac{1}{2x+3} \, dx$

| | | | |
|---|---|---|---|
| 5. | (i) $\displaystyle\int e^x \, dx$ | (ii) $\displaystyle\int e^{8x} \, dx$ | |
| 6. | (i) $\displaystyle\int \frac{1}{\sqrt{49 - x^2}} \, dx$ | (ii) $\displaystyle\int \frac{dx}{\sqrt{100 - x^2}}$ | |
| 7. | (i) $\displaystyle\int \frac{1}{x^2 + 25} \, dx$ | (ii) $\displaystyle\int \frac{dx}{x^2 + 625}$ | |
| 8. | (i) $\displaystyle\int \frac{x + 1}{x} \, dx$ | (ii) $\displaystyle\int \frac{1}{x + 1} \, dx$ | |
| 9. | (i) $\displaystyle\int (2x + 1) \, dx$ | (ii) $\displaystyle\int (2x + 1)^2 \, dx$ | |
| 10. | (i) $\displaystyle\int \frac{1}{5x + 1} \, dx$ | (ii) $\displaystyle\int \frac{1}{\sqrt{x}} \, dx$ | |

### Definite integrals

We can evaluate integrals. Here is the definition:

$$\int_a^b f'(x) \, dx = f(b) - f(a)$$

## Worked Example 12.5

Evaluate the following integrals.

(i) $\displaystyle\int_1^3 6x \, dx$

(ii) $\displaystyle\int_0^{\ln 3} e^x \, dx$

(iii) $\displaystyle\int_{\frac{3}{2}}^3 \frac{dx}{\sqrt{9 - x^2}}$

(iv) $\displaystyle\int_0^{\frac{\pi}{4}} \sin^2 x \, dx$

**Solution:**

(i) $\displaystyle\int 6x \, dx = \frac{6x^2}{2} + c = 3x^2 + c$

$\therefore \displaystyle\int_1^3 6x \, dx = 3x^2 + c \, \Big|_{x=1}^{x=3}$

$= [3(3)^2 + c] - [3(1)^2 + c]$

$= [27 + c] - [3 + c]$

$= 24$

**Note:** When we are finding definite integrals, the constant of integration will always be 'cancelled', as in the example above. So, it is unnecessary to put in the constant of integration when you are asked to do definite integrals.

(ii) $\displaystyle\int_0^{\ln 3} e^x \, dx = e^x \, \Big|_0^{\ln 3}$

$= e^{\ln 3} - e^0 = 3 - 1 = 0$

(Remember! $e^x$ and $\ln x$ are inverse functions.
$\therefore e^{\ln x} = x$ and $\ln e^x = x$)

(iii) $\displaystyle\int_{\frac{3}{2}}^3 \frac{dx}{\sqrt{9 - x^2}} = \sin^{-1} \frac{x}{3} \, \Big|_{\frac{3}{2}}^3$

$= \sin^{-1} 1 - \sin^{-1} \frac{1}{2}$

$= \frac{\pi}{2} - \frac{\pi}{6} = \frac{\pi}{3}$

(iv) To integrate $\sin^2 x$ or $\cos^2 x$ we need the formulae

$$\sin^2 A = \frac{1}{2}(1 - \cos 2A) \text{ and}$$

$$\cos^2 A = \frac{1}{2}(1 + \cos 2A)$$

$\therefore \displaystyle\int_0^{\frac{\pi}{4}} \sin^2 x \, dx = \int_0^{\frac{\pi}{4}} \frac{1}{2}(1 - \cos 2x) \, dx$

$\frac{1}{2} \displaystyle\int_0^{\frac{\pi}{4}} (1 - \cos 2x) \, dx = \frac{1}{2} \left( x - \frac{1}{2} \sin 2x \right) \Big|_0^{\frac{\pi}{4}}$

$\frac{1}{2} \left( \frac{\pi}{4} - \frac{1}{2} \right) - \frac{1}{2}(0 - 0) = \frac{1}{2} \left( \frac{\pi}{4} - \frac{1}{2} \right)$

## Exercise 12 C

1. Evaluate:

(i) $\displaystyle\int_1^3 4x \, dx$

(ii) $\displaystyle\int_0^1 x^2 \, dx$

(iii) $\displaystyle\int_1^2 (2x + 1) \, dx$

(iv) $\displaystyle\int_1^4 (2 - \sqrt{x}) \, dx$

(v) $\displaystyle\int_2^6 \frac{1}{x} \, dx$

(vi) $\displaystyle\int_{-1}^1 x^3 \, dx$

Evaluate the following integrals:

2. $\displaystyle\int_{0}^{\ln 4} e^{x}\,dx$

3. $\displaystyle\int_{0}^{\frac{\pi}{2}} \cos x\,dx$

4. $\displaystyle\int_{\frac{\pi}{4}}^{\frac{\pi}{2}} \sin x\,dx$

5. $\displaystyle\int_{\ln 2}^{\ln 5} e^{x}\,dx$

6. $\displaystyle\int_{\frac{\pi}{6}}^{\frac{\pi}{3}} 2\cos x\,dx$

7. $\displaystyle\int_{0}^{\frac{\pi}{3}} 4\sin x\,dx$

8. $\displaystyle\int_{0}^{\frac{\pi}{4}} (\cos x + \sin x)\,dx$

9. $\displaystyle\int_{\frac{\pi}{4}}^{\frac{\pi}{2}} (\cos x - \sin x)\,dx$

Evaluate:

10. $\displaystyle\int_{2}^{4} \frac{dx}{\sqrt{16 - x^2}}$

11. $\displaystyle\int_{0}^{\log_{e} 2} e^{3x}\,dx$

12. $\displaystyle\int_{0}^{\frac{\pi}{16}} \cos 4x\,dx$

13. $\displaystyle\int_{0}^{\frac{\pi}{6}} \sin 2x\,dx$

14. $\displaystyle\int_{0}^{\frac{\pi}{6}} \cos 3x\,dx$

15. $\displaystyle\int_{0}^{\frac{\pi}{12}} \sin 6x\,dx$

16. Evaluate:

(i) $\displaystyle\int_{0}^{2} \frac{dx}{x^2 + 4}$  (ii) $\displaystyle\int_{0}^{\frac{\pi}{2}} \cos^2 x\,dx$

17. Evaluate:

(i) $\displaystyle\int_{1}^{\sqrt{3}} \frac{dx}{\sqrt{4 - x^2}}$  (ii) $\displaystyle\int_{0}^{\frac{\pi}{3}} \sin^2 x\,dx$

18. Evaluate:

(i) $\displaystyle\int_{0}^{9} \frac{dx}{x^2 + 81}$  (ii) $\displaystyle\int_{0}^{\frac{\pi}{4}} \cos^2 2x\,dx$

19. Evaluate:

(i) $\displaystyle\int_{0}^{1} \frac{dx}{\sqrt{2 - x^2}}$  (ii) $\displaystyle\int_{0}^{\frac{\pi}{8}} \sin^2 2x\,dx$

20. Evaluate:

(i) $\displaystyle\int_{1}^{\sqrt{3}} \frac{dx}{x^2 + 3}$  (ii) $\displaystyle\int_{0}^{\sqrt{2}} \frac{dx}{\sqrt{8 - x^2}}$

## Differential equations

Differential equations are equations with differential coefficients,

e.g. $\qquad 3\dfrac{dy}{dx} = y$

A first order differential equation has, as its highest coefficient, a first derivative

e.g. $\qquad \dfrac{ds}{dt} = 2s$

A second order differential equation has, as its highest coefficient, a second derivative

e.g. $\qquad \dfrac{d^2 s}{dt^2} = 2\dfrac{ds}{dt}$

Differential equations will be divided into four types.
Type 1: First Order Differential Equations: general solutions
Type 2: First Order Differential Equations with definite values
Type 3: Second-order separable differential equations
Type 4: Second order differential equations requiring the chain rule

## Type 1: First order differential equations: general solutions

### Worked Example 12.6

Find the general solution to the differential equation $\dfrac{dy}{dx} = 4\,xy$.

**Solution:**

$$\frac{dy}{dx} = 4xy$$
$$\Rightarrow dy = 4\,xy\,dx$$

Separate the equation so that all terms in $y$ are on one side and all terms in $x$ on the other.

$$\frac{dy}{y} = 4x\,dx$$
$$\int \frac{1}{y}\,dy = \int 4\,x\,dx$$
$$\Rightarrow \log_e y = 4\frac{x^2}{2} + c$$

**Note:** There is no need to put a constant of integration on both sides of the equation. Usually a constant is put only on the right hand side.

$$\log_e y = 2\,x^2 + c$$
$$y = e^{2x^2 + c} : \text{Answer}$$

**Note:** A general solution contains a constant $c$. The solution is valid for all values of $c$.

### Exercise 12 D

Find the general solution to the following differential equations

| | |
|---|---|
| 1. $\dfrac{dy}{dx} = 6\,y.$ | 2. $\dfrac{dy}{dx} = 2xy$ |
| 3. $\dfrac{dy}{dx} = \cos x$ | 4. $\dfrac{dy}{dx} = \dfrac{4\,x^3}{y}.$ |
| 5. $\dfrac{dy}{dx} = 3\,x^2\,y.$ | 6. $\dfrac{dy}{dx} + \dfrac{\sin 2\,x}{y} = 0$ |
| 7. $\dfrac{dy}{dx} = 2x\left(y^2 + 1\right).$ | 8. $\dfrac{dy}{dx} = 2\sqrt{1 - y^2}$ |

## Type 2: First-order differential equations with definite values

### Worked Example 12.7

Find a function $y = f(x)$ such that $\dfrac{dy}{dx} = 2y$ and $y = 1$ when $x = 0$.

**Solution:**

$$\frac{dy}{dx} = 2y$$

Separate the variables by bringing all terms in $y$ to one side and all terms in $x$ to the other.

$$\frac{dy}{y} = 2\,dx$$
$$\therefore \qquad \int \frac{dy}{y} = \int 2dx$$

Now put in limits:
The upper limits are $y$ and $x$. The lower limits are $y = 1$ when $x = 0$ (as given in the question).

$$\int_1^y \frac{dy}{y} = \int_0^x 2dx$$
$$\log_e y \Big|_1^y = 2x \Big|_0^x$$
$$\log_e y - \log_e 1 = 2\,x - 2\,(0)$$
$$\log_e y = 2\,x$$
$$y = e^{2x} : \text{Answer}$$

**Note:** These "separable" differential equations can be solved by bringing the $y$-functions to the $dy$ side and the $x$-functions to the $dx$ side; then integrate both sides.

### Worked Example 12.8

$$\text{Solve } \frac{dy}{dx} = xy,$$

given that $y = 3$ when $x = 0$.

**Solution:**

Bring all terms in $y$ to the left, all terms in $x$ to the right.

$$\frac{dy}{y} = x\,dx$$

Integrate with appropriate limits:

$$\int_3^y \frac{dy}{y} = \int_0^x x\,dx$$

$$\log_e y \Big|_3^y = \frac{1}{2}x^2 \Big|_0^x$$

$$\log_e y - \log_e 3 = \frac{1}{2}x^2 - 0$$

Combine the two logs.

$$\therefore \log_e \frac{y}{3} = \frac{1}{2}x^2$$

$$\therefore \frac{y}{3} = e^{\frac{1}{2}x^2}$$

$$\therefore y = 3\, e^{\frac{1}{2}x^2} \text{ Answer}$$

### Worked Example 12.9

Given the differential equation $\frac{dy}{dx} = xy^2 + 4x$, and given that $y = 2$ when $x = 1$, find (correct to one decimal place) the value of $y$ when $x = 2$.

**Solution:**

$$\frac{dy}{dx} = xy^2 + 4x,$$

$$\therefore \frac{dy}{dx} = x\left(y^2 + 4\right)$$

$$\therefore \int \frac{dy}{y^2 + 4} = \int x\, dx$$

$$\therefore \int_2^y \frac{dy}{y^2 + (2)^2} = \int_1^2 x\, dx$$

$$\therefore \frac{1}{2}\tan^{-1}\frac{y}{2}\Big|_2^y = \frac{x^2}{2}\Big|_1^2$$

$$\frac{1}{2}\tan^{-1}\frac{y}{2} - \frac{1}{2}\tan^{-1}1 = \frac{(2)^2}{2} - \frac{(1)^2}{2}$$

Multiply across by 2:

$$\therefore \tan^{-1}\frac{y}{2} - \tan^{-1}1 = 4 - 1$$

$$\therefore \tan^{-1}\frac{y}{2} - \frac{\pi}{4} = 3$$

$$\therefore \tan^{-1}\frac{y}{2} = \frac{\pi}{4} + 3$$

$$\therefore \frac{y}{2} = \tan\left(\frac{\pi}{4} + 3\right)$$

$$\therefore y = 2\tan\left(\frac{\pi}{4} + 3\right)$$

$$\therefore y = 1.5 \text{ using a calculator in radian mode}$$

### Exercise 12 E

1. Solve $\frac{dy}{dx} = 3y$ given that $y = 1$ when $x = 0$.

2. Solve $\frac{dy}{dx} = 5y$ given that $y = 2$ when $x = 0$.

3. Solve $\frac{dy}{dx} = 2x\sqrt{1 - y^2}$, if $y = 1$ when $x = 0$.

4. Solve $\frac{dx}{dt} = tx$, given that $x = \sqrt{e}$ when $t = 1$.

5. If $\frac{dy}{dx} = \frac{y}{x}$ and if $y = 3$ when $x = 1$, find the value of $x$ when $y = 21$.

6. Solve $\frac{ds}{dt} + \frac{\sin t}{s} = 0$, given $s = \sqrt{2}$ when $t = \frac{\pi}{3}$.

7. Solve $\frac{dy}{dx} - 4x^3 y = 0$, if $y = 3$ when $x = 0$.

8. Solve $\frac{y}{x^2}\frac{dy}{dx} = 1$, given $x = 1$ when $y = 0$.

9. Solve $\frac{dy}{dx} - \frac{\cos x}{y} = 0$ if $y = 1$ when $x = \frac{\pi}{2}$.

10. Solve $\frac{dy}{dx} - \frac{y}{x} = \frac{1}{x}$ if $x = 4$ when $y = 0$.

11. Solve $\frac{dy}{dx} - y^2\sin x = 0$, given $x = \pi$ when $y = 1$.

12. Solve $xy\frac{dy}{dx} = y^2$, if $y = 2$ when $x = 1$.

13. Solve $v\frac{dv}{dx} = \cos^2 x$, if $v = 1$ when $x = 0$.

14. Solve $\frac{dy}{dx} = y\sin x$, if $y = \sqrt{e}$ when $x = \frac{\pi}{3}$.

15. Given the differential equation
    $$\frac{dy}{dx} = y\cos x,$$

    (i) find the general solution given that $y = 2$ when $x = \frac{\pi}{6}$,

    (ii) find the value of $y$ when $x = \frac{\pi}{2}$.

16. If $2\frac{dy}{dx} = xy + x$, and given that $y = 2$ when $x = 1$, find the value of $y$ (correct to two decimal places) when $x = 2$.

17. Given the differential equation:

$x \dfrac{dy}{dx} = \sqrt{4 - y^2}$ find the general solution given that $y = 0$ when $x = 1$. Find the value of $y$ when $x = \sqrt[3]{e^{\frac{\pi}{2}}}$.

## Type 3: Second-order separable differential equations

These are differential equations where

$$\frac{d^2y}{dx^2} = f\left(\frac{dy}{dx}\right)$$

### Worked Example 12.10

Solve $\dfrac{d^2y}{dx^2} = 3 \dfrac{dy}{dx}$,

given that $y = 0$ and $\dfrac{dy}{dx} = 1$ when $x = 0$

**Solution:**

**Step 1:** Let $v = \dfrac{dy}{dx}$. Therefore $\dfrac{dv}{dx} = \dfrac{d^2y}{dx^2}$

The equation becomes $\dfrac{dv}{dx} = 3v$,

given that $y = 0$ and $v = 1$ when $x = 0$.

$$\therefore \int_1^v \frac{dv}{v} = \int_0^x 3dx$$

$$\therefore \log_e v \Big|_1^v = 3x \Big|_0^x$$

$$\therefore \log_e v - \log_e 1 = 3x - 3(0)$$

$$\therefore \log_e v = 3x$$

$$\therefore v = e^{3x}$$

**Step 2:** $v = e^{3x}$

$$\therefore \frac{dy}{dx} = e^{3x} \quad (\text{since } v = \frac{dy}{dx})$$

$$\therefore \int_0^y dy = \int_0^x e^{3x} dx$$

$$\therefore y \Big|_0^y = \frac{e^{3x}}{3} \Big|_0^x$$

$$\therefore y - 0 = \frac{e^{3x}}{3} - \frac{1}{3}$$

$$\therefore y = \frac{1}{3}(e^{3x} - 1) : \text{Answer}$$

### Exercise 12 F

1. Solve $\dfrac{d^2y}{dx^2} = 2 \dfrac{dy}{dx}$, given that $y = 0$ and $\dfrac{dy}{dx} = 1$ when $x = 0$.

2. Solve $\dfrac{d^2y}{dt^2} = \dfrac{dx}{dt^2}$, if $x = 0$ and $\dfrac{dx}{dt} = 1$ when $t = 0$.

3. Solve $\dfrac{d^2s}{dt^2} = 6$, given that $\dfrac{ds}{dt} = 4$ and $s = 0$ when $t = 0$.

4. Solve $\dfrac{d^2s}{dt^2} = -\left(\dfrac{ds}{dt}\right)^2$, if $\dfrac{ds}{dt} = \dfrac{1}{2}$ and $s = 0$ when $t = 0$.

5. Solve $\dfrac{d^2x}{dt^2} = \left(\dfrac{dx}{dt}\right)^2 + 1$, if $\dfrac{dx}{dt} = 0$ and $x = 0$ when $t = 0$.

6. Solve $\dfrac{d^2y}{dx^2} = 2x$, if $\dfrac{dy}{dx} = 1$ and $y = 10$ when $x = 0$.

## Type 4: Second order differential equations requiring the chain rule

We now turn our attention to differential equations of the form $\dfrac{d^2y}{dx^2} = f(y)$

Take the equation $\dfrac{d^2y}{dx^2} = 4y$, given that $\dfrac{dy}{dx} = 4$ when $y = 2$ and that $y = e$ when $x = 0$.

If we let $v = \dfrac{dy}{dx}$, then $\dfrac{dv}{dx} = \dfrac{d^2y}{dx^2}$ and the equation reads $\dfrac{dv}{dx} = 4y$. This new equation has three variables and cannot be solved as it is.

Buy $\dfrac{d^2y}{dx^2} = \dfrac{dv}{dx} = \dfrac{dv}{dy} \cdot \dfrac{dy}{dx} = \dfrac{dv}{dy} \cdot v = v \dfrac{dv}{dy}$

So, the equation can now read $v \dfrac{dv}{dy} = 4y$ which is a first order differential equation in only two variables, and hence solvable. So, let's solve it.

**Step 1:** To find $v$.

$$v \frac{dv}{dy} = 4y$$

$$\therefore \int_4^v v \, dv = \int_2^y 4y \, dy$$

since $v = 4$ when $y = 2$.

$$\therefore \left.\frac{v^2}{2}\right|_4^v = \left.\frac{4y^2}{2}\right|_2^y$$

$$\therefore \frac{1}{2}v^2 - 8 = 2y^2 - 8$$

$$\therefore v^2 = 4y^2$$

$$\therefore v = \pm 2y$$

But $v = -2y$ is rejected since it does not satisfy the condition that $v = 4$ when $y = 2$ so, we continue with the only possible solution $v = 2y$.

**Step 2:** To find $y$.

$$v = 2y$$

$$\therefore \frac{dy}{dx} = 2y$$

$$\therefore \int_e^y \frac{dy}{y} = \int_0^x 2dx$$

$$\therefore \left.\log y\right|_e^y = \left.2x\right|_0^x$$

since $y = e$ when $x = 0$.

$$\therefore \log_e y - \log_e e = 2x - 2(0)$$

$$\therefore \log_e y - 1 = 2x$$

$$\therefore \log_e y = 2x + 1$$

$$\therefore y = e^{2x+1}: \text{Answer}$$

---

**Worked Example 12.11**

Solve $\dfrac{d^2s}{dt^2} = -\dfrac{1}{s^3}$

given that $\dfrac{ds}{dt} = 0.1$ and $s = 10$ when $t = 0$.

**Solution:**

$$\text{Let } v = \frac{ds}{dt}$$

$$\therefore \frac{d^2s}{dt^2} = \frac{dv}{ds} \cdot \frac{ds}{dt}$$

$$= \frac{dv}{ds} \cdot v = v\frac{dv}{ds}$$

**Step 1:** To find $v$.

$$v\frac{dv}{ds} = -\frac{1}{s^3}$$

$$\int_{0.1}^v v\,dv = \int_{10}^s -s^{-3}\,ds$$

---

$$\left.\frac{1}{2}v^2\right|_{0.1}^v = \left.\frac{1}{2}s^{-2}\right|_{10}^s$$

since $v = 0.1$ when $s = 10$.

$$\therefore \frac{1}{2}v^2 - \frac{1}{2}(0.1)^2 = \frac{1}{2}s^{-2} - \frac{1}{2}(10)^{-2}$$

$$\therefore v^2 - \frac{1}{100} = \frac{1}{s^2} - \frac{1}{100}$$

$$\therefore v^2 = \frac{1}{s^2}$$

$$\therefore v = \pm\frac{1}{s}$$

But $v = -\dfrac{1}{s}$ is rejected since it does not satisfy the condition that $v = \dfrac{1}{10}$ when $s = 10$. The only possible solution is $v = +\dfrac{1}{s}$.

**Step 2:** To find $s$.

$$v = \frac{ds}{dt} = \frac{1}{s}$$

$$\int_{10}^s s\,ds = \int_0^t dt$$

$$\left.\frac{1}{2}s^2\right|_{10}^s = \left.t\right|_0^t$$

$$\frac{1}{2}s^2 - \frac{1}{2}(10)^2 = t - 0$$

$$\frac{1}{2}s^2 - 50 = t$$

$$s^2 = 2t + 100$$

$$s = \pm\sqrt{2t + 100}$$

But $s = -\sqrt{2t + 100}$ is rejected since it does not satisfy the condition that $s = 10$ when $t = 0$.

$$\therefore s = +\sqrt{2t + 100}: \text{Answer.}$$

---

**Exercise 12 G**

1. Solve $\dfrac{d^2y}{dx^2} = y$, given that $\dfrac{dy}{dx} = 1$ and $y = 1$ when $x = 0$.

2. Solve $\dfrac{d^2s}{dt^2} = 9s$, given that $\dfrac{ds}{dt} = -6$ when $s = 2$ and that $s = e$ when $t = 0$.

3. Solve $\dfrac{d^2y}{dx^2} = -\dfrac{2}{y^5}$, given that $\dfrac{dy}{dx} = 1$ and $y = 1$ when $x = \dfrac{1}{3}$.

4. Solve $\dfrac{d^2y}{dx^2} = -y$, if $\dfrac{dy}{dx} = 2$ and $x = 0$ when $y = 0$.

5. Solve $\dfrac{d^2x}{dt^2} = 2x\,(9 + x^2)$, given that $\dfrac{dx}{dt} = 9$ when $x = 0$ and $x = 3$ when $t = 0$.

6. Solve $\dfrac{d^2x}{dt^2} = \dfrac{3x^3}{2}$, given that $\dfrac{dx}{dt} = -8$ and $x = 4$ when $t = 0$.

7. If $\dfrac{d^2y}{dx^2} + \dfrac{2}{y^3} = 0$, given that $\dfrac{dy}{dx} = \sqrt{2}$ and $x = \sqrt{2}$ when $y = 1$, find the value of $y$ when $x = \sqrt{18}$.

## Solving real-life problems by means of differential equations

If $s$ = the distance of a particle from a point $P$, then $\dfrac{ds}{dt}$ = the rate at which this distance changes = the velocity of the particle.

$\dfrac{d^2s}{dt^2} = \dfrac{dv}{dt}$ = the rate at which the velocity changes = the acceleration of the particle.

But $\dfrac{dv}{dt} = \dfrac{dv}{ds} \cdot \dfrac{ds}{dt} = \dfrac{dv}{ds} \cdot v = v\,\dfrac{dv}{ds}$

In conclusion, there are two ways of writing acceleration: $a = \dfrac{dv}{dt}$ or $a = v\,\dfrac{dv}{ds}$. The first leads to a relationship between $v$ and $t$, the latter to a relationship between $v$ and $s$.

### Worked Example 12.12

A particle moves so that its deceleration is equal, in magnitude, to the square of its velocity. It starts at a point $P$ with initial velocity 20 m/s.
How far will it have travelled in slowing down to 10 m/s?

**Solution:**

The deceleration equals $v^2$. Therefore the acceleration equals $-v^2$.

This can be written as $\dfrac{dv}{dt} = -v^2$ or $v\,\dfrac{dv}{ds} = -v^2$.

Since we are asked for the distance travelled, we will use $v\,\dfrac{dv}{ds} = -v^2$ which will yield a $v/s$ relationship, which is what we want.

The initial velocity is 20 m/s. That is, $v = 20$ when $t = 0$. It starts at $P$ when $t = 0$. If $s$ = the distance from $P$, the problem reads:

'If $v\,\dfrac{dv}{ds} = -v^2$ given that $v = 20$ when $s = 0$, find $s$ when $v = 10$.'

$$v\,\frac{dv}{ds} = -v^2$$

$$\therefore \int_{20}^{10} \frac{v\,dv}{v^2} = \int_0^s -ds$$

$$\therefore \int_{20}^{10} \frac{dv}{v} = \int_0^s -ds$$

$$\therefore \log_e v \,\Big|_{20}^{10} = -s \,\Big|_0^s$$

$$\therefore \log_e 10 - \log_e 20 = -s + 0$$

$$\therefore s = \log_e 20 - \log_e 10$$

$$\therefore s = \log_e 2 \text{ metres: Answer}$$

### Worked Example 12.13

A particle of mass $m$ falls from rest under gravity. There is an air resistance of magnitude $mkv$, where $k$ is a positive constant and $v$ is the velocity of the particle at any moment.

Show that the velocity at time $t$ is given by

$$v = \frac{g}{k}\left(1 - e^{-kt}\right)$$

Show that as time passes indefinitely, the speed of the particle approaches a 'terminal velocity' of $\dfrac{g}{k}$.

**Solution:**

In all problems where forces are featured, it is important to decide what direction is to be the 'positive' direction. If forces are along this direction, they will be positive; if they are in an opposite direction, they will be negative. The same can be said of accelerations and velocities.

In this case, downwards is regarded as the positive direction. Here, then, are the forces acting on the particle.

Scale        Forces

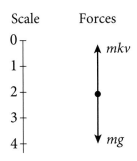

Fig. 12.1

(Note: the force $mkv$ is a resistance force, so it is in the opposite direction to motion.)

$$F = ma$$

$$\therefore\ mg - mkv = ma$$

$$\therefore\ a = g - kv$$

Since the question asks for a $v/t$ relationship, we will use $a = \dfrac{dv}{dt}$. The particle 'starts from rest' means that $v = 0$ at $t = 0$.

$$\therefore\ \frac{dv}{dt} = g - kv$$

$$\therefore\ \int_0^v \frac{dv}{g - kv} = \int_0^t dt$$

$$\therefore\ -\frac{1}{k} \log_e (g - kv) \Big|_0^v = t \Big|_0^t$$

$$\therefore\ -\frac{1}{k} \log_e (g - kv) + \frac{1}{k} \log_e g = t - 0$$

$$\therefore\ \frac{1}{k} \log_e \left( \frac{g}{g - kv} \right) = t$$

$$\therefore\ \log_e \left( \frac{g}{g - kv} \right) = kt$$

$$\therefore\ \frac{g}{g - kv} = e^{kt}$$

$$\therefore\ \frac{g - kv}{g} = e^{-kt}$$

$$\therefore\ g - kv = g\, e^{-kt}$$

$$\therefore\ kv = g\left(1 - e^{-kt}\right)$$

$$\therefore\ v = \frac{g}{k}\left(1 - e^{-kt}\right) \qquad \text{Q.E.D.}$$

As $t \to \infty$, $e^{kt} \to \infty$, $\therefore\ e^{-kt} \to 0$

$\therefore$ As $t \to \infty$, $v \to \dfrac{g}{k}(1 - 0) = \dfrac{g}{k}$

This is the terminal velocity, which parachutists quickly reach—or almost reach!

## Exercise 12 H

1. A particle of mass $m$ is projected along a smooth horizontal surface with initial speed 10 m/s. There is air resistance to motion of magnitude $\frac{1}{3}\, mv$, where $v$ is the velocity of the particle. No other force acts on the particle. Find the velocity of the particle after 3 seconds.

2. A car starts from rest. When it is at a distance $s$ from its starting point, its speed is $v$ and its acceleration is $25v + v^3$.
   Show that $dv = (25 + v^2)ds$ and find (correct to 2 decimal places) its speed when $s = 0.01$.

3. A particle starts from rest at a point $P$ and moves in a straight line subject to an acceleration which is equal to $v^2 + 100$, where $v$ is the particle's velocity. Find, correct to two decimal places the time taken to reach 20 m/s.
   (Hint: Use radian measure, when calculating $\tan^{-1} 2$.)

4. A particle of mass $m$ is projected towards a point $O$ with initial speed $\dfrac{\sqrt{5}}{3}$ m/s from a point $P$ where $|OP| = 3$ metres. The particle is repelled from $O$ by a force of magnitude $\dfrac{4m}{x^3}$ where $x$ is its distance from $O$.
   (i) Show that the equation of motion is $v\, dv = 4 x^{-3}\, dx$.
   (ii) Find how close the particle will get to $O$.
   (iii) Find its speed when it has travelled half the distance from $P$ to this nearest point.

5. A particle of mass 8 kg moves along a line (the $x$-axis) on a smooth horizontal plane under the action of a force in newtons of $(40 - 3\sqrt{x})\, \vec{i}$, where $\vec{i}$ is the unit vector along the $x$-axis and $x$ is the distance of the particle from a fixed point $O$ of the axis. The particle starts from rest at $O$.
   (i) Using acceleration $= v \dfrac{dv}{dx}$ find its speed when $x = 100$.
   (ii) Calculate where it next comes to instantaneous rest.

6. A particle of mass $m$ is projected vertically upwards from the earth's surface with initial speed 120 m/s in a medium where there is a resistance $0.098\, v^2$ per unit mass of the particle, when $v$ is the speed. Calculate the time to reach the highest point, to the nearest tenth of a second.

7. A particle is projected in a straight line from a fixed point $O$ with initial velocity $u$. It is opposed by a resistance $kv^q$ per unit mass, where $q$ is a constant such that $0 < q < 1$. If $s$ is the displacement from $O$ when the particle comes to rest, prove that $s = \dfrac{u^{2-q}}{(2-q)\,k}$.

8. A spherical meteorite in outer space has radius 10 m. A particle of mass $m$ is projected vertically from its surface with initial velocity 20 m/s. It is attracted back towards the centre of the meteorite by a force of magnitude $\dfrac{5000\,m}{x^2}$ where $x$ is its distance from the centre of the meteorite.
   (i) Find the velocity of the particle when it is $\dfrac{30}{7}$ metres above the meteorite's surface.
   (ii) Find also the greatest height that the particle will reach above the surface.

9. A particle of mass $m$ is acted on by a force of magnitude $\dfrac{2m}{x^5}$ directed away from a fixed point $O$, where $x$ is the distance of the particle from $O$. The particle starts from rest at a point, which is a distance $d$ from $O$.
   (i) Show that when $x = \sqrt{3}d$ the speed of the particle is $\dfrac{2\sqrt{2}}{3d^2}$
   (ii) Show that the velocity of the particle tends to a limit of $\dfrac{1}{d^2}$.

10. If $\dfrac{d^2s}{dt^2} = a$, given that $\dfrac{ds}{dt} = u$ and $s = 0$ when $t = 0$, where $a$, $u$ are constants, show that $s = ut + \frac{1}{2}at^2$ using integration.

11. If $\dfrac{d^2s}{dt^2} = a$, given that $\dfrac{ds}{dt} = u$ and $s = 0$, where $a$, $u$ are constants, show that $v^2 = u^2 + 2as$

## Harder problems

In some problems, it is necessary to use both $a = \dfrac{dv}{dt}$ and $a = v\dfrac{dv}{ds}$. Here is an example.

### Worked Example 12.14

A van, free-wheeling on a straight road, experiences a retardation which is proportional to the square of its speed. Its speed is reduced from 50 m/s to 10 m/s in a distance of 200 m. Calculate the time taken to travel the 200 m, to the nearest second.

**Solution:**

The equation of motion is $a = -kv^2$.

At the start $t = 0$, $s = 0$ and $v = 50$. At the end $t = t$, $s = 200$ and $v = 100$.

$$a = v\frac{dv}{ds}$$
$$\therefore \frac{vdv}{ds} = -kv^2$$
$$\therefore \int_{50}^{10} v\frac{dv}{ds} = \int_{0}^{200} -k\,ds$$
$$\therefore \int_{50}^{10} \frac{1}{v}\,dv = \int_{0}^{200} -k\,ds$$
$$\therefore \log_e v\Big|_{50}^{10} = -ks\Big|_{0}^{200}$$
$$\therefore \log_e 10 - \log_e 50 = -200k + 0$$
$$\therefore 200k = \log_e 50 - \log_e 10$$
$$\therefore 200k = \log_e\left(\frac{50}{10}\right)$$
$$\therefore 200k = \log_e 5$$
$$\therefore k = \frac{\log_e 5}{200} \qquad \text{Result 1}$$

Now, let's go back to the start, and solve the equation of motion using $a = \dfrac{dv}{dt}$.

$$a = \frac{dv}{dt} = -kv^2$$
$$\therefore \int_{50}^{10} v^{-2}\,dv = \int_{0}^{t} -k\,dt$$
$$\therefore -\frac{1}{v}\Big|_{50}^{10} = -kt\Big|_{0}^{t}$$

$$\therefore -\frac{1}{10} + \frac{1}{50} = -kt$$

$$\therefore kt = \frac{2}{25} \qquad \text{Result 2}$$

$$\therefore \frac{\log_e 5}{200} t = \frac{2}{25} \qquad \text{Using Result 1}$$

$$\therefore t = \frac{16}{\log_e 5} = 10 \text{ seconds (to the nearest second)}$$

## Exercise 12 I

1. A particle starts from a point $P$ with initial velocity 2 m/s and moves in a straight line subject to an acceleration which is equal to $(v^2 + 4)$ m/s$^2$, where $v$ is the particle's velocity. Find, correct to two decimal places, the time taken to reach 6 m/s, using acceleration $= \frac{dv}{dt}$.

2. A particle moves in a straight line with acceleration equal to minus the square of its velocity. If its initial velocity is 1 m/s, calculate the distance travelled one second later.

3. A particle moves in a straight line so that at any instant its acceleration is, in magnitude, half its velocity. If its initial velocity is 3 m/s, find (correct to one decimal place) the distance it describes in the fifth second.

4. A car, free-wheeling on a straight road, experiences a retardation which is proportional to the square of its speed. Its speed is reduced from 20 m/s to 10 m/s in a distance of 100 m. Calculate the time taken to travel the 100 m.

5. A particle moves in a straight line and undergoes a retardation of $\frac{v^3}{25}$, where $v$ is the speed.
   (i) If the initial speed of the particle is 25 m/s, find its speed when it has travelled a distance of 99 m.
   (ii) Find the time for the particle to slow down from 10 m/s to 5 m/s.

6. A particle of mass 2 kg starts from rest and is acted on by a force, which increases uniformly in 80 seconds from zero to 20 N.
   (i) Prove that $t$ seconds after the particle begins to move, its acceleration is $\frac{t}{8}$ m/s$^2$
   (ii) Prove that when the particle has moved a distance $s$, its speed is $v$, where $9s^2 = 8v^3$.

## Problems involving power

We saw earlier that if the power output of an engine is $P$, and if the tractive effort produced is $T$, then $P = Tv$. This equation is useful when solving problems which involve power.

### Worked Example 12.15

A car of mass $m$ is travelling on a straight road. The power output is a constant $100m$ watts. The car speeds up from $u_0$ to $2u_0$. Show that the time taken is given by

$$t = \frac{3u_0^2}{200}$$

Solution:

$$P = Tv$$

$$\therefore Tv = 100m$$

$$\therefore T = \frac{100m}{v}$$

The car is subject to the tractive effort $T$ driving it forward.

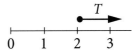

Fig. 12.2

$$F = ma$$

$$\therefore T = ma$$

$$\therefore \frac{100\,m}{v} = ma$$

(Dividing by $m$)

$$\therefore a = \frac{100}{v}$$

$$\therefore \frac{dv}{dt} = \frac{100}{v}$$

$$\therefore \int_{u_0}^{2u_0} v \, dv = \int_0^t 100 \, dt$$

$$\therefore \frac{v^2}{2} \Big|_{u_0}^{2u_0} - 100\,t \Big|_0^t$$

$$\frac{4u_0^2}{2} - \frac{u_0^2}{2} = 100\,t - 0$$

$$\frac{3\,u_0^{\,2}}{2} = 100t$$

$$t = \frac{3\,u_0^{\,2}}{200} \qquad \text{Q.E.D.}$$

## Exercise 12 J

1. A car of mass $m$ is travelling on a straight road. The power output is a constant $25m$ watts. The car speeds up from 1 m/s to 3 m/s. Find the time taken, correct to 2 decimal places.

2. An engine pulls a train. The engine works at a constant power $25\,kmu_0^{\,2}$, where $m$ is the total mass of the train and engine and $k$, $u_0$ are positive constants. Show that

   (i)  the equation of motion is
   $$v^2\,dv = 25\,k\,u_0^{\,2}\,ds$$

   (ii) the distance travelled as the car speeds up from $u_0$ to $4u_0$ is $\dfrac{21\,u_0}{25k}$

3. A car of mass 1 tonne (=1000 kg) moves along a horizontal road. The engine works at a constant rate of 75kW.

   (i)   Show that the acceleration of the car is $\dfrac{75}{v}$ m/s$^2$

   (ii)  How long will it take to speed up from 5 m/s to 25 m/s?

   (iii) What distance does it cover in this time?

## Summary of important points

1. Velocity $\quad = \dfrac{ds}{dt}$

2. Acceleration $= \dfrac{dv}{dt} = v\,\dfrac{dv}{ds}$

3. Force $\quad = ma = m\,\dfrac{dv}{dt} = mv\,\dfrac{dv}{ds}$

4. Power $\quad = Tv$

## DOs and DON'Ts for the exam

### DO

- Do know your methods of integration well
- Do draw a force diagram with a **scale**. Any acceleration or velocity along the positive direction is plus; any acceleration or force along the negative direction is minus.
- Do remember that there are two differential formulae for acceleration: $\dfrac{dv}{dt}$ or $v\,\dfrac{dv}{ds}$, which can also be written as $v\,\dfrac{dv}{dx}$

### DON'T

- Don't put the initial velocity in the diagram as a force
- Don't mix up power and force
- Don't forget the power formula $P = Tv$

# Simple harmonic motion

## Chapter 13

*Ut tensio, sic vis*

(The more the extension the more the force)

*Robert Hooke*

## Contents

## Learning outcomes

**In this chapter you will learn...**

- Hooke's Law and its applications

- The definition of Simple Harmonic Motion (SHM)

- The equations of SHM

- Using the equations of SHM to solve problems

- Solving problems of SHM with elastic bands

- The simple pendulum

## You will need to know...

- $\lim\limits_{A \to 0} \dfrac{\sin A}{A} = 1$
- The derivative of $\sin kx$ is $k \cos kx$
- The derivative of $\cos kx$ is $k \sin kx$
- The period of $a\cos \omega t$ or $a\sin \omega t$ is $\dfrac{2\pi}{\omega}$.
- The amplitude of $a \sin \omega t \pm b \cos \omega t$ is $\sqrt{a^2 + b^2}$

## Hooke's Law

When an elastic string or a spring is stretched beyond its natural length, it exerts a restoring force which is proportional to the length it is extended beyond its natural length.

Let $l_o$ = the natural length of an elastic string, and let $l$ = the actual length, then $l - l_o$ is the extension beyond the natural length. Hooke's law states that the force $F$ exerted by the string is proportional to $l - l_o$. It follows that $F = k\left(l - l_o\right)$. The constant $k$ in this formula is called the elastic constant, and depends on the nature of the string (or spring). It has dimension N/m.

If an elastic string of natural length 1 m and elastic constant 7 N/m is stretched to a length 4 m, it will exert a force $F$, where

$$F = k\left(l - l_o\right)$$
$$= 7\left(4 - 1\right)$$
$$= 21 \text{ N.}$$

This force is exerted on objects at the ends of strings.

### Worked Example 13.1

(i) A particle rests on a smooth horizontal table between two walls. It is connected to the left hand wall by means of a horizontal string of natural length 1 m and elastic constant 4 N/m and to the other wall by means of a horizontal string of natural length 2 m and elastic constant 6 N/m. If the walls are 18 m apart, find the position where the particle would be in equilibrium.

(ii) If the particle is held at a point on the table equidistant from the two walls, find the magnitude and direction of the resultant force on it.

### Solution:

(i) In equilibrium the force to the left $F_l$ will be equal to the force to the right, $F_r$.

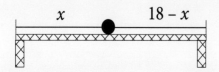

Fig. 13.1

Let $x$ = the distance between the particle and the left hand wall.

$\therefore$ $18 - x$ = the distance between the particle and the right hand wall.

$$F_l = k\left(l - l_o\right)$$
$$= 4\left(x - 1\right)$$
$$= 4x - 4$$
$$F_r = k\left(l - l_o\right)$$
$$= 6\left(18 - x - 2\right)$$
$$= 96 - 6x$$

But $\qquad F_l = F_r$ (in equilibrium)

$$\Rightarrow 4x - 4 = 96 - 6x$$
$$\Rightarrow 10x = 100$$
$$\Rightarrow x = 10 \text{ m}$$

Answer (i): 10 m from the left hand wall.

(ii)
$$F_l = k\left(l - l_o\right)$$
$$= 4\left(9 - 1\right)$$
$$= 32 \text{ N}$$
$$F_r = k\left(l - l_o\right)$$
$$= 6\left(9 - 2\right)$$
$$= 42 \text{ N}$$
$$\therefore F = F_r - F_l$$
$$= 42 - 32$$
$$= 10 \text{ N, to the right}$$

Answer (ii): The force has magnitude 10 $N$ and is to the right.

### Worked Example 13.2

A particle of mass $\frac{1}{2}$ kg is attached to one end of an elastic string of natural length 1 m and elastic constant 6 N/m. The other end is fixed to a point on a smooth horizontal surface. The particle moves in a circle on the surface with constant angular speed 2 rad/s. Find the radius of the circle of motion.

### Solution:

Let $r$ = the radius = the length of the extended string. The force, $F = k\left(l - l_o\right) = 6\left(r - 1\right)$. But this must equal $m\omega^2 r$, so that the particle moves in a circle.

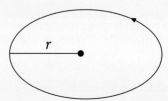

Fig. 13.2

$$6(r-1) = m\omega^2 r$$
$$\therefore 6r - 6 = \tfrac{1}{2}(4)r$$
$$\therefore 6r - 6 = 2r$$
$$\therefore 4r = 6$$
$$\therefore r = \tfrac{3}{2} : \text{Answer}$$

## Exercise 13 A

1. A string has natural length 5 m and elastic constant 10 N/m. Find the force on a particle at the end of the string when the length is
   (i) 6 m
   (ii) 10 m
   (iii) 5.2 m.

2. A string has natural length 2 m and elastic constant 9 N/m. Find the force on a particle at the end of the string when the length is
   (i) 3 m
   (ii) 5 m
   (iii) $3\tfrac{1}{3}$ m.

   What is the length of the string if the force exerted is of magnitude 54 N?

3. A particle rests on a smooth horizontal table. It is attached to the ends of two horizontal elastic strings, the other ends being fixed to points on two vertical walls. The left hand string has natural length 1 m and elastic constant 2 N/m; the other has natural length 1 m and elastic constant 4 N/m. The walls are 20 m apart. Find
   (i) the resultant force on the particle when it is midway between the walls
   (ii) the position where the particle would be in equilibrium.

4. A particle rests on a smooth horizontal table between two vertical walls which are 19 m apart. It is attached to the left hand wall by means of a string of natural length 1 m and elastic constant 5 N/m. It is attached to the other wall by means of a string of natural length 2 m and elastic constant 3 N/m. Find
   (i) the position of equilibrium
   (ii) the point where there is a resultant force of magnitude 16 newtons acting on the particle to the right.

5. A particle rests on a smooth horizontal table between two vertical walls which are 35 m apart. It is attached to the left hand wall by means of an elastic string of natural length 2 m and elastic constant 7 N/m and to the other by means of a string of natural length 3 m and elastic constant 3 N/m. Find
   (i) the position of equilibrium
   (ii) two positions where the resultant force on the particle would be of magnitude 40 N.

6. A particle of mass 1 kg is attached to one end of an elastic string of natural length 1 m and elastic constant 50 N/m. The other end of the string is fixed to a point on a smooth horizontal table. The particle moves in a circle of radius 2 m. Find its angular speed.

7. A particle of mass 10 kg is attached to one end of an elastic string of natural length 1 m and elastic constant 49 N/m. The other end of the string is attached to the ceiling so that the particle hangs freely. Find how far the particle will be below the ceiling when it is in equilibrium.

8. A particle of mass 2 kg hangs from the ceiling by means of an elastic string of natural length 2 m and elastic constant 7 N/m. Find the length of the string when the system hangs in equilibrium.

   If the particle is stretched a further distance *x*, show that the force on the particle is of magnitude 7*x*.

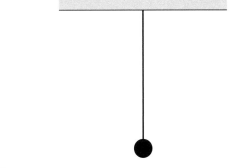

Fig. 13.3

221

9. A conical pendulum consists of a particle of mass $m$ attached to an elastic string of natural length 3 m which is fixed to a point $P$ at its other end. The particle rotates in a horizontal circle of radius 3 m, the centre of the circle being 4 m vertically below $P$. Show that

    (i) the elastic string is extended 2 m beyond its natural length,

    (ii) the elastic constant $k = \dfrac{5mg}{8}$

    (iii) the angular speed of the particle is $\sqrt{\dfrac{g}{4}}$ rad/s.

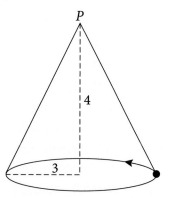

Fig. 13.4

10. A particle is hung from two points $P$ and $Q$ on the same horizontal line, where $|PQ| = 8$ m by means of two elastic strings of equal length. The strings have natural lengths 2 m and 1 m; they have elastic constants 10 N/m and 7 N/m respectively.

    (i) Show that the angle $A$ which the two strings make with the vertical is given by $\sin A = \dfrac{12}{13}$.

    (ii) Find the weight of the particle.

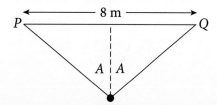

Fig. 13.5

11. A heavy particle is hung from two points on the same horizontal line and a distance $2d$ apart by means of two light, elastic strings of natural length $l_1$, $l_2$ and elastic constants $k_1$, $k_2$ respectively. In the equilibrium position the two strings make equal angles $\theta$ with the vertical.

Prove that:
$$\sin\theta = \frac{d(k_1 - k_2)}{k_1 l_1 - k_2 l_2}$$

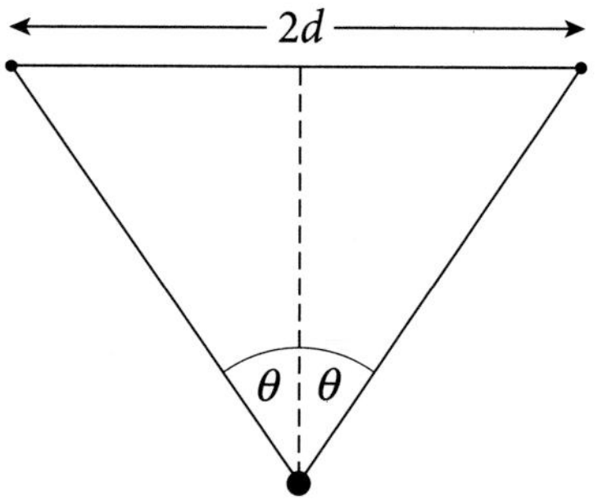

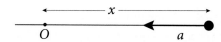

Fig. 13.6

## Simple harmonic motion

**Definition:** When a particle moves so that its acceleration is proportional to its displacement from a fixed point $O$ and is directed towards $O$, the particle is said to move with **simple harmonic motion** (SHM).

Fig. 13.7

Let $x$ = the displacement of the particle from $O$. The acceleration is proportional to $x$, but it is directed back towards $O$, so it has opposite sign to $x$. If $a$ = the acceleration, then $a = -\omega^2 x$ (letting the constant be $-\omega^2$ ensures that $a$ is negative when $x$ is positive)

$$a = -\omega^2 x \qquad \text{Equation 1}$$

$$\therefore v\frac{dv}{dx} = -\omega^2 x$$

$$\therefore \int v\, dv = \int -\omega^2 x\, dx$$

But the particle must stop at some point. The greatest distance from $O$ reached by the particle is called the amplitude and is denoted by the positive constant $A$.

Hence $v = 0$ when $x = A$.

$$\therefore \int_0^v v\, dv = -\omega^2 \int_A^x x\, dx$$

$$\therefore \frac{v^2}{2}\bigg|_0^v = -\omega^2 \frac{x^2}{2}\bigg|_A^x$$

$$\therefore \frac{v^2}{2} - 0 = -\frac{\omega^2 x^2}{2} + \frac{\omega^2 A^2}{2}$$

$$\therefore v^2 = \omega^2 A^2 - \omega^2 x^2$$

$$\therefore v^2 = \omega^2(A^2 - x^2) \qquad \text{Equation 2}$$

It can be proven that $x = A \sin(\omega t + \varepsilon)$ is a solution of equation 1: $a = -\omega^2 x$.

Proof: Let $x = A \sin(\omega t + \varepsilon)$
$$\therefore v = \frac{dx}{dt} = A\omega \cos(\omega t + \varepsilon)$$
$$\therefore a = \frac{dv}{dt} = -A\omega^2 \sin(\omega t + \varepsilon)$$
$$\therefore a = -\omega^2 x \qquad \text{Q.E.D}$$

It can also be proven that $x = A \cos(\omega t + \varepsilon)$ is a solution of $a = -\omega^2 x$. This should be verified by the student.

There are two special cases:

**Case 1:** $x = A \sin \omega t$ is used when the particle starts at the centre (since when $t = 0$, $x = 0$).

**Case 2:** $x = A \cos \omega t$ is used when the particle starts at the extreme (since when $t = 0$, $x = A$).

### Mnemonic
Look at the second letter of s**i**n: it is *i* for inside.
Look at the second letter of c**o**s: it is *o* for outside.

The time for a full cycle ($T$) is given by $\boldsymbol{T = \frac{2\pi}{\omega}}$ ... Equation 3

The maximum velocity (which occurs when $x = 0$), is given by $\boldsymbol{v_{max} = \omega A}$... Equation 4

The maximum acceleration (which occurs when $x = \pm A$) is given by $\boldsymbol{a_{max} = \omega^2 A}$ ... Equation 5

## Summary

1. $^*a = -\omega^2 x$

2. $^*v^2 = \omega^2(A^2 - x^2)$

3. $^*$Periodic time $T = \frac{2\pi}{\omega}$

4. $v_{max} = \omega A$

5. $a_{max} = \omega^2 A$

6. $x = A \sin \omega t$ (starting at the centre)
   $x = A \cos \omega t$ (starting at extreme point)
   $^*x = A \sin(\omega t + \varepsilon)$ or $x = A \cos(\omega t + \varepsilon)$
   otherwise

7. $A$ and $\omega$ are taken to be positive constants.

8. $x$ and $a$ are always of opposite sign; if one is positive the other is negative.

9. Average speed $= \frac{4A}{T}$

The equations marked with an asterisk appear on page 54 of *Formulae and Tables*.

### Worked Example 13.3

A particle, moving with simple harmonic motion, has speeds 6 m/s and 8 m/s when its distances from the centre of oscillation are 4 m and 3 m respectively. Find
(i) the amplitude
(ii) the periodic time
(iii) the average speed
(iv) the maximum velocity
(v) the maximum acceleration.

Solution:

(i) We know $v^2 = \omega^2(A^2 - x^2)$
$v = 6$ when $x = 4$
$\therefore 36 = \omega^2(A^2 - 16)$ equation I
$v = 8$ when $x = 3$
$\therefore 64 = \omega^2(A^2 - 9)$ equation II
Dividing I by II we get
$$\frac{36}{64} = \frac{\omega^2(A^2 - 16)}{\omega^2(A^2 - 9)}$$
$$\therefore \frac{A^2 - 16}{A^2 - 9} = \frac{9}{16}$$
$$\therefore 16A^2 - 256 = 9A^2 - 81$$
$$7A^2 = 175$$
$$\therefore A^2 = 25$$
$$\therefore A = 5 \text{ m.}$$

(ii) Equation I $\Rightarrow 36 = \omega^2(A^2 - 16)$
$\therefore 36 = \omega^2(25 - 16)$
$\therefore 4 = \omega^2$
$\therefore \omega = 2$
$T = \frac{2\pi}{\omega} = \frac{2\pi}{2} = \pi$ seconds

(iii) The distance covered in one full cycle is $4A = 20$ m. The time taken is $\pi$ seconds.
$\therefore$ the average speed $= \frac{20}{\pi} = 6.366$ m/s.

(iv) $v_{max} = \omega A = 2(5) = 10$ m/s.

(v) $a_{max} = \omega^2 A = 4(5) = 20$ m/s$^2$.

## Exercise 13 B

1. A particle performs SHM with amplitude 5 m and periodic time $\frac{2\pi}{7}$ seconds. Find
   (i) the maximum velocity
   (ii) the maximum acceleration
   (iii) the average speed throughout one full cycle.

2. A particle performs SHM about a fixed point $O$. When its distance from $O$ is $\sqrt{7}$ m, its speed is 9 m/s. When it is 2 m distant from $O$, its speed is $6\sqrt{3}$ m/s. Find the amplitude and the periodic time.

3. A particle performs SHM. Its maximum velocity is 6 m/s and its maximum acceleration is 12 m/s². Find the periodic time and the amplitude. Find also the magnitude of its acceleration when its speed is $2\sqrt{5}$ m/s.

4. A particle performs SHM about a fixed point $O$. When it is 1 cm from $O$ its speed is 8 cm/s. When it is 7 cm from $O$ its speed is 4 cm/s. Find
   (i) the amplitude
   (ii) the periodic time
   (iii) the speed of the particle when it passes through $O$.

5. A particle performs SHM about a fixed point $P$. When its distance from $P$ is 1 m, its speed is 3 m/s and its acceleration is of magnitude 3 m/s². Find the maximum acceleration.

6. A particle performs SHM about a fixed point $O$. When it is 5 m from $O$, its velocity is of magnitude 24 m/s and its acceleration is of magnitude 20 m/s².
   (i) Find the amplitude.
   (ii) Find the periodic time.
   (iii) How many complete oscillations does it perform in one minute?

7. A particle of mass 2 kg performs SHM about a fixed point $O$. When its distance from $O$ is $\sqrt{2}$ m its speed is 2 m/s and its acceleration is of magnitude $4\sqrt{2}$ m/s². Find the time taken for the particle to move from $O$ to where its distance from $O$ is 1.5 m. What is the force on the particle at this point?

8. The tides are assumed to rise and fall with Simple Harmonic Motion. At 12 noon, the depth of water in a harbour is at its lowest and shows a depth of 3 metres. At 5.30 pm that evening, the depth is at its greatest at 13 m. A yacht needs a depth of 10 m to sail out of the harbour.
   (i) What is the amplitude?
   (ii) What is the periodic time?
   (iii) What is the earliest time that afternoon that the yacht can sail?

9. A particle moves with SHM, through two points $P$ and $Q$ which are 1.2 m apart. Its speed is the same at $P$ as at $Q$. It takes 3 seconds to go from $P$ to $Q$ and 3 seconds to go from $Q$ to $Q$ (i.e. passing $Q$ the next time).
   (i) Find the period of motion.
   (ii) Find the amplitude.

10. The depth of water in a harbour is assumed to rise and fall with SHM. On a certain day the low tide has a depth of 13 m at 12.58 pm and the following high tide had a depth of 18 m at 6.58 pm.

    If a ship requires a depth of 16.5 m of water before it can leave the harbour, find the latest time on that day that the ship can leave the harbour.

## Worked Example 13.4

A particle moves so that its displacement $x$ (in metres) from a point $O$ after $t$ seconds is given by $x = 2 \sin 4t$

   (i) Show that it will perform SHM.
   (ii) Find its distance from $O$, $\frac{\pi}{16}$ seconds after it leaves the point $O$.
   (iii) Find the magnitude of the acceleration when the velocity $4\sqrt{3}$ m/s.
   (iv) Find the time taken to reach a point 1.5 m from $O$.

**Solution:**

   (i)
$$x = 2 \sin 4t$$
$$\therefore v = \frac{dx}{dt} = 8 \cos 4t$$
$$\therefore a = \frac{dv}{dt} = -32 \sin 4t$$
$$\therefore a = -16\,x$$

Since the acceleration, $a$ is proportional to $x$ but of the opposite sign, the particle moves with SHM.

When $t = \dfrac{\pi}{16}$,

$$x = 2 \sin 4t$$
$$= 2 \sin \frac{\pi}{4}$$
$$= 2 \frac{1}{\sqrt{2}}$$
$$= \frac{2}{\sqrt{2}}$$
$$= \sqrt{2} \text{ m.}$$

(ii) Comparing $x = 2 \sin 4t$ with the general solution $x = A \sin \omega t$ we see that $A = 2$ and $\omega = 4$.

Unfortunately, we have no equation relating the acceleration $a$ to the velocity $v$. Instead, we use $x$ as a go-between. From $v$ we find $x$; from $x$ we find $a$.

$$v^2 = \omega^2 (A^2 - x^2)$$

But $\omega = 4$, $A = 2$ and $v = 4\sqrt{3}$.

$$\therefore 48 = 16 (4 - x^2)$$
$$\therefore x^2 = 1$$
$$\therefore x = \pm 1$$

Now
$$a = -\omega^2 x$$
$$= -(16)(\pm 1)$$
$$= \pm 16 \text{ m/s}^2.$$

The acceleration is of magnitude 16 m/s$^2$.

(iii) We want to find $t$ when $x = 1.5$.

$$x = 2 \sin 4t$$
$$\therefore 1.5 = 2 \sin 4t$$
$$\therefore \sin 4t = 0.75$$
$$\therefore 4t = \sin^{-1}(0.75)$$
$$= 0.8480 \text{ (Using calculator in RAD mode.)}$$
$$\therefore t = 0.2120 \text{ s.} \qquad \text{Answer}$$

## Worked Example 13.5

A particle moves so that its displacement $x$ from a fixed point $O$ at time $t$ is given by

$$x = 8 \cos 5t + 15 \sin 5t.$$

(i) Prove that the particle will perform SHM.
(ii) Find the periodic time.
(iii) Find the amplitude.
(iv) Find when $x = 0$ for the first time.

## Solution

(i) $x = 8 \cos 5t + 15 \sin 5t$

$\therefore \dfrac{dx}{dt} = 8 (-\sin 5t)(5) + 15 (\cos 5t)(5)$

$$= -40 \sin 5t + 75 \cos 5t$$

$\therefore \dfrac{d^2x}{dt^2} = -40(\cos 5t)(5) + 75(-\sin 5t)(5)$

$$= -200 \cos 5t - 375 \sin 5t$$
$$= -25(8 \cos 5t + 15 \sin 5t)$$

$\therefore a = \dfrac{d^2x}{dt^2} = -25x$

Since the acceleration is proportional to the displacement but in the opposite direction, the particle will perform SHM,

with $\omega = \sqrt{25} = 5$ (since $a = -\omega^2 x$).

(ii) $T = \dfrac{2\pi}{\omega} = \dfrac{2\pi}{5}$ seconds

(iii) It can be proven that the amplitude of $a \cos \omega t \pm b \sin \omega t$ is $\sqrt{a^2 + b^2}$

In this case the amplitude is given by
$$A = \sqrt{8^2 + 15^2}$$
$$= \sqrt{64 + 225}$$
$$= \sqrt{289}$$
$$= 17 \text{ m}$$

(iv) $x = 0$

$\therefore 8 \cos 5t + 15 \sin 5t = 0$ (divide by $\cos 5t$)

$$\therefore 8 + 15 \tan 5t = 0$$
$$\therefore \tan 5t = -\frac{8}{15}$$

Now there are many solutions to this equation. The first positive one will be when the angle $5t$ is in the second quadrant: the equivalent of 151.9° in radians.

$$\therefore 5t = 2.65$$
$$\therefore t = 0.53 \text{ sec. : Answer}$$

## Exercise 13 C

1. A particle moves so that its distance $x$ (in metres) from a fixed point $O$ is given by $x = 3 \sin 5t$. Show that it will perform SHM and find the periodic time. How long does it take to move from $O$ to a point 1.5 m from $O$?

2. A particle moves so that its displacement $x$, in metres, from a point $P$ after $t$ seconds is given by $x = 4 \cos 2t$
   (i) Show that it will perform SHM.
   (ii) What is the greatest distance between the particle and the point $P$?
   (iii) How long will it take to go from a point where its velocity is zero to a point 2.5 m from $P$?

3. A particle moves in SHM, so that its displacement $x$, in metres, from a point $P$ after $t$ seconds is given by $x = 9 \cos 3t$

(i) How far from $P$ is the particle when $t = 0$?

(ii) How long does the particle take to travel 2 metres? Give your answer to the nearest thousandth of a second.

4. A particle moves so that its distance $x$, in metres, from a fixed point $O$ after $t$ seconds is given by $x = 13 \sin(\omega t + \varepsilon)$. When $t = 0$, $x = 5$ and the velocity $v = 24$ m/s. Find

(i) the value of $\varepsilon$

(ii) the value of $\omega$

(iii) the value of $t$ when $x = 0$ for the first time.

5. Given that the amplitude of $a \cos \omega t \pm b \sin \omega t$ is $\sqrt{a^2 + b^2}$ and that the period is $\frac{2\pi}{\omega}$, find the amplitude and period of the following cases of SHM:

(i) $x = 3 \cos 2t + 4 \sin 2t$

(ii) $x = 8 \cos 4t + 6 \sin 4t$

(iii) $x = 12 \cos t + 5 \sin t$

(iv) $x = 3 \cos \pi t + \sqrt{7} \sin \pi t$

(v) $x = \sin 3t + \cos 3t$

(vi) $x = 21 \sin 2\pi t + 20 \cos 2\pi t$

(vii) $x = \sqrt{3} \sin 5t - \cos 5t$

(viii) $x = 2 \sin \frac{1}{2} t + 3 \cos \frac{1}{2} t$

(ix) $x = 24 \sin \frac{1}{4} t - 7 \cos \frac{1}{4} t$

(x) $x = 2 \sin \frac{1}{3} t + \cos \frac{1}{3} t$

6. A particle moves so that its displacement $x$ from a fixed point $O$ at time is given by
$x = 12 \cos t + 35 \sin t$.

(i) Prove that the particle will perform SHM.

(ii) Find the periodic time.

(iii) Find the amplitude.

(iv) Find when $x = 0$ for the first time.

7. A particle moves so that its displacement $x$ from a fixed point $O$ at time $t$ is given by
$x = 12 \sin 2t + 5 \cos 2t$.

(i) Prove that the particle will perform SHM.

(ii) Find the periodic time.

(iii) Find the amplitude.

(iv) Find when $x = 0$ for the first time.

(v) Find when $x = 0$ for the second time.

8. Define simple harmonic motion. The distance, $x$, of a particle from a fixed point, $O$, is given by $x = A \cos(\omega t + \alpha)$ where $A$, $\omega$, $\alpha$ are positive constants.

(i) Show that the particle is describing simple harmonic motion about $O$ and calculate $\omega$ and $\alpha$ if the velocity $v = -2A$ and $x = \frac{3A}{5}$ when $t = 0$.

(ii) After how many seconds from the start of the motion is $x = 0$ for the first time?

9. A horizontal platform, on which bodies are resting, oscillates vertically with simple harmonic motion of amplitude 0.2 m. What is the maximum integral number of complete oscillations per minute it can make, if the bodies are not to leave the platform?

10. (a) A particle is moving in a straight line such that its distance $x$ from a fixed point at time $t$ is given by $x = r \cos \omega t$

Show that the particle is moving with simple harmonic motion.

(b) A particle is moving in a straight line with simple harmonic motion. When it is at a point $P_1$ of distance 0.8 m from the mean-centre, its speed is 6 m/s and when it is at a point $P_2$ of distance 0.2 m from the end-position on the same side of the mean-centre as $P_1$ its acceleration is of magnitude 24 m/s$^2$.

(i) If $r$ is the amplitude of the motion, show that $\frac{2}{3} = \frac{r - 0.2}{r^2 - 0.64}$

(ii) Hence find the value of $r$.

(iii) Find also the period of the motion and the shortest time taken between $P_1$ and $P_2$ correct to two places of decimals.

## SHM with elastic strings or springs

In cases where you are asked to prove that a particle (attached to elastic strings or a spring) performs SHM, follow these steps:

1. Find the position of equilibrium $O$.
   There are 3 ways of doing this:

(i) By inspection – it is the position of zero force.

(ii) By finding (mathematically) the position of zero force.

(iii) It is sometimes given in the question.

2. Examine the forces on the particle when it is displaced a distance $x$ from $O$.

(i) If motion is horizontal, displace the particle to the right.

(ii) If motion is vertical, displace the particle downwards.

3. Find the resultant force on the particle.
   (i) If motion is horizontal,
   $$F_{resultant} = F_{right} - F_{left}$$
   (ii) If motion is vertical,
   $$F_{resultant} = F_{down} - F_{up}$$

4. Find the resultant acceleration, using $F = m\,a$.

5. Show that the acceleration $a$ is proportional to the displacement $x$, but in the opposite direction. This proves that the particle will perform SHM.

## Worked Example 13.6

A particle of mass 10 kg rests on a smooth horizontal table between two vertical walls, which are 8 m apart. It is connected to the walls by means of horizontal elastic strings, both of natural length 1 m and elastic constant 20 N/m. Initially the particle is held so that the right-hand string is just slack and it is then released from rest. Show that it will perform SHM. Find how long it will take to reach a point 2.5 m from the right-hand wall.

**Solution:**

Due to symmetry, the position of equilibrium is midway between the walls. To show that it will perform SHM, we examine the forces on the particle, not in the initial position, but when it is displaced any distance $x$ from the position of equilibrium.

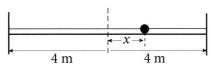

Fig. 13.8

The force to the right =
$$F_r = k\,(l - l_o)$$
$$= 20\,(4 - x - 1)$$
$$= 60 - 20\,x$$

The force to the left =
$$F_l = 20\,(4 + x - 1)$$
$$= 60 + 20\,x$$

The resultant force =
$$F_{resultant} = F_r - F_l$$
$$= (60 - 20\,x) - (60 + 20\,x)$$
$$= -40\,x$$

$$\therefore F = -40\,x$$
$$\therefore ma = -40\,x$$
$$\therefore 10\,a = -40\,x$$
$$\therefore a = -4\,x$$

This shows that the acceleration is proportional to $x$ but in the opposite direction, so the particle will perform SHM. Comparing the equations $a = -4\,x$ and $a = -\omega^2\,x$ it is clear that $\omega^2 = 4 \Rightarrow \omega = 2$. But how can the amplitude be found? The amplitude is determined by the *distance between the initial position and the equilibrium position*. This is because the particle will never be further from the position of equilibrium than at the start. In the initial position the right-hand string is just slack, so that its length is 1 m. The particle is therefore 3 m from the centre of oscillation. Therefore, $A = 3$ m.

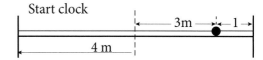

Fig. 13.9

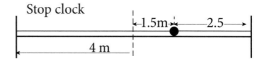

Fig. 13.10

When the particle is 2.5 m from the right-hand wall, it is 1.5 m from the centre of oscillation, i.e. $x = 1.5$. We want to find $t$ when $x = 1.5$. Since the "clock" starts when the particle is at the extreme position, we will use the formula
$$x = A \cos \omega t.$$
$$\therefore x = 3 \cos 2t$$
$$\therefore 1.5 = 3 \cos 2t \text{ (since } x = 1.5)$$
$$\therefore 0.5 = \cos 2t$$
$$\therefore 2t = \frac{\pi}{3}$$
$$\therefore t = \frac{1}{2}\left(\frac{\pi}{3}\right) = \left(\frac{\pi}{6}\right) = 0.5236 \text{ s : Answer}$$

### Strings which go slack

Let us imagine an elastic string is tied at one end to a fixed point $P$ on a wall and at the other end to a particle on a horizontal surface. Let us now drag the particle so that the string is extended beyond its natural length. When we let the particle go, it will slide across the floor and crash into the wall. So, where is the simple harmonic motion here? Surely, when SHM takes place a particle moves back and forth indefinitely? In this case the particle does perform SHM, but only as long as the string remains taut. We can use this fact to time the particle, or to find its speed or acceleration.

Fig. 13.11

### Worked Example 13.7

An elastic string has natural length 1 m and elastic constant 16 N/m. One end of the string is tied to a point $P$ on a smooth horizontal floor, the other to a small particle of mass $\frac{1}{4}$ kg. The particle is dragged across the floor to a point $Q$, which is 1.8 m from $P$ and released from rest.

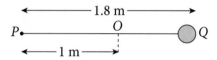

Fig. 13.12

(i)  Show that the particle will perform SHM as long as the string remains taut.

(ii)  Find the time taken for the particle to reach $P$ correct to four decimal places.

### Solution

(i)  When the particle is at a point $O$, 1 m from $P$, there is no force on it. We will examine the force on the particle when it is a further distance $x$ beyond $O$. The force will be negative as it is in the opposite direction to the displacement.

$$F = -k(l - l_o)$$
$$= -16(1 + x - 1)$$
$$= -16x$$
$$\therefore ma = -16x$$
$$\therefore \frac{1}{4}a = -16x$$
$$\therefore a = -64x$$

Since the acceleration is proportional to the displacement but in the opposite direction, the particle will perform SHM, with
$$\omega = \sqrt{64} = 8 \qquad \text{Q.E.D.}$$

(ii)  We will divide the journey from $Q$ to $P$ into two parts: $Q$ to $O$ and $O$ to $P$.

The journey from $Q$ to $O$ is one quarter of a full cycle. The time taken $(t_1)$ is given by
$$t_1 = \frac{1}{4}\left(\frac{2\pi}{\omega}\right)$$
$$= \frac{1}{4}\left(\frac{2\pi}{8}\right)$$
$$= \frac{\pi}{16}$$
$$= 0.19635 \text{ seconds.}$$

The journey from $O$ to $P$ is travelled at a constant speed, since the string has now gone slack. The speed reached is the maximum speed $= \omega A = (8)(0.8) = 6.4$ m/s.

(The amplitude is 0.8, since that is the greatest displacement from $O$.)

The time taken $(t_2)$ is given by
$$t_2 = \frac{\text{distance}}{\text{speed}}$$
$$= \frac{1}{6.4}$$
$$= 0.15625 \text{ seconds.}$$

The total time $= t_1 + t_2$
$$= 0.19635 + 0.15625$$
$$= 0.3526 \text{ seconds: Answer}$$

### Exercise 13 D

1.  A particle of mass 1 kg rests on a smooth horizontal table which stands between two vertical walls 6 m apart. The particle is joined to each wall by means of horizontal elastic strings. Both strings have natural length 1 m and elastic constant 2 N/m. The particle is released from rest from a point 2 m from one wall.

    (i)  Show that it will perform SHM.

    (ii)  Find its periodic time.

    (iii)  Find its speed when it is midway between the walls.

2.  A particle of mass $\frac{1}{2}$ kg rests on a smooth horizontal table which stands between two walls, 10 m apart. It is attached to the walls by means of two horizontal strings – both of natural length 1 m and elastic constant 9 N/m. It is released from rest when it is 3 m from the right-hand wall.

    (i)  Show that the particle will perform SHM.

    (ii)  Find how long it will take to reach a point 4 m from the right-hand wall.

    (iii)  Find also its speed at this point.

3. A particle of mass 5 kg rests on a smooth horizontal table between two walls, 8 m apart. It is connected to the walls by means of two horizontal strings, both of natural lengths 1 m and elastic constants 20 N/m. Initially, the particle is held so that one string is just slack and then it is released from rest.

   (i)   Show that the particle will perform SHM.

   (ii)  Find its maximum speed.

   (iii) How far from the centre of oscillation will the particle be when its speed is one third of its maximum speed?

   (iv)  When will it reach this speed for the first time? (Give your answer correct to two decimal places.)

4. A particle of mass 5 kg rests on a smooth horizontal table between two vertical walls, 7 m apart. It is attached to the left-hand wall by means of an elastic string of natural length 1 m and elastic constant 12 N/m, and to the right-hand wall by means of an elastic string of natural length 1 m and elastic constant 8 N/m.

   (i)   How far from the left-hand wall is the position of equilibrium?

   (ii)  By examining the forces on the particle when it is a distance $(3 + x)$ from the left-hand wall, show that it will perform SHM.

   (iii) If the particle is released from rest midway between the walls, show that the periodic time is $\pi$ seconds and find the maximum speed.

   (iv)  Find the magnitude of the force on the particle when its velocity is $\dfrac{\sqrt{3}}{2}$ m/s.

5. A particle of mass $\dfrac{1}{6}$ kg rests on a smooth horizontal table. It is attached to two vertical walls, 20 m apart, by means of elastic strings, both of natural lengths 2 m but of elastic constants 15 N/m and 9 N/m, respectively, as shown. Show that the position of equilibrium is 8 m from the left-hand wall.

   (i)   By examining the forces on the particle when it is displaced a distance $x$ from equilibrium show that it will perform SHM.

   (ii)  If the particle was initially released from rest at a point 9 m from the left hand wall, find the maximum acceleration.

(iii) What is the speed of the particle when its acceleration is $\dfrac{3}{5}$ of its maximum acceleration?

Fig. 13.13

6. An elastic string has natural length 1 m and elastic constant 5 N/m. One end of the string is tied to a point $P$ on a smooth horizontal floor, the other to a small particle of mass 20 kg. The particle is dragged across the floor to a point $Q$, which is 2 metres from $P$ and released from rest.

   (i)   Show that the particle will perform SHM as long as the string remains taut.

   (ii)  Show that the time taken for the particle to reach $P$ is $(\pi + 2)$ seconds.

7. An elastic string has natural length 1 metre and elastic constant 8 N/m. One end of the string is tied to a point $P$ on a smooth horizontal floor, the other to a small particle of mass $\dfrac{1}{2}$ kg. The particle is dragged across the floor to a point, which is 1.5 metres from $P$, and released from rest.

   (i)   Show that the particle will perform SHM as long as the string remains taut.

   (ii)  Find the maximum speed.

   (iii) Find the time taken for the particle to travel 0.2 metres (correct to two decimal places).

8. An elastic string has natural length $a$ and elastic constant $k$ N/m. One end of the string is tied to a point $P$ on a smooth horizontal floor, the other to a small particle of mass $k$ kg. The particle is dragged across the floor to a point $Q$, which is a distance $2a$ from $P$ and released from rest.

   (i)   Show that the particle will perform SHM as long as the string remains taut.

   (ii)  Find the time taken for the particle to reach $P$.

9. A particle of mass 1 kg rests on a rough horizontal table. The coefficient of friction between the particle and the table is $\dfrac{1}{2}$. The particle is attached to a fixed point $P$ by means of a horizontal elastic string of natural length

1 m and elastic constant 7 N/m. It is released from rest at a point 3.7 m from $P$.

Fig. 13.14

(i)  Show the forces on the particle when it is a distance $(1.7 + x)$ metres from $P$.

(ii)  Show that until the string goes slack it will perform SHM and that the periodic time is $\frac{2\pi}{\sqrt{7}}$ seconds.

(iii)  Find, correct to two decimal places, the time which the particle will take to reach a point 2 m from $P$.

10. A particle $P$, of mass 5 kg, is connected by a light elastic string, of natural length 2 m and elastic constant 140 N/m to a fixed point $Q$ on a rough horizontal surface where the coefficient of friction is 1. $P$ is released from rest at a point $A$ where $|QA| = 3$ m.

(i)  By considering the forces acting on $P$ when its distance is $(2.35 + x)$ m from $Q$, prove that $P$ moves in simple harmonic motion as long as the string remains taut.

(ii)  State the position of the centre, $O$, of the simple harmonic motion, i.e. $|QO|$.

(iii)  Write down the amplitude.

(iv)  Show that the period of motion is $\frac{\pi}{\sqrt{7}}$ s.

(v)  Calculate the time taken by the particle to travel from $A$ to a point 2 m from $Q$.

## Vertical SHM

### Worked Example 13.8

A particle of mass $\frac{1}{4}$ kg hangs freely from a ceiling by means of an elastic string of natural length 2 m and elastic constant 49 N/m. It is released from rest from a point $P$ which is 2 m below the ceiling.

(i)  Show that it will perform SHM.

(ii)  Find the periodic time.

(iii)  Find also the time taken for the particle to reach a point $Q$ which is 2.08 m below the ceiling. Give the answer correct to two decimal places.

**Solution:**

(i)  The first step is to find the position of equilibrium, $O$. Let $d$ = the distance from the ceiling to $O$. The forces on the particle at this point are as follows:

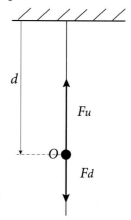

Fig. 13.15

$$F_{down} = m\,g$$
$$= \frac{1}{4}g = \frac{1}{4}9.8$$
$$= 2.45$$
$$F_{up} = k\,(l - l_o)$$
$$= 49\,(d - 2)$$

But at $O$ $F_{down} = F_{up}$

$$\therefore 2.45 = 49\,(d - 2)$$
$$\therefore 0.05 = d - 2$$
$$\therefore d = 2.05 \text{ m.}$$

The second step is to examine the forces on the particle when it is displaced a further distance $x$ beyond the equilibrium position. In this case we have these forces:

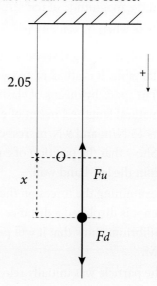

Fig. 13.16

$$F_{down} = \frac{1}{4}g$$

$$= 2.45$$

$$F_{up} = k\,(l - l_o)$$

$$= 49\,(2.05 + x - 2)$$

$$= 2.45 + 49\,x$$

Taking downwards as our "positive" direction, the resultant force

$$F_{resultant} = F_{down} - F_{up}$$

$$= 2.45 - (2.45 + 49\,x)$$

$$= -49\,x$$

$$F = -49\,x$$

$$\therefore m\,a = -49\,x$$

$$\therefore \frac{1}{4}\,a = -49\,x$$

$$\therefore a = -196\,x$$

Since the acceleration is proportional to $x$ but of the opposite sign, the particle will perform SHM about $O$.

| (ii) | $a = -196\,x$ |
|---|---|

$$\therefore \omega^2 = 196$$

$$\therefore \omega = 14$$

The periodic time $T = \dfrac{2\pi}{14}$

$$= \frac{\pi}{7} \text{ secs}$$

(iii) The amplitude is found from the initial position. How far is the initial position from the centre of oscillation? The answer is 0.05 m, since the particle was released from rest at a point 2 m from the ceiling, while the centre of oscillation $O$ is 2.05 m from the ceiling. It follows that $A = 0.05$ m.

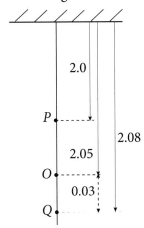

Fig. 13.17

The time for the particle to move from $P$ to $Q$ can be divided into two parts: $P$ to $O$ and $O$ to $Q$.

Firstly, $P$ to $O$: This is $\frac{1}{4}$ of a full cycle.

The time taken is $\dfrac{1}{4}\dfrac{\pi}{7} = \dfrac{\pi}{28} = \dfrac{3.142}{28} = 0.112$ secs

Next, $O$ to $Q$: We will "Start the clock" when the particle is at $O$. We will therefore use

$$x = A \sin \omega t \text{ or (in this case)}$$

$$x = 0.05 \sin 14\,t$$

But when the particle is at $Q$, $x = 0.03$

$$\therefore 0.03 = 0.05 \sin 14t$$

$$\therefore \sin 14t = 0.6$$

$$\therefore 14t = \sin^{-1} 0.6$$

$$= 0.6434$$

$$\therefore t = 0.046\ s.$$

The total time $= 0.112 + 0.046$

$$= 0.158$$

$$= 0.16\ s. \text{ (correct to two decimal places)}.$$

### Worked Example 13.9

A cylinder of radius $r$ and height $h$ has relative density $s$. It is floating in water with its axis vertical. It is then depressed vertically a further small distance into the water and released. Show that it will perform SHM and find an expression for the periodic time.

**Solution:**

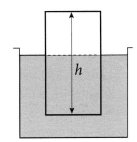

Fig. 13.18

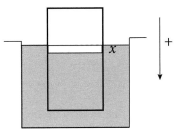

Fig. 13.19

When the cylinder floats in equilibrium, its weight $W$ must equal its buoyancy $B$. We will take downwards as the positive direction. When the cylinder is depressed downwards a further distance $x$, extra buoyancy $B'$ is called into play. This buoyancy is in an upward direction, and therefore negative, and is equal to the weight of the extra water displaced.

$$B' = -V\rho g$$

$$= -(\pi r^2 x)(1000)g$$
$$= -1000\,\pi r^2 g\,x$$

But what is the mass of the whole cylinder?

$$\text{Mass} = V\rho = (\pi r^2 h)(1000\,s)$$
$$= 1000\,\pi r^2 h\,s$$

$$\text{Now } F = m\,a$$
$$\therefore B' = m\,a$$
$$\therefore -(1000)\pi r^2 g x = (1000\,\pi r^2 hs)\,a$$
$$\therefore a = -\frac{g}{hs}x$$

Since the acceleration is proportional to $x$ and in the opposite direction, the cylinder will perform SHM.

$$a = -\omega^2 x$$
$$\therefore \omega = \sqrt{\frac{g}{hs}}$$
$$T = \frac{2\pi}{\omega}$$
$$= 2\pi\sqrt{\frac{hs}{g}}$$

The cylinder will bob up and down with SHM, completing a full cycle in $2\pi\sqrt{\dfrac{hs}{g}}$ seconds.

## Exercise 13 E

1. A string has natural length 1 m and elastic constant 98 N/m. One end is fixed to a point $P$ on a ceiling. The other end is attached to a particle of mass 2 kg, which is then released from rest 1 m vertically below $P$.
   (i) Find the position of equilibrium.
   (ii) By examining the forces on the particle when it is displaced a further distance $x$ below the position of equilibrium, show that it will perform SHM.
   (iii) Find the period of motion.
   (iv) Find the maximum speed.
   (v) How long will it take to fall a distance 0.15 metres (correct to three decimal places)?

2. A particle of mass $\frac{1}{2}$ kg hangs vertically from a point $P$ on the ceiling by means of a light elastic string of natural length 1 m and elastic constant 7 N/m. It is released from rest at a point 1.2 m below the ceiling.
   (i) Show it will perform SHM.
   (ii) Find the maximum acceleration and hence the maximum force on the particle.

   (iii) How long does it take to reach a point 2 m below $P$? Give your answer correct to two decimal places.

3. A particle of mass $m$ is suspended from a point $p$ on the ceiling by means of a light elastic string of natural length $d$ and elastic constant $\frac{49m}{d}$. It is pulled down a distance $\frac{8d}{5}$ below $P$ and released from rest.
   (i) Show it will perform SHM as long as the string remains taut.
   (ii) Find, in terms of $d$, when the string becomes slack for the first time.

4. A mass of 4 kg suspended by a light spiral spring extends the spring 8 cm when in equilibrium. A second mass of 2 kg is then attached to the first without moving it and the combined mass is then released from rest.
   (i) Prove that the motion is simple harmonic.
   (ii) Find the period of the ensuing motion.
   (iii) Find the maximum velocity of the resulting motion.

5. A cubic block of wood of side $h$ and relative density $s$ floats in water with all sides either vertical or horizontal. It is depressed a distance $x$ into the water, and released from rest.
   (i) Show that it will perform SHM and find an expression for the periodic time.
   (ii) If the water had been a liquid of relative density $k$, what would the periodic time have been?

6. A rectangular block of wood of relative density 0.6 has height 80 cm, breadth 50 cm and width 20 cm. It floats in water with its height vertical.
   (i) Show that 48 cm of its height is submerged.
   (ii) If it is depressed so that 50 cm of its height is submerged and then released from rest, show that it will perform SHM and find its maximum acceleration.

# The simple pendulum

Before studying the simple pendulum, it is worth noting that if angles are measured in radians and if $\theta$ is a small angle, then $\theta \approx \sin \theta$ (approximately equal). Here is a table which shows how close the values of $\theta$ and $\sin \theta$ are:

| Angle (degrees) | Angle (radians) | $\sin \theta$ |
|---|---|---|
| 1° | 0.0175 | 0.0175 |
| 3° | 0.0523 | 0.0524 |
| 5° | 0.0873 | 0.0872 |
| 7° | 0.1222 | 0.1219 |
| 10° | 0.1745 | 0.1736 |

Even when $\theta = 10°$ the difference between $\theta$ and $\sin \theta$ is less than 0.001.

In general, if $\theta$ is small then $\theta \approx \sin \theta$. This is sometimes written in this way:

$$\lim_{\theta \to 0} \frac{\sin \theta}{\theta} = 1$$

The simple pendulum consists of a particle of mass $m$ attached to a weightless inelastic string of length $l$. We will show that if it is allowed to swing with small oscillations in a vertical plane, then it will perform simple harmonic motion. We will also show that the periodic time $T$ is given by

$$T = 2\pi\sqrt{\frac{l}{g}}.$$

Consider the particle when the string makes an angle $\theta$ (which must be small) with the vertical. Let $x$ = the length of the arc through which the particle has travelled since the string was last vertical. We will take motion to the right as "positive". It follows that $x = r\theta$ or, in this case, $x = l\theta \Rightarrow \theta = \frac{x}{l}$.

Here are the forces acting on the particle:

Forces:

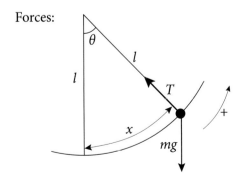

Fig. 13.20

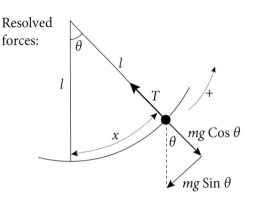

Resolved forces:

Fig. 13.21

It is clear that the force acting on the particle along its line of motion is $-mg \sin \theta$ (why is it negative?)

$$\therefore F = -mg \sin \theta$$
$$\therefore F = -mg \theta$$

(since $\theta = \sin \theta$ if $\theta$ is small)

But $F = ma$ and $\theta = \frac{x}{l}$

$$\therefore ma = -mg\left(\frac{x}{l}\right)$$
$$\therefore a = -\frac{g}{l}x \text{ (where } g \text{ and } l \text{ are constants)}$$

So, the pendulum performs simple harmonic motion with $\omega = \sqrt{\frac{g}{l}}$.

The periodic time $T = \frac{2\pi}{\omega}$

$$= 2\pi\sqrt{\frac{l}{g}} \qquad \text{Q.E.D.}$$

---

### Worked Example 13.10

(i) A **seconds pendulum** completes a full oscillation every two seconds. Find its length correct to three decimal places.

(ii) If the pendulum were brought to the moon — where the gravitational acceleration is $\frac{1}{6}g$ — find its periodic time there, correct to one decimal place.

**Solution:**

(i)
$$T = 2\pi\sqrt{\frac{l}{g}}$$
$$\therefore T^2 = \frac{4\pi^2 l}{g}$$
$$\therefore (2)^2 = \frac{4\pi^2 l}{9.8}$$
$$\therefore l = \frac{9.8}{\pi^2}$$
$$= \frac{9.8}{9.8722}$$
$$= 0.993 \text{ metres. Answer.}$$

(ii)
$$l = 0.993,$$
$$\text{"}g\text{"} = \frac{1}{6}g = \frac{9.8}{6} = 1.633$$

$$T = 2\pi \sqrt{\frac{l}{g}}$$

$$= 2\,(3.142)\sqrt{\frac{0.993}{1.633}}$$

$$= 4.9 \text{ s. Answer.}$$

## Exercise 13 F

1. A simple pendulum consists of a particle attached to one end of a light inelastic string of length 50 cm, the other end being fixed. Find the periodic time.

2. A simple pendulum consists of a particle attached to one end of a light inelastic string, the other end being fixed. The periodic time is 3 s. Find the length of the string.

3. A simple pendulum consists of a particle attached to one end of a light inelastic string of length 4 m, the other end being fixed. Find the periodic time.

4. A simple pendulum consists of a particle attached to one end of a light inelastic string, the other end being fixed. The periodic time is 5.5 s. Find the length of the string to the nearest centimetre.

5. The periodic times of two simple pendula are in the ratio 2:1. Find the ratio of their lengths.

6. The lengths of two simple pendula are in the ratio 4:9. Find the ratio of their periodic times.

7. If a grandfather clock were moved to the moon, would it go fast or slow? Justify your answer.

8. A simple pendulum has period 1 second. How many times will it oscillate in a day? If the pendulum is lengthened by 2%, find how many times fewer will it oscillate in a day.

9. A seconds pendulum performs 30 complete oscillations per minute. It is shortened so that it performs 31 complete oscillations per minute. Calculate the percentage reduction in its length.

10. If a simple pendulum's length is doubled, find the percentage increase in its periodic time to the nearest integer.

11. Acceleration due to gravity on the moon is $\frac{1}{6}$ of that on the earth. A pendulum on the earth and one on the moon have lengths in the ratio 8:3. Find the ratio of their periodic times.

12. (i) A simple pendulum has length $k$. Prove that it will perform simple harmonic motion and that the periodic time $T$ is given by $2\pi \sqrt{\frac{k}{g}}$.

(ii) Deduce that $g = \frac{4\pi^2 k}{T^2}$.

(iii) A student wishes to measure $g$. She makes a simple pendulum of length 0.6 m and finds that it oscillates 39 times in one minute. Find the value of $g$ which this experiment yields (correct to one decimal place), using the formula in part (ii).

(iv) Find the percentage error in this experimental result to the nearest whole number.

# Summary of important points

1. Hooke's Law: $F = k\,(l - l_o)$
2. $a = -\omega^2 x$
3. $v^2 = \omega^2\,(A^2 - x^2)$
4. $v_{max} = \omega A$
5. $a_{max} = \omega^2 A$
6. Periodic time, $T = \frac{2\pi}{\omega}$
7. $x = A \sin \omega t$ (Starting at the centre).
   $x = A \cos \omega t$ (starting at the extreme position)
   $x = A \sin(\omega t + \varepsilon)$ or
   $x = A \cos(\omega t + \varepsilon)$ in all other cases.
8. Simple pendulum: $T = 2\pi\sqrt{\frac{l}{g}}$

## DOs and DON'Ts for the exam

### DO
- Know (in English) the definition of SHM
- Do use the RADIAN mode for your calculator when doing trigonometrical calculations
- Do remember that $x$ represents the displacement from the centre, not the distance travelled
- In questions with elastic strings, find the position of equilibrium ($O$) and then let $x$ be the displacement from $O$.

### DON'T
- Don't use the initial forces (in questions about elastic strings) to derive the equation of motion. The initial position is the key to finding the amplitude.
- Don't forget that the amplitude of $a \cos \omega t + b \sin \omega t$ is $\sqrt{a^2 + b^2}$

# Rigid body rotation

## Chapter 14

"The world is round and the place which may seem like the end may also be only the beginning."

*Ivy Baker Priest*

## Contents

## Learning outcomes

**In this chapter you will learn...**

- How to calculate the potential energy and kinetic energy of a rotating body

- The definition of moment of inertia

- How to prove the formulae for the moment of inertia of rods, rectangles, discs and annuli

- How to use the Principle of Conservation of Energy to solve problems of rotating rigid bodies

- The periodic time of the compound pendulum

- How to find the minimum periodic time of a compound pendulum

## You will need to know...

- How to integrate $x^n$
- How to find the minimum value of a function using calculus

**Greek notation**: the meaning of $\Delta$ and $\Sigma$.
The Greek letter $\Delta$ (**delta**) is used to mean "a small piece of". For example $\Delta x$ means a small piece of the $x$-axis, $\Delta m$ a small piece of mass, $\Delta A$ a small area. Another Greek capital letter, $\Sigma$ (**sigma**) is used to mean "the sum of". For example, if we divide a body into small pieces of mass $\Delta m$, then $\Sigma \, \Delta m$ would mean "the sum of all the small masses", i.e. the mass of the whole body.

Fig. 14.1

Here is another example: Take a **lamina** (a body which has area but not volume, like a thin piece of cardboard). We divide the lamina into small pieces of area $\Delta A$. In this case, $\Sigma \, \Delta A$ would mean "the sum of all the small areas", i.e. the area of the entire lamina.

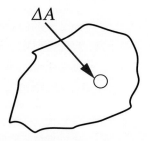

Fig. 14.2

## Moment of inertia

We have already seen that, if no forces other than gravitational forces act on a body, then the sum of the potential energy (PE) and the kinetic energy (KE) remains a constant. Mathematically, we write:
$PE + KE = m \, g \, h + \frac{1}{2} m \, v^2 = $ constant.
But if a rigid body is rotating with constant angular speed $\omega$ rad/s about some axis, how can we measure its potential and kinetic energy?

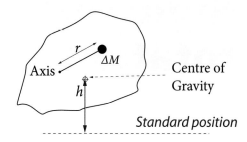

Fig. 14.3

Firstly, the potential energy $PE = mg\bar{h}$, where $m$ is the mass of the body and $\bar{h}$ = the height of the centre of gravity of the body above some standard position. Secondly, the kinetic energy (KE) of the rotating body is the sum of the KE of each small piece of mass ($\Delta m$) in the body:

$$KE = \sum \frac{1}{2} \Delta m \, v^2$$
$$\therefore KE = \sum \frac{1}{2} \Delta m \, (\omega \, r)^2$$

(since $v = \omega \, r$, where $r$ is the radius of each piece's circle of motion about the axis of rotation).

$$\therefore KE = \sum \frac{1}{2} \Delta \, m \, \omega^2 \, r^2$$
$$\therefore KE = \frac{1}{2} \omega^2 \sum \Delta m \, r^2$$

(since $\frac{1}{2}$ and $\omega^2$ are the same for each piece).
Now $\sum \Delta m \, r^2$ is defined as the moment of inertia of the body about this particular axis. It is depicted by the letter $I$.

$$\text{Hence } KE = \frac{1}{2} I \, \omega^2 \text{ where } I = \sum \Delta m \, r^2.$$

The **Principle of Conservation of Energy** for a rotating body reads:

$$PE + KE = mg\bar{h} + \frac{1}{2} I \, \omega^2 = \text{constant}$$

The definition $I = \sum \Delta m \, r^2$ shows that the moment of inertia of a body about a fixed axis depends not only on the mass of the body but also on how that mass is distributed.

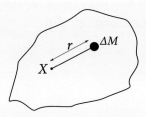

Fig. 14.4

If mass is a measure of a body's "difficultness to move" then moment of inertia is a measure of a body's "difficultness to turn".

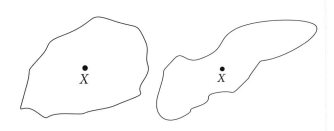

Fig. 14.5          Fig. 14.6

Two bodies might have equal masses but the second might require more turning force to rotate it about an axis than the first because of the way the mass is distributed. The further the mass is from the axis, the greater the turning force required to rotate it about the axis.

## Moments of inertia of regular bodies

We will now establish and prove formulae for the moment of inertia of certain regular bodies, such as a rod, a rectangular lamina and a disc. We use integration to find the sum of the near-infinite number of $\Delta m \, r^2$.

### Theorem 14.1:

The moment of inertia of a uniform rod of mass $m$ and length $2\,l$ about an axis through its midpoint, perpendicular to its length, is $\frac{1}{3}\,m\,l^2$.

**Proof**: Let $C$ be the midpoint of the rod. The rod has length but not area or volume. It is like a line segment. We will define $\rho$ as the mass per unit length.

$$\rho = \frac{\text{mass}}{\text{length}}$$

$$\therefore \text{ mass (of rod)} = \rho \times \text{length}$$

$$\therefore m = \rho\,(2l)$$

$$= 2\,\rho\,l.$$

We now break up the rod into infinitesimally small pieces, each of length $\Delta x$, where $x$ is the distance between this piece of mass and $C$.

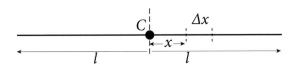

Fig. 14.7

What is the mass $(\Delta m)$ of each piece?

$$\text{Mass} = \rho\,(\text{length})$$

$$\therefore \Delta m = \rho\,\Delta x$$

$$\text{Now } I = \sum \Delta m \, r^2$$

$$= \sum \rho \, \Delta x \, x^2$$

$$= \sum \rho \, x^2 \, \Delta x$$

Summations in a continuum are, in fact, integrals. The "$\Delta x$" of the summation becomes the "d$x$" of integration. The $\sum$ becomes $\int$ .
The limits of the integration are determined by the limits on the variable $x$. A glance at the diagram shows that $x$ can vary from a maximum value of $+\,l$ to a minimum value of $-\,l$.

$$I = \sum \rho \, x^2 \, \Delta x$$

$$= \int_{-e}^{e} \rho \, x^2 \, \mathrm{d}x$$

$$= \rho \, \frac{x^3}{3} \, \Big|_{-e}^{e}$$

$$= \left[ \rho \, \frac{l^3}{3} \right] - \left[ -\rho \, \frac{l^3}{3} \right]$$

$$= 2\,\rho \, \frac{l^3}{3}$$

$$= 2\,\rho \, l \, \frac{l^2}{3}$$

But          $m = 2\,\rho l$

$$\therefore I = m \, \frac{l^2}{3}$$

$$= \frac{1}{3}\,m\,l^2 \qquad \text{Q.E.D.}$$

### Theorem 14.2:

The moment of inertia of a uniform rectangular lamina of mass $m$, length $2l$, and width $2k$ about an axis which bisects its length, is $\frac{1}{3}\,m\,l^2$.

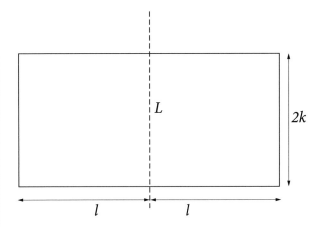

Fig. 14.8

Proof: Let $L$ be the axis which bisects the length. The lamina has area but not volume. We will define $\rho$ as the mass per unit area.

$$\rho = \frac{\text{mass}}{\text{area}}$$

$$\therefore \text{ mass} = \rho \times \text{area}$$

$$\therefore m = \rho\,(2\,l)\,(2\,k) = 4\,l\,k\,\rho$$

We now break up the rectangular lamina into

237

infinitesimally small strips, parallel to $L$, each of length $2k$ and of width $\Delta x$, where $x$ is the distance between the strip and $L$.

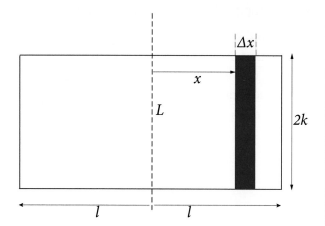

Fig. 14.9

The mass $(\Delta m)$ of each strip is given by

$$\Delta m = \rho \,(\text{area})$$
$$= \rho \,(2\,k)\,(\Delta x)$$
$$= 2\,k\,\rho\,\Delta x$$
$$\text{Now } I = \sum \Delta m\, r^2$$
$$= \sum (2\,k\,\rho\,\Delta x)\,x^2$$
$$= \sum 2\,k\,\rho\, x^2\,\Delta x$$

This sum in a continuum becomes an integral. The limits of the integration are determined by the limits on the variable $x$. A glance at the diagram shows that $x$ can vary from a maximum value of $+\,l$ to a minimum value of $-\,l$.

$$I = \sum 2\,k\,\rho\, x^2\,\Delta x$$
$$= \int_{-l}^{l} 2\,k\,\rho\, x^2\,\mathrm{d}x$$
$$= 2\,k\,\rho\, \frac{x^3}{3}\bigg|_{+l}^{-l}$$
$$= \left[2\,k\,\rho\, \frac{l^3}{3}\right] - \left[-2\,k\,\rho\, \frac{l^3}{3}\right]$$
$$= \frac{4\,k\,\rho\, l^3}{3}$$
$$= \frac{(4\,l\,k\,\rho)\,l^2}{3}$$

But $\qquad m = 4\,l\,k\,\rho$

$$\therefore I = m\, \frac{l^2}{3}$$
$$= \frac{1}{3}\,m\, l^2 \qquad \text{Q.E.D.}$$

## Theorem 14.3:

The moment of inertia of a uniform circular disc of mass $m$ and radius $r$ about an axis through its centre perpendicular to the plane of the disc is $\frac{1}{2}\,m\, r^2$.

Proof: Let $c$ be the centre of the disc. The lamina has area but not volume. We will define $\rho$ as the mass per unit area.

$$\rho = \frac{\text{mass}}{\text{area}}$$
$$\therefore \text{mass} = \rho\,(\text{area})$$
$$\therefore m = \rho\,\pi\, r^2.$$

We now break up the rod into infinitesimally thin hoops (or annuli), centre $c$, each of width $\Delta x$, where $x$ is the radius of the hoop (or annulus).

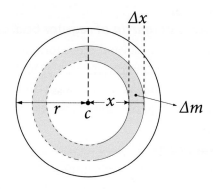

Fig. 14.10

If a hoop were cut out by a scissors and opened out, it would have length $2\,\pi\, x$ and width $\Delta x$. Its area, therefore, would be $2\,\pi\, x\,\Delta x$.

The mass $(\Delta m)$ of each strip is given by

$$\Delta m = \rho\,(\text{area})$$
$$= \rho\, 2\,\pi\, x\,\Delta x$$
$$= 2\,\pi\,\rho\, x\,\Delta x$$
$$\text{Now } I = \sum \Delta m\, r^2$$
$$= \sum (2\,\pi\,\rho\, x\,\Delta x)\,x^2$$
$$= \sum 2\,\pi\,\rho\, x^3\,\Delta x$$

This sum becomes an integral. The limits of the integration are determined by the limits on the variable $x$: the range of values of $x$ is from 0 to $r$.

$$\therefore I = \sum 2\,\pi\,\rho\, x^3\,\Delta x$$
$$= \int_{0}^{r} 2\,\pi\,\rho\, x^3\,\mathrm{d}x$$
$$= 2\,\pi\,\rho\, \frac{x^4}{4}\bigg|_{0}^{r}$$
$$= \left[\frac{1}{2}\,\pi\,\rho\, r^4\right] - [0]$$
$$= \frac{1}{2}\,\pi\,\rho\, r^4$$

$$= \frac{1}{2} \left( \pi \rho \, r^2 \right) r^2$$

But $m = \pi \rho \, r^2$.

$$\therefore I = \frac{1}{2} m r^2 \qquad \text{Q.E.D.}$$

**Theorem 14.4:**

The moment of inertia of a point mass $m$, rotating about an axis in such a way that the distance between the point mass and the axis is a constant $r$, is $m r^2$.

Proof:
$$I = \sum \Delta m \, r^2$$
$$= r^2 \sum \Delta m$$
$$= r^2 \, m$$
$$= m \, r^2$$

(since $r$ is a constant throughout).

## *Radius of gyration*

**Definition:** If the entire mass of a body is imagined to be concentrated as a point mass at a fixed distance $k$ from its axis of rotation such that the point mass has the same moment of inertia as the body, then $k$ is called the **radius of gyration** of the body about that axis.

Mathematically, $I = m k^2$

$$\therefore k = \sqrt{\frac{I}{m}}.$$

For example, the radius of gyration of a uniform rod of length $2\,l$ about an axis through its centre perpendicular to its length is given by

$$k = \sqrt{\frac{I}{m}}$$
$$= \sqrt{\frac{\frac{1}{3} m l^2}{m}}$$
$$= \sqrt{\frac{1}{3} l^2}$$
$$= \sqrt{\frac{1}{3}} \, l$$

This means that a point mass $m$ at a distance $\sqrt{\frac{1}{3}}\, l$ from the axis would have the same moment of inertia about the axis as the rod.

---

**Exercise 14 A**

1.  (i)  Prove that the moment of inertia of a uniform rod of mass $m$ and length $2l$ about an axis through an endpoint, perpendicular to its length, is $\frac{4}{3} m l^2$

    (ii)  What is its radius of gyration?

---

2.  (i)  Prove that the moment of inertia of a uniform square of mass $m$ and side $d$ about an axis through its centre, parallel to a side, is $\frac{1}{12} m d^2$.

    (ii)  What is its radius of gyration?

3.  A uniform annulus consists of a disc of radius 3 metres with a disc of radius 1 metre removed from its centre. The mass of the annulus is $m$. Prove that the moment of inertia of the annulus about an axis through its centre, perpendicular to its plane is $5m$.

Fig. 14.11

4.  A uniform rod has length $6l$ and mass $m$. An axis is fixed a distance $l$ from one end, perpendicular to the length of the rod. Find the moment of inertia of the rod about this axis.

5.  A uniform rectangular lamina has length $2l$ and width $2k$. Its mass is $3m$.

    (i)  Prove that the moment of inertia about an axis along the side of length $k$ is $4\,ml^2$.

    (ii)  Show that the radius of gyration is $2\,l$.

6.  A uniform annulus consists of a disc of radius $R$ with a disc of radius $r$ removed from its centre. The mass of the annulus is $m$. Prove that the moment of inertia of the annulus about an axis through its centre, perpendicular to its plane is $\frac{1}{2} m(R^2 + r^2)$

7.  Prove that the moment of inertia of a uniform annulus of internal diameter $y$ and external diameter $7y$ and mass $8m$ about an axis through its centre perpendicular its plane is $50\,my^2$.

8.  Prove that the moment of inertia of a uniform square of mass $3m$ and side $2p$ about an axis through its centre, parallel to a side, is $mp^2$.

**Theorem 14.5: The Perpendicular Axes Theorem**

If $I_X$ and $I_Y$ are the moments of inertia of a lamina about two perpendicular axes $X$ and $Y$ (respectively) in the plane of the lamina which intersect at $o$, then the moment of inertia $I_Z$ of the lamina about the axis $Z$, through $o$, perpendicular to the plane of the lamina is given by $I_Z = I_X + I_Y$.

**Proof:**

Let $x$, $y$ and $z$ be the distances of a small piece of mass $\Delta m$ about the axes $X$, $Y$ and $Z$, respectively.

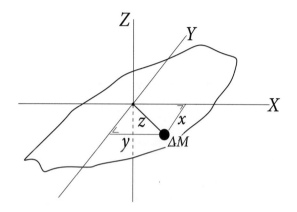

Fig. 14.12

By Pythagoras' Theorem, $z^2 = x^2 + y^2$.

$$I = \sum \Delta m \, z^2$$
$$= \sum \Delta m \left(x^2 + y^2\right)$$
$$= \sum \Delta m \, x^2 + \sum \Delta m \, y^2$$
$$= I_X + I_Y \qquad \text{Q.E.D.}$$

**Theorem 14.6: The Parallel Axes Theorem**

If $I_c$ is the moment of inertia of a body of mass $m$ about an axis $c$ through its centre of gravity, then the moment of inertia of the body about an axis $l$, parallel to $c$, is given by $I_l = I_c + md^2$, where $d$ is the distance between the axes $l$ and $c$.

**Proof:**

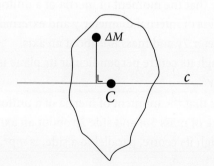

Fig. 14.13

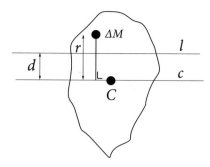

Fig. 14.14

It is worth noting, before starting the theorem proper, that if the variable $r$ represents the distance between each piece of mass $\Delta m$ and the axis $c$, then $I = \sum r \, \Delta m = 0$. This is because, by the very definition of centre of gravity, the sum of all the moments of the gravitational forces on the parts of the body about $c$ is zero. The moments on one side of $c$ balance out with those on the other side – that is what makes the centre of gravity what it is.

Take a piece of mass $\Delta m$ and let $r$ be its distance from the axis $c$. Its distance from $l$ is, therefore, $(r - d)$.

$$I_l = \sum \Delta m \, (r - d)^2$$
$$= \sum \Delta m \left(r^2 - 2\,rd + d^2\right)$$
$$= \sum \Delta m \, r^2 - \sum \Delta m \, (2rd) + \sum \Delta m \, d^2$$
$$= \sum \Delta m \, r^2 - 2d \sum r \, \Delta m + d^2 \sum \Delta m$$
$$\text{(since } d \text{ is a constant)}$$
$$= I_c - 2d\,(0) + d^2\,(m)$$
$$= I_c + md^2 \qquad \text{Q.E.D.}$$

---

### Worked Example 14.1

(i) A uniform rod $[PQ]$ has length $2l$ and mass $m$. The end $Q$ is attached to the circumference of a disc of mass $m$ and radius $l$, so that the rod is along the line of the diameter of the disc. Find the moment of inertia of this system about an axis through $P$ perpendicular to the plane of the disc.

(ii) This system is free to rotate about a horizontal axis at $P$, perpendicular to the plane of the disc. It is released from rest when the rod is horizontal. Find its angular speed, $\omega$, when the rod is vertical.

**Solution:**

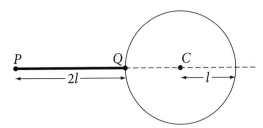

Fig. 14.15

(i) Let $p$ be the axis through $P$, perpendicular to the plane of the disc.

The rod: According to *Formulae & Tables* (page 53), $\quad I_p = \frac{4}{3}m l^2$.

The disc: Let $c$ be the axis through the centre of the disc, parallel to $p$.

$$I_c = \frac{1}{2}m l^2 \text{ (Theorem 14.3)}$$

In accordance with the Parallel Axes Theorem,

$$I_p = I_c + m d^2,$$

where $d$ is the distance between the axes $c$ and $p$.

$$I_p = I_c + m d^2$$
$$= \frac{1}{2}m l^2 + m(3l)^2$$
$$= \frac{1}{2}m l^2 + 9 m l^2$$
$$= \frac{19}{2}m l^2.$$

The system $I_{system} = I_{rod} + I_{disc}$
$$= \frac{4}{3}m l^2 + \frac{19}{2}m l^2$$
$$= \frac{65}{6}m l^2$$

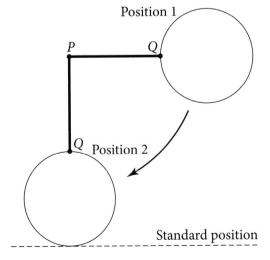

Fig. 14.16

(ii) This part of the question is solved using the new energy equation:

$$m g \bar{h}_1 + \frac{1}{2}I\omega_1{}^2 = m g \bar{h}_2 + \frac{1}{2}I\omega_2{}^2$$

Usually, we treat the potential energies of the different parts separately, but the kinetic energy of the entire system together. In this case:

$$mg\bar{h}_{1(rod)} + mg\bar{h}_{1(disc)} + \frac{1}{2}I\omega_1{}^2 (system) =$$
$$mg\bar{h}_{2(rod)} + mg\bar{h}_{2(disc)} + \frac{1}{2}I\omega_2{}^2 (system)$$

$$mg(4l) + mg(4l) + \frac{1}{2}I(0)^2 =$$
$$mg(3l) + mg(l) + \frac{1}{2}\left(\frac{65}{6}m l^2\right)\omega^2$$

$$\therefore 8 mgl = 4 mgl + \frac{65}{12}m l^2\omega^2$$
$$\therefore 4 mgl = \frac{65}{12}m l^2 \omega^2$$
$$\therefore 4 g = \frac{65}{12}l \omega^2$$
$$\therefore \omega^2 = \frac{48 g}{65}$$
$$\therefore \omega = \sqrt{\frac{48 g}{65 l}} \quad : \text{Answer}$$

**Worked Example 14.2**

(a) The diagram shows a uniform rectangular lamina of mass $m$, measuring $6l$ by $2l$. The centre of gravity of the rectangle is at $C$. Find the moment of inertia of the lamina about

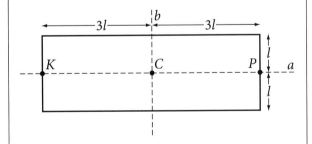

Fig. 14.17

(i) the axis $a$ in the plane of the lamina
(ii) the axis $b$ in the plane of the lamina
(iii) the axis $c$ through $C$ perpendicular to the plane of the lamina
(iv) the axis $k$ through $K$ perpendicular to the plane of the lamina.

(b) A point mass $2m$ is fixed to the point $P$. This system is free to rotate about a horizontal axis through $K$, perpendicular to the plane of the lamina. The system is released from rest when $P$ is vertically above $K$. Find the angular speed and the speed of the point mass when $P$ is vertically below $K$.

**Solution:**

(a)

(i) Theorem 14.3 states that the moment of inertia of a rectangular lamina of mass $m$ about a line $L$ in the plane of the lamina, bisecting one side is $\frac{1}{3} m l^2$, where $l$ = half the length that is bisected by $L$.

Hence $I_A = \frac{1}{3} m (3 l)^2 = 3 m l^2$

(ii) Similarly, $I_B = \frac{1}{3} m (l)^2 = \frac{1}{3} m l^2$

(iii) In accordance with the Perpendicular Axes Theorem,

$$I_C = I_A + I_B$$
$$= 3 m l^2 + \frac{1}{3} m l^2$$
$$= \frac{10}{3} m l^2$$

(iv) In accordance with the Parallel Axes Theorem,

$$I_k = I_c + m d^2$$
$$= \frac{10}{3} m l^2 + m (3 l)^2$$
$$= \frac{10}{3} m l^2 + 9 m l^2$$
$$= \frac{37}{3} m l^2$$

(b) **Point mass:** The moment of inertia of the point mass about $k$ is given by

$$I_P = m r^2$$
$$= (2m) (6 l)^2$$
$$= 72 m l^2$$

System:

$$I_{system} = I_{lamina} + I_{point\ mass}$$
$$= \frac{37}{3} m l^2 + 72 m l^2$$
$$= \frac{253}{3} m l^2$$

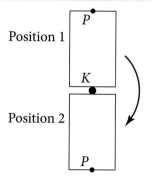

**Fig. 14.18**

$$m g \overline{h}_1 + m g \overline{h}_1 + \frac{1}{2} I \omega_1^2$$
$$= m g \overline{h}_2 + m g \overline{h}_2 + \frac{1}{2} I \omega_2^2$$

The energy equation in this case is:

$$\underset{point\ mass}{m g \overline{h}_1} + \underset{lamina}{m g \overline{h}_1} + \underset{system}{\frac{1}{2} I \omega_1^2} =$$
$$\underset{point\ mass}{m g \overline{h}_2} + \underset{lamina}{m g \overline{h}_2} + \underset{system}{\frac{1}{2} I \omega_2^2}$$

$$\therefore (2m) g (12 l) + m g (9 l) + \frac{1}{2} I (0)^2$$
$$= (2m) g (0) + m g (3 l) + \frac{1}{2} \left( \frac{253}{3} m l^2 \right) \omega^2$$

$$\therefore 24\ mgl + 9\ mgl + 0 = 0 + 3 mgl + \frac{253}{6} m l^2 \omega^2$$

$$\therefore 30\ mgl = \frac{253}{6} m l^2 \omega^2$$

$$\therefore 180\ g = 253\ l \omega^2$$

$$\therefore \omega = \sqrt{\frac{180 g}{253\ l}}$$

= the angular speed

The speed of the point mass is given by

$$v = \omega r$$
$$= \sqrt{\frac{180\ g}{253\ l}} (6\ l)$$
$$= 6 \sqrt{\frac{180\ g\ l}{253}}$$

**Exercise 14 B**

1. A rod has length $6 l$ and mass $m$. Find its moment of inertia about an axis perpendicular to its length

   (i) through its midpoint

   (ii) through one end

   (iii) through a point which is $l$ from one end

2.

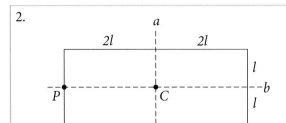

Fig. 14.19

(a) This rectangular lamina has mass $m$. Find its moment of inertia about

    (i) the axis $a$ in the plane of the lamina

    (ii) the axis $b$ in the plane of the lamina

    (iii) the axis through $c$ perpendicular to the plane of the lamina, through $C$

    (iv) the axis through $P$ perpendicular to the plane of the lamina.

(b) If a point mass $3m$ is attached to the lamina at $C$, which of (i), (ii), (iii), and (iv) are increased and by how much?

3. Find the moment of inertia of each of the following compound bodies about an axis through the point marked $X$, perpendicular to the plane of the body:

(i)

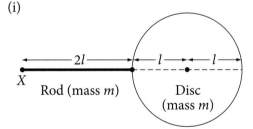

(ii)

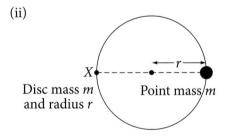

(iii)

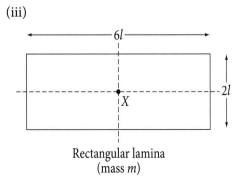

Rectangular lamina (mass $m$)

(iv)

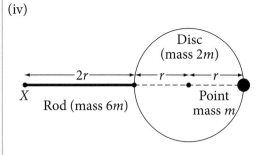

(v)

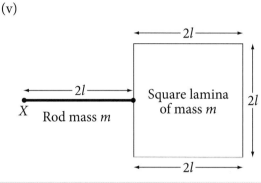

4. A rod $[PQ]$ has length $4l$ and mass $m$. A disc of radius $l$ and mass $2m$ is attached to the rod at $Q$, so that $PQ$ is continuous with a diameter of the disc. Find the moment of inertia of the compound body about an axis through $P$ perpendicular to the plane of the disc.

5. $A$ and $B$ are perpendicular diameters of a disc of mass $m$. $A$ and $B$ intersect at the centre $C$.

(i) If $c$ is an axis through $C$, perpendicular to the plane of the disc, say why $I_C = I_A + I_B$.

(ii) Hence show that the moment of inertia of a disc of radius $r$ and mass $m$ about a diameter is $\frac{1}{4} m r^2$.

6. A uniform rod $[PQ]$ has length $2l$ and mass $m$. It is free to rotate about a horizontal axis through $P$, perpendicular to its length. It is released from rest when $PQ$ is horizontal. Find its angular speed when $PQ$ is vertical.

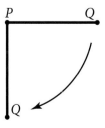

Fig. 14.20

7. (i) A uniform rod [PQ] has length $4l$ and mass $m$. The point $Q$ is attached to the circumference of a disc of mass $m$ and radius $l$, in such a way that $P$ and $Q$ are collinear with the centre of the disc and the two pieces do not overlap. Find the moment of inertia of the system about an axis through $P$ perpendicular to the plane of the disc.

   (ii) This system is free to rotate about a horizontal axis through $P$, perpendicular to its length. It is released from rest when $Q$ is vertically above $P$. Find its angular speed when $Q$ is vertically below the point $P$.

8.

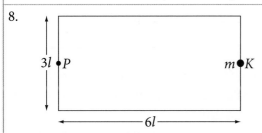

Fig. 14.21

   The diagram shows a rectangular lamina of mass $m$, length $6l$ and width $3l$. A point mass $m$ is attached at $K$, the midpoint of one side. The system is free to rotate about a horizontal axis through $P$ (another side's midpoint) perpendicular to the plane of the lamina. The system is released from rest when [PK] is horizontal. Find the speed of the point mass when [PK] is vertical.

9. A thin rod [XY] of length $2l$ and mass $3m$ has a point mass $m$ attached to the endpoint $Y$. The compound body is free to rotate about a horizontal axis through $X$, perpendicular to $XY$. Initially, the system is projected with angular speed $\sqrt{\dfrac{g}{l}}$ from a position where $Y$ is vertically above $X$. Find the angular speed when the system is next vertical.

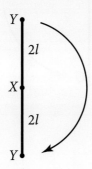

Fig. 14.22

10. (i) A uniform rod [PQ] has length $6l$ and mass $m$. The point $Q$ is attached to the midpoint of the side of a uniform rectangular lamina of mass $3m$, length $4l$ and width $2l$, in such a way that $P$ and $Q$ are collinear with the centre of the rectangle and the two pieces do not overlap. Find the moment of inertia of the system about an axis through $P$ perpendicular to the plane of the disc.

   (ii) This system is free to rotate about a horizontal axis through $P$, perpendicular to its length. It is released from rest when $Q$ is vertically above $P$. Find its maximum angular speed subsequently.

## Problems where there is both linear motion and rotation

In some problems, there will be objects moving in a straight line (whose kinetic energy is $\frac{1}{2}mv^2$) and objects rotating (whose kinetic energy is $\frac{1}{2}I\omega^2$). The connection between the variables $v$ and $\omega$ is determined by the equation $v = \omega r$.

### Worked Example 14.4

A fixed pulley is a disc of mass $m$ and radius $r$ which is free to rotate without friction about an axis through its centre, perpendicular to its plane. One end of a light inextensible string is attached to a point on the rim of the disc. The string is then wound around the rim of the disc and a particle of mass $3m$ hangs freely from the other end. The system is released from rest. Find the linear acceleration of the $3m$ mass and the tension in the string.

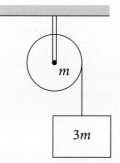

Fig. 14.23

**Solution:**

Let us find the speed of the $3m$ mass after it has fallen a distance $s$.

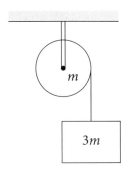

Fig. 14.23

**Solution:**

Let us find the speed of the $3m$ mass after it has fallen a distance $s$.

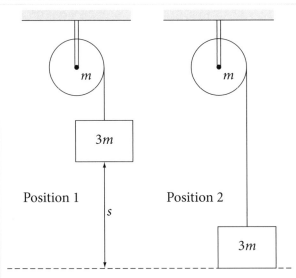

Fig. 14.24

The potential energy in position 1 is transformed into two kinds of kinetic energy in position 2 : the linear motion of the $3m$ mass and the rotation of the disc. Let $v$ be the speed of the $3m$ mass in position 2 and let $\omega$ be the angular speed of the disc at this point. The disc is rotating about its centre, so that its moment of inertia is given by $I = \frac{1}{2} m r^2$.

The energy equation is:

$$m g \overline{h}_{1(mass)} + m g v_{1(mass)} + \frac{1}{2} I \omega_1{}^2 (disc)$$
$$= m g \overline{h}_{2(mass)} + m g v_{2(mass)} + \frac{1}{2} I \omega_2{}^2 (disc)$$

$$\therefore (3m)gs + \frac{1}{2}(3m)(0)^2 + \frac{1}{2} I (0)^2 =$$
$$mg(0) + \frac{1}{2}(3m) v^2 + \frac{1}{2}\left(\frac{1}{2} m r^2\right)\omega^2$$

$$\therefore 3 mgs = \frac{3}{2} m v^2 + \frac{1}{4} m r^2 \omega^2$$

But
$$v = \omega r$$
$$\therefore v^2 = r^2 \omega^2$$

$$\therefore 3 mgs = \frac{3}{2} m v^2 + \frac{1}{4} m v^2$$

$$\therefore 3 mgs = \frac{7}{4} m v^2$$

$$\therefore 12 gs = 7 v^2$$

$$\therefore v = \sqrt{\frac{12 g s}{7}}$$

To find the acceleration, we use the equation
$$v^2 = u^2 + 2 a s.$$
$$\therefore \frac{12}{7} g s = (0)^2 + 2 a s$$
$$\therefore a = \frac{6}{7} g : \text{Answer}$$

To find the tension in the string we use the formula $F = ma$ on the $3m$ mass.

$$F = ma$$
$$\therefore 3 m g - T = (3 m)\left(\frac{6}{7}g\right)$$
$$\therefore 3 m g - T = \frac{18}{7} m g$$
$$\therefore T = \frac{3}{7} m g : \text{Answer}$$

## Exercise 14 C

1. A disc of mass $m$ and radius $r$ rolls down a slope of incline 30°. The slope is rough enough to prevent slipping. The disc travels from rest a distance 120 metres down the slope.
   (i) Show that the final linear velocity of the disc is 28 m/s.
   (ii) Find the time taken to travel 120 m.

2. A disc of mass $m$ and radius $r$ rolls down a slope of incline $\tan^{-1}\frac{3}{4}$. The slope is rough enough to prevent slipping. The disc travels from rest a distance $s$ metres straight down the slope.
   (i) Show that the linear acceleration of the disc is $\frac{2}{5} g$.
   (ii) Show that if the disc is on the point of slipping then the coefficient of friction between the disc and the slope is $\frac{1}{4}$.

3. A fixed pulley is a disc of mass $m$ and radius $r$ which is free to rotate without friction about an axis through its centre, perpendicular to its plane. One end of a light inextensible string is attached to a point on the rim of the disc. The string is then wound around the rim of the disc and a particle of mass $2m$ hangs freely from the other end. The system is released from rest. Find the acceleration of the $2m$ mass and the tension in the string.

4. A disc of mass $m$ and radius $r$ has a light inextensible string wound around its circumference. One end of the string is attached to a ceiling, so that the disc falls freely under gravity. The plane of the disc and the string remain vertical, as the disc falls vertically from rest. The disc falls a distance $s$. Show that

   (i) the linear speed of the disc reaches $\sqrt{\frac{4}{3} gs}$.

   (ii) the linear acceleration of the disc is $\frac{2}{3} g$.

   (iii) the tension in the string is $\frac{1}{3} mg$.

5. A disc of radius 2 metres has a circular hole of radius 1 metre removed from its centre, to form an annulus of mass $m$. Show that the moment of inertia of the annulus about an axis through its centre perpendicular to its plane is $\frac{5}{2} m$.

   (i) This annulus is set to roll from rest down a slope of incline 45°. The annulus rolls without slipping. Find the linear acceleration of the annulus.

   (ii) Show that if $\mu$ is the coefficient of friction between the annulus and the slope then $\mu \geq \frac{5}{13}$.

6. A fixed pulley of mass $m$ and radius $r$ turns on a fixed frictionless axis.

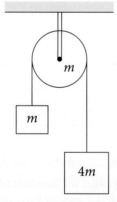

Fig. 14.25

   Particles of mass $m$ and $4m$ hang freely from the ends of a light inextensible string which passes over the pulley. The string turns the pulley with no slipping.

   (i) Show that the common acceleration of the particles is $\frac{6}{11} g$.

   (ii) Find the tension in each part of the string.

7. A hoop rolls down a hill of incline 30°(without slipping). Find its linear acceleration. [The moment of inertia of a hoop about an axis through it centre perpendicular to its plane is given by $I = m r^2$]

8. An annulus of mass $m$ has outer radius $R$ and inner radius $r$.

   (i) Prove that the moment of inertia of the annulus about an axis through its centre perpendicular to its plane is $\frac{1}{2} m (R^2 + r^2)$

   (ii) A light inextensible string is wound around the outer rim of the annulus. The free end is fixed to a point on a ceiling so that the annulus falls freely under gravity. If the annulus and the string remain vertical show that the linear acceleration of the annulus is given by

   $$a = \frac{2 R^2 g}{3 R^2 + r^2}$$

   (iii) Show that the tension in the string is given by

   $$T = mg \left( \frac{R^2 + r^2}{3R^2 + r^2} \right)$$

## The principle of angular momentum

**Definition:** The angular momentum of a body which is rotating with angular speed $\omega$ about a fixed axis, where $I$ is the moment of inertia of the body about that axis, is $I \omega$.

Newton's Second Law, which states that the rate of change of linear momentum is proportional to the applied force, is sometimes called the Principle of Linear Momentum. Mathematically, this law can be written $F = m a$ or $F = m \frac{d^2x}{dt^2}$. We accept it because it leads to results which agree with observation.

There is a very similar law for bodies which are rotating. It is called the **Principle of Angular Momentum:** The rate of change of the angular momentum of a rigid body rotating about a fixed axis is proportional to the moment about that axis of the external forces acting on that body.

Mathematically, if $M$ is the moment of the external forces about the fixed axis, then

$$M = \frac{d}{dt} (I \omega) = I \frac{d\omega}{dt} = I \frac{d^2\theta}{dt^2}.$$

(In the mks system, the constant of proportionality

is 1).

## The compound pendulum

The simple pendulum has all of its mass concentrated at a point, at the end of a weightless string of length $l$. Its period of motion (for small oscillations) is given by $T = 2\pi\sqrt{\frac{l}{g}}$. A compound pendulum is any rigid body which is free to rotate about a fixed axis.

## The periodic time of compound pendulums

### Theorem 14.6

A compound pendulum performing small oscillations will move with simple harmonic motion. The period of small oscillations is $T = 2\pi\sqrt{\frac{I}{mgh}}$, where $h$ is the distance from the centre of gravity of the body to the axis, $I$ is the moment of inertia of the body about the axis and $m$ is the mass of the body.

### Proof:

The only forces acting on the body at any stage will be the reaction $R$ at the axis and $mg$, the weight of the body, acting at $C$ the centre of gravity of the body. The moment of $R$ about the axis is zero. The line of action of $mg$ is at a distance $h \sin \theta$ from the axis. This moment is negative, because it is clockwise. Applying the Principle of Angular Momentum, we get:

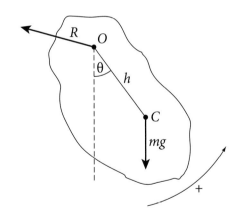

Fig. 14.26

$$M = I\frac{d^2\theta}{dt^2}$$
$$\therefore -(mg)\, h \sin\theta = I\frac{d^2\theta}{dt^2}$$
$$\therefore I\frac{d^2\theta}{dt^2} = -mgh \sin\theta$$

But $\qquad \sin\theta = \theta$ if $\theta$ is small

$$\therefore I\frac{d^2\theta}{dt^2} = -mgh\,\theta$$
$$\therefore \frac{d^2\theta}{dt^2} = -\frac{mgh}{I}\,\theta$$

This proves that the body will move with Simple Harmonic Motion, with $\omega^2 = \frac{mgh}{I}$.

Hence the periodic time will be

$$T = \frac{2\pi}{\omega}$$
$$= \frac{2\pi}{\sqrt{\frac{mgh}{I}}}$$
$$= 2\pi\sqrt{\frac{I}{mgh}} \qquad \text{Q.E.D.}$$

### Worked Example 14.5

A compound pendulum consists of a rod $[XY]$ of mass $m$ and length $6\,l$ attached (as shown) to the rim of a disc of mass $3m$ and radius $l$, so that the centre of the disc is on the line $XY$ and no overlapping occurs. The pendulum performs small oscillations about a horizontal axis through $X$ perpendicular to the plane of the disc.

(i) Find the periodic time.

(ii) Find the length of the equivalent simple pendulum.

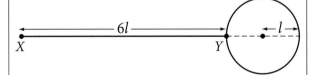

Fig. 14.27

### Solution:

(i) Let $C$ be the centre of the disc. Let $c$ be the axis through $C$ perpendicular to the plane of the disc. Let $x$ be the axis through $X$ parallel to $c$.

**Step 1:** Find the moment of inertia.

**Rod:**
$$I_x = I_{\text{endpoint}}$$
$$= \text{``}\tfrac{4}{3}\,m\,l^2\text{''}$$
$$= \tfrac{4}{3}\,m\,(3\,l)^2$$
$$= 12\,m\,l^2$$

**Disc:**
$$I_c = \text{``}\tfrac{1}{2}\,m\,r^2\text{''}$$
$$= \tfrac{1}{2}\,(3m)\,l^2$$
$$= \tfrac{3}{2}\,ml^2$$

**247**

$$I_x = I_c + md^2$$

$$= \frac{3}{2}ml^2 + (3m)(7l)^2$$

$$= \frac{3}{2}ml^2 + 147\,ml^2$$

$$= \frac{297}{2}ml^2$$

**System:** $\quad I_{system} = I_{rod} + I_{disc}$

$$= 12\,ml^2 + \frac{297}{2}ml^2$$

$$= \frac{321}{2}ml^2$$

**Step 2:** Find $h$, the distance from the centre of gravity to the axis $x$.

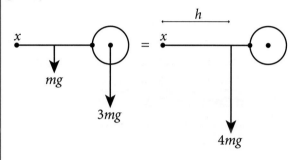

**Fig. 14.28**

We apply the Principle of Moments, taking moments about $X$ of the weights and their resultant:

|  | Rod | Disc | System |
|---|---|---|---|
| Weight | $mg$ | $3mg$ | $4mg$ |
| Distance to axis $x$ | $3l$ | $7l$ | $h$ |

$$mg\,(3l) + 3\,mg\,(7l) = 4\,mg\,(h)$$

$$\therefore 24\,mgl = 4\,mgh$$

$$\therefore h = 6l$$

**Step 3:**

$$T = 2\pi\sqrt{\frac{I}{mgh}}$$

$$= 2\pi\sqrt{\frac{\frac{321}{2}ml^2}{(4m)\,g\,(6l)}}$$

$$= 2\pi\sqrt{\frac{321ml^2}{48\,mgl}}$$

$$= 2\pi\sqrt{\frac{107\,l}{16\,g}} : \qquad \text{Answer}$$

(ii) Let $L$ be the length of the equivalent simple pendulum.

$$\therefore 2\pi\sqrt{\frac{L}{g}} = 2\pi\sqrt{\frac{107\,l}{16\,g}}$$

$$\therefore L = \frac{107}{16}l \qquad : \text{Answer}$$

---

**Exercise 14 D**

1. A rod of length $2\,l$ and mass $m$ is free to rotate about a horizontal axis through one end, perpendicular to the length of the rod. It performs small oscillations. Find the periodic time.

2. A disc of radius $r$ and mass $m$ is free to rotate about a horizontal axis through a point on its rim, perpendicular to the plane of the disc. It performs small oscillations. Find the periodic time.

3. A uniform square lamina of side $2l$ and mass $m$ is free to rotate about a horizontal axis through one corner, perpendicular to the plane of the lamina. Find the periodic time of small oscillations about this axis.

4. A compound pendulum consists of a uniform rod of mass $m$ and length $2l$ with a point mass $m$ attached to its endpoint. It is free to rotate about a horizontal axis through the other end of the rod, perpendicular to the rod. Find the periodic time of small oscillations about this axis.

5. A compound pendulum consists of a uniform rod of mass $m$ and length $2l$ attached to the rim of a disc of radius $l$ and mass $2m$, so that no overlapping occurs and the centre of the disc is along the line of the rod. It is free to rotate about a horizontal axis through the free end of the rod, perpendicular to the plane of the disc. Find the periodic time.

6. The diagram shows a compound pendulum that consists of a rod of mass $m$ attached to a rectangular lamina of mass $m$. It is free to rotate about a horizontal axis through the free end of the rod, perpendicular to the plane of the lamina.

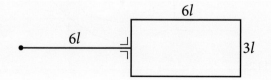

**Fig. 14.29**

(i) Find the periodic time.

(ii) Find the length of the equivalent simple pendulum.

7. A pendulum consists of a uniform rod of mass $m$ and length $2l$. It is free to rotate about a horizontal axis perpendicular to its length, through a point which is a distance $x$ from its midpoint. If a simple pendulum of length $\frac{7}{6}l$ has the same periodic time, show that $x$ can equal $\frac{1}{2}l$ or $\frac{2}{3}l$.

8. (a) Show that the moment of inertia of a uniform square lamina of side $2l$ and mass $m$ about an axis perpendicular to the plane of the lamina through its centre of mass is $\frac{2}{3}ml^2$.

   (b) A thin uniform rod of length $2l$ and of mass $m$ is attached to the midpoint of the rim of the square, as shown.

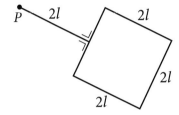

Fig. 14.30

   (i) Find the moment of inertia of the system about an axis through $P$ perpendicular to the plane of the lamina and rod.

   (ii) When this system makes small oscillations in a vertical plane about the axis, show that the period of oscillation is $2\pi\sqrt{\dfrac{11\,l}{4\,g}}$.

9. A uniform disc has mass $m$ and radius $r$. It is free to rotate about a horizontal axis through a point $P$ on its rim, perpendicular to the plane of the disc. A particle of mass $2m$ is attached to the disc at $Q$ on its rim diametrically opposite $P$, as shown.

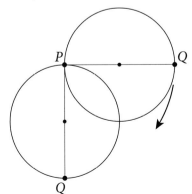

Fig. 14.31

   (i) The disc is held with $PQ$ horizontal and released from rest. Find, in terms of $r$, the angular velocity when $Q$ is vertically below $P$.

   (ii) If the system were to oscillate as a compound pendulum, prove that it would have a periodic time equal to that of a simple pendulum of length $\frac{19}{10}r$.

10. A uniform rod $[AB]$ of length $2p$ and of mass $3m$ has a mass $m$ attached to it at a distance $y$ from $A$.

   (i) Prove that the moment of inertia of this system about a smooth horizontal axis through $a$ is $4mp^2 + my^2$.

   (ii) The system oscillates in a vertical plane about $a$. If the length of the equivalent simple pendulum is $\frac{40}{33}p$, show that $y$ is either $\frac{2}{3}p$ or $\frac{6}{11}p$.

11. (i) Prove that the moment of inertia of a uniform square lamina of mass $m$ and side $2l$, about an axis through its centre in the plane of the lamina is $\frac{1}{3}ml^2$.

   (ii) Deduce the moment of inertia of the lamina about an axis through a vertex, perpendicular to the plane of the lamina.

   Four thin uniform rods, each of length $2l$ and mass $m$ are attached to the sides of this square lamina.

   (iii) Show that the moment of inertia of the system about an axis through a vertex, perpendicular to the common plane of the lamina and rods is $16\,ml^2$.

   (iv) If this system were used as a compound pendulum, making small oscillations in a vertical plane about a horizontal axis through a vertex perpendicular to the common plane of the lamina and rods, show that the periodic time of each oscillation is $2\pi\sqrt{\dfrac{8\sqrt{2}l}{5g}}$

### Problems with minimum times

When we are trying to find the minimum periodic time of a compound pendulum, we use calculus.

#### Worked Example 14.6

A uniform rod of mass $m$ and length $2l$ has a point mass $m$ attached to its midpoint. It is free to rotate about a horizontal axis perpendicular to its length, through a point a distance $x$ from the midpoint. This compound pendulum performs small oscillations about the axis with periodic time $T$.

(i) Show that $T^2 = \dfrac{2\pi^2}{3g}\dfrac{(l^2 + 6x^2)}{x}$

(ii) Find the value of $x$ for which this periodic time is a minimum.

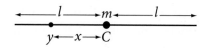

Fig. 14.32

**Solution:**

(i) Let $C$ be the midpoint and $c$ a horizontal axis through $C$ perpendicular to the rod. Let $y$ be the axis of rotation, parallel to $c$.

**Step 1:** Find the moment of inertia.

**Rod:**
$$I_c = I_{midpoint}$$
$$= \tfrac{1}{3} m l^2$$
$$I_y = I_c + md^2$$
$$= \tfrac{1}{3} ml^2 + mx^2$$

**Point Mass:** $I_y = m x^2$

**System:**
$$I_{system} = I_{rod} + I_{point\ mass}$$
$$= \tfrac{1}{3} ml^2 + mx^2 + mx^2$$
$$= \tfrac{1}{3} ml^2 + 2mx^2$$

**Step 2:** Find $h$: Since the centre of gravity of the system is at $C$, $h = x$.

**Step 3:** The mass of the compound pendulum is $2m$.

$$T = 2\pi\sqrt{\frac{I}{mgh}}$$
$$= 2\pi\sqrt{\frac{\tfrac{1}{3}ml^2 + 2mx^2}{(2m)g(x)}}$$
$$= 2\pi\sqrt{\frac{ml^2 + 6mx^2}{6mgx}}$$
$$= 2\pi\sqrt{\frac{l^2 + 6x^2}{6gx}}$$
$$\therefore T^2 = 4\pi^2\left(\frac{l^2 + 6x^2}{6gx}\right)$$
$$= \frac{4\pi^2}{6g}\left(\frac{l^2 + 6x^2}{x}\right)$$
$$= \frac{2\pi^2}{3g}\left(\frac{l^2 + 6x^2}{x}\right) \quad \text{Q.E.D.}$$

(ii) To find a minimum for $T$ is to find a minimum for $T^2$, because the smaller $T$ is, the smaller $T^2$ must be.

The minimum value for $T^2$ is

where $\dfrac{dT^2}{dx} = 0$

and $\dfrac{d^2T^2}{dx^2} > 0$

$$\frac{dT^2}{dx} = 0$$
$$\therefore \frac{2\pi^2}{3g}\left(\frac{x(12x) - (l^2 + 6x^2)(1)}{x^2}\right) = 0 \quad \text{(using Quotient rule)}$$
$$\therefore \frac{2\pi^2}{3g}\left(\frac{12x^2 - l^2 - 6x^2}{x^2}\right) = 0$$
$$\therefore \frac{2\pi^2}{3g}\left(\frac{6x^2 - l^2}{x^2}\right) = 0$$
$$\therefore 6x^2 - l^2 = 0$$
$$\left(\text{Since if } \frac{A}{B} = 0, \text{ then } A = 0\right)$$
$$\therefore x = \frac{l}{\sqrt{6}} \quad : \text{Answer}$$

**Step 4:** It is nice to show that $\dfrac{d^2T^2}{dx^2} > 0$ when $x = \dfrac{l}{\sqrt{6}}$.

$$\frac{d^2T^2}{dx^2} = \frac{2\pi^2}{3g}\left(\frac{x^2(12x) - (6x^2 - l^2)(2x)}{(x^2)^2}\right)$$
$$= \frac{2\pi^2}{3g}\left(\frac{2l^2 x}{x^4}\right)$$
$$= \frac{2\pi^2}{3g}\left(\frac{2l^2}{x^3}\right) > 0, \text{ since } x > 0$$

Therefore $x = \dfrac{l}{\sqrt{6}}$ gives a minimum periodic time.

## Exercise 14 E

1. A rod of length $2l$ and mass $m$ is free to oscillate about a horizontal axis perpendicular to the length of the rod, through a point which is a distance $x$ from the midpoint of the rod. It performs small oscillations. Find the value of $x$ for which the periodic time is a minimum.

2. A rod of length $2l$ and mass $m$ has a point mass $2m$ attached to its midpoint. This system is free to oscillate about a horizontal axis perpendicular to the length of the rod, through a point which is a distance $x$ from the point mass. Find the value of $x$ for which the periodic time of small oscillations is a minimum.

3. A uniform square $ABCD$ of mass $m$ and side $2l$ is free to oscillate about a horizontal axis perpendicular to the plane of the lamina through a point $P$ which is at a distance $x$ from the centre of mass of the lamina, along the diagonal $AC$.
   Prove that when the period of small oscillations is a minimum $x = \sqrt{\frac{2}{3}}\, l$.

4. (i) A uniform disc of mass $m$ and radius $r$ performs small oscillations in a vertical plane about a horizontal axis through a point which is a distance $x$ from the centre. Find the periodic time when $x = \frac{1}{2}r$.
   (ii) Prove that the periodic time is a minimum when $x = \frac{r}{\sqrt{2}}$. Verify that the periodic time in this case is less than that in part (i).

5. A uniform square lamina $ABCD$ of mass $3m$ and side $\sqrt{2}$ is free to rotate with its plane vertical about a smooth horizontal axis through a point $P$ on the diagonal $AC$. The point $P$ is at a distance $x$ from the centre of mass of the lamina. A mass $m$ is attached at each of the points $A$ and $C$.

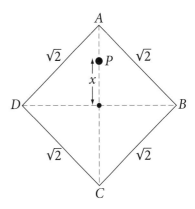

Fig. 14.33

   (i) Prove that the moment of inertia of the system about a horizontal axis through $P$ is $m(3 + 5x^2)$.
   (ii) Show that if $T$ is the period of small oscillations, then
$$T^2 = \frac{4\pi^2}{5g}\left(\frac{3 + 5x^2}{x}\right).$$
   (iii) Find the value of $x$ which gives the minimum periodic time.

6. (a) Prove that the moment of inertia of a uniform circular disc, of mass $m$, and radius $r$, about an axis through its centre perpendicular to its plane in $\frac{1}{2}mr^2$

   (b) Deduce that the moment of inertia of the disc about a diameter is $\frac{1}{4}mr^2$

   (c) A thin rod AB of mass $m$, and length $2a$ can turn freely in a vertical plane, about a fixed horizontal axis through A. A uniform circular disc of mass $24m$ and radius $\frac{a}{3}$ has its centre C clamped to the rod so that the length $|AC| = x$ and the plane of the disc passes through the axis of rotation.

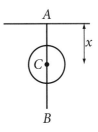

Fig. 14.34

   (i) Show that the moment of inertia of the system about the axis is $2m(a^2 + 12x^2)$
   (ii) The system makes small oscillations. Find the period and show that the period is a minimum when $x = \frac{a}{4}$.

## Summary of important points

1. The kinetic energy of a rotating body is $\frac{1}{2} I \omega^2$

2. $I = \sum \Delta M r^2$

3. Rod: $I_{\text{midpoint}} = \frac{1}{3} m l^2$;
   $I_{\text{endpoint}} = \frac{4}{3} m l^2$

4. Rectangle: $I = \frac{1}{3} m l^2$

5. Disc: $I_{\text{centre}} = \frac{1}{2} m r^2$;
   $I_{\text{diameter}} = \frac{1}{4} m r^2$

6. Point mass: $I = m r^2$

7. Perpendicular Axes Theorem: $I_z = I_x + I_y$

8. Parallel Axes Theorem: $I_l = I_c + md^2$

9. Principle of Conservation of Energy:
   $mgh + \frac{1}{2} I \omega^2 =$ a constant

10. Compound Pendulum: $T = 2\pi \sqrt{\dfrac{I}{m g h}}$

## DOs and DON'Ts for the exam

### DO
- Do know the three proofs (rod, rectangular lamina and disc) and their variations off by heart
- Do draw large clear diagrams on graph paper

### DON'T
- Don't mix up a disc which rotates about its diameter with a disc which rotates about an axis through a point on its rim, perpendicular to the plane of the disc. In the former case, $I = \frac{1}{4}mr^2$; in the latter case $I = \frac{3}{2}mr^2$.
- Don't forget how to locate the centre of gravity of a compound body

# Answers

### Exercise 1 A

6.  Yes.
9.  5 cm; E 53°N.
10. Approximately 7 cm due East.
11. 13 cm.

### Exercise 1 B

1.

  (i) $\sqrt{29}, E\, 21°48'N.$

  (ii) $\sqrt{8}, NE.$

  (iii) $5, E\, 36°52'S.$

  (iv) $13, W\, 67°23'S.$

  (v) $\sqrt{20}, W\, 26°34'N.$

  (vi) $\sqrt{2}, NE.$

  (vii) $\dfrac{1}{\sqrt{2}}, SE.$

  (viii) $1, W\, 53°8'S.$

  (ix) $2, W\, 30°\, N.$

  (x) $\sqrt{12}, E\, 30°\, N.$

  (xi) $4,$ due west.

2.

  (i) $5\vec{i} - 4\vec{j}$

  (ii) $\vec{i} + 2\vec{j}$

  (iii) $-\vec{i} + 2\vec{j}$

  (iv) $7\vec{j}.$

3.

  (i) $\sqrt{13}$

  (ii) $\sqrt{104}$

  (iii) $13$

4.

  (i) $4\vec{i} + 8j$

  (ii) $\sqrt{82}$

6.

  (i) $\dfrac{3}{5}\vec{i} + \dfrac{4}{5}\vec{j}$

  (ii) $\dfrac{1}{\sqrt{5}}(\vec{i} + 2\vec{j})$

  (iii) $\dfrac{1}{\sqrt{2}}(\vec{i} - \vec{j})$

  (iv) $\dfrac{1}{\sqrt{10}}(-3\vec{i} - \vec{j}).$

  (v) $\dfrac{1}{2}(\sqrt{3}\vec{i} + \vec{j})$

7. $k = 5, t = -2.$

8. $t = \frac{2}{5}$

9. $k = \pm 4$

10. $p = \pm 5$

11. $k = \pm 2$

12. $k = \pm 5$

16. 3

17. -2

### Exercise 1 C

1.

$|AB| = H\cos\theta, |BC| = H\sin\theta$

$|AB| = H\sin\theta, |BC| = H\cos\theta$

$|AC| = H\cos\theta, |BC| = H\sin\theta$

$|AB| = H\sin\theta, |AC| = H\cos\theta$

2.

  (i) $\frac{12}{13}, \frac{5}{13}$

  (ii) $\dfrac{\sqrt{10}}{\sqrt{11}}, \dfrac{1}{\sqrt{11}}$

  (iii) $\frac{\sqrt{7}}{4}, \frac{\sqrt{7}}{3}$

  (iv) $\frac{40}{41}$

3.

  (i)   $|AB| = 4\sqrt{3};$  $|BC| = 4$
  (ii)  $|XY| = 2;$        $|YZ| = 2$
  (iii) $|AB| = 6.63;$     $|BC| = 7.66$
  (iv)  $|XY| = 16.38;$    $|XZ| = 11.47$
  (v)   $|PQ| = 37.59;$    $|QR| = 13.68$
  (vi)  $|PQ| = 6;$        $|QR| = 6\sqrt{3}$
  (vii) $|AB| = 12;$       $|BC| = 9$
  (viii) $|PQ| = 72;$      $|QR| = 30$
  (ix)  $|XY| = 3;$        $|YZ| = 2$
  (x)   $|AB| = 4;$        $|BC| = 2$

4. (a) $X = H\sin\theta\cos\varnothing$
   (b) $X = 3$

5. (a) $X = H\cos\alpha\cos\beta$
   (b) $H : X = 10.7$

## Exercise 1 D

1.

   (i) $\vec{i} + \sqrt{3}\vec{j}$

   (ii) $9.511\vec{i} + 3.09\vec{j}$

   (iii) $4\sqrt{2}\vec{i} - 4\sqrt{2}\vec{j}$

   (iv) $-18.794\vec{i} + 6.84\vec{j}$

   (v) $-5\vec{i} - 5\vec{j}$

   (vi) $9.3252\vec{i} - 7.5516\vec{j}$.

2. $\vec{u} + \vec{v} = 4\vec{i} - 11j$ :

   (i) $\vec{w} = -4\vec{i} + 11j$ :

   (ii) $|\vec{w}| = 11.7$; Direction : $70°$ N of W

3. $(2 + 2\sqrt{3})\vec{i} + 0\vec{j}$.

4. $-2.6\vec{i} + 5.8\vec{j}$.

5. (i) $\vec{a} = 12\vec{i}; \vec{b} = -12\vec{i} + 5\vec{j}$

   (iii) 5

6. (i) $\vec{x} = -20\vec{i} + 15\vec{j}; \vec{y} = 8\vec{i} - 15\vec{j}$

   (iii) 12

## Exercise 1 E

1. $\frac{12}{5}$; 24.

2. $\vec{a} + \vec{b} = -\vec{j}$.

3. $8; 4\sqrt{3}$

4. 3.42.

5. $k = 8$

6. (i) $33\vec{i} + 33\vec{j}$.

7. 15.8

9. $p = 5$

10. 22.88.

## Chapter 2
## Uniform Acceleration

## Exercise 2 A

1. (i) 2m/s (ii) 25m.

2. (i) 8s (ii) 96m.

3. 6 m/s

4. 4m/s²; 5s.

5. 5 m/s

6. 42 m

7. $\frac{3}{4}$ m/s²; 4s

8. $2\frac{1}{2}$ m/s²; 480m; 500m

   (i) 36m (ii) 144m.

10. (a) 20m/s (b) $\frac{2}{9}$ m/s²; 30s; 400m.

11. 2.5 m/s²; 45 m.

12. 6s; 23m/s; 19m/s.

13. (i) 10 s (ii) 230 m and 170 m

14. (i) $\frac{25}{6}$ s (ii) $\frac{625}{9}$ m (iii) $\frac{625}{9}$ m/s²

## Exercise 2 B

1. (i) 15s (ii) 735m (iii) 3m/s²

2. (i) 4m/s² (ii) 50m (iii) 15s.

3. (i) 1625 m (ii) 40.625 m/s

4. (i) 5 s (ii) 5250 m (iii) 52.5 m/s

5. (i) 400m (ii) 160m (iii) 39s.

6. (i) 3 m/s² (ii) 6 ¾ m/s²

   (iii) 13 ½ m/s; (iv) when $t = 5$, $10\frac{7}{9}$.

7. 2.5 m/s².

8. 2.5 m/s².

9. 8 s

10. 30 s

11. (i) 1200 m; 7200 m; 400 m. 260 s

## Exercise 2 C

1. 12.5 s

2. (i) 4.5 s (ii) 219.375 m

3. (i) 12 s; 4 s (ii) 12 m/s

4. 10 s; 200 m

5. (i) $10 + 3t$, $20 + 2t$;

   (ii) $10t + 1.5\,t^2$, $20t + t^2$ (iii) $t = 10$ (iv) $t = 20$

6. $a = 1$ m/s²

7. (i) 3 m/s² (ii) 6 m/s (iii) 42 m

8. (i) 3.5 m/s² (ii) 7 m

9. 289 m

10. 2.4 s

11. 25 m/s; 125 m, 800 m, 75 m.

12. (i) 15 s, 5 s (ii) 15 m/s (iii) 150 m

13. 6.3 km

14. (i) 20 m/s (ii) 20 s, 280 m

15. 0.772 s

16. (i) 30.75 s (ii) 30 s

17. (i) 75 m (ii) 2 seconds later

18. 30 s

19. 132 m

21. (i) 2 s (ii) 20 s more

22. 1.2 m/s² and 2 m/s²

23. $\frac{5}{6}$ m/s²

24. (i) $\frac{3}{5}$ m/s² (ii) (a) 6 s (b) 48 m

## Exercise 2 D

1. (i) $\frac{50}{7}$ s (ii) 62.5 m

2. (i) 21 (ii) 22.5 m (iii) $\frac{30}{7}$ s
3. (i) 2 s from start (ii)19.6 m
4. (i) 2 s (ii) 109.6 m
5. $u = 56$; $t = \frac{10}{7}$
6. (i)18.5 (ii) 30.5 m/s

## Exercise 2 E

2. (i)10$k$ s (ii) $4\sqrt{6}k$ s
4. (i) 5$u$
6. (b) (i) 65 m (ii) $(6n + 5)$ m
   (iii) 20$^{th}$ & 21$^{st}$

## Chapter 3
## Projectiles on a horizontal plane

## Exercise 3 A

1. (i) 39.9 m (ii) 40 m (iii)120 m
2. (i)160 m (ii) 640 m (iii) $56\vec{i} + 16.8\vec{j}$ m/s
3. (i) 70.35 m/s, 5°43' N of E (ii)1500 m
4. (i) 16.1 m (ii) $\frac{16}{7}$ or 2 s
5. (i)122.5 m (ii)100 m (iii) $10\vec{i} - 9.8\vec{j}$ m/s
6. (i)114.8 m/s, 52.43° N of E (ii) 2000 m
7. (i) 39.9 m (ii) 22.92 m/s
8. (i) $\frac{25}{7}$ s (ii) $\frac{5}{2}$ s (iii) $\frac{65}{14}$ s
10. (i)10 s (ii) $100\vec{i} + 490\vec{j}$ m
11. (i) 8 and12 s (ii)110 m/s
12. $\frac{110}{49}$ s, $\frac{170}{49}$ s.

## Exercise 3 B

1. (i) $14\vec{i} + 7\vec{j}$ m/s (ii) 20 m
2. (i) $28\vec{i} + 21\vec{j}$ m/s (ii) 32.08 m/s
3. (i) $\frac{100}{7}$ m (ii)1.875 m
4. (i) $\frac{128}{245} = 0.522$ m (ii) $\frac{32}{49}$ s
5. (b) 100 m
6. 500 m
7. (i) 10 m (ii) $\frac{5}{7}$ or $\frac{15}{7}$ s
8. 60 m
9. (i) 4 s (ii) 11.4 s
10. (i) $30t\vec{i} + (40t - 4.9t^2)\vec{j}$ m
    (ii) 43 m/s, 11 45° N of E (iii) 245 m
11. $k = 16$
12. (iii) 45°, 500m
13. 76°
14. 83°
15. (i) tan $A = 0.75$, $u = 14$ m/s (ii) 20 m
16. (i) 30° or 150° (ii) 15° or 75°

17. 0.7
19. (i) $p = 28$, $q = 10.5$ (ii) 15 m
20. 49°

## Exercise 3 C

1. 37° or 66°
2. 45° or 72°
3. (i) 72° or 79° (ii) 1.4 s, 2.3 s
4. (i) 63° or 79° (ii) 10 s, 23.43 s
   (iii) 13.5 s
5. (i) $\frac{11}{7}$ or 2 (ii) 8.33 s or 10 s
6. $\frac{30}{7}$ s
8. (ii) $\frac{3}{4}$ or $\frac{11}{2}$ ; $\frac{10}{7}$ or $\frac{20}{7}\sqrt{5}$ s
10. (i)14.7 m/s and 9 m/s (ii) 7.056 m
    (iii) 12.6 m/s
11. (i) $\frac{1}{7}$ s (ii) 14 m/s (iii) 14.07 m/s
13. 70 m/s
14. (ii) $\frac{10}{7}$ s; 60m

## Chapter 4
## Relative Velocity

## Exercise 4 A

1. (i) $5\vec{i}$ m/s (ii) 200 s
2. (i) $3\vec{i}$ m/s (ii) 180 m (iii) 200 s
3. (i) $10\vec{i}$ m/s (ii)$25\vec{i}$ ; (iii) 20 s
4. (i) $1.2\vec{i}$ m/s (ii) $2.5\vec{i}$ m/s (iii) 100 s
5. (i) $3\vec{i} + 4\vec{j}$ km/h (ii) 5 km/h (iii) 4 h
6. (i) $\sqrt{8}$ m/s, SW (ii) $\sqrt{5}$ m/s, 26°34' N of E
7. $-7\vec{i} + 4\vec{j}$ m, $-8\vec{i}$ m; B is farther
8. (i) $-5\vec{i} + 3\vec{j}$ (ii) $-8\vec{i} + 8\vec{j}$
9. 26 m/s, 67°23' S of E
10. 10 s
11. (i) $-5\vec{i}$ km/h (iii) 8 hours later
12. (i) $-12\vec{i}$ km/h (iii) 5 hours later
13. (a) $t = 4$ (b) (i) $4\vec{i} + 3\vec{j}$ km/h (ii)10 h
14. (i) $5\vec{i} + 5\vec{j}$ m/s (ii) $-12\vec{i} + 5\vec{j}$ m/s
    (iii) 200 s
15. (i) 6 m/s due North (ii) 36.87°N of W or
    36.87°N of E;150 s, 750 s
16. (ii) 2.309 h = 2 h19 mins
17. (ii) 17.00 hours
18. (ii) 16.00
19. (i)14 (ii)10.00
20. (i) 3 (ii)17.00 (5 o'clock)

## Exercise 4 B

1. (i) $3\vec{i} + 4\vec{j}$ m/s (ii)16 m
2. (i) $-15\vec{i} + 8\vec{j}$ m/s (iii) 56 m
3. (i) $6\vec{i} + 8\vec{j}$ m/s (ii) 4000 m
4. (i) $8.66\vec{i} - 5\vec{j}$ km/h, $-14.14\vec{i} + 14.14\vec{j}$ km/h,
   $22.8\vec{i} - 19.14\vec{j}$ km/h
   (ii) 29.77 km/h, 40° S of E (iii) 64.3 km
5. (i) $7\vec{i} - 24\vec{j}$ m/s (ii) 96 m
6. (i) $4\vec{i} - 3\vec{j}$ km/h (ii) 5 km/h, 36°52' S of E
   (iii) 210 km (iv) 80 h
7. (i) $4\vec{i} - 3\vec{j}$ m/s (ii) 180 m (iii) 54 s
8. (i)160 m (ii) 7.2 s
9. (i) $-2.83\vec{i} + 25.46\vec{j}$ m/s (ii) 1104 m
   (iii) 130.2 s
10. (i) $14.14\vec{i} + 4.14\vec{j}$ km/h (ii) 56.20 km
    (iii) 58.10 km
11. (i) $17.32\vec{i} - 2\vec{j}$ km/h,17.43 km/h, 6.59°S of
    E (ii)11.47 km (iii) 36.70 km
12. (i) $8.66\vec{i} + 2\vec{j}$ m/s (ii) 8.88 m/s, 13°N of E
    (iii) 24.2 m (iv) 4.47 s
13. (i) $-35.36\vec{i} + 5.36\vec{j}$ km/h, 35.76 km/h,
    8.62°N of W (ii)11.24 km (iii)15.09

## Exercise 4 C

1. (i) 5 s (ii) 26 m (iii) $5\vec{i} - 12\vec{j}$ m/s (iv) 24 m
2. (i) 2.5 s (ii) 50 m (iii) $6\vec{i} - 8\vec{j}$ m/s (iv) 40 m
3. (i) $21\vec{i} + 20\vec{j}$ m/s (ii) 100 m (iii) 3.62 s
4. (i) 20 s (ii) 40 m (iii) 5 m/s, 36.87°S of E
   (iv) 24 m (v) 26.4 s (vi) $33\frac{1}{3}$ s
5. $v = 19.2$ (i) 61.44 m (ii) 69 m
6. 44.72 m
7. 1.92 km
8. (a) $-28\vec{i} - 13.856\vec{j}$ m/s
   (b) (i) 6.25 s (ii) 6.94 s

## Exercise 4 D

1. (i) 20 s (ii) 20 m
2. 5 s, 25 m
3. (i)12 s (ii)15 s
4. (i) 30 s (ii) 32.5 s
5. (i) 24 s (ii) 25 s
6. (i) 300 s (ii) 340 s
7. (i) 42 m (ii) 29 s
9. (i) Straight across (ii) 90 s (iii) 75 m
10. 100.5 km/h, 5°43' S of E
11. 50 s; No, 32 s

12. 8 s less
13. (i)13 m/s (ii) 20 s;100 m
14. 17 m/s
15. (i) 73°44' (ii) 5 s
16. 2 h; Yes
17. 60°
18. 1.47 m/s
19. 83.28 km/h
20. 161.5 km/h
21. 80 s; 39 s
22. $a = 0, b = 14 - 8\sqrt{2}$ ; $t = \dfrac{4.25}{14 - 8\sqrt{2}}$ .
    Total time $= 1.75$ h
23. $t = \dfrac{d\sqrt{4x^2 - 2v^2}}{x^2 - v^2}$
26. (a) $\cos A = \sqrt{1 - \sin^2 A}$
    (b) (i) $-4\vec{i} + 3\vec{j}$ or $-3\vec{i} + 4\vec{j}$ m/s
    (ii) $\vec{i} + \vec{j}$ or $2\vec{i} + 2\vec{j}$ m/s

## Exercise 4 E

1. (i) $4\vec{i} - 5\vec{j}$ m/s (ii) $\sqrt{41}$ m/s, 51.34°S of E
   (iii) 66°S of E
2. $2\vec{i} + \vec{j}$ m/s
3. (i) $6\vec{i} - 8\vec{j}$ m/s (ii) 10 m/s
4. 5 m/s, 53.13°N of E
5. $2\vec{i} + 3\vec{j}$ m/s
6. $7\vec{i} - 2\vec{j}$ m/s
7. (i) $3\vec{i} + 6\vec{j}$ m/s (ii) 6 m/s
8. (i) $6\vec{i} - 8\vec{j}$ m/s (ii) From 59°N of W
9. (i) $6\vec{i} - 2\vec{j}$ m/s (ii) 1.75 m/s
10. $16\vec{i} - 12\vec{j}$ m/s
11. (i) $24\vec{i} + 7\vec{j}$ m/s (ii) 29 km (iii) 93 minutes

## Exercise 4 F

1. 37 s and 77 s
2. (i) 72.9° to the downstream direction or
   27.66° to the upstream (ii) 52 s or 108 s
3. (i) $p = 0.6, q = 0.45$ (ii) 357 s
4. (i) 59.4°N of W (ii) 264 s
5. (i) 39.5° or 18.6°N of E (ii) 22 s or 44 s

## Chapter 5
## Newton's Laws and Connected Particles

### Exercise 5 A

1. (i) $2\,\text{m/s}^2$ (ii) $400\,\text{m}$.
2. $\frac{1}{2}\,\text{m/s}^2$; $\frac{1}{3}\,\text{m/s}^2$.
3. $115\,\text{N}$; $160\,\text{N}$.
4. $25\,\text{N}$
5. $75\,\text{cm}$
6. $40\,\text{N}$
7. (i) $1\,\text{m/s}^2$ (ii) $1150\,\text{N}$
8. (i) $1000\,\text{N}$ (ii) $4\,\text{m}$
9. (i) $400\,\text{m}$ (ii) $1200\,\text{m}$
10. $100$ grams; $18\,\text{cm}$
11. $\dfrac{mu^2}{2s}$ ; $v = 2u$ ; $t = \dfrac{2s}{u}$
12. $20\,\text{cm}$
13. $0.798\,\text{N}$
14. $\dfrac{4h}{7}$. No, $h$.

### Exercise 5 B

1. $2.08\,\text{m/s}^2$
2. $0.12\,\text{m/s}^2$
3. (i) $1.4\,\text{N}$ (ii) $1.4\,\text{m/s}^2$
   (iii) $4.375\,\text{m}$
4. (i) $2450\,\text{N}$ (ii) $10$ (iii) $0.05\,\text{m/s}^2$
5. (i) $980\,\text{N}$ (ii) 5 dogs (iii) $0.025\,\text{m/s}^2$
6. (d) (i) $2.2\,\text{m/s}^2$ (ii) $840\,\text{N}$
7. $1.4\,\text{m/s}^2$; 5 seconds; $17.5\,\text{m}$
8. $0.2$
9. (i) $R = 38\,\text{N}$; $a = 8\,\text{m/s}^2$
   (ii) $R = 38\,\text{N}$; $a = 6.1\,\text{m/s}^2$
10. (i) $6.12\,\text{m/s}^2$ (ii) $5.41\,\text{m/s}^2$

### Exercise 5 C

1. (i) $5.6\,\text{m/s}^2$ (ii) $46.2\,\text{N}$
2. (i) $8.4\,\text{m/s}^2$ (ii) $25.2\,\text{m/s}$
3. (i) $2.8\,\text{m/s}^2$ (ii) $12.6\,\text{m}$
4. (i) $4.2\,\text{m/s}^2$ (ii) $4.1\,\text{m/s}$ (iii) $\frac{6}{7}\,\text{m}$
5. (i) $7\,\text{m/s}^2$ (ii) $7\,\text{m/s}$ (iii) $2.5\,\text{m}$
6. (i) $2.8\,\text{m/s}^2$ (ii) $12.6\,\text{N}$ and $28\,\text{N}$
7. (i) $\frac{3}{5}g$ (ii) $\frac{7}{15}g$
8. (i) $\frac{1}{9}g$ (ii) $\frac{40}{9}g$ N (iii) $\frac{2}{81}g$ m
9. $\mu = \frac{1}{2}$
10. (i) $\frac{7}{32}g$ (ii) $\frac{15}{16}g$ N and $\frac{75}{32}g$ N
11. (i) $1.5\,\text{s}$ (ii) $0.75\,\text{s}$

### Exercise 5 D

1. (i) $\frac{1}{5}g$ (ii) $6g$ N
5. (i) $\frac{1}{5}g$ (ii) $\frac{3}{5}mg$
6. (iii) $\frac{1}{3}mg$
7. $\frac{1}{2}g$
8. $T = 63\,\text{N}$ ; Particles: $1.4\,\text{m/s}^2$, $5.6\,\text{m/s}^2$.
   Pulley: $3.5\,\text{m/s}^2$
9. Particles: $0.3g$, $0.1g$. Pulley: $0.2g$

### Exercise 5 E

1. (i) $2\,\text{m/s}^2$ (ii) $0.04\,\text{m/s}^2$
2. $\frac{9}{13}g$ ; $\frac{40}{13}g$ N
3. (i) $0.28\,\text{m/s}^2$ (ii) It rises
4. (i) $\frac{17}{33}g$ (ii) $\frac{14}{33}g$
5. $a = \frac{1}{6}g$; $T = \frac{32}{5}g$ N
6. (i) $a = \frac{1}{3}g$; $T = \frac{28}{3}g$ N
   (ii) $a = \frac{5}{33}g$; $T = \frac{329}{330}g$ N

### Exercise 5 F

1. $\frac{1}{15}g, \frac{2}{15}g$
2. $\frac{11}{29}g, \frac{6}{29}g$
3. $\frac{5}{17}g, \frac{4}{17}g$ ; $\frac{1}{17}g, \frac{9}{17}g$ (both downward)
4. (ii) $\frac{1}{11}g, \frac{2}{11}g$ ; $\frac{1}{11}g, \frac{5}{11}g$

### Exercise 5 G

1. $\frac{\sqrt{3}}{9}g, \frac{2}{3}g$
2. $\frac{1}{15}g, \frac{8\sqrt{2}}{15}g$ ; $0.125\,\text{m/s}$
3. $\frac{1}{7}g, \frac{4\sqrt{2}}{7}g$
4. $\frac{12}{109}g$
5. $0\,\text{m/s}^2$
7. $\frac{1}{9}g$
8. (ii) $4\,\text{m}$
9. $\left(3g - T\right) = 5\left(f - \dfrac{4}{5}a\right)$
   $\left(4g - R\right) = 5\left(\dfrac{3}{5}a\right)$;
   $\left(T - g\right) = f$;
   $S = a$
   $\dfrac{3}{5}R - \dfrac{4}{5}T - S = 8a$,
   where $R$ and $S$ are the reactions and $T$ is the tension.
10. $T - \dfrac{3}{5}g = 1\left(f - \dfrac{4}{5}a\right)$; $R - \dfrac{4}{5}g = 1\left(\dfrac{3}{5}a\right)$; $5g - T\cos\theta = 5f\cos\theta$;
    $T\sin\theta = 5\left(a - f\sin\theta\right)$; $\dfrac{4}{5}T - \dfrac{3}{5}R - T\sin\theta = 8a$.

## Chapter 6
## Work, Power, Energy & Momentum

### Exercise 6 A

1. 2400 J; 240 W
2. 2400 J; 300 W
3. 6000 J;100 W
4. 12,000 W
5. 20,000 N
6. (i) 182 N (ii) 26 N (iii) 1440 J
   (iv) 1.1 m/s$^2$ (v) 72 W
7. 9000 W
8. 296 kW
9. 5 m/s
10. (i) 40 kW (ii) 40 m/s
11. (i) 69.28 N, 40 N (ii) 156 N
    (iii) 0.864 m/s$^2$ (iv) 34.64 J
12. (i) 0.24 m/s$^2$ (ii) 0.03 m/s$^2$

### Exercise 6 B

1. 14.28 m/s
2. 20 cm
3. 3.13 m/s$^2$
4. 3.5 m
5. $\sqrt{\frac{g}{5}}$ m
6. (i) 10.5 m (ii) 14.35 m
7. 14 m/s
8. 10 m/s
9. (i) $mga$ (ii) $a$ (iii) $\sqrt{ga}$
10. 1.4 m/s

### Exercise 6 C

1. 5 Ns
2. 15 Ns
3. 8 m/s; $-8\vec{j}$ Ns; $8\vec{j}$ Ns
4. 0.8 Ns
5. 10 Ns
6. (i) 9.6 m/s (ii) $n = 3$
7. 5 m/s
8. 12.9 m/s
9. 1.9 kg
10. 120 m/s
11. 420 m/s

### Exercise 6 D

1. (i) $\frac{1}{3}g$ m (ii) $\frac{5}{8}g$ m
2. $\frac{81}{22}g$
3. (i) $\frac{14}{13}g$ (ii) $\frac{38}{15}g$
4. (i) $\frac{8}{9}g$ m (ii) $\frac{2}{9}g$ m    6. (ii) No

## Chapter 7
## Impacts & collisions

### Exercise 7 A

1. (i) $6\vec{j}$ m/s (ii) 32 Ns
   (iii) 64 J
2. (i) 10 m/s (ii) 6 Ns (iii) 30 J
3. (i) 7 m/s (ii) 4 m/s (iii) $11\vec{j}$ Ns (iv)16.5 J
4. (i)14 m/s (ii)$84\vec{j}$ Ns (iii) 588 J
5. (i) 21 m/s (ii) 15 m/s (iii) 3.6 $\vec{j}$ Ns
   (iv)10.8 J
6. (i) $5\vec{i}+6\vec{j}$ m/s (ii) 28 J (iii) $28\vec{j}$ Ns
7. (i) $8\vec{i}+6\vec{j}$ m/s (iii)18.9 J
8. (i) $\frac{2}{3}$ (ii) 20% (iii) $\frac{2}{3}$
9. (i) $-3\vec{i}+3\vec{j}$ m/s (ii) 28 %
10. (i) 28 m/s (ii)14 m/s (iii)10 m
11. (i) $\sqrt{2gh}$ (ii) $e\sqrt{2gh}$ (iii) $e^2h$
13. (i) $12\sqrt{2}$ m/s (ii) $28m$ Ns (iii) $56m$ J (iv) 7
14. (i) 24.2 m/s (ii)1 Ns (iii) 2 J
15. $\frac{1}{3}$

### Exercise 7 B

1. (i) $5\vec{i}$ m/s ; $6\vec{i}$ m/s (ii)1 joule
2. (i) $-5$ m/s, 1 m/s (ii) $\pm7$ Ns (iii) 35%
3. (i) $\frac{7}{9}$ (ii) 7 m/s (iii) $\pm30\vec{i}$ Ns ;(iv)12.25m/s$^2$
4. (i) $v = 2$ (ii) $e = \frac{4}{5}$ (iii)12%
5. (i) 1, $\frac{13}{3}$ (ii) 87.5 J (iii) $25\vec{i}$ Ns
6. (i) 1,6 m/s (ii) 45 J (iii) 27 W
7. (i) 3 m/s (ii) 0.75 m/s. Yes since $v_A > v_B$
8. (ii) $e = \frac{1}{2}$ (iii) $66\frac{2}{3}$%
9. (i) 1.375 m/s;1.625 m/s (ii) $\frac{1}{4}$
10. (i) 1, 5, 0 (ii) 1,$\frac{5}{6}$,$\frac{25}{6}$ (iii) $\frac{31}{36}$,$\frac{35}{36}$,$\frac{25}{6}$. Since
    $v_A < v_B < v_C$
11. 1.25 m/s; 8.75 m/s.187.5 Ns
12. (a) 12.544 m (b)1.5 m/s; 45 N
14. $\frac{1}{2}$
16. (i) 0.6
19. (i) 2.2 (ii) 0.8 m/s, 1.0 m/s
20. (i) $\frac{u}{4}(1-3e)$; $\frac{u}{4}(1+e)$ (iii) 70%,
    (iv) 75%

### Exercise 7 C

1. (i) $2\vec{i}+3\vec{j}$ m/s ; $3\vec{i}+2\vec{j}$ m/s (ii) 4 joules
2. (i) $-3\vec{i}+4\vec{j}$ m/s ; $3\vec{j}$ m/s (ii) 24 J (iii) 12 Ns

3. (i) $\vec{i} - 5\vec{j}$ m/s (ii) $\frac{1}{8}$

4. (i) $2.5\vec{i} + 5\vec{j}$ m/s ; $5\vec{i}$ m/s (ii) $\pm 5m\vec{i}$ Ns
   (iii) 12.5% (iv) 18°26′

5. (i) $4\vec{i} + 3\vec{j}$ m/s ; $-4\vec{i} + 4\vec{j}$ m/s
   (ii) $-5\vec{i} + 3\vec{j}$ m/s ; $2\vec{i} + 4\vec{j}$ m/s (iii) 9 J

6. (i) $-\frac{1}{3}\vec{i} + 4\vec{j}$ m/s ; $\frac{2}{3}\vec{i} - 3\vec{j}$ m/s (iii) 46°

7. $m = 7$

8. (i) $-2\vec{i} + 4\vec{j}$ m/s (ii) $5\vec{i}$ (iii) $\frac{7}{8}$

10. (ii) $-\frac{6}{7}u\vec{i}$ (iii) $286.53u^2$ J

## Exercise 7 D

4. (iii) $\frac{1}{3}$

5. (ii) $\frac{2}{3}$

6. (a) $ac + bd = 0$

7. (ii) $u\sqrt{2}$ and $2\sqrt{2}\,u$

# Chapter 8
# Statics

## Exercise 8 A

1. (a) 10 $\vec{j}$, 35 cm from $P$.

   (b) 5 $\vec{j}$, 2.4 m from $P$.

   (c) $-5$ $\vec{j}$, 1 m from $P$.

   (d) $-3$ $\vec{j}$, 4 m from $P$.

   (e) $-3$ $\vec{j}$, $4\frac{1}{3}$ cm from $P$.

2. $6W$, 3.5 and 2.5 m

3. 30 cm

5. (i) 3 (ii) 5

## Exercise 8 B

1. (4, 3)
2. (2, 3)
3. (6, -3), (6, 3)
4. (9, 13)
5. $3\vec{i} + 2\vec{j}$, (9, –4)
6. $k = 3$, $h = 10$
7. (0, 1)
8. (i) (5,4) (ii) $k = -8$, $y = -14$
9. $x = 1$, $y = -10$
10. $x = 5$, $y = 3$
11. (38,18)
12. (2, 2.5)
13. $\left(\frac{8}{3}, \frac{7}{9}\right)$

## Exercise 8 C

1. (i) (0.75,1.25), 23°12′
   (ii) (1.25, 2), 32°

(iii) $\left(\frac{3}{2}, \frac{37}{18}\right)$ 37°39′
(iv) (5.15, 1.65), 75°19′

2. 1 cm away
3. (1.9, 1.9)
4. (i) (3, 2) (ii) (7, 3)
   (iii) (3.25,1.25) (iv) $\left(8, \frac{31}{11}\right)$
5. 3.5 cm
6. 38 cm
7. (4.27, 2.94)
8. (a) $x = 2$, $y = -1$ (b) $-\frac{2}{15}r$
9. 54 mm
10. (i) 57.5 cm (ii) 60.9 cm
11. (i) 108 and 270 (ii) (6,10)
    and (16, 6) (iii) (13.14, 7.14)
12. (ii) (4, 8) and (18, 6) (iii) (14.5, 6.5)

## Exercise 8 D

1. (i) 12 cm (ii) 6 cm (iii) 9 cm (iv) 12 cm
2. 2 cm
3. (i) 20 (ii) $60\pi$ cm$^3$
4. (i) 8 (ii) $\frac{1024\pi}{3}$ cm$^3$
5. (i) 6 (ii) $72\pi$ cm$^3$
6. 7 cm
7. 10 cm
8. 19 mm
9. 7 mm
11. (ii) 27.5 cm
12. (ii) 18.25 cm
13. 10.2 cm
14. (ii) $2.5r$

## Exercise 8 E

1. $\sqrt{8}$ N, $\sqrt{26}$ N
2. 10 N; 70 cm; $\frac{7}{6}$ m from $a$
3. (i) $-5\vec{i} - 12\vec{j}$ (ii) 13 N (iii) $\frac{11}{13}$ m
4. (i) 13 N (ii) $\frac{14}{13}$ m (iii) 2 m
5. 10 N; 4.8 m
6. (i) 12 N (ii) $\frac{l}{\sqrt{3}}$ m; $4\sqrt{3}l$ Nm

## Exercise 8 F

1. $\frac{5}{4}W$ , $\frac{3}{4}W$
2. $\frac{5}{8}W$ and $\frac{11}{8}W$
3. (i) $\frac{8}{7}$ N, $\frac{6}{7}$ N (ii) 2.5 cm from $A$
4. (i) $R = W$ ; $S = \frac{1}{3}W$; $\mu = \frac{1}{3}$
5. $\frac{5}{11}$
6. (a) (i) Friction (ii) Moment (b) $\frac{5}{8}$

7.  $A = 45°$
8.  37°
10. (ii) 6.5 m (ii) $\frac{25}{24}$

## Exercise 8 G

1.  (ii) $\frac{1}{4}$
2.  (ii) $\frac{5}{8}$
3.  $\frac{7}{20}$
4.  (i) $\frac{11}{13}W$ and $\frac{8}{13}W$ (ii) $\frac{11}{13}$
5.  (b) (i) $\frac{1}{\sqrt{3}}W$ , $W$; $\frac{1}{\sqrt{3}}$
6.  $\frac{7}{9}W$, $W$ and $\frac{5}{9}W$

## Exercise 8 H

1.  40 N
2.  40 N
3.  20 N
4.  $\frac{1}{3}$
7.  (i) 36.87° (iii) $\frac{196}{\sqrt{5}}$ N
8.  (i) $\dfrac{W\sin(\alpha+\lambda)}{\cos\lambda}$
    (ii) $W\tan(\alpha+\lambda)$ (iii) $W\sin(\alpha+\lambda)$

## Exercise 8 I

1.  $\frac{2}{3}W$, $\frac{1}{2}W$ ; $T=\frac{5}{6}W$
2.  (i) $\frac{6}{5}W$ ; $\frac{17}{5}W$ (ii) 53°
3.  (ii) 41.81° (iii) $\frac{\sqrt{5}}{3}W$ ; $\frac{7}{3}W$
4.  (i) $\frac{6}{5}W$ ; $\frac{1}{2}W$ (ii) $\frac{13}{10}W$
5.  (ii) $\frac{9}{4}W$ ; $\frac{11}{4}W$ (iv) $\tan^{-1}\frac{5}{3}=59°$
6.  $\frac{9}{8}W$ ; $\frac{5}{4}W$, $\frac{7}{4}W$
9.  (i) Friction $=W$; $R=\frac{1}{2}W\tan\phi$
12. (iii) 0.6
14. (iv) 28 N

## Exercise 8 J

1.  $\frac{4}{\sqrt{15}}W$, $\frac{1}{\sqrt{15}}W$
2.  $10\sqrt{3}$ N
3.  (i) 90 N (ii) 256 N
4.  (iii) $\frac{5}{3}W$ , $\frac{4}{3}W$
5.  $\frac{15}{4}g$
6.  5: 7
7.  (iii) $\frac{3}{4}W$ (iv) $\frac{3}{5}W$
8.  $\frac{4}{\sqrt{17}}$ , $\frac{4}{5}$; $\frac{10}{3\sqrt{17}}W$, $\frac{5}{3\sqrt{17}}W$

## Chapter 9
## Hydrostatics

### Exercise 9 A

1.  830 kg/m³
2.  0.375
3.  (i) 13600 kg/m³ (ii)13.6
4.  9; 9000 kg/m³
5.  $\frac{1}{14}$ m³; 175 kg
6.  0.98
7.  7.182
8.  60 ml
9.  24g
10. 0.072$\pi g$
11. (a) 1.026$\pi g$ N (b) 0.2413$\pi g$ N (c) 0.99

### Exercise 9 B

1.  (i) 2000g Pa
2.  (i) 93.5g Pa (ii) 0.23375$\pi g$ N
    (iii)0.23375$\pi g$ N
3.  4:13
4.  (a)1.2 cm (b) 7.16 cm
5.  (a)15.75 cm (b)16.8 cm
6.  3000g Pa,12000g Pa (i) 0.25 m
    (ii) 250g Pa (iii)1000g N
7.  (i) 2.25 cm (ii) 22.5g Pa
    (iii) 360$\pi g$ N
8.  (i) 1 cm (ii) 9g Pa
    (iii) 0.0324$\pi g$ N
9.  0.1 Pa
10. 150.92 kN; 3.675 kN

### Exercise 9 C

1.  3
2.  0.65
3.  0.9
4.  6; $\frac{2}{3}$
5.  25 N; 25.5 N
6.  40 N
7.  (i) 10 (ii) 0.8 (iii) 0.75
8.  0.8
9.  (i) 0.036$\pi$ m³ (ii) 90$\pi g$ N
    (iii) 54$\pi g$ N
10. (i) 0.066 m³ (ii) 5,174.4 N
    (iii) 4527.6 N

### Exercise 9 D

1.  0.75; 75g; 25g
2.  $33\frac{1}{3}$%
3.  (i) 0.99 (ii) 0.99

4. $1\frac{1}{3}$ kg
5. Lead
6. 87%
7. 2822.4 N
8. (i) 0.005 m$^3$ (ii) 4 kg (iii) 83.3 N
9. (i) 0.0016 m$^3$ (ii) 12.5 cm
10. 8; 1.6 m$^2$; 4 cm
11. 14 cm
12. 98000 Pa
13. (i) $\frac{2000}{3}\pi g$ N (ii) $2000\pi g$ N (iii) $\frac{4000}{3}\pi g$ N
14. (i) $7.2\pi g$ kN (ii) $25.2\pi g$ kN (iii) $18\pi g$ kN
15. 12:7
16. (i) $500g$ Pa (ii) $\frac{125\pi}{16}$ N (iii) 7 :1
17. 0.9
18. (i) $6.8t$ (ii) 801.6 kg/m$^3$; 507 mm
19. (i) $\pi r^3 \rho g$ ; $2\pi r^3 \rho g$
20. $\frac{29}{34}$

## Exercise 9 E

1. (i) $\frac{2}{5}W$ (ii) $\frac{5}{9}$
2. (ii) $\frac{1}{4}W$ (iii) $\frac{2}{3}$
3. (i) $\frac{31}{240}W$ (ii) $\frac{5}{48}W$
4. 20 cm
5. (i) $\frac{101}{240}W$ (ii) $\frac{103}{240}W$
6. (i) $\frac{13}{20}$ (ii) $\frac{7}{13}W$

## Chapter 10
## Projectiles on the inclined plane

### Exercise 10 A

1. $v_x = u\cos\alpha - g\sin\beta t$
   $v_y = u\sin\alpha - g\cos\beta t$
   $s_x = u\cos\alpha t - \frac{1}{2}g\sin\beta t^2$
   $s_y = u\sin\alpha t - \frac{1}{2}g\cos\beta t^2$

2. $v_x = u\cos\alpha + g\sin\beta t$
   $v_y = u\sin\alpha - g\cos\beta t$
   $s_x = u\cos\alpha t + \frac{1}{2}g\sin\beta t^2$
   $s_y = u\sin\alpha t - \frac{1}{2}g\cos\beta t^2$

3. $v_x = u\cos(\alpha+\theta) + g\sin\theta t$
   $v_y = u\sin(\alpha+\theta) - g\cos\theta t$
   $s_x = u\cos(\alpha+\theta)t + \frac{1}{2}g\sin\theta t^2$
   $s_y = u\sin(\alpha+\theta)t - \frac{1}{2}g\cos\theta t^2$

4. $v_x = 5\sqrt{3} - \dfrac{g}{\sqrt{2}}t$

   $v_y = 5 - \dfrac{g}{\sqrt{2}}t$

   $s_x = 5\sqrt{3}t - \dfrac{g}{2\sqrt{2}}t^2$

   $s_x = 5t - \dfrac{g}{2\sqrt{2}}t^2$

### Exercise 10 B

2. $\dfrac{2u^2(\sqrt{3}-1)}{3g}$ ; $\dfrac{\sqrt{3}u^2}{6g}$

3. $\dfrac{143}{2g}$

4. (i) $\dfrac{200(\sqrt{3}-1)}{3g}$, (ii) $\dfrac{200}{3g}$

6. $\dfrac{260}{19g}$

9. (i) $55°$, (ii) $45°$

# Exercise 10 C

1. $\dfrac{\sqrt{5}u^2}{4g}$

3. (i) 2 (ii) 3 (iii)1.5

4. (ii) $\dfrac{u^2}{\sqrt{3}g}$

6. $\dfrac{\sqrt{5}u\sin\theta}{g}$ ; $\dfrac{\sqrt{5}u^2}{4g}$

7. (a) $45°$ or $\tan^{-1}\frac{1}{2}$
   (b) (i) $4g$
       (ii) $16mg^2 (= 8mg^2 + 8mg^2)$

# Exercise 10 D

1. (i) $\frac{9}{16}h$ (ii) $\frac{32}{7}h$

2. (i) $\frac{6400}{9g}$ (ii) $12°$

3. $\dfrac{5u^2\sin A}{8g}$ ; $\dfrac{25u^2\sin A}{128g}$

5. (i) $\dfrac{2u^2}{g}$ (ii) $e = 1$

# Chapter 11
# Circular motion

## Exercise 11 A

1. (i) 2 rad/s (ii) 5 rad (iii) $\frac{3}{4}$ rad (iv) 0.55 rad
2. (i)15 cm (ii) 4 cm (iii) 6 cm (iv) 8.5 cm
3. 4 cm
4. 1.15 cm
5. 1.8 rad/s
6. 1.75 cm
7. 4.7 rad/s
8. 95; 4 m/s
9. 21 rad/s
10. 3.58 m/s

## Exercise 11 B

1. 100 N
2. 14 N
3. (i) 3 m (ii) 29 N (iii) 25 N
4. (i) $45°$ (ii) $50\sqrt{2}$ N (iii) 48 N
6. (i) $T = \frac{2}{\sqrt{3}}mg$ (ii) 3.364 rad/s
7. (i) 1.2 m (ii) $R = 254.8$ N
   (iii) 4.427 rad/s
8. (i) 0.3 m (ii) $T = 97.5$ N
   (iii) 4.4 rad/s
9. 3.5 rad/s
10. (i) $T\cos\theta = mg$ ; $T = m\omega^2 l$ (ii) 6.3 rad/s
11. (iii) 0.1 m

## Exercise 11 C

1. 0.9
2. (i) 12.52 m/s (ii) $\frac{5}{24}$
3. 3.5 rad/s
4. 6 m
5. 7 m/s
6. 4 km
7. 141 m/s
8. (i) 3 m (ii) $\sqrt{\frac{2}{3}g}$ rad/s
9. (i) 0.7 m (ii) $\sqrt{\frac{40}{21}g}$
10. (i) $mg$ ; $\frac{2}{15}$ m (ii) $5mg$ ; $\frac{22}{15}$ m
11. $\frac{1}{2}\sqrt{g}$
12. 112 N; 84 N; 70°

## Exercise 11 D

2. $\cos^{-1}\frac{5}{6}$ , $\sqrt{\frac{5}{6}gr}$
3. $\frac{7}{2}mgr$
4. $120°$ , $\frac{3}{2}r$

## Chapter 12
## Differential Equations

### Exercise 12 A

1.
  (i) $\log_e 12$
  (ii) $\log_e \frac{6}{7}$
  (iii) $\log_e 72$
  (iv) $\log_e \frac{32}{25}$
  (v) $\log_e 6$
  (vi) $\log_e 2$
  (vii) $\log_e \frac{75}{8}$
  (viii) $\log_e x^3$
  (ix) $\log_e 2\sqrt{\frac{x}{7}}$.

2. (i) $1$.
  (ii) $e^2$
  (iii) $-1$
  (iv) $\frac{1}{3}$
  (v) $8$
  (vi) $4$
  (vii) $2$
  (viii) $49$
  (ix) $3$
  (x) $64$
  (xi) $2e$
  (xii) $\frac{e^3}{5}$
  (xiii) $\sqrt{\frac{e}{3}}$
  (xiv) $\frac{27}{e^2}$

### Exercise 12B

1. (i) $\frac{x^5}{5} + c$  (ii) $\frac{3x^5}{5} + c$

2. (i) $\sin x + c$  (ii) $\frac{\sin 3x}{3} + c$

3. (i) $-\cos x + c$  (ii) $-\frac{\cos 4x}{4} + c$

4. (i) $\ln x + c$  (ii) $\frac{\ln(2x+3)}{2} + c$

5. (i) $e^x + c$  (ii) $\frac{1}{8} e^{8x} + c$

6. (i) $\sin^{-1}\frac{x}{7} + c$  (ii) $\sin^{-1}\frac{x}{10} + c$

7. (i) $\frac{1}{5}\tan^{-1}\frac{x}{5} + c$  (ii) $\frac{1}{25}\tan^{-1}\frac{x}{25} + c$
  $\frac{1}{45}\tan^{-1}\frac{9x}{5} + c$

8. (i) $x + \ln x + c$  (ii) $\ln(x+1) + c$

9. (i) $x^2 + x + c$  (ii) $\frac{4}{3}x^3 + 2x^2 + x + c$

10. (i) $\frac{\ln(5x+1)}{5} + c$  (ii) $2\sqrt{x} + c$

### Exercise 12 C

1. (i) $16$  (ii) $\frac{1}{3}$  (iii) $4$  (iv) $\frac{4}{3}$  (v) $\ln 3$  (vi) $0$

2. $3$

3. $1$

4. $\frac{1}{\sqrt{2}}$

5. $3$

6. $\sqrt{3} - 1$

7. $2$

8. $1$

9. $1 - \sqrt{2}$

10. $\frac{\pi}{3}$

11. $\frac{7}{3}$

12. $\frac{1}{4\sqrt{2}}$

13. $\frac{1}{4}$

14. $\frac{1}{3}$

15. $\frac{1}{6}$

16. (i) $\frac{\pi}{8}$  (ii) $\frac{\pi}{4}$

17. (i) $\frac{\pi}{6}$  (ii) $\frac{\pi}{6} - \frac{\sqrt{3}}{8}$

18. (i) $\frac{\pi}{36}$  (ii) $\frac{\pi}{8}$

19. (i) $\frac{\pi}{4}$  (ii) $\frac{\pi}{15}$

20. (i) $\frac{\pi}{12\sqrt{3}}$  (ii) $\frac{\pi}{6}$

### Exercise 12 D

1. $y = e^{6x+c}$

2. $y = e^{x^2+c}$

3. $y = \sin x + c$

4. $y = \pm\sqrt{2(x^4+c)}$

5. $y = e^{x^3 + c}$

6. $y = \pm\sqrt{\cos 2x + 2c}.$

7. $y = \tan(x^2 + c).$

8. $y = \sin(2x + c)$

## Exercise 12 E

1. $y = e^{3x}.$

2. $y = 2e^{5x}$

3. $y = \sin\left(x^2 + \dfrac{\pi}{2}\right).$

4. $x = e^{(1/2)t}$

5. $y = 3x$

6. $s = \sqrt{2\cos t + 1}.$

7. $y = 3x^{x^4}.$

8. $y = \sqrt{2(x^3 - 1)/3}.$

9. $y = \sqrt{2\sin x - 1}.$

10. $y = \frac{1}{4}(x - 4).$

11. $y = \dfrac{1}{\cos x + 2}.$

12. $y = 2x$

13. $v = \sqrt{x + \frac{1}{2}\sin 2x + 1}.$

14. $y = e^{1 - \cos x}.$

15. (i) $y = 2\,e^{\sin x - 0.5}$
    (ii) $2\sqrt{e} = 3.3$

16. 5.35

17. $y = \sin(\ln x); y = 1$

## Exercise 12 F

1. $y = \frac{1}{2}(e^{2x} - 1).$

2. $x = \log_e\left(\dfrac{1}{1 - t}\right).$

3. $s = 3t^2 + 4t.$

4. $s = 3t^2 + 4t$

6. $s = \frac{1}{3}[(2t + 16)^{\frac{3}{2}} - 64].$

7. $y = \dfrac{x^3}{3} + x + 10$

## Exercise 12 G

1. $y = e^x.$

2. $s = e^{1 - 3t}.$

3. $y = \sqrt[3]{3x}.$

4. $y = 2\sin x.$

5. $x = 3\tan(3t + \frac{\pi}{4})$

6. $x = \left(\dfrac{2}{t + 1}\right)^2.$

7. 3

## Exercise 12 H

1. (i) $\frac{10}{e} = 3.68$ m/s

2. 1.28 m/s

3. 0.11 s

4. (ii) 2 m (iii) 0.6 m/s

5. (i) $\sqrt{500} = 22.36$ m/s (ii) $x = 400$ m

6. 1.5 s

8. 10 m; $\frac{20}{3}$ m

## Exercise 12 I

1. 0.80 m

2. $\log_e 2 = 0.69$ m

3. 28.8 m

4. 7.2 s

5. (i) $\frac{1}{4}$ m/s (ii) $\frac{3}{8}$ s

## Exercise 12 J

1. 0.16 s

3. (ii) 4 s (iii) 68.89

# Chapter 13
## Simple Harmonic Motion

## Exercise 13 A

1. (i)10 N (ii) 50 N (iii) 2 N
2. (i) 9 N (ii) 27 N (iii) 12 N; 8 m
3. $18\vec{i}$
   13 m from the left hand wall (LHW)
4. (i) 7 m from LHW
   (ii) 5 m from LHW
5. (i)11 m from LHW
   (ii) 7 m,15 m from LHW
6. 5 rad/s
7. 3 m
8. 4.8 m
10. 17.95 N

## Exercise 13 B

1. (i) 35 m/s (ii) 245 m/s (iii) $\frac{70}{17} = 22.28$ m/s
2. 4 m; $\frac{2\pi}{3}$ s
3. (i) $\pi$ s (ii) 3 m (iii) 8 m/s$^2$
4. (i) $\sqrt{65}$ m (ii) $2\pi$ s
   5(iii) $\sqrt{65}$ m/s
5. 6 m/s
6. (i) 13 (ii) $\pi$ s (iii)19
7. $\frac{\pi}{6}$ s ; 12 N
8. (i) 5 m (ii) 11 hours (iii) 3.29 pm
9. (i) 12 s (ii) $\frac{3\sqrt{2}}{5}$
10. 9.10 pm

## Exercise 13 C

1. $\frac{2\pi}{5}$ ; $\frac{\pi}{30} = 0.1047$ s
2. (ii) 4 m (iii) 0.4478 s
3. (i) 9 m (ii) 0.227 s
4. (i) 0.3948 (ii) 2 (iii)1.37 s
5. (i) 5; $\pi$
   (ii) 10; $\frac{\pi}{2}$
   (iii) 13; $2\pi$
   (iv) 4; 2
   (v) $\sqrt{2}$ ; $\frac{2\pi}{3}$
   (vi) 29; 1
   (vii) 2; $\frac{2\pi}{5}$
   (viii) $\sqrt{13}$ ; $4\pi$
   (ix) 25, $8\pi$
   (x) $\sqrt{5}$ ; $6\pi$

6. (ii) $2\pi$ s (iii) 37 (iv) $t = 2.811$
7. (ii) $\pi$ s (iii) 13
   (iv) 1.373 (v) 2.944 s
8. $\omega = 2.5$ ; $\alpha = 0.9273$; 0.2575 s
9. 66
10. $r = 1.7$ ; $\frac{\pi}{2}$ s ; 0.15 s

## Exercise 13 D

1. (ii) $\pi$ s (iii) 2 m/s
2. (ii) $\frac{\pi}{18} = 0.1745$ s (iii) $6\sqrt{3} = 10.4$ m/s
3. (ii) $3\sqrt{8}$ m/s (ii) $\sqrt{8}$ m
   (iii) 0.12 m/s (iv) 0.12 m/s
4. (i) 3 m (ii) 1 m/s (iii) 5 N
5. 144 m/s$^2$; 9.6 m/s
7. (ii) 2 m/s (iii) 0.23 s
8. (ii) 2.57 s
9. (iii) 0.54 s
10. (ii) 2.35 m (iii) 0.65 m (v) 0.404 s

## Exercise 13 E

1. (i)1.2 m below
   (iii) $\frac{2\pi}{7}$
   (iv)1.4 m/s
   (v) 0.188 s
2. (ii) 7 m/s$^2$; 3.5 N
   (iii) 0.59 s
3. (ii) $\frac{2\pi\sqrt{d}}{21}$
4. (ii) $2\pi\sqrt{\frac{3}{25g}}$ (iii) $\frac{1}{5}\sqrt{\frac{g}{3}}$
5. $2\pi\sqrt{\frac{hs}{g}}$ ; $2\pi\sqrt{\frac{hs}{kg}}$ ;
6. 0.408 m/s

## Exercise 13 F

1. 1.419 s
2. 2.234 m
3. 4.014 s
4. 751 cm
5. 4:1
6. 2:3
7. Slow
8. (i) 86400, (ii) 851
9. 6.35%
10. 41%
11. 2:3
12. (iii) 10.0 s (iv) 2%

# Chapter 14
# Moments of inertia

## Exercise 14 A

1. (ii) $\sqrt{\frac{4}{3}}l$

2. (ii) $\sqrt{\frac{1}{12}}d$

4. (ii) $7ml^2$

## Exercise 14 B

1. (i) $3ml^2$

   (ii) $12ml^2$

   (iii) $7ml^2$

2. (a) (i) $\frac{1}{3}ml^2$

   (ii) $\frac{4}{3}ml^2$

   (iii) $\frac{5}{3}ml^2$

   (iv) $\frac{17}{3}ml^2$

   (b) Only (iv) and by $12ml^2$

3. (i) $\frac{65}{6}ml^2$

   (ii) $\frac{11}{2}ml^2$

   (iii) $\frac{10}{3}ml^2$

   (iv) $43mr^2$

   (v) $11ml^2$

4. $56\frac{1}{3}ml^2$

6. $\sqrt{\frac{3g}{2l}}$

7. (i) $\frac{185}{6}ml^2$  (ii) $\sqrt{\frac{168g}{185l}}$

8. $6l\sqrt{\frac{24g}{65l}}$

9. $\sqrt{\frac{7g}{2l}}$

10. (i) $209ml^2$  (ii) $\sqrt{\frac{108g}{209l}}$

## Exercise 14 C

1. (ii) $\frac{60}{7} = 8.57$ s

3. $a = \frac{4}{5}g$ ; $T = \frac{2}{5}mg$

5. (ii) $\frac{2}{3\sqrt{2}}g$

6. (ii) $T = \frac{20}{11}g$ ; $S = \frac{17}{11}g$

7. $\frac{1}{4}g$

## Exercise 14 D

1. $2\pi\sqrt{\frac{4l}{3g}}$

2. $2\pi\sqrt{\frac{3r}{2g}}$

3. $2\pi\sqrt{\frac{8l}{3\sqrt{2}g}}$

4. $2\pi\sqrt{\frac{16l}{9g}}$

5. $2\pi\sqrt{\frac{61l}{21g}}$

6. (i) $2\pi\sqrt{\frac{129\,l}{4\,g}}$ (ii) $\frac{129\,l}{4}$

8. (b) (i) $11ml^2$

9. (i) $\sqrt{\frac{20g}{19r}}$

11. (ii) $\frac{8}{3}ml^2$

## Exercise 14 E

1. $\frac{1}{\sqrt{3}}l$

2. $\frac{1}{3}l$

4. (i) $2\pi\sqrt{\frac{3r}{2g}}$

5. (iii) $\sqrt{\frac{3}{5}}$

6. (ii) $2\pi\sqrt{\frac{2(a^2+12\,x^2)}{g(24x+a)}}$